E-Business Process Management:

Technologies and Solutions

Jayavel Sounderpandian
University of Wisconsin-Parkside, USA

Tapen Sinha
Instituto Tecnológico Autónomo de México, Mexico and
University of Nottingham, UK

IDEA GROUP PUBLISHING

Hershey • London • Melbourne • Singapore

Acquisition Editor: Kristin Klinger
Senior Managing Editor: Jennifer Neidig
Managing Editor: Sara Reed
Assistant Managing Editor: Sharon Berger
Development Editor: Kristin Roth
Copy Editor: Angela Thor
Typesetter: Jamie Snavely
Cover Design: Lisa Tosheff
Printed at: Yurchak Printing Inc.

Published in the United States of America by
        Idea Group Publishing (an imprint of Idea Group Inc.)
        701 E. Chocolate Avenue
        Hershey PA 17033
        Tel: 717-533-8845
        Fax: 717-533-8661
        E-mail: cust@idea-group.com
        Web site: http://www.idea-group.com

and in the United Kingdom by
        Idea Group Publishing (an imprint of Idea Group Inc.)
        3 Henrietta Street
        Covent Garden
        London WC2E 8LU
        Tel: 44 20 7240 0856
        Fax: 44 20 7379 0609
        Web site: http://www.eurospanonline.com

Library of Congress Cataloging-in-Publication Data

E-business process management : technologies and solutions / Jayavel Sounderpandian and Tapen Sinha, editors.
     p. cm.
   Summary: "This book explores the issues of supply chain management with new perspective providing examples of integrated framework for global SCM, novel ways of improving flexibility, responsiveness, and competitiveness via strategic IT alliances among channel members in a supply chain network, and techniques that might facilitate improved strategic decision making in a SCM environment"--Provided by publisher.
   Includes bibliographical references and index.
   ISBN 978-1-59904-204-6 (hbk.) -- ISBN 978-1-59904-206-0 (ebook)
   1. Electronic commerce--Management. I. Sounderpandian, Jayavel. II. Sinha, Tapen.
   HF5548.32.E17754 2007
   658.70285--dc22
                              2006033750

British Cataloguing in Publication Data
A Cataloguing in Publication record for this book is available from the British Library.

E-Business Process Management:

Technologies and Solutions

Table of Contents

Preface

The prevalence of electronic commerce that we see today makes it necessary for any employee to be familiar with e-business processes. Whether it is a government, a business, or a nonprofit organization, the employer is invariably found to engage in some form of online transactions. Governments publish policies online, businesses sell goods online, and universities offer courses online. Almost all of them accept payments online. It is no surprise, therefore, that there is a demand for e-business literature meant for specialists as well as nonspecialists. We believe this book will satisfy a good part of that demand. In a single volume, it presents an eclectic compilation of the most relevant details about today's e-business processes. We also believe that business managers and academic researchers alike will find this book useful.

Business Process Management and E-Business Process Management

With the rise of large scale production in the eighteenth century, business process management became the focal point of the business of economics. Adam Smith (1776), in his classic book, discussed business process management by examining the production of pins. He was the first to examine in detail how specialization brings efficiency into production processes. Not coincidentally, it was also the time when humanity witnessed the first rise of multinational corporations in the form of limited liability charters offered to shipping companies by English, French, Dutch, and Spanish governments.

E-business process management is strictly a product of the 21st century. In earlier centuries, it would have been unthinkable even to contemplate e-business process management. Rising computer literacy, falling cost of computers, cheaper communications, and deregulation have all played mutually reinforcing parts in the rise of e-business process management. As e-business grew, so did the research on e-business. The growth in e-business research demanded more journal outlets. Many new journals were started. The most recent among them is the *Journal of Electronic Commerce in Organizations,* introduced in 2003.

E-business process management is important because information and communications technologies (ICTs) play an increasing role in the economy of every country. In the case of poor countries like India, ICTs play an increasing role in freeing the country out of the poverty trap. In any country, the ICT sector is pivotal in raising the productivity of the economy by raising the productivity of the government, the businesses, and the households. The nature of ICT is distinctly global as it makes physical distance almost insignificant in many types of business processes such as order processing and customer services.

We start our discussion with an in-depth look at e-governance. Without the government setting up rules of the game and actively participating in enhancing the efficiency of the system, all e-business developments would be futile.

Overview of Section I: E-Governance

It has been shown in economics literature that the biggest obstacle for economic growth in developing countries is the lack of good governance. When a government allocates $1, say, for building roads or for flood relief, only a fraction (sometimes even less than 50%) ever reaches the people for whom it is intended. The remaining fraction is eaten up by inefficiencies in the system and by downright corruption. Just a decade ago, the logistics of accounting, bookkeeping, correspondence, and approvals was slow and costly. With interactive use of the World Wide Web, it has become cheaper and faster to execute such logistics.

Chapter I in this book shows how this is done in governance; hence, this chapter is titled e-governance. The technology has become the enabler of this process. Of course, to execute the whole process, there are certain prerequisites. For example, without computers, the execution would not be possible. To run computers, you will need a reliable supply of electricity. To connect computers over long distances, you will need reliable telephone and other networks. These requirements are not trivial in developing countries. In addition, you will need software that is platform independent. Most of all, you will need human resources, people who are capable of handling such a technological leap. In many developing countries, illiteracy itself runs high. For them, even computer literacy is a tall order.

In any given region, three types of agents are involved in e-governance communications: the government, the citizens, and the businesses. The author of the first chapter argues that e-governance can facilitate interaction between governments and citizens, and between governments and business entities. It will increase efficiency just the way automated teller machines have done with withdrawal of money from bank accounts. It will increase flexibility by streamlining the processes and reduce corruption by digitizing the processes. Land registry and electronic booking of railway tickets in India are good examples.

To facilitate orderly e-business processes, channels of communication have to be secure. Without security, any form of trade is restricted to only those parties that trust one another. A global market system of economic transactions is far more efficient than a tribal system. This compels any government to bring about a security based market system.

In **Chapter II**, the author discusses four elements of cryptology on which modern electronic systems of communications rely for security. The first element is privacy, which requires a scheme that will keep the content of a transaction secret from all but those authorized to access it. The second is digital signature scheme, which requires a mechanism whereby a person can electronically sign a document. The third element is data integrity, which needs a method that can detect insertion, substitution, or deletion of data. Finally, the system will require authentication, which requires a mechanism whereby both parties can be assured of the identity of the other. This chapter provides a primer on cryptology, and addresses all four elements.

E-business does not operate in a vacuum. It has to have legal standing. For example, the degree of legal acceptance of digital signatures varies from country to country. In some countries, even a scanned copy of a check is accepted as a basis for certain kinds of payments. The main legal basis in almost all countries are trademark, copyright, and patents. E-business needs to operate in that context.

Chapter III deals with the five important issues. They are: (1) Digital Millennium Copyright Act (DMCA), (2) digital rights management (DRM), (3) posting copyrighted material on Web sites including appropriate and inappropriate linking to other Web sites, and (4) liability of the Internet service providers (ISPs). The extent of liability is not simply a problem of the ISPs alone. For example, in May 2005, Google was sued by a U.S. Congressman for benefiting from child pornography sites that showed up in Google searches.

Chapter IV reviews e-market literature in scholarly journals. The reviews have one clear goal: to identify the technological trends that have appeared in the last decade. Some specific areas are discussed in detail: architecture, interoperability, technologies, protocols, and services. It then discusses important contributions. The aim of this chapter is to provide a blueprint of the literature related to e-business technologies for e-markets.

As we noted at the beginning of this section, e-business requires many types of interactions between many types of parties over the Internet. This was not possible until clear standards were established. First, such standards were set as the electronic data interchange (EDI) standards. Such standards were used for business-to-business transactions such as automated purchase of goods and services. The first EDI standard set up for North American companies (mostly for American and Canadian companies) in 1985 was called American National Standards Institute (ANSI) standards. Later, a special global standard was set up by the United Nations. With the introduction of the extensible markup language (XML) in 1997, the entire panorama changed. The advantage of XML is its platform and language-independence. It also allowed interactions between parties.

Chapter V shows that there are two classes of XML standards emerging: vertical and horizontal. The vertical standards are industry specific while the horizontal standards cut across different industries. Because the initial development of the World Wide Web operated in the confines of a scientific consortium, security was not an issue. However, today, with complete anonymity available in the Internet, security is a major concern. Different standards are emerging in different industries based on their specific needs. Thus, one can find different standards used in industries such as agriculture, accounting, automobile, banking, insurance, and other services.

Interoperability was a theme touched on in Chapter IV. Government-to-business interaction was discussed in Chapter I. In **Chapter VI**, the authors bring these two themes together. It offers a case study to develop a generic, standardized, interoperable platform (CCIGOV platform) that is able to model and manage administrative business-related processes and content. The motivation is to follow a one-stop approach, where Chambers of Commerce and Industry operate seamlessly across Europe with transactions between various government and business platforms.

Overview of Section II: Mobile Computing

With severe restrictions on the use of airwaves put on by governments around the globe, it was impossible to use private communications channels or personal communications services (PCS). New Zealand started the trend by auctioning off spectrum rights in 1990. In 1993, the U.S. government auctioned off PCS spectrum rights to private operators. Selling such rights would not make sense until it became feasible to have digital communications. On the demand side, the decade of the 1990s has been extraordinary. By 2002, the number of mobile telephones in the world has exceeded the number of land line telephones. It is now recognized that the Internet, television, telephones, and computers can all be rolled into one, making mobile computing very important.

Chapter VII starts with the history of different generations of mobile telephone. From the first generation (known as bricks and now called 1G) to the second generation (2G) where signals became digital with the capability of short message service (SMS) and circuit switched data (CSD). The next generation devices (called 2.5G) became Internet enabled. For example, by 2002, more than half the cellular phones in South Korea and more than 80% of cellular phones in Japan were Internet enabled. Wireless local area network (WLAN) has been growing since the IEEE set up the first standards in 1997. It became known as the IEEE 802.11 standard. They were capable of transmitting signals of up to 2Mbps. New products are expected to come to the market with 802.11n standards that will be capable of handling data rates of 600Mbps. For metropolitan areas, IEEE 802.16 standard called WiMAX are being set up. In Europe, this has become known as HiperMAN (high performance radio metropolitan area network). All of this will blur the distinction between computers, telephones, and television for the third generation (3G) devices.

One special type of networking is very popular today: wireless fidelity or WiFi. **Chapter VIII** discusses WiFi in-depth. First, pure WiFi and its limitations are discussed. WiFi depends on radio frequency that can be propagated within short distances such as inside a home or inside a store. Because it is wireless, it is extremely convenient. For that very reason, it is also very vulnerable. Snooping is extremely easy in wireless networks, and therefore warrants special security measures.

Expanding a wireless network across a city can offer access through moving vehicles, called vehicular ad hoc networks. This method is helping distribution of goods and services in cities. In the future, it can become very useful in rural areas, especially in developing countries. The only problem with such networks is that they are subject to congestion rather rapidly.

While the previous two chapters discuss supply side issues of mobile computing, **Chapter IX** gives a consumer's view of it. Any available technology may not mean much unless a sufficient number of consumers use it. One of the puzzling facts in the European Union (in the so-called E-15 region) is that even though more than 80% of the population could access broadband in 2005, less than 10% actually did so. This chapter discusses a number of issues from the point of view of the consumer. Specifically, perceived usefulness, compatibility with existing values, perceived ease-of-use, result demonstrability, and perceived risks are important elements of any new technology. For example, if consumers perceive that broadband connections could easily lead to identity theft, they may not use the technology, even if it is very cheap.

Overview of Section III:
Global Outsourcing of Business Services

An important element of e-business process management is globalization. As economies have moved towards service orientation, agriculture and manufacturing are becoming less and less important. An upshot of this is that more and more jobs require less and less face-to-face interaction. At the same time, long-distance communication is becoming cheaper. The cost of sending an e-mail with an attachment is the same whether it is sent to the next room or to the other end of the world. With Internet telephony, voice message cost is also going down the same path.

Chapter X discusses the issue of outsourcing by taking two particular countries: United States and India. India has become the largest recipient outsourced e-business. The United States has become the largest outsourcer. Thus, a discussion of these two countries throws a revealing light on outsourcing processes. The chapter discusses how India got to such a place through the Y2K problem. Although businesses in the U.S., always looking for ways to cut costs, embraced outsourcing wholeheartedly, the U.S. government, pushed by the voters, has resisted it. Outsourcing has unexpectedly become an exporter of jobs without people physically moving from one country to another. The authors discuss where this trend will lead to in the future.

The process of business process outsourcing is discussed more generally in **Chapter XI**. It distinguishes between inshoring and offshoring, and between insourcing and outsourcing. It points out that offshoring is becoming more popular for four principal reasons: execution of work can become 24/7, cheaper labor is accessible across the globe, communications have become cheaper, and businesses have become more modular. It discusses various strategies from the point of view of the customer, and then goes on to discuss the risks inherent in business process outsourcing.

Overview of Section IV:
Web Delivery of College Level Courses

It has been long believed that education at the university level cannot be offered efficiently over long distances. In the past, there have been correspondence courses offered by some universities. But, they left a lot to be desired. There were three main areas of problem. First, they were only as fast as the mail. Second, feedback from the teachers was minimal. Third, it was difficult to cross national boundaries because of the first problem. Fourth, there was no interaction among the students. With the development of XML technology, all four problems are attacked head-on through online delivery of course materials. In this section, two papers discuss this final frontier of education.

Chapter XII discusses business education through the World Wide Web. The earliest form of distance education started with closed circuit television. The technology was clumsy and expensive. With the advent of the Internet, the process has become much more flexible. Videos and online teaching material can be stored in secure locations. They can be viewed anytime, anywhere. Not surprisingly, business education, specifically the Master of Business Administration (MBA) programs, are being offered online more than other programs because most business students are already working full time in some business. The chapter therefore pays more attention to online MBA programs.

A critical element in online programs is quality because there seems to be widespread belief that online programs are inferior in quality compared to on-site programs. Universities therefore concentrate on getting their online programs accredited by premier accrediting bodies. For MBA programs, the premier accrediting body is the AACSB International (Association for Advancement of Collegiate Schools of Business, International). Therefore, Chapter XII lists relevant accreditation guidelines of AACSB International wherever appropriate. Additionally, the strengths and weaknesses of online education are discussed. Online programs also require detailed infrastructure to provide the needed technological support.

Chapter XIII tackles the business of online education. Like any other business, we need to discuss costs and revenue of this form of education. It can cost less because it does not require physical infrastructure. On the other hand, it can reduce the opportunity cost of studying as it becomes unnecessary to travel to study. Online education has significant benefits including support for self-paced learning and better discussion between learners and teachers. The design of an online curriculum requires convergence of several dimensions. It requires coordinated efforts of teacher, learner, media designers, communication methods, administration, and marketing. The developers need to consider the power of the suppliers, power of the buyers, substitutes, barriers to entry, and the current degree of rivalry. These factors can be addressed by long-range planning, defining the student target, and forming partnerships with stakeholders in the online education industry.

Overview of Section V: Risk Management

Any new business model comes with its own risks, at times very novel forms of risks. E-business process risks are fundamentally different from traditional business process risks. There are elements of fraud and theft that are truly global in scope. The scale of such risks is unprecedented in history.

Chapter XIV tackles these risks in five dimensions: risks in services, risks in business models, risks in technology, risks in processes, and risks in fulfillment. Probably the most important services risks today arise in banking through fraud. These frauds include bogus invoices, cramming, slamming, loan scams, and phishing. New technologies can accidentally release private information when it is not intended. For example, a laptop computer was stolen, in May 2006, that contained information about 26.5 million veterans in the U.S. The burglars did not know the content of the laptop. Somebody else can do the same to exploit the vulnerability of a company for blackmailing. Any process of risk management requires five dynamic steps: identification, quantification, taking mitigating actions, monitoring, and having a feedback process to make it dynamic.

Chapter XV takes a legal approach to e-risk management. It focuses on a series of risks of legal liability arising from e-mail and Internet activities that are a common part of many e-businesses. Some of the laws governing these electronic activities are new and especially designed for the electronic age, while others are traditional laws only, whose application to electronic activities is novel. E-business not only exposes companies to new types of liability risk, but also increases the potential number of claims and the complexity of dealing with those claims. The international nature of the Internet, together with a lack of uniformity in the laws governing the same activity in different countries, means that companies need to proceed with caution.

This book contains different facets of e-business process management. The strength of this volume arises from the fact that the contributors are specialists in their areas. They have had many years of experience dealing with the issues they discuss both as academics and as practitioners. We are happy to bring out this collection of chapters on the important topic of e-business process management. We are grateful to Idea Group Inc. for giving us the opportunity to edit this volume. We are particularly thankful of Ms. Kristin Roth for cheerfully guiding us throughout the editing process. Finally, we thank the authors, who have contributed a very informative collection of articles. Tapen Sinha wishes to thank Instituto Tecnológico Autónomo de México and the Associatión Mexicana de Cultura AC for their generous support.

Jayavel Sounderpandian
University of Wisconsin-Parkside

Tapen Sinha
Instituto Technológico Autónomo de México

Section I

E-Governance

Chapter I

E-Governance

Srinivas Bhogle, National Aerospace Laboratories, India

Abstract

E-governance uses Internet and communication technologies to automate governance in innovative ways, so that it becomes more efficient, more cost-effective, and empowers the human race even more. E-governance exercises are being attempted for more than a decade now, but have so far achieved only mixed success. The long-term prognosis for e-governance, however, remains extremely positive. The emergence of Web-services technologies, the continually proliferating computer networks, and the irreversible migration towards digital information strongly confirm the view that e-governance is here to stay. The eventual success of any e-governance project is intimately linked to the methodology used, and to that complex mesh between men, machines, and mindsets. We explain the "what," "why," and "how" of e-governance. We also talk of e-governance concerns, and discuss a few illustrative case studies.

What is E-Governance?

Definitions

The biggest problem in developing countries is good governance, not poverty. It is, for example, well known that only a miniscule fraction of the money earmarked for development, relief, or rehabilitation eventually filters down to fulfill its mandated objective. There are also numerous instances where the concern is not how to *find* the money, but how to go through the maze of complicated procedures to *spend* the available money before the financial year ends.

Until a decade ago, the sheer logistics of accounting, bookkeeping, correspondence, and approvals was an onerous overhead. But the World Wide Web completely changed things. With e-mail, correspondence across the globe became almost instantaneous, and richer, because mail attachments were possible. The technologies to make Web pages interactive, and connect them to databases, worked wonders on the approval processes: approvals became faster, were based on more intelligent inputs, and could be securely archived. It was now possible, and indeed highly desirable, to use the Web for real governance.

Electronic governance (or e-governance) could therefore be defined as the use of Internet and communication technologies to automate governance in innovative ways, so that it becomes more efficient, more cost-effective, and empowers the human race even more.

Since "governance" is normally associated with a "government," may authors choose to explicitly mention the government while defining e-governance. Backus (2001), for example, defines e-governance as the "application of electronic means in the interaction between government and citizens and government and businesses, as well as in internal government operations to simplify and improve democratic, government and business aspects of governance." The strategic objective of e-governance, as Backus explains, is simply to use electronic means to support and stimulate good governance.

Governance vs. E-Governance

Both governance and e-governance are based on the same principles, and aim to achieve the same end objective. But the means used are widely different. Consider, for example, the requirement of a publicly funded national R&D lab to recruit scientists. A decade ago, the following procedure was probably adopted: (a) advertise widely in national newspapers indicating the job requirement and eligibility, (b) identify the format in which applications must be submitted, (c) receive, sort, and classify the applications sent, (d) shortlist the applicants and invite them for a test or interview, and (e) select the candidates and issue them appointment letters.

This entire process usually took almost a year—so long that the applicants often got tired of waiting and flew away to some other opportunity. The excuse offered for the delay was that prescribed government procedures were too complex and tedious. It was ironical that these classical governance procedures were actually sending away the best talent instead of bringing it in.

The e-governance approach would dramatically change things: the job requirement and eligibility would appear as hyperlinked Web pages on the lab's Web site. The application format would be a Web page template, with thoughtful validations to improve data quality. Upon submission, the applicant's data would instantaneously flow into database tables on the lab's server. The short-listing process would merely involve making lists based on a wide variety of database queries and, finally, the selected candidates would be issued appointment letters via an e-mail attachment.

The advantages offered by this e-governance procedure are abundantly clear, but let us list them for the record. First, the "time-to-recruit" is dramatically reduced: 12 months could be reduced to 1-2 months. Second, the quality of the selected candidates is significantly better because of timely selection and improved data quality and search procedures. Third, the procedure is much less expensive; there are no advertisement or data tabulation costs. Fourth, the e-recruitment procedure reaches a much larger number of applicants right across the globe because of the growing ubiquity of the Web, and because the application window is open 24 × 7. And, finally, the e-governance procedure automatically guarantees data or content in digital form, making them more amenable for future knowledge management or data mining exercises.

On the down side, e-governance procedures frequently raise security concerns, for example, could someone access or modify information? Electronic procedures also require widespread, efficient, and reliable computer networks. But the biggest concern relates to mindsets: officials involved in governance fiercely resist change.

Table 1 summarizes the arguments for and against e-governance. It can be seen that the advantages significantly outweigh the concerns.

Table 1. Advantages and concerns of e-governance

Advantages	Concerns
Significant time saving ("there are no delays")	Mindsets of governance teams
Improved information quality	Security concerns ("can information be tampered or delayed?")
Less expensive (especially after e-governance infrastructure is set up)	Requirement of widespread, efficient and reliable computer networks and software
Wider reach ("can reach the whole world")	
Digital content (data capture is digital)	

Evolution of E-Governance

E-governance became possible only after the appearance of the World Wide Web and the widespread use of browsers like Netscape and Internet Explorer. In the early years (until about 1997), browsers simply displayed "static" Web pages. These pages were attractive, available on different computer platforms, allowed you to "mix" text with multimedia content, and could be hyperlinked.

From an e-governance viewpoint, this still was not good enough. Imagine that the task is to secure admission in a school or college. With Web pages, you could display all kinds of information about the college: its history, its courses, names of teachers on its faculty, pictures of the college buildings and swimming pools, college maps, and so forth. You could also post formats of application forms that must be submitted. But you could not *actually fill up such forms online*. With static Web pages, you could only "inform," but you could not "interact."

The chief reason was that Web pages use the Hypertext Markup Language (HTML), and HTML simply was not meant to be interactive. It was a one-way street: the college could reach its information to you, but you could not get back to the college using the same browser.

One could, of course, still print the application form off the Web page, fill it up off-line, and then mail or fax it to the college. The college could then, if it wished, reenter the details on an electronic database. But this did not seem right. If you could "connect" to the college, why could you not "reach" its database as well?

HTML's inability to directly connect to a database had to be corrected; one had to get HTML to talk to SQL (the structured query language that all databases use). The early efforts (1997-99) to achieve this involved the use of a common gateway interface (CGI) and a programming language like PERL. It worked rather well, although the programming overhead was a little severe. Later, especially after the widespread use of a platform-independent language like Java (by 2001), the database connectivity problem was solved much more elegantly.

From an e-governance perspective, this meant that we had moved from the "inform" to the "interact" phase. Our college applicant was now only required to fill up an online form and "submit." The data would seamlessly flow into the college's backend database. Better still, the student could also obtain an online or e-mail response, for example, to say that the application has been received or accepted.

A typical governance transaction, however, involves much more than filling or submitting a form. The conventional procedure is to put this application form on a file or dossier. The file then travels from one "governance desk" to the next. At each desk, the concerned individual is required to carry out a process involving either "scrutiny and verification" or "decision-making and judgment." Each process therefore involves information addition or manipulation. In the college application example, the process might involve seeking referee reports, administering a test, determining qualification criteria, and eventually reaching a decision.

How would one achieve an electronic adaptation of this governance transaction? We would first of all store the applicant's information and documents into carefully structured databases ("files") or similar digital repositories. Every participant in the governance transaction ("desk") would then access the databases in the prescribed sequence, and either add or manipulate data. As the transaction proceeds, information is continually updated digitally. The eventual verdict is based on the same information inputs, albeit in the digital format.

A transaction therefore involves multiple, and usually richer, interactions. We are therefore moving higher in the e-governance hierarchy: after "inform" and "interact," it is now "transact." In terms of technology, a transaction is considerably more complicated. Basically, transactions involve workflows (a supply chain is an example of a workflow). There are now more participants, and issues relating to security now require greater attention. Even workflow management can get sufficiently complicated, because workflows may not be straightforward. For example, after traveling through desks A -> B -> C -> D, D might suddenly decide to revert the file back to B for a clarification; or, in certain situations, one may be directly required to jump from desk B to desk D.

Technologies relating to such electronic transactions matured by about 2003. In most cases, these were Web-enabled implementations of the enterprise resource planning (ERP) solutions that had been around for many years.

But even as e-governance solutions became more sophisticated technologically, a very different sort of problem was becoming increasingly evident. The technology was "ready," but the people required to use the technology were "not ready"; in fact, often "not willing" to change. This mindset problem was apparent even earlier, when full-blown ERP solutions started being implemented, because such solutions required considerable process reengineering, and established organizations with aging managers simply refused to change.

While developing technologies for e-governance transactions constitutes a very big forward step, it is not the end of the story. These transactions must eventually go on to "transform" businesses; they must change business paradigms. There are still serious problems in migrating from the "transact" stage to the "transform" stage.

Consider again the case of an applicant to College A. If College A rejects the applicant, he would like to be considered for College B, College C … and so on until he eventually gains admission somewhere. Unfortunately, it is still unlikely that College A and College B can seamlessly exchange the applicant's information. Their information systems would be engineered at least a little differently, making such information exchanges difficult and expensive. Consider another example where Enterprise A takes over Enterprises B. Sadly, the billing procedures in Enterprises A and B are significantly different, although each procedure is, by itself, efficient and streamlined. Exchanging information between Enterprises A and B will therefore become a major handicap. So severe, in fact, that many information managers might find it more convenient (Hagel III, 2002) to adopt a "no tech" solution—backroom boys (perhaps outsourced from India!) would manually "convert" formats and then throw the data back into the system.

This difficulty arises because we do not have standardized information formats and processes. One recalls the electronic data interchange (EDI) initiative of the 1990's that fell through because it was not sufficiently versatile, and because it allowed the business "big brother" to become the "big bully" by "controlling" data formats. The way out seems to be to evolve universal (and "open") frameworks, and then build supporting frameworks for interoperability so that every enterprise's formats are "reduced" to this universal format. This approach should hopefully usher in true e-governance.

Table 2. Different phases in the evolution of e-governance

E-Governance phase	Attributes
'Inform' (<1997)	Web pages containing 'static' information (featuring text, pictures, or even multimedia clips) posted on a Web site. Pages are hyperlinked.
'Interact' (1997-2001)	Web pages with database connectivity. Now possible to submit queries and receive responses.
'Transact' (>2001)	Improved interactivity. Transactions across workflows. Security features. ERP-like formulations
'Transform' (?)	Universal frameworks. Enterprises can seamlessly exchange information over distributed networks.

G2B, G2C, G2G

The three principal participants in e-governance are the government, the citizen, and the business entities. So e-governance is essentially about interactions between these participants in which the government plays the pivotal role.

It is customary to classify these interactions. G2C, for instance, refers to interactions between the government (G) and the citizen (C). Obtaining a driving license is an example of such an interaction. The citizen approaches the government for a license with the relevant supporting documentation. The government eventually grants him the license and ensures that the citizen's details enter the government's information repositories. These details can then be used in governance, for example, to fine the citizen after a traffic violation.

G2B refers to the interactions between the government (often as a regulatory authority) and business enterprises. The procedures involved in receipt and payments of taxes are an example of G2B e-governance. There could be very complex underlying processes such as date management, discounts, payment policies, and so forth, in G2B e-governance.

Finally, G2G refers to interactions between two government departments, for example, between a state and federal government or between government agencies respectively involved in development and funding projects. The real G2G e-governance challenge is to create a monolithic government entity in which the citizen or the business interacts with an apparently single entity (a "single window") for all governance transactions. This is a very formidable task given the wide disparity in governance procedures between two government departments.

An E-Governed Future

E-governance is a very attractive and compelling concept. But the path towards this ideal is exceedingly difficult and complicated.

First of all, we need the *infrastructure*: every enterprise, every government department, and every home must hold electronic devices such as computers, mobile handsets, or wireless sensors that must be "connected" with robust, fast, and reliable networks. The networking technologies could be different (wired, wireless, terrestrial, satellite-based), but this variety need not be a concern.

Second, we need *enabling software* that is compatible across these diverse hardware platforms: ideally, software with open architectures. Software solutions must seamlessly support (a) browsers or other communication devices at the "front-end," (b) the information repositories and databases at the "back-end," and (c) the business logic and intelligence in the "middle-tier."

Third, we need *digitization*. All data or information in the archives, in administrative ledgers, in books, in court proceedings, and so forth, must eventually get digitized. This is an onerous task, but, thankfully, not an urgent prerequisite. A pragmatic approach would be to choose a cutoff date and make sure that at least all future records are digital. We also need supporting instruments such as scanners, document management systems, and so forth, for digitization.

Fourth, we need *security*, operating at different levels: (a) user identification and authentication using smart cards and digital signatures, (b) data protection using encryption and fault-tolerant software, and (c) protection from other external threats such as hackers, viruses, spam mails, and service denial programs.

Finally, we need *universal standards and frameworks* to facilitate data exchange. The eventual success of e-governance would depend on how good these standards are, and how faithful and widespread is the compliance with these standards. Such standards would grow into frameworks, and the emergence of robust Internet technologies like XML, or more generally, Web services, would eventually package these standards and frameworks into successful e-governance implementations.

Thus, in tomorrow's e-governed future, anyone, any time, from anywhere, using any connection device, can ask for any service. This looks like a pipe dream right now … but there is no reason to believe that it cannot happen tomorrow, or the day after, if there is a shared collective will.

Table 3. The prerequisites for e-governance

Prerequisite	Attributes
Infrastructure	Participants must have electronic interfaces such as computers or mobile handsets. There must be a robust, reliable, and fast network to connect these participants
Enabling software	Software with open architectures to seamlessly connect the front-end, back-end and middle tiers
Digitization	Data must become digital: new data must be entered in digital formats, legacy data must be digitized using scanners and document management systems
Security	User authentication, data protection, and protection from external threats
Universal standards and frameworks	Development and compliance of universal standards to exchange data and applications.

Why E-Governance?

Empowerment

In historical narratives, a king was considered virtuous and benign if each of his subjects had the freedom to approach the king's court with a request or a grievance. In many ways, this continues to be the ideal of democratic societies even today. But the governance agencies are getting more "distant" because of growing populations, growing procedures and, sadly, growing indifference.

One of the chief merits of e-governance is that it can again empower the citizen. To take a trivial example, most governance procedures are initiated with an application form. It is common, especially in developing countries, to deny a citizen even access to this form! One has to know an influential contact, or pay a modest bribe, to obtain this form. In an e-governed world, this form would be available almost instantaneously … in fact it could be filled out and submitted almost as easily.

The citizen is also often completely ignorant of procedures, and of his rights. He needs counseling or advice before he can choose his preferred option. Such advice, however, is often denied or only made available at a price. In e-governed societies, the citizen could have access to video films or interactive help routines to permit him to make a better-informed decision. He could also join discussion groups where individuals share their personal experiences in working around procedures.

E-governance offers a 24 × 7 service desk, and this too is a major instrument for empowerment. Government offices worldwide are known to have an abnormally large number of holidays, and, even on working days, service counters are often not manned all the time ("Mr. X still isn't back from lunch").

E-governance will also empower businesses. Every businessman knows how difficult it is to bid for, and perhaps eventually obtain, a lucrative government contract. The associated paperwork requires him to interact with a large number of different government offices and officials who have no worthwhile information exchange processes between their establishments. This significantly delays the award of the contract and proves to be an unnecessary and expensive overhead.

Finally, e-governance will empower because of its wider reach. It is, for example, well known that a cartel of big vendors often gobbles up most of the big government contracts. Likewise, citizens residing in a country's capital often run away with most of the lucrative international opportunities. When such tenders or announcements are put on easily accessible Web sites, they will reach practically every entrepreneur or citizen.

Profitability

E-governance will make businesses and enterprises more profitable. One route to greater profits will emerge because of reduced lead times. Every business process can be streamlined to a greater degree, parallel activities can be initiated and the project can be completed faster. It is always more profitable if projects are completed on time.

E-governance will offer significant gains because businesses can deploy a reduced, but more skilful, manpower component. All project teams have a team of core technical experts and a second team of "facilitators." These facilitators are not really productive in a business sense; they are needed to cover up the deficiencies in the governance processes. As e-governance implementations improve, we will need fewer facilitators.

E-governance has also opened up the extremely profitable opportunity of outsourcing. Project tasks can be transferred, for example, from Boston in the U.S. to Bangalore in India, because businesses are electronically wired up, and a country like India offers manpower of matching quality at a fraction of the international costs. Starting from about 2003, the outsourcing business is booming; it even easily survived a campaign debate in the 2004 U.S. presidential elections.

Efficiency

Anyone visiting Asia after a gap of about 5 years would be struck by two very visible phenomena: the ubiquity of bank ATM counters and the pervasive use of mobile telephones. This is a strongest possible signal that e-governance is coming.

The example of mobile telephones is most interesting. Starting off as a status symbol that every rich man was supposed to flaunt, it has now made deep inroads into the middle-class income groups and the small business or service segments. Plumbers, electricians, car and scooter mechanics, and even cooks and priests are now just a phone call away! Mobile phones have provided decent livelihood to a significant fraction of the population and made businesses much more efficient.

ATM counters too have dramatically improved efficiency. ATM services have often served as "robots" to reduce the burden on banking clerks, and ensure that fewer citizens crowd bank offices. Best of all, the ATM experiment has made signatures less sacrosanct. Two of the most dreadful requirements of classical governance are (a) to ask that every request be written out on paper, and (b) to insist that every governance agent affixes his signature after even the most trivial transaction. The acceptance of an ATM card with its secret pin code, instead of a printed signature, to disburse money is a step forward.

Flexibility

One often encounters administrative procedures that are extremely tedious, and for no apparent reason. Both the administrators and the customers are aware of this, but seem incapable of changing things. This is largely because the established governance procedures are inflexible. You realize, for example, that A -> D -> C -> E is a better way of going about things than A -> B -> C -> D -> E, but you are told that this cannot be done because it would disturb the existing administrative set-up, and require reprinting of all the stationery and the bound ledgers. An e-governance set-up that would easily permit modification of workflows would solve the problem.

We need flexibility in a wide variety of other situations as well, for example, while changing from summer times to winter times, if we decide to shift a particular business operation from Location A to Location B, or if we wish to transfer a responsibility from Mr. A to Ms. B.

Anticorruption

Corruption is arguably the biggest obstacle to good governance, at least in the poorer states and countries. E-governance can counter corruption in at least two ways: first by introducing *transparency* in all governance processes, and, second, by being a very effective *deterrent*. For example, consider all governance procedures associated with land or property records. These procedures are so seeped in corruption that even a legal owner of land or property can never feel secure. Ownership is normally established based on an appropriate entry in an official governance record—but what if this record is modified for a bribe? Farmers in poorer countries are often the biggest victims; their land can be "grabbed," and their land records "destroyed" by the evil nexus of politicians, lawyers, and the land mafia. Digitizing all land records securely, and educating the local farmer to use electronic procedures to protect his ownership rights, could defeat such corruption. Another example of the transparency of e-governance is the management of examinations by universities: all worries about exam paper leaks, faulty evaluation, and manipulation of results can be banished once the entire process becomes publicly visible, and thus accountable. Even corrupt practices in elections, arguably the greatest scourge of democratic societies, can be countered by e-governance.

The role of e-governance as a corruption deterrent is more subtle, but equally effective. Information about every high value government transaction can be posted on a public Web site for citizens, public interest groups, and the media to peruse. This will ensure that every transaction is publicly watched, and every decision fiercely debated. This simple e-broad-casting ploy can keep every official on his toes, and make him think twice before making a wrong move! Aggressive e-advocacy can also help reverse decisions where corruption has been spotted.

Digital Repositories

In an e-governed world, all records will be entered or sensed into electronic repositories, and will therefore be automatically digital. This "forced digitization" is extremely useful because digital content is easiest to manipulate, and also potentially the most durable (although the rapid obsolescence of the data capture and storage devices is a matter of concern). The ability to easily manipulate or play with data will enable more efficient "knowledge" extraction, or discovery, for example, using data mining or using algorithms based on artificial intelligence (AI) methodologies.

The digital medium also embraces multimedia content. We already see many instances of multimedia in governance: "in-camera" court depositions from geographically distant locations, animated weather forecasts and hurricane alerts on TV, tracking a criminal's movement using GPS/GIS devices, and so forth. Digital multimedia is therefore poised to become a powerful and versatile force in e-governance.

Table 4. The benefits of e-governance

Benefit	Reasons
Empowerment	Empowers the citizen or business because of unfettered access to governance, education on governance procedures, 24 x 7 service, and wider reach
Profitability	Reduced lead times, better manpower deployment, possibility of outsourcing
Efficiency	Opportunities for mobile connectivity, sophisticated devices to automate mechanical and repetitive tasks, faster transfer of money, encourages digital signatures
Flexibility	Reengineering or reconfiguring business processes, easy transfer of business locations or individual responsibilities
Anticorruption	Introduces transparency in the governance process, acts as a deterrent
Creates digital repositories	Forces data digitization, this allows easier data manipulation and more efficient knowledge retrieval. Supports multimedia content.

Once Again, Why E-Governance?

It is interesting that while practically everyone advocates e-governance, the reasons cited are widely different, although each is thought provoking. The following one-liners (W'O Okot-Uma, 2001) are in response to the question: "Why good governance?". If we assume that e-governance is the most likely vehicle to deliver good governance, then these are also answers to "why e-governance?"

We therefore see that e-governance is much more than just an implementation of information and communication technologies. It is also intimately linked to a wide variety of social, economic, and political factors such as "freedom," "social justice," "openness," "globalization," "economic liberalization," and "human development." E-governance could, one day, redefine human civilization itself.

Table 5. One-line responses to "Why good governance?"

Respondent	Response
Amartya Sen	Development of freedom
John Paul II	Freedom of a person to live out his/her creative potential
John Rawls	Social justice as fairness
Mahathir Mohamed	Global civilized society
George Soros	Global open society
UNDP	Human development
Atlantic Charter	World free from fear and want

How E-Governance?

Climb the Mountain

How does one actually begin the business of ushering in e-governance? There is really only one way: start climbing the mountain that takes you from the "inform" phase to the "interact" phase, and thereafter, to the "transact" and "transform" phases.

It is also still not completely clear how we will scale the ultimate peak; but if we keep climbing, and equip ourselves with the essential "tools" to trudge upwards, we will surely get there. Better still, the benefits start coming in almost as soon as we harness this resolve to climb; and they grow incrementally as we conquer each intermediate peak.

For the "inform" phase, we need rather modest tools: at the "governance end" we will need a Web server to host the Web site, and at the "citizen end" we will need no more than a networked desktop computer with browser software. As we move to the "interact" phase, the governance end will have to be bolstered: faster servers, and a database server to complement the Web server. At the citizen end, the same desktop computer would still do the job, but it would help if the network connect speed improves, and if the connectivity can be sustained over longer time periods.

The climb up to the "transact" phase is significantly more difficult, and we need more powerful and versatile technology tools. More importantly, we have to steel our human resolve. The inform phase is great fun; no one protests … in fact, everyone says: "hey, I didn't know this was so easy, and so cool!" The honeymoon endures as we enter the "interact" phase … we are now gushing: "I didn't have to wait in long queues to get this done, I applied right from my home, and in the middle of the night!". The "transact" phase brings in the big worries; at the governance end there are concerns about the performance of the servers and fidelity of the processes. Officials are also alarmed by a perceived loss of power, since they no longer physically hold official records and the office hierarchy gets disturbed. At the citizen end, there are widespread concerns especially about security, and confusion about the process workflows. By the time we reach the "transform" phase, the big action has shifted to the backend: the concerns are about how to exchange and manage data seamlessly and share the same processes. At the citizen end, things have now become rather simple: a single, completely configured, and customized desktop provides that ultimate "window to the whole world."

We will now introduce the many underlying e-governance building blocks. It must be mentioned that the real technological challenge is significantly greater than what this narrative might suggest.

Hypertext Markup Language

The Hypertext Markup Language (HTML) is used to create Web pages. The general procedure is to first key in the text, and then add "tags" to (a) embellish the page appearance, (b) insert multimedia content, and (c) hyperlink the Web page to other related Web pages.

Table 6. The major steps in e-governance implementation

Phase	"Governance end"	"Citizen or client end"	Technology prerequisites
Inform	Host an attractive and informative Web site on a Web server with hyperlinked Web pages and multimedia content	A desktop computer with browser software; at least a rudimentary network connection	HTML, browsers, devices for content digitization (scanners, optical character recognition software, conversion to pdf) TCP/IP network connectivity
Interact	Database server to complement the Web server. Ability to connect to databases. Design front-end forms with suitable validations. Routines to populate and query back-end databases	A desktop computer with browser software, and an improved network connection. Logins and passwords to identify and authenticate user	HTML, browsers, digitization, improved network connectivity, database design and development, programming for database connectivity (e.g., using Java)
Transact	Cluster of servers for specialized functions such as database management Web hosting, Web application management, security and fault tolerance. Design and coding of process workflows, and of user-friendly and secure front-end interface. Data encryption.	A desktop computer with browser software, and a fast and reliable network connection. Logins, passwords, and digital signatures or security tokens to identify and authenticate user	HTML, browsers, digitization, reliable and secure network connectivity, database design and development, programming for database connectivity (e.g., using Java), software to support workflows, process integration, rights and privileges. Hardware devices and software tools for information security
Transform	Cluster of servers for specialized functions like database management, Web hosting, Web application management, security, and fault tolerance. Design and coding of process workflows, and of user-friendly and secure front-end interface. Data encryption. Standards and frameworks to connect diverse data and application implementations.	A desktop computer with browser software and a fully user-specific configured desktop. Fast, reliable, and persistent network connection. Wide slew of features to authenticate and protect the user.	HTML, browsers, digitization, reliable and secure network connectivity, database design and development, programming for database connectivity (e.g., using Java), software to support workflows, process integration, rights and privileges. Hardware devices and software tools for information security. XML and Web services. Data format standardization. Frameworks for interoperability.

Internally, HTML identifies the IP address of the server holding the referred Web page, and requests the server to send the page across the Internet.

From an e-governance perspective, HTML provides the richest possible machinery to inform. In spite of its apparent simplicity, designing a Web page is still a considerable challenge. The Web pages must be appealing, must contain compelling links to other information sources, and must have an intelligent underlying structure. Web pages must also be frequently updated, with old pages being promptly weeded out.

Internet

There would be no e-governance without the Internet. The Internet is a worldwide computer network created by interconnecting computers. The most popular connecting "topology" uses a switch (earlier, a hub) with multiple ports. Every computer in the local neighborhood connects into this switch. Then the switch itself connects into another switch, and so the network telescopes out. Computers are identified by a unique IP address (that is, quite like a phone number; IP addresses currently are "dotted quads," 202.12.13.14, for example), and there are searching and connecting mechanisms on the Internet to quickly identify computers and then exchange data packets. When a user types in http://www.google.com on his browser, the domain name server on the network (that is like a telephone book) quickly identifies the IP address of the server hosting the Google site, and then attempts to establish the connection. Things happen very fast, and the data packets are delivered at great speed and with uncanny precision.

Networks are now turning "wireless"; instead of cables, networks use radio as the primary carrier. Wireless networks, using associated technologies like WiMAX (Vaughan-Nichols, 2004), will provide a major fillip to e-governance because they allow use of *mobile* devices. So if you want to book an airline ticket, you could use the handset of your mobile telephone instead of a "wired" computer. If you are a soldier patrolling a border area, you could use a palmtop computer to update the army's database on enemy positions. If you are a fisherman on the high seas, you could connect to a database indicating the supply requirement at different points on the coastline to plan and optimize your catch.

Indeed it appears increasingly likely that "full-blown" e-governance will eventually be achieved using wireless networks, and wireless data collection technologies, such as RFID (Want, 2004), that use electronic tags to store data. RFID tags can make any object "visible" to a network—anywhere and at any time. RFID tags are still rather expensive, and so used rather sparingly (to track expensive goods in transit, for example). But their use will proliferate once they become more affordable. Every book in a library or bookstore, every commodity in a supermarket, every inventory in an engineering or medical establishment, every car on an auto route, and even every child's schoolbag could then be tagged. Indeed, these tags could go on to redefine the very art of governance.

Databases

A lot of governance involves the collection, storage, and retrieval of data. Databases store data intelligently so that it can be retrieved easily and quickly using powerful querying options.

As data gets more complex and interlinked, database design becomes important in e-governance. For example, if a database field seeks a respondent's *age*, instead of his *date of birth*, things will become very awkward a few years down the line.

One of the challenges in database design is to ensure that the data locked in different database tables always remain consistent; this is usually achieved by the normalization technique (Gilfillan, 2000), where the designer works his way through the first, second, and third normal forms.

Another e-governance challenge was to connect "front-end" HTML-based user interfaces to "back-end" SQL-based databases. Such database connectivity initially tended to be specific to the database software product used, and that was obviously not very comfortable. Now the connectivity issue has been resolved more elegantly with the appearance of platform-independent "middle-tier" *Web servers*, for example, using Java.

A related problem arises when the number of "hits" becomes very large. Simple Web servers can no longer cope up with the traffic of users wishing to connect to databases at practically the same instant. One way out is to use the more powerful *Web application servers*. A second option is to move the data out of the database and store it between customized Extensible Markup Language (XML) tags. Since XML pages show up almost instantaneously on browsers, the user receives a much quicker response to his query. In fact, XML is now emerging as the preferred choice for data exchange across disparate networks.

Workflows

Most transactions in e-governance depend on workflows. After an applicant initiates a process, the application normally travels from one official desk to the next, until the process is eventually terminated. For example, an application for a loan will involve a careful scrutiny of the applicant's credit-worthiness before a decision on the loan request is made.

Most of the "bad" governance, especially in developing countries, can be attributed to faulty workflows. To start with, the workflow could be clumsy and tedious, and spread across geographically distant locations. This involves multiple queues and much grief. Then, bad workflows tend to introduce unacceptable lead times in the governance procedures. Finally, and rather sadly, flawed workflows promote corrupt practices. A file containing valuable documents and endorsements might, for example, simply vanish into thin air, and reappear only after a hefty bribe is paid.

"Good" workflows, on the other hand, provide the surest route to good governance. Like all evolutionary processes, good workflows evolve over time. Paths or chains in workflows must be trimmed, elongated, diverted, or concatenated until the optimal procedure evolves. The recent appearance of powerful workflow engines greatly simplifies such business process reengineering exercises.

ERP

Enterprise resource planning (ERP) is about tightly integrating all the business processes, usually *within* the enterprise. Most enterprises have very similar sort of functions: inventory management, manufacture, sales, marketing, human resource development, payrolls, budgeting, and so forth, and they usually operate in the "project mode," It would obviously be a great advantage if all these functions, and their interdependencies, are continually watched and monitored by a single information system. Successful ERP solutions, therefore, allow the enterprise to be much more alert and responsive, and make more intelligent business decisions.

On the down side, ERP solutions have proved to be expensive and rather difficult to implement. The difficulty in implementation is directly proportional to the extent of process reengineering ("customization") that the ERP solutions demand. But ERP solutions still provide a very valuable platform and facilitate the eventual migration to full-blown e-governance.

Security

As e-governance implementations grow, so too will security concerns. Most enterprises work around a security policy that outlines rules for network access. Security threats can be internal or external, could involve men or machines, be either willful or accidental … or be a combination of some or all of these factors.

To counter internal security threats, users are required to use passwords, or passwords in combination with other devices (smart cards, synchronized tokens, biometric matching) if the perceived threat is greater. All data and information are encrypted, and multiple back ups are maintained on diverse media. Software routines also archive detailed transaction logs so that security breaches can be investigated.

External threats are controlled by firewalls. These threats are largely from hackers or malicious software such as viruses, spasm, worms, or Trojan horses that seek to disrupt or deny service. Firewalls typically try to cut off most of the network access "ports." Because of the ubiquity of the Web, the "80 port," which brings in all the HTTP traffic, has necessarily to be kept open. The effort therefore is to funnel *all* network traffic through this single (well-guarded) port. This partly explains the growing popularity of the Web services framework.

Finally, security threats can be significantly reduced by good user practices. An ongoing training program on correct user behavior is often the first, and vital, step in the wider social engineering that enterprises must undertake.

XML and Web Services

HTML's greatest merit is that it is based on *open* standards. That is why Web pages can show up on any browser sitting on any operating system. But HTML can only *display* data; it cannot *describe* data, or facilitate the *exchange* of data. XML corrects this weakness. XML too is based on open standards, but it can also encode data or information.

XML therefore provides a wonderful opportunity to exchange data across disparate information systems. Suppose Enterprise A, having all its data on the Oracle database, wishes to exchange information with Enterprise B using the SQL Server database. Both Enterprises A and B could encode their data using XML, and the platform-independent XML could then easily facilitate the information exchange via the Web route (Hagel III, 2002).

Table 7. The e-governance building blocks

Technology	Role
HTML	Open standard for displaying Web pages. The first step in e-governance is to build a Web site that is visible to all users
Internet	The information carrier. All users participate in e-governance by using a computer or mobile device connected to the Internet. Networks are built using cable or radio
Databases	All information used in e-governance is usually stored on databases. Databases allow easy and secure storage, and quick and smart data retrieval.
Workflows	Workflows describe the paths of the e-governance processes. Most transactions are modeled using workflow engines
ERP	A tool to tightly couple business processes in an enterprise. Enterprises with ERP solutions are significantly better equipped to implement full-blown e-governance
Security	Software and hardware solutions to protect e-governance implementations from internal and external threats
XML and Web services	Open standards to exchange disparate data and applications across the Web. The recommended model to implement e-governance, especially in the "transform" phase.

Indeed, as the Web and Web protocols become ubiquitous, it is now even possible for two different Web-based applications to interact dynamically! A connection can be set up, for example, between an application using Java and another using .Net. Such connection technologies (Web services) will allow e-governance to move up from the "transact" phase to the "transform" phase.

Implementation Strategies

E-governance is not just about technology; the social, political, and economic challenges in its implementation are just as daunting. The citizens and officials must be willing to accept change; the political leadership must have a roadmap and aggressively push it; and the project funding must be committed and available. It also helps if good (but not electronic) governance practices are already in place.

To get e-governance off the ground, Andersen Consulting (Backus, 2001) recommends a strategy of "think big, start small and scale fast." At the top end of the e-governance implementation spectrum, John Hagel et al (Hagel, Brown, & Layton-Rodin, 2004) suggest that the secret to creating value from Web services is to "keep it simple, keep it incremental, and learn, learn, learn."

E-Governance Concerns

The Three Big Worries

To make e-governance a reality, "soft" leadership and management skills must complement "hard" technology skills. There are many instances where the technology development and infrastructure creation has been impeccable, but e-governance implementations have failed because the "soft" concerns were not addressed.

Three worries will be apparent as we take the long road to e-governance, and at different stages in the implementation life cycle. The first barrier, which we face soon after an e-governance project starts, relates to *human mindsets*. We often do not appreciate how radically e-governance will change human interactions and affect the "power" that people feel by physically "holding" information repositories.

Midway through a successful e-governance implementation, we worry about the *digital divide*. E-governance apparently favors "digitally well-connected" governments and enterprises. Imagine a scenario where e-governance causes the trusted postman to disappear, but the e-mail connection, which is supposed to replace the postman, has not been installed, or is unreliable. The fear, therefore, is that, for the less privileged, the old order will change, but a new order will not replace it.

Finally, in full-blown or near full-blown e-governance implementations, there is a real concern that the citizen will lose all his *privacy*: the citizen's bank balance, medical condition, voting preference, physical movements, and even his love life will be visible as e-governance radars relentlessly scan every moment of his life. We already hear protests about mobile phones being unacceptably intrusive. Tomorrow's e-governance processes could blow the privacy lid wide open.

Human Mindsets

Human reaction to an e-governance initiative can be widely different. While many enthusiastically embrace Web connectivity, others strongly resist change. It is important to understand why they respond this way, and see how we can correct that response.

Often, there is a *fear of technology*, or of interacting with "alien" machines instead of familiar humans. The attitude is: "I will submit my form to the office clerk, not a dumb computer." This is also why many callers are not comfortable leaving a message on a voice recorder, or of typing in a credit card number on a Web interface.

In most cases, however, there is the *fear of losing power or authority*. E-governance brings in sweeping process changes that make officials very uncomfortable. Most officials enjoy the power of receiving files, making remarks on files, signing on them with a flourish, and entertaining visitors soliciting favors. E-governance initiatives dilute this power and make their hallowed role rather redundant. And, if indeed this is a corrupt official receiving bribes for a favorable verdict, the pinch is felt even more.

In the early days of e-governance, there was also the very genuine *fear of losing your job* and livelihood. That is why labor unions stoutly resisted electronic initiatives. Now that fear is fading, but this is still no guarantee that an employee or official will change his mental makeup.

These mindsets must be corrected gradually. A continuous and intensive training program will be very useful. Enterprises could also start with e-governance projects of the "win-win' type; for example, showing a clerk how a click of the mouse will generate a report that took him 5 hours to write. Incentive and rewards for the best participants in e-governance projects also help in swinging things.

Digital Divide

A frequently articulated concern is that e-governance will create a digital divide between the technology "haves" and "have not's." One reason cited is the wide divergence in Internet access: while practically every citizen of a developed country would soon have Internet access, the access percentage in an under-developed country could be abysmally low. According to a recent estimate, only 7% of the human race has Internet access.

It is feared (Norris, 2001) that this wide gap between the information rich and poor will actually exacerbate social tensions, not reduce them. It is also feared that this divide, caused by e-governance, will actually weaken democracy, not strengthen it. The counterview is that "the simple binary notion of technology haves and have not's doesn't quite compute" (Warschauer, 2003) and that the "divide is not caused by just physical hardware availability, but also by the ability to engage technologies" (Warschauer, 2004).

It does indeed seem that the early concerns on the digital divide are now receding. Computer hardware and networking costs continue to decline rapidly, and the growing usage of open standards in e-governance is also diminishing software costs. The availability of cheap mobile interfaces, and the growing geographical reach through wireless networking are also encouraging developments. So although the digital divide will not disappear, it does appear that this divide will be no deeper than the other divides that have always plagued human civilizations.

Loss of Privacy

At a recent seminar of Indian CIOs in Bangkok, one of the technology solution vendors surprised the audience by openly declaring that he was not a nice man to know because he did a lot of nasty things: for example, buy up the old laptop computer that the CIO had recently sold after formatting its hard disk. "I can recover every byte on that computer using special software tools ... and then threaten to publish all your valuable data," he said only half in jest.

E-governance indeed poses a very serious threat to a citizen's privacy. For example, software for tracking a voter's preference would give a political party the sort of inputs it needs to win the next election. The e-governance tool that uses a sophisticated GIS-based software to track down criminals could just as easily be used to blackmail an innocent citizen—and things would become even easier when RFIDs start flooding the marketplace! The infrastructure created for e-governance implementations can also facilitate serious sexual misconduct on the Web.

We already see minor privacy invasions: mobile phone operators, for instance, cheerfully sell customer databases to banks and market research agencies without the customer's permission! While the menace can be partly countered by better security implementations, and by legislating more punitive legal measures to counter cyber crimes (Sinha & Condon, 2005), it does look as though, with e-governance, citizens are doomed to suffer at least a certain loss of privacy forever.

How to Address E-Governance Concerns

In a very detailed appraisal of e-governance implementations worldwide ("eGovernment for development," 2004), the "eGovernment for Development Information Exchange" project, coordinated by the University of Manchester's Institute for Development Policy and Management, has identified the "enablers" and "constraints" for every individual case study. In Tables 8 and 9, we summarize the major e-governance enablers and constraints. In Table 10, we run through the major recommendations retrieved from this study.

Table 8. Enablers of e-governance

Enabler	Remarks
Champion	Someone in the enterprise, preferably the CEO himself or one of his trusted advisers, must aggressively support e-governance and facilitate its implementation
Political will	Things become a lot simpler if the political leadership shows its willingness and keenness to usher in e-governance
Funding	The timely availability of the requisite funds is a big advantage
Frequent awareness and promotion campaigns	Many of the human mindset problems can be overcome this way
Continuous training	Even after the e-governance solution is put in place, training must continue on a regular basis
User acceptance	Start with e-governance applications offering win-win option for both the employee and the enterprise
User pressure	Once a user feels empowered by e-governance, he will ask for more
Correct location	A location with the right mix of resources is a better enabler; for example, Bangalore in India is better than Dhaka in Bangladesh
Government-citizen partnership	If both the government and the citizen perceive a shared stake in e-governance, both cooperate to make it happen. If the government fails to involve the citizen, it is less likely to work.

Table 9. E-governance constraints

Constraint	Remarks
Lack of leadership	An e-governance project without a champion, and without strong government support may not succeed
Scale	A big vision is desirable, but scales must be manageable and grow incrementally. Goals should not be overambitious
Technology availability	Projects launched without sufficient infrastructure, or using the wrong technology, tend to fail
Legislation	Even the best e-governance solution cannot be successful without supporting legislative action, for example, to permit business process reengineering
Political interference	A feud between rival political parties may hurt e-governance plans
Official disinterest	Officials will scuttle e-governance if they fear a loss of power or opportunity; a video conferencing initiative in Africa failed because officials thought it would deny them opportunities for foreign jaunts
Hostile work conditions	Implementations are not likely to succeed if work conditions are inimical
Apathy or resistance	If the participants are not excited by e-governance, or are illiterate, it will not work
Poor research	If the e-governance solution is poorly designed, it will fail far too often.

Table 10. E-governance recommendations

•	Get the technology right	•	Provide intensive training
•	Start small	•	Use a phased approach
•	Match e-governance to organizational reality	•	Look for 'win-win' situations
•	Encourage transparency	•	Undertake risk management

E-Governance Case Studies

We will look at e-governance case studies drawn from different parts of the world. The case studies highlight the many phases in an e-governance implementation. A very large number of case studies are available on the WWW; see, for example, UN Public Administration compilations ("UNPAN: Virtual Library ..", 2006) or the collection put together by the University of Manchester's Institute for Development Policy and Management ("eGovernment for development," 2004).

Citizen's Web Portal in Estonia

Every citizen in Estonia, as indeed in many other parts of Europe, has the right to know the information stored about him on the government's official databases. Typical queries could be: "give me my data from the population register," or "show me my entries in the motor vehicles register." This service had to be offered to each of Estonia's 1.4 million citizens.

Estonia, therefore, created its special citizens' Web portal (Kalja & Ott, 2004) with standard database services, at a cost of about a million euros. This service, which became fully operational by 2002, offered access to about a hundred government databases. Interactions with some of these databases could be intense and frequent; each of the 10 most popular databases recorded a few thousand hits daily. This portal could be accessed both by the citizens and the authorized civil servants.

The challenge in this relatively simple e-governance project was to ensure that the data was *secure* and *comprehensive*. To authenticate users, the portal required citizens to either log in using their ID-card, or ride on the authentication service of the country's commercial banks (this ensured access to about 75% of the citizens). Another highlight of this project was the use of open architectures to create the portal.

The project has been quite successful and triggered off other similar citizen friendly services. This project is likely to be replicated in neighboring Latvia and Lithuania.

E-Procurement in Brazil

Brazil's federal government set up an e-procurement system called COMPRASNET around 2000. Two years later, more than 1,000 federal government purchase units used this Web-based system for online quoting and reverse auction commodity purchases.

The procedure was rather simple. Every department of the federal government was required to post the specifications of its required purchase online. If the value of the commodity was

Table 11. Citizen's portal in Estonia

Attribute	Details
Why?	To guarantee the right to information to every Estonian citizen.
Who gains?	The citizen and the civil servant in Estonia, because both can quickly and securely access official records. The State, because its records get digitized.
Technology inputs	Open standards with internationally accepted protocols. The alpha version used XML RPC. The final version uses SOAP.
Lesson	Web technology could be used to offer citizens an information service that was practically free. The quality of data could be improved because citizens e-mailed corrections. There were some problems because suitable legislation did not precede the project implementation.
E-governance phase	"Inform"

Table 12. E-procurement by Brazil's federal government

Attribute	Details
Why?	Automate procurement process, make it more transparent and uniform, reduce procurement costs, speed up procurement, increase pool of suppliers.
Who gains?	The Brazilian federal government because of reduced costs, improved quality, and faster procurement. The suppliers because of better opportunity and a more level playing field.
Technology inputs	Classical client-server architecture with Windows-based servers and clients, Web application services, and application software from Vesta Business Services Suite
Lesson	Even a relatively simple e-governance implementation improves efficiency, increases profits, empowers suppliers, and builds goodwill for the federal government.
E-governance phase	"Inform" and "interact"

relatively low, the federal procurement officer opted for online quoting; for higher value purchases he recommended the reverse auction procedure.

In a review of this system, Marcos Ozorio de Almeida (2002) notes: "COMPRASNET was introduced to automate the procurement process. The aim of the automation was to make the procurement process uniform without centralizing the buying process of the federal organizations. It was also intended to reduce procurement costs and give more transparency to the process. Other aims were to increase the number of government suppliers, reduce participation cost for these suppliers, and increase competition among suppliers to reduce costs and improve the quality of goods or services acquired."

The COMPRASNET system was rated to be "largely successful." In its first 2 years it recovered about 30% of its investment cost, chiefly because it achieved an average reduction of about 20% in the cost of goods or services. Procurement times were substantially reduced; in typical cases, the time came down from 2 months to 15 days. The project was a success because it was backed by "political will inside the government" and the "external pressures" from the suppliers for a fair playing ground. The project also benefited because "it got the technology right," "provided intense training," and "adopted a phased approach." The idea of using the Web for a reverse auction, to whittle down prices, was also sufficiently innovative (Joia & Zamot, 2002).

eChoupal to Empower Indian Farmers

In Indian agriculture, the farmer often benefits the least although he does the most work and takes the biggest risks. The farmer is obliged to sell his produce at the village marketplace for ridiculously low prices to "middlemen"; these middlemen, who have better storage, transport, and marketing resources, often go on to make big profits.

Table 13. The eChoupal project for the Indian farmer

Attribute	Details
Why?	Empower the Indian farmer by educating him about good agricultural practices and enabling him to sell his produce at more attractive prices.
Who gains?	The Indian farmer and ITC who run eChoupal. ITC's investments allowed it to replace the old "middlemen" and profit from commercial transactions. It is a win-win for both.
Technology inputs	Computers with Internet connectivity; the best results were achieved using the VSAT technology.
Lesson	E-governance can be successful even in the sparsely networked Indian countryside. The project succeeded because it was visionary and ITC had the financial muscle to push it through. The project illustrates how human mindsets can indeed be changed.
E-governance phase	"Inform" and "interact"

The eChoupal software (Annamalai & Rao, 2003), from ITC, electronically recreates the village meeting place—where farmers meet to discuss crop prospects and selling rates—by positioning computers in the village with Internet connectivity. At these kiosks, often located in the house of the educated village head, farmers can order seeds, fertilizer, and other products at prices lower than those available with the village trader. They also obtain information about new farming techniques.

This e-governance project, which started gathering steam by 2003, has reached thousands of villages and helped millions of farmers. Although it started off as a project to "inform" the farmer, and help him in his trade "interactions," eChoupal is now acquiring a community center character by also advising farmers on health and creating e-learning portals for farmer education. The project should receive a significant fillip when wireless connectivity becomes more widespread.

Beijing's Business E-Park

The Zhongguancun Science Park was established in Beijing in 1988 following China's decision to open its economy to the outside world. By 2000, there were 6,000 business houses operating out of the Science Park, including international giants such as IBM, Microsoft, and Motorola.

Managing all these business establishments was proving to be very difficult because of diverse administrative procedures and workflows, a large number of approving and monitoring government departments, and long operational lead times. These business establishments contributed $12 billion in revenue and $200 million in foreign investment, so it was essential not to lose goodwill.

Table 14. Beijing's Zhongguancun E-Park

Attribute	Details
Why?	It was becoming very difficult to manage the operations of the 6,000 business establishments in the Zhongguancun Science Park. These businesses brought in valuable revenue and investments.
Who gains?	The business establishments because of efficient and streamlined governance. The Chinese government because of better trade and positive goodwill.
Technology inputs	A conventional Web-faced solution by Beijing Beauty Beard Ltd. with enhanced security and workflow management systems. Major investments in hardware, fiber, and application software.
Lesson	E-governance brings about a dramatic increase in efficiency, revenue, and goodwill, but it is important to manage mindsets and legal bottlenecks. Legislation must be in step with implementation.
E-governance phase	"Inform," "interact," and "transact."

In 2000, therefore, the Chinese government set up the Zhongguancun E-Park as a pilot project to improve the efficiency and responsiveness of the Government (Lin, Zhu, & Hachigian, 2006). Over 30 G2B and G2C functions such as "apply for license," "submit tax reports," or "file monthly statements" were introduced in a comprehensive software solution that had modules for e-application, e-registration, e-reporting, e-administration, and e-consulting. The solution also contained "reminder routines" and options to monitor the workflow progress online.

The Zhongguancun E-Park initiative has been very successful. Ninety percent of the application and approval procedures are now performed online, with as many as 4,400 companies actively interacting with the e-governance system. Application filing can now be completed in 3 days, instead of 15 days. The number of visits to complete the application filing is down from a dozen or more to just one. In fact, the Mayor of Beijing has gone on record to say that *all* administrative procedures in Beijing will be converted to this E-Park model by 2010.

The chief difficulty involved in this $1.5 million implementation was the unwillingness of officials to accept this e-governance solution because of a decrease in their power and autonomy. There were also several legal hurdles encountered during the process. Continuous and intensive training was very useful. An attractive spin-off is that there are now no traffic jams around Beijing's government establishments since most of the activity happens online!

Electronic Reservation in Indian Railways

The Indian Railways use 7,000 passenger trains to carry 5 billion train passengers every year across a network spanning 63,000 km and 7,000 railway stations. Because of overcrowding and long journey times, the recommended procedure is to board an Indian train only after prior reservation.

Table 15. Summary of e-governance initiative for Indian Railway ticket reservation

Attribute	Details
Why?	Indian Railways only have about 3,000 automated reservation counters. These counters are always crowded and expensive to manage.
Who gains?	(a) Every passenger using Indian Railways. (b) Indian Railways, because it can manage its business processes much more efficiently, offer its customers a 24x7 service, and eventually downsize its expensive reservation counters to smaller kiosks.
Technology inputs	Conventional interactive Web architecture with the provision to link the disparate railway and bank databases.
Lesson	Political pressure required the Indian Railways to innovate almost 15 years ago. Now user pressure and user acceptance ensures that there is no going back.
E-governance phase	"Inform," "interact," "transact," and fledgling elements of "transform"

While software solutions to manage train reservations were implemented over a decade ago, the procedure still required the passenger *to physically visit* a reservation booth to make his booking and payment. From 2003 or so, however, a comprehensive online booking system is now operational.

The new procedure seeks the passenger's travel details, offers an interactive session to verify seat availability online, and eventually prepares a travel bill with the option to connect to the passenger's preferred bank. An electronic payment is made using a secure connection and the passenger either has the option of printing an e-ticket or receiving the ticket by courier.

References

Annamalai, K., & Rao, S. (2003). *ITC's eChoupal and profitable rural transformation: Web-based information and procurement tools for the Indian farmer.* World Resources Institute.

Backus, M. (2001). *E-governance and developing countries: Introduction and examples.* Retrieved September 1, 2005, from http://www.ftpiicd.org/files/research/reports/report3.pdf

eGovernment for development. (2004). *Cases of eGovernment success and failure from developing/transitional countries.* Retrieved September 10, 2005, from http://www.egov4dev.org/topic1cases.htm

Gilfillan, I. (2000, March). Database normalization. *Database Journal.* Retrieved February 13, 2006, from http://www.databasejournal.com/sqletc/article.php/1428511

Hagel III, J. (2002). *Out of the box: Strategies for achieving profits today and growth tomorrow through Web services.* Boston: Harvard Business School Press.

Hagel, J., Brown, J. S., & Layton-Rodin, D. (2004). *The secret to creating value from Web services today: Start simply*. Retrieved September 17, 2005, from http://www.johnhagel.com/paper_startsimply.pdf

Joia, L. A., & Zamot, F. (2002). Internet-based reverse auctions by the Brazilian government. *The Electronic Journal on Information Systems in Developing Countries, 9*(6), 1-12.

Kalja, A., & Ott, A. (2004). *Special citizens Web portal with standard DB-services (Estonia)*. Retrieved February 8, 2006, from http://unpan1.un.org/intradoc/groups/public/documents/Other/UNPAN022018.pdf

Lin, Zhu, & Hachigian. (2006). *Beijing's buisiness e-park*. Retrieved December 11, 2006 from http://unpan1.un.org/intradoc/groups/public/documents/APCITY/UNPAN002122.pdf

Norris, P. (2001). *Digital divide: Civic engagement, information poverty, and the Internet worldwide*. Cambridge: Cambridge University Press.

Ozorio de Almeida, M. (2002). *eProcurement by Brazil's federal government*. Retrieved February 10, 2006, from http://unpan1.un.org/intradoc/groups/public/documents/Other/UNPAN022347.pdf

Sinha, T., & Condon, B. J. (2005). *Legal liabilities in a brave new cyberworld: Making electronic risk management work*. Retrieved September 8, 2005, from http://ssrn.com/abstract=800890

UNPAN Virtual Library. (2006). *Information by content type*. Retrieved February 13, 2006, from http://www.unpan.org/autoretrieve/content.asp?content=case%20studies

Vaughan-Nichols, S. J. (2004). Achieving wireless broadband using WiMAX. *Computer, 37*(6), 10-13.

Want, R. (2004). RFID: A key to automating everything. *Scientific American, 290*(1), 46-55.

Warschauer, M. (2003). Demystifying the digital divide. *Scientific American, 289*(2), 34-39.

Warschauer, M. (2004). *Technology and social inclusion: Rethinking the digital divide*. Cambridge, MA: The MIT Press

W'O Okot-Uma, R. (2001). *Electronic governance: Re-inventing good governance*. Retrieved September 2, 2005, from http://www1.worldbank.org/publicsector/egov/Okot-Uma.pdf

Chapter II

Introduction to Cryptography

Rajeeva Laxman Karandikar, Indian Statistical Institute, India

Abstract

The chapter introduces the reader to various key ideas in cryptography without going into technicalities. It brings out the need for use of cryptography in electronic communications, and describes the symmetric key techniques as well as public key cryptosystems. Digital signatures are also discussed. Data integrity and data authentication are also discussed.

Introduction

With a many-fold increase in digital communication in the recent past, cryptography has become important not only for the armed forces, who have been using it for a long time, but for all the aspects of life where Internet and digital communications have entered. *Secure and authenticated communications* are needed not only by the defense forces but, for example, in banking, in communicating with customers over the phone, automated teller machines (ATM), or the Internet.

Cryptography has a very long history. Kahn (1967) describes early use of cryptography by the Egyptians some 4,000 years ago. Military historians generally agree that the outcomes of the two world wars critically depended on breaking the codes of secret messages. In World War II, the breaking of the Enigma code turned the tide of the war against Germany. The term cryptography comes from the Greek words kryptós, meaning "hidden," and gráphein, meaning "to write." The first recorded usage of the word "cryptography" appears in Sir Thomas Browne's Discourse of 1658 entitled "The Garden of Cyrus," where he describes "the strange Cryptography of Gaffarel in his Starrie Booke of Heaven."

This chapter provides an introduction to the basic elements of cryptography. In the next section, we discuss the need for cryptography. The following four sections describe the four pillars of cryptology: confidentiality, digital signature, data integrity, and authentication. The final section concludes the chapter.

Why We Need Cryptology

First, if a company that has offices in different locations (perhaps around the globe) would like to set up a link between its offices that guarantees secure communications, they could also need it. It would be very expensive to set up a separate secure communication link. It would be preferable if secure communication can be achieved even when using public (phone/Internet) links.

Second, e-commerce depends crucially on secure and authenticated transactions–after all the customers and the vendors only communicate electronically, so here too secure and secret communication is a must (customers may send their credit card numbers or bank account numbers). The vendor (for example, a bank or a merchant), while dealing with a customer, also needs to be convinced of the identity of the customer before it can carry out instructions received (say the purchase of goods to be shipped or transfer of funds). Thus, authenticated transactions are required. Moreover, if necessary, it should be able to prove to a third party (say a court of law) that the instructions were indeed given by said customer. This would require what has come to be called a *digital signature*. Several countries have enacted laws that recognize digital signatures. An excellent source for definitions, description of algorithms, and other issues on cryptography is the book by Menezes, van Oorschot, & Vanstone (1996). Different accounts can be found in Schneier (1996), and Davies and Price (1989).

Thus, the objectives of cryptography are:

1. **Confidentiality-secrecy-privacy:** To devise a scheme that will keep the content of a transaction secret from all but those authorized to have it (even if others intercept the transcript of the communication, which is often sent over an insecure medium).

2. **Digital signature:** Requires a mechanism whereby a person can sign a communication. It should be such that at a later date, the person cannot deny that it (a communication signed by him) was indeed sent by him.

3. **Data integrity:** Requires a method that will be able to detect insertion, substitution, or deletion of data (other than by the owner). (Say on a Web server or in a bank's database containing the information such as the balance in various accounts.)

4. **Authentication:** Two parties entering into a communication identify each other. This requires a mechanism whereby both parties can be assured of the identity of the other.

Confidentiality-Secrecy-Privacy: Encryption

Encryption is necessary to secure confidentiality or secrecy or privacy. This requires an understanding of the encryption process. Most of such encryption in the past involved linguistic processes.

Consider the following example. Suppose two persons, A and B, would like to exchange information that may be intercepted by someone else. Yet A and B desire that even if a transmitted message is intercepted, anyone (other than A and B) should not be able to read it or make out what it says. Two friends may be gossiping or two senior executives in a large company may be exchanging commercially sensitive information about their company. This may be executed via e-mail (which can be intercepted rather easily). The most widespread use of secure communication is in the armed forces, where strategic commands are exchanged between various officers in such a fashion that the adversary should not be able to understand the meaning, even if they intercept the entire transcript of communication.

Let us first see how this objective could be achieved. Consider a *permutation* of the 26 letters of the Roman alphabet:

abcdefghijklmnopqrstuvwxyz

sqwtynbhgzkopcrvxdfjazeilm

Suppose that A and B both have this permutation (generated randomly). Now when A would like to send a message to B, he/she replaces every occurrence of the letter a by the letter s, letter b by q, and so on (a letter is replaced by the letter occurring just below it in the list given). Since B knows this scheme and also has this permutation, he can replace every letter by the letter occurring just above it in the list, and he can recover the message. This scheme has the disadvantage that word lengths remain the same and thus could be a starting point for *breaking the code*. This could be done using the same techniques that linguists have used to decode ancient scripts based on a few sentences written on stone. The word length remaining the same could be rectified by adding a *space* to the character set used (for ease of understanding we will denote a space by &). We will also add the punctuations , . and ?. Let us also add the 10 digits 0,1,2,3,4,5,6,7,8,9. Thus, our character set now has 40 elements. Let us write the character set and its permutation (randomly generated) as follows:

abcdefghijklmnopqrstuvwxyz0123456789&.,?

s&q69w5ty.n,b4hg0zk7opc8r?vxd1fjaze2ilm3

Now the coding scheme is a goes to s, b goes to & (space) and so on. Now even the word lengths would not be preserved, and so the attack based on word lengths would not be a threat. However, if a rather long message is sent using this scheme, say 15 pages of English text, then the scheme is not safe. A statistical analysis of the coded message would be a giveaway. It is based on the observation that frequencies of characters are different: vowels, in particular the letter e, occur most frequently in any large chunk of English text. Thus, word frequencies in the encoded text are a starting point for an attack in an attempt to recover an original message.

These are naive examples of encoding schemes. We can construct more complicated schemes, thereby making it more difficult for an attacker to recover an original message. For example, instead of one character at a time, we can form words of two characters, and have a permutation of two character words that could act as an encoding scheme. Perhaps too difficult to encode or decode manually, machines or computers could be used for these operations. For schemes that have these characters as the basic alphabet, linguists, along with mathematicians, could attempt to break the code, as was done for the Wehrmacht Enigma cipher used by Nazis during World War II. Different Enigma machines have been in commercial use since the 1920s. However, the German armed forces refined it during the 1930s. The breaking of the Werhmacht version was considered so sensitive that it was not even officially acknowledged until the 1970s.

Today, the information to be communicated is typically stored on a computer, and is thus represented using a binary code (as a string of 0s and 1s). So coding and decoding is of strings of 0s and 1s and in such a scheme, linguists have a minimal role, if any.

Basic Nuts and Bolts of Cryptology

Let us now introduce terminology that we will use in the rest of the article. The message to be sent secretly is called *plaintext* (though it could be say a music file, or a photograph). We will assume that the text or the music file or photograph has been stored as a file on a storage device (using a commonly used format such as ASCII, mp3, or jpg). We will regard the plaintext as a string of 0s and 1s. The scheme, which transforms the plaintext to a secret message that can be safely transmitted, is called an *encryption algorithm,* while the encrypted message (secret message) is called the *ciphertext*. The shared secret, which is required for recovery of original plaintext from the ciphertext, is called the *key*. The scheme that recovers the ciphertext from plaintext using the key is called *decryption algorithm*.

The encryption/decryption algorithms that require a common key to be shared are known as the *symmetric key ciphers*. In this framework, there is an algorithm, Encrypt, that takes a plaintext M_0 and a key K_0 as input and outputs ciphertext C_0 :

$$\text{Encrypt: } (M_0, K_0) \longrightarrow C_0$$

and an algorithm, Decrypt, that takes a ciphertext C_1 and a key K_1 as input and outputs plaintext M_1:

$$\text{Decrypt: } (C_1, K_1) \longrightarrow M_1.$$

The two algorithms, Encrypt and Decrypt, are related as follows: If the input to Decrypt is C_0, the output of Encrypt, and the key is K_0, the same as the key used in Encrypt, then the output of Decrypt is the plaintext M_0 that had been used as input to Encrypt. Thus, if A and B share a key K, A can take a plaintext M, use Encrypt with input (M,K) to obtain ciphertext C, and transmit it to B. Since B knows K, using (C,K) as input to Decrypt, B gets back the original message M that A had encrypted. The important point is that even if an interceptor obtains C, unless he has the original key K that was used as input to Encrypt, the message M cannot be recovered.

An adversary will try to systematically recover plaintext from ciphertext, or even better, to deduce the key (so that future communications encrypted using this key can also be recovered). It is usually assumed that the adversary knows the algorithm being used (i.e., the functions Encrypt and Decrypt), and he has intercepted the communication channel and has access to the ciphertext, but he does not know the true key that was used. This is the worst-case scenario. The algorithm has to be such that the adversary cannot recover the plaintext, or even a part of it in this worst-case scenario. The task of recovering the message without knowing the key or recovering the key itself is called cryptanalysis.

Here are different situations against which we need to guard the algorithm depending upon the usage:

- A *ciphertext-only attack* is one where the adversary (or cryptanalyst) tries to deduce the decryption key or plaintext by only observing ciphertext.
- A *chosen-plaintext attack* is one where the adversary chooses plaintext and is then given corresponding ciphertext in addition to the ciphertext of interest that he has intercepted. One way to mount such an attack is for the adversary to gain access to the equipment used for encryption (but not the encryption key, which may be securely embedded in the equipment).
- An *adaptive chosen-plaintext attack* is a chosen plaintext attack wherein the choice of plaintext may depend on the ciphertext received from previous requests.
- A *chosen-ciphertext attack* is one where the adversary selects the ciphertext and is then given the corresponding plaintext. One scenario where such an attack is relevant is if the adversary had past access to the equipment used for decryption (but not the

decryption key, which may be securely embedded in the equipment), and has built a library of ciphertext-plaintext pairs. At a later time without access to such equipment, he will try to deduce the plaintext from (different) ciphertext that he may intercept.

One kind of attack that an adversary can always mount (once he knows the algorithm being used) is to sequentially try all possible keys one by one, and then the message will be one of the outputs of the decryption function. It is assumed that based on the context, the adversary has the capability to decide which of the decrypted outputs is the message. Thus, the total number of possible keys has to be large enough in order to rule out exhaustive search. Note that if all keys of p-bits are allowed, then p = 128 would suffice for this purpose, for now, as there will be 2^{128} possible keys. Let us examine why.

Suppose we have a machine that runs at 4GHz clock speed, and we have an excellent algorithm that decides in one cycle if a given p-bit string is the key or not. Then in 1 second, we will be able to scan through $4 \times 1024 \times 1024 \times 1024 = 2^{32}$ keys. In 1 year, there are approximately 2^{25} seconds, and thus in 1 year, we can scan 2^{57} keys. Even if we use 1,000 computers in parallel, we would still have covered only 2^{67} keys. Thus, the fact that there are 2^{128} possible keys assures us that exhaustive search will not be feasible or *exhaustive search is computationally infeasible*. While designing crypto algorithms, the designer tries to ensure that the total number of possible keys is so large that exhaustive search will take a very long time (given the present computing power), and at the same time ensuring that no other cryptanalytic attacks can be mounted.

We will now describe a commonly used family of ciphers, known as *stream ciphers*.

Many of the readers may be aware of *pseudo random number generators*. These are algorithms that start from a seed (or an initial value, typically an integer) that generates a sequence of 0s and 1s that appear to be random or generated by tossing of fair coin, where 0 corresponds to tails and 1 corresponds to heads. Another way to put it is the output is indistinguishable from the output of a sequence of fair coin tosses. For any integer N, this algorithm, with the seed as input, produces $x_1, x_2, \ldots , x_N$, where each x_i is 0 or 1. Such algorithms are part of every unix/Linux distribution, and also of most C/C++ implementations.

Suppose A wants to send plaintext (message) $m_1, m_2, \ldots, m_N$ (each m_i is either 0 or 1) to B. Let the shared secret key be an integer K. Using K as the seed, it generates random bits $x_1, x_2, \ldots , x_N$ and defines:

$$c_i = x_i \oplus m_i$$

(Here $\oplus$ is the addition modulo 2, $0 \oplus 0=0$, $0 \oplus 1=1$, $1 \oplus 0=1$, $1 \oplus 1=0$).

Now $c_1, c_2, \ldots, c_N$ is the ciphertext that can be transmitted by A to B. On receiving it, B uses the shared key K as the seed, generates the bits $x_1, x_2, \ldots , x_N$ and computes:

$$d_i = c_i \oplus x_i.$$

It can be verified easily that for all a, b in {0,1}, (a $\oplus$ b) $\oplus$ b=a, and thus $d_i = (x_i \oplus m_i) \oplus$ m_i for all i.

Thus, having access to the same random number generator algorithm and the same seed enables B to generate the same random bit-sequence $x_1, x_2, \ldots, x_n$ and thereby recover the message $m_1, m_2, \ldots, m_N$ from the ciphertext $c_1, c_2, \ldots, c_N$.

It should be noted that even if an adversary knew the algorithm or the scheme being used including the random number generator, as long as she does not know the secret shared K, the generation of $\{m_i\}$ would not be possible, and hence recovery of $\{x_i\}$ will not be possible.

So the strength of this algorithm is in the pseudorandom number generator. There are algorithms that are very good for simulation (for example, the Mersenne Twister algorithm), but are not good for using in a stream cipher in the manner described, since the entire sequence can be computed if we know a few of the previous bits. This can be utilized to mount an attack on a stream cipher based on the Mersenne Twister random number generation algorithm. There are other methods to generate pseudorandom numbers for cryptographic purposes that yield good stream ciphers. Most commonly used stream ciphers are based on linear feedback shift registers (LFSR). Several LFSRs are combined via a nonlinear combining function to yield a good random bit generator. The stream cipher encrypts the binary digits of the plaintext one by one using an encryption transformation that varies with time or the position of the bit to be encrypted in the sequence (Golomb, 1967).

Another type of symmetric key (or shared key) cipher that is commonly used is a *block cipher*. This divides the plaintext into blocks of fixed size (m-bits, say), and transforms each block into another block (preferably of the same size) in such a way that the operation can be inverted (necessary for decryption). This transformation is dependent on the key, and thus decryption is possible only when we know the key that was used for encryption. The encryption transformation that operates on a block does not vary with the position of the block (in contrast with the stream cipher). Also, if the ciphertext encrypted using a block cipher is transmitted over a noisy channel, a single transmission error would lead to erroneous decryption of the entire block. Thus, errors propagate over an entire block. When ciphertext encrypted using a stream cipher is transmitted over a noisy channel, errors do not propagate. Apart from this advantage that errors do not propagate, stream ciphers are faster than block ciphers when implemented in hardware. However, as of now, no single algorithm is accepted as a standard. Lots of algorithms that are in use are proprietary.

In the early 1970s, IBM established a set of standards for encryption. It culminated in 1977 with the adoption as a U.S. Federal Information Processing Standard for encrypting unclassified information. The data encryption standard (DES) thus became the most well-known cryptographic mechanism in history. It remains the standard means for securing electronic commerce for many financial institutions around the world. (see, Menezes et al., 1996, chapter I). Block ciphers have been extensively studied from the point of view of cryptanalysis. Two techniques, called differential cryptanalysis and linear cryptanalysis, are used in cryptanalysis. In differential cryptanalysis, two plaintexts are chosen with specific differences, and each is encrypted with the same key. The resulting ciphertexts are then studied for possible mathematical relationships. If a relationship can be found that, in turn, can be used to mount an attack, it is thus a chosen plaintext attack. It is widely believed that designers of DES were aware of this technique and thus ensured that DES is secure against differential cryptanalysis. Linear cryptanalysis consists of studying the relationship between specific bits of plaintext, key, and ciphertext. If it can be established that such a linear relationship exists with high probability, it can be used to recover (a part of) the plaintext.

With increasing computing power, experts realized in the nineties that they need a new standard. Several proposals were considered and finally, in 2000, an algorithm named, *Rijndael* had been chosen by experts as a standard, now known as *dvanced Encryption Standard* or AES (see Daemen & Rijmen, 2002, also see AES1, AES2, AES3). It is used extensively in many communication devises. This uses a 128-bit key, and is considered secure for commercial transactions.

While symmetric key ciphers (stream-ciphers and block-ciphers) require that the encryption and decryption is done using the *same* key, thus requiring the sender and receiver to share the key, another framework, called *public key encryption*, does away with this requirement. Originally proposed by Diffie and Hellman (1976), this scheme consists of two algorithms, encryption algorithm and decryption algorithm, and uses a pair of (distinct) keys, one for encryption and one for decryption. The scheme works as follows: each person (or entity) in a group generates a pair of keys; one key, called the *public key*, is available in a directory of all members (or stored with a trusted third party), and the other key, called the *private key*, is kept secret by each member. A public key E_0 and the corresponding private key D_0 are related as follows: a message encrypted with the key E_0 can be decrypted using the key D_0.

Let us denote the public keys of A, B by E_A and E_B, and private keys by D_A and D_B respectively. When A wants to send a message M to B, A obtains the public key E_B of B from the directory of members, and then encrypts the message M using this key- E_B and sends the ciphertext (encrypted message) to B. Now since B knows his/her private key D_B, he/she can decrypt the ciphertext using D_B and recover the message. Also, since D_B is known only to B, only B can recover the message.

Thus, public key encryption also has two algorithms, Encrypt and Decrypt. In this framework Encrypt that takes a plaintext M_0 and a key K_0 as input and outputs ciphertext C_0:

$$\text{pubEncrypt: } (M_0, K_0) \longrightarrow C_0$$

and an algorithm, Decrypt that takes a ciphertext C_1 and a key K_1 as input and outputs plaintext M_1:

$$\text{pubDecrypt: } (C_1, K_1) \longrightarrow M_1.$$

The two algorithms, pubEncrypt and pubDecrypt, are related as follows: Let K_0 be the public key of an individual and K_1 be the corresponding private key (of the same entity). If the ciphertext input to pubDecrypt is C_0 (the output of pubEncrypt) and the key is K_1, then the output of pubDecrypt is the plaintext M_0 that had been used as input to Encrypt. Note that in symmetric key encryption, the requirement was that K_0 is the same as K_1, where as in public key encryption, the requirement is that the pair (K_0, K_1) are respectively the public and private keys of the same entity.

Thus, A and B no longer need to share a key K, A only needs to know the public key K_0 of B and then he/she can take a plaintext M, use Encrypt with input (M, K_0) to obtain ciphertext

C, and transmit it to B. Since B has the corresponding private key K_1, using (C, K_1) as input to Decrypt, B gets back the original message M that A had encrypted. The important point is that even if an interceptor obtains C, (and knows K_0, which is usually the case since the public key of all entities can be obtained) unless he/she has the corresponding private K_1, the message M cannot be recovered.

It is of course required that it should not be possible to compute the private key from the public key. Here, the phrase "not possible" is to be interpreted as computationally difficult in the sense that even several computers working in parallel would take years to compute the same. A commonly used algorithm used for public key cryptography is known as the RSA (The name RSA comes from the initials of the last names of authors Ron Rivest, Adi Shamir, and Len Adleman, who first described it). Yet another algorithm is ElGamal. The ElGamal algorithm is an asymmetric key encryption algorithm for public key cryptography, which is based on the Diffie-key agreement. Taher Elgamal discovered it in 1984.

The RSA was proposed in 1977. Initially, the computational requirements were thought to be so large, that it remained a mathematical curiosity. In fact, Clifford Cocks, in the British Intelligence Agency, proposed the same algorithm in 1973. MIT took out a patent in 1983 (which expired in 2000). Had Cocks' work been made public, it would not have been possible for MIT to patent it.

RSA is based on the widely accepted belief among experts that if p and q are two *large* prime numbers and n is their product, then given n is computationally difficult to factorize n (i.e., given n to determine p,q). What is large depends on the computational power available. Even in the late nineties, 24-bit primes, (prime numbers which in binary would require 24 bits to represent, roughly 8 digits in the decimal system) were considered very safe (p, q have to satisfy some additional restrictions). In this case n is about 48 bits. Currently, 64-bit primes are considered large enough for commercial applications, though for military and defense application, 512- or 1024-bit primes are used.

Why not use only public key cryptography and forget about symmetric key cryptography, since the former does not require sharing of a common secret key? Moreover, why not use 1024-bit primes even for commercial applications? The answer to both of these questions lies in the fact that the computational power required to encrypt or decrypt a message using public key cryptography is high, and it grows with the size of n. So public key cryptography has its limitations. Also, for a commercial communication involving a few thousand dollars, the adversary is not going to spend huge sums on breaking the code, whereas when it comes to a nation's security, the adversary can (and probably will) have a lot more resources (in terms of computing power) to try and break the code. Thus, we see that we can increase the *cost* of breaking the code for the adversary, but in turn we have to put in more resources for encryption and decryption. So like many other things in life, we have to strike a balance between costs and benefits.

So if a small piece of plaintext is to be sent, it can be encrypted using RSA. But if a long plaintext (say several pages of text along with some data files) is to be sent, it would be too time (and resource) consuming to encrypt it using RSA and we have to use a symmetric key cipher. An interesting solution is to use a combination of both. First a (random) key K of required size (for the chosen symmetric key cipher) is generated by the sender, and then this key K is encrypted using RSA and sent to the receiver, who retrieves K. Subsequently, the plaintext is encrypted using the agreed symmetric key algorithm and the key K and the ciphertext so generated is sent. The receiver already has K, and so she can decrypt it to get the plaintext.

In the evolution of the Internet, secrecy and authentication were not built into the design. Thus, unless otherwise instructed, the information is exchanged as it is and can be retrieved easily as other users also have access to the "packets" of information that are being exchanged. To be specific, say a student or a professor at a university accesses the server at her university via Telnet. After typing the login id, she types her password, which on her terminal shows as ******** so that someone looking at her screen cannot see it. However, it is very easy for someone at a university with access to another terminal on the same local area network (LAN) to capture the entire transcript of her session (all communications between her terminal and the server) including her password. The same is the story when someone accesses his or her Web-mail account through the "http" protocol from a browser. Thus, if someone gives her credit card number to a vendor while she has connected over a connection that is not "secure," the same information can be trapped by anyone who is monitoring the traffic.

To work around this is to build a secure layer over the Internet. Let us explain this with ssh, namely "secure shell" (which replaces Telnet), and sftp, "secure FTP" (which replaces FTP). Both ssh and sftp are built in most Linux distributions and are also available for Windows/Mac operating systems. At installation, the ssh client as well as the ssh server both generate a public key/private key pair. When an ssh client seeks a connection to an ssh server, they agree on one symmetric key algorithm and one public key algorithm to be used that are supported by both the server and client, then exchange their public keys. The ssh client then generates a session key for the agreed symmetric key cipher, encrypts it with the server's public key using the agreed public key algorithm, and transmits the resulting ciphertext. The ssh server now decrypts this and has the session key for a symmetric key cipher. Once this is done (all this is over in fraction of a second), all further communications are encrypted (and on receiving decrypted) using the session key. The same protocol applies when we use the sftp.

When a user accesses a Web site with an https protocol, the same steps as are carried out (provided the Web site is running the https server and the browser at the client end has the capability). So over a secure https connection, secret information can be transmitted safely. The user still has to ensure that others do not have access to his/her computer for the private key; (in principle) the session key as well as the information transmitted can be recovered from the user computer unless special precautions are taken. This now brings us to an important question. When a user accesses a Web site that he/she believes to be his/her bank and receives (or in the background, the browser receives) what is supposed to be his/her banks public key, how can he/she protect against the possibility that someone has intervened and replaced the bank's public key with another key? If indeed this happens, the user will send the session key to the imposter and subsequently, the information sent (could be his/her PIN or credit card number or other identification information) may be compromised. Thus there should be a way for the user to verify that the public key indeed belongs to the bank. This can be achieved via *digital signatures,* which we now discuss. This was introduced by Diffie and Hillman (1976).

Digital Signature

When two persons/entities enter into a contract over the Internet (an e-contract), it is necessary that they put their *signature* on the contract so that, at a later date, either party cannot repudiate the fact that they had agreed to the terms of the contract. Of course this cannot be achieved by appending a signature at the end of the e-contract as in the paper contract since, in the e-form, parts can be changed, leaving the rest intact.

A digital signature will have to be something that binds the identity of signatory and the contents of the document being signed. The framework discussed earlier about public key cryptography can be used as a framework for the digital signature.

Once again we assume that various individuals (and entities) generate a public key and a private key pair for an agreed algorithm, say RSA. A trusted third party stores identities of individuals, along with their public keys. Suppose A wants to send a digitally signed document to B. Now A encrypts the document using his/her private key, and then the resulting ciphertext is now taken as the digitally signed document and sent to B. On receiving the document, B can obtain A's public key and recover the document and, at the same time, be assured that it was signed by A. Moreover, in case of a dispute later, B can prove to a third party, say a court, that indeed A had signed the document; all he/she has to do is to preserve the ciphertext received and produce that as evidence.

Let us closely examine the last statement. The argument goes as follows: The ciphertext received is such that when decrypted using the public key of A it yields a meaningful text. Thus, it could only have been generated by someone who has access to A's private key. Since it is assumed that only A knows his/her private key, it must have been signed by A.

At the outset it looks to be a weak argument. The probability that someone can produce a bit stream that, when decrypted with A's public key, would yield meaningful text is very small, therefore, it must have been generated by A. It may still seem a rather weak argument, but it is accepted and indeed recognized by law in several countries. Indeed, this is the backbone of all e-commerce and e-transactions.

Let us assume that all individuals or entities that may exchange signed messages store their public key with a trusted third party. This trusted third party (TTP) itself generates a private key/public key pair, and its public key is available with each user. For each user, the TTP generates a digital certificate, it generates a document giving the identity of the user and the users public key, and signs it with its own private key. When A sends a digitally signed document to B, A also sends the digital certificate issued by TTP. Then B first decrypts the certificate using TTP's public key, thus recovering the identity as well as the public key (authenticated) of the sender, and can proceed to decrypt the ciphertext using the public key of the sender to recover the signed message.

Note that this system requires that there exists a trusted third party whose public key is known to all users; each user gets a digital certificate from TTP that binds his/her identity with his/her public key. Beyond this, the system does not require anything else. The individual users communicating with each other may be total strangers to each other.

In the scenario described, anyone who intercepts the communication can recover the document since all it needs is the public key of the sender. However, the same infrastructure can be used to have secret authenticated communication as follows: let KA1, KA2 be the public key and the private key of A ,and KB1 and KB2 be the public key and the private key of B. Suppose A wishes to send B a secret document, say M, signed by A. He/she follows the following steps.

Sign the document (using his/her private key) to generate C1, which is the signed document as described:

pubEncrypt: $(M, KA2)$ ———→ C1.

Encrypt C1 using public key of B to generate signed ciphertext C2:

pubEncrypt: $(C1, KB1)$ ———→ C2.

Transmit C2 to B:

B can now decrypt the transmitted message C2 using his/her private key:

pubDecrypt: $(C2, KB2)$ ———→ C3.

C3 is the same as C1. Thus, B has the digitally signed document C1. Now B can get the document (message) M by decrypting it using the public key of A. Moreover, B can retain the signed document C1 as proof that, indeed, A has signed the document M. Even if an adversary intercepts the transmission C2, (and knows or can find out the public keys of both A and B, but does not know the private key of B), he/she cannot recover C1 from C2, and so he/she cannot decrypt to get M.

Thus, the infrastructure for public key cryptography, a TTP, with a registry of users' identities and their public keys (while the users keep their private keys to themselves), suffices for digital signatures.

We had earlier remarked that if a large document is to be encrypted using a public key cryptoprotocol, say RSA, it needs a huge computational effort for encryption as well as decryption. Instead, it is common to exchange a session key for a symmetric key algorithm via public key algorithm, and then encrypt the message using this session key and symmetric key algorithm.

This does not work for a digital signature. The signature has to be something that depends on the full document and the identity of the person signing the document. However, there is one way to avoid signing the full document; it uses the notion of *hash function*, which we will discuss next.

Data Integrity

One way to ensure data integrity is to use hash functions. A hash function, or more precisely cryptographic hash function, h, is a function that takes as an input a message M (or a file) of arbitrary length and produces an output h(M) of fixed length, say n bits. The output h(M) is often referred to as the hash or hash value of M. Of course this would mean that there are bound to be collisions, that is, two distinct messages M_1, M_2 can lead to identical hash values ($h(M_1)$=$h(M_2)$). However, if the size of the output n is large, say 1,024, then the chance that two messages M_1, M_2 (chosen independently) could lead to the same hash value is very small – $2^{\{-1024\}}$. This is smaller than the probability that two randomly chosen persons have the same DNA!

Uses of the hash function: Suppose two users have downloaded a large file from the Web and, at a later date, would like to know if the two files are identical? Suppose they are in two locations far away from each other and can communicate over the Internet. Can this be done without the whole file being transferred from one location to the other? Yes, the two users can compute the hash value of their files and then compare the hash values. If they are identical, the chances are very high that the two files are the same. Another usage is in the distribution of public domain software, say *FileUtilities,* that is downloadable from several Web sites. How does the distributor and the buyer ensure that someone else is not passing off a malicious software in the name of *FileUtilities* name that has a virus embedded in it? One way to do this is (that along with the executable file) the creator publishes its hash value and before installing the software, the buyer cross-checks the hash value of the downloaded version with the value published by the creator.

In order that a hash function be useful for this purpose given, it is necessary that a change in the input leads to an unpredictable change in the hash value. If not, a malicious person can first change the file and then make other changes that have no effect on the virus, but lead to the same hash value as the original.

Desirable properties of a hash function:

- **Pre-image resistance:** given any y for which a corresponding input is not known, it is computationally infeasible to find any pre-image M such that h(M) =y.

- **2nd-pre-image resistance:** given M, it is computationally infeasible to find a 2nd-pre-image M* different from M such that h(M) = h(M*).

- **Collision resistance:** It is computationally infeasible to find any two distinct inputs M_1, M_2 that hash to the same output, that is, such that $h(M_1)$ = $h(M_2)$. (Note that here there is free choice of both inputs.)

If h is a hash function with these properties, then for a message (or file) M, its hash value h(M) can be taken as a representative for the purposes described. Thus, if we are presented a copy M* of a message M (M* may be sent over an insecure channel, which is subject to tampering) and the hash value y=h(M) (say sent over a secure channel), we can compute the hash value h(M*), and if this equals y, we can conclude that M* is indeed a copy of the message M. This would follow from the 2nd pre-image resistance property.

Hash functions can be used for data integrity checks as follows: as soon as an authorized modification of a database (or some other data source) is carried out, the administrator can generate its hash value and store it securely. Now any modification (addition, deletion) would change the database and would disturb the hash value. Thus, the administrator can periodically compute the hash value and compare it with the value stored with him. If the hash values match, the administrator can be (almost) certain that the data has not been altered.

Hash functions can also be used in the context of a digital signature, where we wish to avoid huge computations involved in digitally signing a large document. Given a hash function h with the properties of pre-image resistance, 2nd-pre-image resistance, and collision resistance, in order to digitally sign a message M, first the hash value y of M is computed (h(M) = y) and y is digitally signed using RSA. Note that irrespective of the size of M, y has a fixed predetermined size. Of course M cannot be recovered from y, but M is sent along with the digitally signed copy of y. Now y is recovered from its signature and the hash value of M is computed. If these two quantities coincide, we can conclude that M was signed by the person who signed y.

We will now see the reasons for demanding the listed properties of the hash function. Here h should be 2nd-pre-image resistance, otherwise, an adversary may observe the signature of A on h(M), then find an $M^{\#}$ such that h(M) = h($M^{\#}$), and claim that A has signed $M^{\#}$. If the adversary is able to actually choose the message that A signs, then C need only find a collision pair (M, $M^{\#}$) rather than the harder task of finding a second pre-image of y=h($M^{\#}$), thus collision resistance is also required. This forgery may be of concern if the attacker can find a pair (M, $M^{\#}$) with same hash such that M seems harmless and so the person agrees to sign it, while $M^{\#}$ is something that the adversary could use (say a promise to pay $10,000!).

Number theory has played an important role in development and analysis of various algorithms described. As the computing power increases, there is need to develop new algorithms that need a lot more computing power to break, especially in defense applications. Elliptic curves are playing an increasing role in developments on the cryptography front. These days, the computing power available on desktops (and other low-cost computing environments such as Linux clusters) is large and is increasing. Thus, elliptic curve-based algorithms would become essential even for commercial algorithms.

Authentication

All users of e-mail are used to logging into their accounts, where they choose a user name (or user_id) and then a password at the time of account set up and then, subsequently, when they wish to access their account, they have to identify themselves to the system by providing the user_id and password. The system checks this combination with the stored records and if it matches, then the user is allowed to access the account. In Unix/Linux systems, the password is not stored directly, but its hash value is stored (in some implementations, the password and user_id are concatenated to produce a string whose hash is stored). The same operation is done when a user tries to access the account and if hash values match, the access is allowed. A disadvantage of this system is that once a user has given password, someone having access to his/her system can trap it and, thereafter, impersonate him/her.

There are alternatives to this scheme; these are interactive and are based on challenge-response, Here when a user is trying to identify and authenticate himself, the system sends one or more challenges (a different set each time) and the user is to give an appropriate response. One such protocol, Feige-Fiat-Shamir (FFS) protocol (Feige, Fiat, & Shamir, 1988) relies on the computational difficulty of the problem of finding the square root modulo composite integers n that are the product of two large "RSA like" primes p,q (n=pq). This, and some other identification protocols, are known as *zerokKnowledgepProtocols(ZK)*.

They have a property that, at the end of the identification, they have passed on no other information than the identification itself. Thus, anyone having the full transcript of the communications by one user A over a period of time would still not be able to impersonate A.

We will discuss a simpler version of FFS called Fiat-Shamir protocol (Fiat & Shamir, 1987).

Setup time:

- A trusted third party generates RSA-like modulus n=pq and publishes n, but keeps p, q secret.

- Each user generates a random number s, $0<s<n$ (not equal to p,q) and computes $v=s^2$ modulo n and registers v (the users signature) with the trusted third party. The users signature is public knowledge.

Identification protocol: A user (prover) identifies himself/herself to the trusted party (verifier) and the verifier retrieves the prover's registered signature v. The following steps 1-4 are carried out say 20 times.

1. The user (prover) generates a random number r, $0<r<n$ and computes $x=r^2$ and sends x (called a witness) to the trusted party.

2. The trusted party (verifier) generates e=0 or e=1 with probability ½ each and sends e to the prover. (e is called challenge).

3. If e=0, the prover sends y=r and if e=1 sends y=rs to the verifier.

4. If e=0 and $y^2=x$ or if e=1 and $y^2=xv$ then accept the prover's claim.

If the prover's claim is accepted in all the rounds, then the prover's identity is accepted. At first glance, it would appear strange that in step 2, the verifier may select e=0 and would require the user to send only the random number r. This step is required to prevent forgery: suppose the prover always generates e=1 and a malicious person knows this (and also v, which is public knowledge), then the user can generate a number t, compute $x=t^2/v$ (modulo n) and send as witness and in step 3, send y=t. Without knowing s, the malicious person would have satisfied the condition $y^2=xv$. In this case, if e=0 is allowed, then the malicious person will not be able to send the square root of $x= t^2/v$ (modulo n) in step 3.

This protocol can be thought of as follows: in step 1, the prover sends a witness x and claims to have answers to the questions "what is r?" and "what is y=rs?", but in one instance would answer any of the two questions but not both (as it would reveal his/her secret).

Concluding Comments

In this chapter, we have four pillars of cryptology: confidentiality, data signature, data integrity, and authentication. Thus, we have discussed the problems that can occur when data is transmitted over *insecure* lines.

There are other dangers as well. Starting from someone observing the keystrokes when a person enters a key or password via a keyboard, to someone running a simple program on a person's computer that traps (and record) all keystrokes, an adversary can recover a key or password that was typed. Likewise, unless one is careful, one can recover files that were deleted (even after the recycle bin on Windows operating system has been emptied!). Garfinkel and Shelat (2003) analyzed 158 second-hand hard drives. They found that less than 10% had been sufficiently cleaned, and a wide variety of personal and confidential information was found in the rest. Thus, there are simple measures that most people ignore to secure information. No amount of cryptographic safeguards can save us from human follies.

References

Advanced Encryption Standard 1. (n.d.). Retrieved August 16, 2006 from http://csrc.nist. gov/publications/fips/fips197/fips-197.pdf

Advanced Encryption Standard 2. (n.d.). Retrieved August 16, 2006 from http://csrc.nist. gov/CryptoToolkit/aes/round1/conf2/papers/biham2.pdf

Advanced Encryption Standard 3. (n.d.). Retrieved August 16, 2006 from http://csrc.ncsl. nist.gov/CryptoToolkit/aes/rijndael/misc/nissc2.pdf

Daemen, J. & Rijmen, V. (2002). *The design of Rijndael: AES—the advanced encryption standard.* Berlin: Springer-Verlag.

Davies, D. W., & Price, W.L. (1989). *Security for computer networks* (2nd ed.). New York: JohnWiley & Sons.

Diffie, W., & Hellman, M. E. (1976). New directions in cryptography. *IEEE Transactions on Information Theory, IT-22*(6), 644-654.

Feige, U., Fiat, A., & Shamir, A. (1988). Zero-knowledge proofs of identity. *Journal of Cryptography, 1,* 66-94.

Fiat, A., & Shamir, A. (1987). How to prove yourself: Practical solutions to identification and signature problems. *Advances in Cryptology—Crypto '86* (pp.186-194). Berlin: Springer-Verlag.

Garfinkel, S. L., & Shelat, A. (2003). Rememberance of data passed: A study of disk sanitation practise. *IEEE Security and Privacy, 1*(1), 17-27.

Golomb, S. W. (1982). *Shift register aequences.* San Francisco: Holden-Day. Walnut Creek: Aegean Park Press.

Kahn, D. (1967). *The codebreakers.* New York: Macmillan Publishing Company.

Menezes, A., van Oorschot, P., & Vanstone, S. (1996). *Handbook of applied cryptography.* Boca Raton: CRC Press.

Rivest, R. L., Shamir, A., & Adleman, L. (1978). A method for obtaining digital signatures and public-key cryptosystems. *Communications of the ACM, 21*(2), 120-126.

Schneier, B. (1996). *Applied cryptography: Protocols, algorithms, and source code in C* (2nd ed.). New York: John Wiley & Sons.

Chapter III

E-Business Process Management and Intellectual Property:
Issues and Implications

Kathleen Mykytyn, Southern Illinois University, USA

Peter Mykytyn, Southern Illinois University, USA

Abstract

The emergence of e-business as a viable business model is unquestioned and global in its involvement and impact. Further, the value that intellectual property (IP) in the form of trademarks, copyrights, and patents plays in that medium of doing business impacts businesses, information technology (IT) professionals, academics responsible for IT coursework and programs, and, of course, the legal community. This chapter reviews these IP types with particular emphasis on their relationship and impact on e-business. Relevant legal cases are cited and discussed to provide additional foundation to the e-business community. The chapter also provides appropriate recommendations for e-business in light of these IP issues, and identifies some possible future trends and research issues.

E-Business Process Management and
Intellectual Property: Issues and Implications

The advent of the Information Age has brought about a different way of thinking about how information should be used in both the public and private domain. It has also challenged businesses to take advantage of information technology (IT) in conducting everyday tasks. The introduction of the Internet into the business model, that is, electronic commerce, has not only provided new opportunities and efficiencies for firms, but has also posed threats to them. In particular, firms are confronting numerous issues that today are impacting their intellectual property (IP) assets. All of this is truly a new, virtual frontier. However, computers and the Internet are presenting new and challenging legal questions that may take many years to become well-settled points of law. One area of the law that has been dramatically affected by computer technology is in the field of IP, for example, trademarks, copyrights, and patents. Referring to intellectual property, Ghosh (2002, pp. 454-455) states that:

The field is hot, so to speak, and often eclipses other more compelling issues in the media and legal fora. Intellectual property issues are ubiquitous precisely because intellectual property is the final frontier. Market economies expand and thrive by conquest, and our world has expanded as much as it can geographically. Real property, or land-based systems, offer very few prospects for further exploitation. Personal property similarly offers few remaining challenges for entrepreneurial enterprise..... It is not hard to fathom the importance of intellectual property in commodifying the intangible inputs and outputs of an economy based on the selling of services, whether medical, legal, financial, or entertainment.

Caught in the middle of these emerging e-business issues are the IT professionals, for example, Webmasters, who create and/or maintain a company's Web site and e-commerce systems. They may feel that their technological expertise in developing and maintaining Web sites is their only responsibility, that is, any social, political, or legal issues are not their concern. Consequently, Webmasters not only have no noticeable knowledge regarding the applicable IP laws, they also have a large dose of disdain for them (Kamarck, 1999). They believe that their job is to drive users to a corporate Web site efficiently and effectively, and without any knowledge of, or belief in, IP laws, they can be creative and successful in their abilities to do so. Consequently, firms may have manipulated the technical aspects of Web-site development without regard for the IP rights of others (Kamarck, 1999).

Underscoring the important role played by IT professionals today is the nature and amount of e-business being conducted today. The U.S. Department of Commerce's Economics and Statistics Administration publishes an annual report about the digital economy. Its 2003 report, the latest available, indicates that retail e-business activity has shown a 28% increase over the second quarter of 2002, but that the B2B e-business arena has not shown as much improvement and has fallen short of expectations (Digital Economy, 2003). At the same time, as shown in Figure 1, the rise in e-commerce-related lawsuits from 1995 to 2005, comprising trademark, patent, and copyright litigation, attests to the apparent lack of knowledge of IP law by either firms or Webmasters. As shown, the number of Internet-related lawsuits is increasing dramatically, which should be a cause of concern for organizations and information technology (IT) researchers who are investigating various e-commerce issues today.

Figure 1. E-commerce-related IP lawsuits, 1994-2004

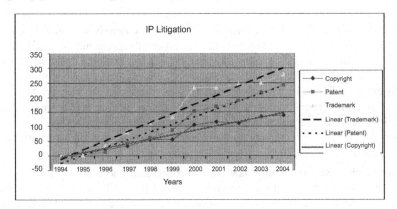

Note: All data was obtained using LexisNexis. A search was conducted for trademark, patent, and copyright court cases using each word, for example, "copyright," as a keyword, followed by the keyword "Internet." We have added a trendline for each type of lawsuit extending beyond 2004 to suggest that the number of such lawsuits is not declining.

The overall purpose of this chapter is to provide an awareness of the relationship between e-business and IP for IT professionals and others, including business professionals. In doing so, we hope that many readers may have an increased awareness of the importance of these issues that impact business professionals, IT professionals, and many in the academic community. We will define the law dealing with the three areas of protection covered in the chapter–trademarks, copyrights, and patents. We will also integrate how these forms of IP relate to e-business. It is important to understand just why these forms of IP are an important area of consideration involving today's e-commerce. The chapter will conclude with areas of suggested research appropriate for academic researchers, and our assessment of some future trends involving IP and e-business. For further support, the chapter will cite relevant court cases involving IP and e-business.

Intellectual Property Law: Trademarks, Copyrights, and Patents

Intellectual property is a broad area of the law related to protecting ideas, concepts, and products. For purposes of this chapter, the relevant topics addressed will be limited to trademarks, copyrights, and patents.

Trademarks

Today, trademarks are used by businesses to distinguish themselves from their competition. They are also used to protect commercial goodwill, and could be regarded as an intangible benefit. Intangible benefits may have direct organizational benefits, but cannot be easily measured in dollars or with certainty. The reputation of a firm is too valuable to risk misunderstanding what trademarks are and how to use them to preserve legal rights in them. The importance of trademarks to current business practice is undisputed. Perhaps Field said it best when he stated that, "Assuming that its owners are not the type to write their name in chalk on the company truck, no business is small enough that it can afford to ignore trademarks" (Field, 2000).

Trademark rights exist at common law and are recognized and enforced by most states. The U.S. Congress recognized these rights and extended them by way of federal statute; this source of trademark rights has become predominant in the U.S. (15 U.S.C. §§1051, 1988). This statute, commonly known as the Lanham Act, provides a national registry for trademarks that carries with it national protection for registered marks (15 U.S.C. §§1114, 1988). Once registered, the trademark is valid for 10 years and may be renewed for like periods as long as the mark is in constant use. Failure to use the mark can result in the loss of the rights in the mark.

The fundamental purpose for the trademark statute is to protect the public against misidentification of a product or service so that there is little likelihood of confusion as to the manufacturer of a product. The statute also protects a trademark owner, who generally has made a substantial investment in the promotion of the product or service being placed in the marketplace, from its misappropriation by competitors. Under this statute, trademark holders can sue for trademark infringement if they can show that they possess a protectable mark. Protectability is generally a function of the strength of a mark and the likelihood of confusion in the marketplace.

A trademark can be viewed as any word, phrase, symbol, design, sound, smell, color, or product structure that is adopted and used by a business to identify and distinguish its products and/or services (Guillot, 2000). Trademarks can be considered synonymous to brand names, and are determined to be important intellectual properties that distinguish one company's products or services from another's. In addition to trademarks, there are service marks; technically, a trademark is a symbol used to identify a specific source of goods, while a service mark is used to identify a service. Such "marks" are denoted as any symbol that can be legally used by only one organization or a group of legally related organizations. Whatever types of "marks" are used, they enable consumers to look for, or avoid, products or services that are marketed under those names or symbols (Field, 2000).

When consumers perceive a name, symbol, and so forth, to be associated with a product or service as indicative of its source, then that name, symbol, and so forth, is entitled to legal protection as a trademark. It would not serve consumer interests if businesses could duplicate a product or service but not identify it in a manner that the consumer would recognize. Field (2000) notes that consumers may even create a trademark or create a second trademark using a nickname; "Coke" was accorded legal protection before the company used it.

Trademark Applicability to E-Business

Until the Internet was developed, only companies that conducted business on a national or international level needed to be concerned about trademark law. If a business was local, there was little likelihood of customer confusion with other local businesses and, thus, little concern over trademark conflicts. Regarding e-commerce, however, there is no such thing as a local business, and the names of businesses, products, and/or services must be given attention to ensure that legal benefits are obtained and legal threats are avoided. When a company invests heavily in consumer goodwill, it needs to understand how to protect its investment. More succinctly, a company wishing to ensure the viability of its trademarks must ensure that its trademarks are not infringed upon by others.

One of the more important areas dealing with e-business and trademark infringement pertains to domain names. When doing business on the Internet, trademark law determines when the use of a domain name infringes someone else's trademark. In the recent past, trademark owners who desired to use their marks as domain names found that the name had already been taken. Further, trademark owners found that unauthorized parties were using their marks as domain names, many times in a deliberate attempt to free ride on the goodwill of the mark's owner (Dueker, 1996). Others have obtained domain names for the purpose of selling them back to a trademark owner. With the passing of the Anticybersquatting Consumer Protection Act (ACPA) in 1999, a domain name that is the same, or confusingly similar to an existing trademark anywhere in the U.S., cannot be used for the purpose of selling the name back to the mark's owner (ACPA, 2000). Two fundamental rules of trademark law and domain names are:

1.   Names, logos, or domain names cannot be used if they can confuse consumers as to the source of goods or services:
     - If a domain name is in conflict with an existing mark and is likely to cause customer confusion, a court could force the infringer to relinquish the name. Further, if the infringement is deemed willful, compensation to the mark's owner for losses and statutory damages may be ordered.
2.   Names, logos, or domain names cannot be used if they invoke a famous product or service, even if consumers would not be confused.

If a domain name is the same or similar to an existing known mark, the owner of the mark may file a suit preventing any further use of the domain name, even though there is little likelihood that consumers would be confused. For example, if a marriage counselor decided on the domain name withfidelity.com, fidelity.com, the domain name of Fidelity brokerage, would probably prohibit the use of the name simply because it causes fidelity.com to come to mind.

One example emphasizes the importance of this point. In September 1998, former Stanford University graduate students incorporated the search engine, Google, and registered its domain name a year later. In December 2000 and January 2001, Sergey Gridasov of St. Petersburg, Russia registered the domain names googkle.com, ghoogle.com, gfoogle.com and gooigle.com. The practice of deliberately misspelling registered domain names for the purpose of creating confusion has become known as "typosquatting." In May 2005, Google filed a complaint with The National Arbitration Forum, a legal alternate to litigating in court, complaining that Gridasov had engaged in this practice. Gridasov didn't respond to Google's complaint, meaning that the arbitrator could accept all reasonable allegations as true. The arbitrator endorsed Google's contention that the misspelled addresses were part of a sinister plot to infect computers with programs, known as "malware," that can lead to recurring system crashes, wipe out valuable data, or provide a window into highly sensitive information. As a result of this decision, the rights to the above referenced domain names were transferred to Google.com (National Arbitration Forum, 2005).

Trying to piggyback on the popularity of a heavily trafficked Web site like Google.com is not new. For instance, the address Whitehouse.com used to display ads for pornography was a surprise for Web surfers looking for Whitehouse.gov, the president's official online channel. Whitehouse.com now operates as a private Web site that sells access to public records.

Besides domain name issues, the selection of a trademark should involve serious consideration. Just because a business may acquire a domain name registration, that does not give it priority in obtaining a trademark on that name. The registration of a domain name on the Internet does not override long-established principles of trademark law. The utilization of a competitor's trademark in a domain name would likely confuse users as to its source or sponsorship, and this form of confusion is precisely what the trademark laws are designed to prevent.

It is also important to recognize that e-business encompasses many dimensions, dimensions that are broader than what is often labeled as e-commerce today. For example, in the case of Planned Parenthood Federation of America, Inc. vs. Bucci, (Planned Parenthood, 1997), the district court found that Bucci impeded Planned Parenthood's ability to use its service mark, Planned Parenthood. Bucci, a pro-life advocate, registered the domain name http://www.plannedparenthood.com and posted antiabortion literature on that site. Although Bucci did not promote a good or service on that site, the court found that Bucci was still engaging in a commercial use of the domain name based on the fact that Bucci affected Planned Parenthood's ability to offer its services over the Internet. This case illustrates quite emphatically the degree/breadth of infringing activities that can violate the ACPA.

Copyrights

Basically, copyrights in the U.S. are a collection of rights, defined by federal statute, that give the copyright owner the exclusive right to do or authorize others to do any of the following: (1) reproduce the copyrighted work; (2) prepare a derivative (adaptation) work based upon the copyrighted work; (3) distribute copies of the copyrighted work to the public by sale or other transfer of ownership or by rental, lease, or lending; (4) publicly perform the work, (5) publicly display the work, and (6) perform a sound recording publicly through digital transmission when the copyrighted work is a sound recording. See Lipson (2001) and Blaise (2005) for additional information regarding copyright history and characteristics.

Creations that can be copyrighted comprise: literary works; musical works; dramatic works; pantomimes and choreographic works; pictorial, graphic, and sculptural works; motion pictures; sound recordings; architectural works; and computer software. Copyright has generally been associated with the "arts" since it has been applied to most forms of artistic works, such as plays, paintings, novels, poetry, music, and so forth.

Copyrights do not exist in facts, ideas, procedures, processes, systems, methods of operation, and so forth, regardless of the form in which they are described or embodied. Copyright does not protect a blank form or commonplace phrases, images, or organizational choices. Essentially, it only protects expression–the way an author, artist, or performer expresses an idea or describes facts.

Over the years, much of IP, and copyright in particular, did not generate that much interest or enthusiasm by businesses and organizations. Rather, these entities were most likely concerned about other more physical assets such as buildings, plants, equipment, and the land upon which those assets rested (Hunter, 2005). In dealing specifically with copyright, that form of IP was considered most relevant to stop commercial reproduction of, say, a book, similar to the previous discussion. Focusing on copyright, in order to preserve the balance between property rights and the ability of the public to have appropriate access to copyrighted works, a copyright owner was never granted complete control over his/her work. Rather, the copyright holder's rights are limited to the six rights listed previously. With the commercialization of the Internet and the development of e-business, the older view of copyright and what businesses must be concerned with changed significantly.

Copyright and The Evolution of Electronic Business

What is often not addressed, at least from an IT research point of view, are some of the legal issues and ramifications encompassing e-business and copyrights that can affect organizations. Essentially, organizations need to be aware that some actions that they take may lead to infringing on others' copyrights. Likewise, those same organizations need to take appropriate measures to ensure that others do not infringe on the organization's copyrighted material.

Realistically, there are a countless number of issues involving copyright and copyright infringement that might arise in the course of e-business. For our purposes, we feel that the topics addressed next are very relevant today as they might impact businesses. These topics are the Digital Millennium Copyright Act (DMCA), digital rights management (DRM), the posting of copyrighted material on Web sites, appropriate and inappropriate linking to other Web sites, liability issues related to Internet service providers (ISPs), and steps that can be taken by organizations to protect their copyrighted material from being infringed by others.

In 1998, the Digital Millennium Copyright Act (DMCA) was enacted in direct response to what were seen as critical challenges from the Internet (Digital, 1998). The U.S. Congress was concerned about the ease with which exact copies of copyrighted materials could be made with hardly any loss of quality, possibly leading to the unauthorized distribution of perhaps millions of copies. The DMCA involved two basic changes to the copyright law. First, it directly prohibited the use of specific technologies: those that can be used to circumvent technological protection measures (Samuelson, 1999). In other words, the protection of expression is, for the first time, achieved through the regulation of devices (Merges 2000). Second, this regulation was attached to a new list of infringing activities focusing on the circumvention of technical protection schemes. In reality, the two sets of provisions–those regulating the deployment of devices, and those defining illicit acts of circumvention-are so distinct that the detailed exemptions to the latter provisions do not apply at all to the former (Samuelson, 1999).

The DMCA is not without its opponent. After 7 years since enactment of the DMCA, critics have stated that the act infringes on a person's free speech and allows copyright owners to override fair use (Fitzdam, 2005). Still others believe that the DMCA stifles competition and innovation and even serves as an impediment to accessing computer networks (Fitzdam, 2005). The Act has thus far withstood all constitutional challenges, and even though Congress has proposed some changes to the Act in order to quiet some of the more discordant critics, it appears to be here to stay.

An important part of copyright today relates to digital rights management (DRM), which is various technologies and methods that can control or restrict users' access to and use of digital media, for example, movies, music, computer games, on various devices, for example, personal computers, that have such technology installed (McCullagh & Homsi, 2005). Early applications of DRM dealt with security and encryption as a means of solving the issue of unauthorized copying. The second-generation of DRM covers the description, identification, trading, protection, monitoring, and tracking of all forms of rights usages over both tangible and intangible assets including management of rights holders' relationships (Iannella, 2001).

With the importance of all types of digital media as relates to e-business today, it is important that all parties involved are cognizant of DRM. Holders of copyrighted material, such as movies, music, photos, and other digital media, have the right to ensure that they receive appropriate rewards for the digital media that they have copyrighted, media that may easily find itself in the stream of e-commerce; these individuals or organizations would be classified as DRM proponents. On the other hand, opponents of DRM are fearful that inappropriate restrictions will be placed on consumers and others who use the Internet lawfully.

Suffice it to say that DRM is an evolving concept that has strong proponents and opponents. Hardware and software technologies are also evolving with regard to how best to implement DRM. Those engaged in e-business, whether they are businesses themselves or end users/consumers who are making purchases of digital media online, need to be aware of the issues so as to ensure that the rights of all parties are protected.

Notwithstanding the importance of the DMCA as discussed, another section of the DMCA has received considerable attention of late that is extremely important to e-business. That concerns the possible liability incurred by ISPs that post copyrighted material on others' Web sites.

ISPs run the risk of substantial liability for passively providing for the opportunity for their subscribers to commit acts that could lead to copyright infringement (Croman 2005). This has become one of the most contentious issues surrounding e-business and copyright, and is perhaps best represented as an issue in terms of the inappropriate, that is, illegal download of copyrighted music, videos, and even software. For the most part, however, the DMCA exempts ISPs from liability for monetary, injunctive, or other equitable relief regarding copyright infringement, even if the ISP transmits, routes, or even provides a connection for such material, including just temporarily storing the material (Albert, Sanders, & Mazzaro, 2005). The caveat for ISPs is that they must not have actual knowledge of the infringing activity, they cannot be aware of information indicating that the material is infringing, and does not receive financial benefit directly attributable to the infringing activity (Albert et al., 2005). These have often been referred to as the "safe harbor" provisions of the DMCA. However, even though the law does not require an ISP to monitor activity on its network or attempt to obtain information that might indicate that an infringing activity is occurring, the ISP must remove the material or disable access to it once the ISP becomes aware of the activity.

Although many of the references are directed toward ISPs, non-ISPs may find that they too may have committed copyright infringement. In the case of A&M Records vs. Napster, Inc. (A&M Records, 2000), Napster allowed uploading of music recordings for access by its customers who had allegedly acquired proper copies of the files. Napster claimed that it should be protected under the safe harbor provisions of the DMCA. The Court found otherwise, and also raised questions about whether Napster's copyright policies were adequate with regard to what the DMCA requires. Further appeals by Napster were denied, leading to significant business problems for Napster.

Another practice that may have negative impacts involving e-business is inappropriate linking of Web sites/Web pages; the practice is often referred to as deep linking. Essentially, deep linking occurs if Web site A links to pages within Web site B and in so doing bypasses the homepage of Web site B. On the one hand, given the relative free nature and free access to the Web, one might not even give such a technique a second thought. However, a number of court cases have led to injunctions against e-business companies that occurred as a result of inappropriate linking.

One of the first hyperlinking cases occurred in Scotland and involved the *Shetland Times* vs. *The Shetland News*. *The Shetland Times* (*Times*) was a well-established newspaper, and *The Shetland News* (*News*) was an electronic paper. The *News* used headlines of *Times* newspaper articles as captions for its hyperlinks, with the links connecting users to the *Times* Web site and the stories themselves, bypassing the *Times'* homepage. The *Times* claimed copyright infringement, while the *News* argued that the Internet in based on free access. The Court found that *News* violated the *Times* copyrights and circumvented the advertising on the *Times'* homepage. The case was eventually settled out of court. (*Shetland Times*, 1996).

In another case involving copyright infringement and hyperlinking, Intellectual Reserve, Inc. vs. Utah Lighthouse Ministry, Inc., the Court ruled in 1999 that the defendant, Utah Lighthouse Ministry, Inc., had engaged in copyright infringement. Its Web page contained copyrighted materials of Intellectual Reserve, Inc. as well as hyperlinks that linked users to three Web sites that they knew contained infringing copies of Intellectual Reserve's copyrighted material. The Court issued a preliminary injunction against Utah Lighthouse Ministry (Dockins, 2005) and made specific mention of the infringing activities associated with deep linking.

With regard to deep linking, some Courts have concluded that this activity does not constitute copyright infringement, for example, Ticketmaster Corp. vs. Tickets.com, Inc. (Ticketmaster, 2000). This uncertainty only serves to lead to confusion and doubt for those engaged in e-business activities. On the one hand, those engaged in e-business as well as most Internet users are accustomed to seeing and using hyperlinks constantly. It follows then that e-businesses should ensure that any linking from their sites to others' sites are appropriate and covered by hyperlinking agreements between the parties.

E-businesses should aggressively pursue those that may infringe on their copyrighted material, especially if the infringing activities could lead to financial harm. With the importance of the Internet and related commerce today, e-businesses should seriously consider securing appropriate legal counsel to protect their interests and also to keep them from infringing on others' copyrighted material. It would be unwise for e-businesses to rely solely on IT professionals, such as Webmasters and Web designers, who generally know very little about the legal issues involved and their ramifications (Mykytyn, Mykytyn, & Harrison, 2005).

The seriousness of copyright infringement was emphasized in the MP3.com case: a case that received much public attention. Judge Rakoff "sent a message" to would-be copyright infringers, stating that:

...while the difficult issue of general deterrence must always be approached with caution, there is no doubt in the Court's mind that the potential for huge profits in the rapidly expanding world of the Internet is the lure that tempted an otherwise generally responsible company like MP3.com to break the law and that will also tempt others to do so if too low a level is set for the statutory damages in this case. Some of the evidence in this case strongly suggests that some companies operating in the area of the Internet may have a misconception that, because their technology is somewhat novel, they are somehow immune from the ordinary applications of laws of the United States, including copyright law. They need to understand that the law's domain knows no such limits. (UMG, 2000, pp. 17-18)

Patents

The U.S. Constitution, dating back to the late 1700s, provides the basis for patent laws in the U.S. These laws are intended to advance science and industry by providing inventors, as well as their assignees, with financial incentives for their inventions for 20 years from the date that a patent application is filed (Voet, 1995). Inventors or assignees are also provided with exclusive rights to the invention during that same period. These rights include the right to exclude others from making, selling, or even using the invention. In addition, the patent holder is also provided with the right to license others to make, sell, or use an invention for a period of 20 years from the patent filing date.

One of the important aspects of patent protection is the rights afforded to the patent holder should someone engage in infringing activities against the patented invention. This makes perfect sense because of the time and/or money to develop the invention and obtain a patent on it. Essentially, patent infringement is defined as any activity by someone who makes, sells, or uses a patented product or process that is substantially the same as the invention even though there may be no knowledge of the existence of a patent on that product or process (Koffsky, 1995). When a patented product or process is copied exactly, infringement is fairly easy to prove. One example of this occurred in 1994 between Microsoft Corporation and Stac Electronics. Stac had received a patent for data compression software, which Microsoft wanted to license. When licensing negotiations broke down, Microsoft decided to use its own technology, which was essentially the same as Stac's. Stac then sued Microsoft for patent infringement. Not only did Microsoft lose the case, the jury awarded Stac $120 million in damages (Chin, 1994).

Based on the Doctrine of Equivalents, a product or process that is substantially the same can also infringe. This doctrine is founded on the theory that "...*if two devices do the same work in substantially the same way and accomplish substantially the same result, they are the same, even though they differ in name, form or shape*" (Graver, 1950, p. 605). Remedies for infringement can include injunctive relief; adequate compensation to the patent holder that, when appropriate, can be trebled and, under no circumstances, would be less than a reasonable royalty plus interest for the use of the invention by the infringer; and in exceptional cases—those cases where a defendant knowingly infringes–the awarding of attorneys' fees.

During the 1980s, actions were taken by the government to strengthen and revitalize the patent system. This revitalization has come with legislation—much of it intended to curb infringement—and, more significantly, with the creation of the Court of Appeals for the Federal Circuit (CAFC) in 1982, which has been granted exclusive jurisdiction over patent appeals (Merz & Pace, 1994). The impact the CAFC has had on patent prosecution through enforcement was studied by Merz and Pace (1994). Using data for the period from July 1971 through December 1991, they questioned whether patent litigation had also increased since the CAFC increased enforceability. Their results indicated that a significant increasing trend in litigation occurred some time after April, 1982. This may be due in part to the creation of the CAFC and a more patent friendly environment. Further, they theorize that the increase in enforceability and, thus, the value of patents, may explain the dynamic increase in patent application filings. Although the data presented in Figure 1 deals with Internet-related patent lawsuits only, there is ample evidence of the growing importance for businesses and IT researchers as well regarding the relationship between IP in general and e-business activities. We address this relationship next.

Patents and The Evolution of Electronic Business

With regard to e-business activities and computer software related thereto, some might raise the question as to whether software is even patentable. For a very long time, such was the case. That changed, however, in 1981, when the U.S. Supreme Court held that software could be patented (Diamond, 1981). The U.S. Supreme Court's decision to provide for the patentability of software in the Diamond vs. Diehr case is significant. The Court declared that a claim for an invention using a computer for one or more steps of a process was valid subject matter for patent protection. Since that time, the number of patents for computer software is measured in the thousands. For example, the following well-known companies have been assigned software-related patents (the number in parentheses is the number of software-related business method patents assigned through late August 2005): Electronic Data Systems – 46; Merrill Lynch – 24; MasterCard International – 15; Priceline.com – 14; Amazon.com – 24 (USPTO, 2005).

The software patents awarded to Priceline.com and Amazon.com are significant in that these organizations deal directly with e-business. In fact, their only method of doing business is based on the Internet. Thus, some of the patents that have been awarded for e-commerce are, in fact, patents for ways of doing business; these are often referred to as business method patents (Wiese, 2000).

Much of the impetus to secure business method patents rests with a now-famous case involving State Street Bank & Trust Co. vs. Signature Financial Group, Inc. Signature had developed and patented a program to calculate changes in the allocation of assets of mutual funds. State Street attempted to negotiate a license with Signature, but was unable to do so. Subsequently, State Street sued Signature, claiming that Signature's patent was invalid. A U.S. District Court in Massachusetts agreed with State Street, finding that the patent was for a business method, which, in its opinion, would invalidate the patent. The case ultimately reached the CAFC, which stated that even though the patented application involved an algorithm (algorithms by themselves are not patentable), the idea itself was applied in such a way as to produce a useful and practical application, which is patentable (State Street, 1998). The aftermath of this decision has seen a flood of business method patent applications being submitted to the U.S. Patent and Trademark Office (Cantzler, 2000), many, as stated, involving e-business initiatives.

As stated, business method patents are especially relevant to the e-business environment. Notwithstanding their importance, many have argued that this type of patent should, for the most part, not be granted because in many instances the method being patented is not a unique business process, or that it tends to stifle e-business. One of the requirements for an invention to be patented is that it not exist as "prior art;" rather, it must be novel and nonobvious. Interesting research by Allison and Tiller (2003) found results that support the position that business method patents are no more invalid than nonbusiness method patents. They found that patents, in general in the late 1990s, as compared with business method patents, are not any better in terms of their quality. More specifically, applications for business method patents spent more time with the USPTO than patents in general; for example, they received more scrutiny, and business method patent applications cited nonpatent prior art of a similar quality to that in the average patent (Allison & Tiller, 2003). These results tend to question the belief that business method patents should be eliminated.

Another interesting and highly relevant patent infringement case is currently being litigated and resides with the CAFC. The case, MercExchange vs. eBay, involves one of the better-known e-businesses, eBay, and a small one-man company called MercExchange owned by Tom Woolston. Woolston's three patents, one for a method and apparatus for Internet-worked auctions, one for using search agents to return a list of matched goods from a number of different sources, and a third patent dealing with the creation of a computerized market for goods for sale or auction. This lawsuit is considered very relevant not only to e-business in general, but also to eBay since the patents at issue allegedly covered significant parts of eBay's Web-based business. These parts include the auction activity, fixed price sales, and a search activity that links a buyer's interest to the database containing the merchandise (GuFN, 2005). The patent infringement issue dealing with the Internet-worked auction patent was dismissed, but the issues involving the remaining two patents were adjudicated. In May 2003, the jury found that eBay and Half.com, a subsidiary company, had willfully infringed the two remaining patents and assessed damages in the amount of $35 million. Appellate proceedings before the CAFC are pending (GuFN, 2005).

The role of patents as they relate to computer software extends far beyond the e-business perspective. Some would suggest that patents are not appropriate for computer software because software innovation is a cumulative activity rather than something that is sequential in nature (Campbell-Kelly, 2005). There are other views. For instance, a number of IT researchers, for example, Mata, Fuerst, and Barney (1995) conclude that software patents are ineffective in protecting software because the patented software could easily be reverse engineered, thereby eliminating any value. What is not considered, however, is that reverse engineering of a patented protected invention, that is, computer software, is grounds for patent infringement if such reverse engineering activity leads in any way to the development of an invention that is based on what was learned through the reverse engineering process (Moffat, 2004). Yet, focusing on e-business in the global environment in which many businesses must compete today, the number of e-business-related software patents, that is, business method patents, continues to increase. This type of protection for software assets cannot be ignored by businesses or IT professionals.

Avoiding Patent Infringement

At first glance, one might suggest that it would be easy to avoid infringing on another's patented software application, especially since any application that is patented is readily available from the USPTO. In fact, a copy of any patent can be obtained from the USPTO and, in most cases, it is available at the USPTO's Web site (http://www.uspto.gov). In addition to the description of the patent, all diagrams and figures related to it, as well as all of the claims for what the application does, are also available. With all of this information available, it would seem that merely developing a different application that does not infringe on any of the claims included with the patented application would suffice. While that is true, it ignores the amount of time, effort, and money that would need to be invested to accomplish that task. Recall that the Doctrine of Equivalents can make it quite difficult to avoid infringing. And recall too that reverse engineering of patented inventions in order to develop follow-up processes to be patented that are based on the original patented process is not allowed. To avoid the time and expense associated with being accused of infringing, there are a number of things an organization can do.

- **Be aggressively vigilant:** Organizations should consider hiring or retaining attorneys who specialize in IP law, with special emphasis on software. These firms can conduct appropriate searches of existing patents, and they are well aware of what to look for. Organizations themselves can be alert by examining patents that have been awarded and comparing those patented applications with business methods they may be using or considering to use.

- **Consider licensing arrangements:** Rather than take the time to attempt to "invent around" another's existing patented application and to possibly risk infringing that way, organizations can attempt to develop licensing agreements with the patent holder. The patent holder may view this quite positively, especially if the firm attempting to arrange for the license has, itself, patents that it could license back. Cross-licensing agreements can benefit both parties.

- **Consider following a "defensive patenting" strategy:** This strategy essentially mirrors a first mover strategy in that an organization would engage the services of a patent attorney to submit a patent application in the hopes of being first. Such a strategy could also prove beneficial later on, in that another organization might wish to attempt to arrange for a licensing arrangement. There are possible strategic advantages that could follow from this action.

The Internet presents interesting and significant opportunities for e-businesses today. Many of these involve the development and use of patented software applications for use in those ventures. These include patented applications for online auctions, for example, patents awarded to Priceline.com and online credit card payments, for example, Open Market, Inc. and BroadVision, Inc. In addition, as of late August 2005, there were in excess of 23,000 patent applications pending in patent class 705, which is defined as Data Processing: Financial, Business Practice, Management, or Cost/Price Determination. Not surprisingly, nearly 2,800 of these pending applications are in class 705/26, which is defined as Electronic Shopping (USPTO, 2005). It is obvious that the protection of e-business-related software applications and the potential value made possible by patenting these processes is a critical segment of e-business today. Organizations engaged in e-commerce activities must rethink their business approaches and strategies if they are not only to be competitive, but also to survive!

Multiple IP Pitfalls

In many instances involving both large and smaller businesses, the strategy of driving users to a Web site may not be reviewed by attorneys or even marketing personnel, but rather handed over to a Webmaster running the site. This may be especially true for some e-businesses that may be small and who may rely on an IT person for many critical aspects of the site. While these issues may appear to be applicable to only the U.S., they have also resonated globally. Of course, e-business today is a global enterprise. A number of issues addressed previously are relevant specifically to trademark, copyright, and patent infringement. Still other possible infringing activities can relate to more than just one of the types of IP. That is, some types of activity can infringe on a copyright as well as a trademark. Some examples of these activities, among others, that can lead to copyright and trademark infringement include:

- The **posting** of copyrighted material from one organization onto another's Web site. This technique involves the practice of obtaining images or literature, even if copyrighted, from selected Web sites on the Internet, and placing them on your Web site. This activity can infringe a copyright and, depending on what is downloaded and posted, it could also lead to trademark infringement.

- **Metatags:** Improper use of metatags to trick search engines by placing another's name or key word within the metatag, is a technique used by Web developers to attract visitors to a Web site. Many search engines rely on metatags in determining ranking, and is an invaluable technique for getting a Web site to the top of a search engine. A series of cases have found such usage impermissible under trademark and unfair competition theories.

- **Misspelling** of famous trademarks in defining domain names as noted earlier in the Google case. Since people often misspell trademark names, a common technique is to register domain names of misspelled trademarks. For example, the following sites were pornographic Web sites registered by Global Net 2000, Inc.: usaday.com, abcnewss. com, busnessweek.com, Playboyy.com and windos95.com. Courts have uniformly enjoined the use of misspelled trademarks as domain names, even characterizing them as a "misuse of the Internet."

- **Framing:** improper framing, which is viewing contents of one Web site that is framed in another site, may trigger a dispute under copyright and trademark law theories, because a framed site possibly alters the appearance of the content and creates the impression that its owner sanctions or voluntarily chooses to associate with the framer.

Other Legal Issues

One of the more contentious topics being addressed today is IT outsourcing. It is an issue that affects individual IT professionals, IT organizations, and client organizations that employ outsourcing vendors. Although IT researchers have invested considerable time in examining the issues, the relationship between outsourcing and IP is normally not addressed. Consider the following scenario. A client organization contracts with an outsourcing vendor to develop some type of software application that will be used by the client organization. Once the application has been developed, the client uses it throughout the term of the outsourcing contract. Unless the contract specifies otherwise, it is possible that the vendor could patent the application and essentially own it. At the end of the contract, the vendor could require the client to pay licensing revenue or even deny access and use of the application to the client, thereby causing considerable disruption to the client's business. Furthermore, the application could even be licensed to the client's competitors, and the client would have no say in the matter. With the continuing growth in the e-business economy today, it is conceivable that many organizations might consider outsourcing arrangements. It would behoove them to ensure that any legal contract is secure for them.

E-business today is global! There is no mistaking that fact. Emphasizing this importance, Biddinger (2001) indicated that globalization involving businesses has led to an increase in the awareness and importance of IP rights, especially involving patents. Along with IP issues today, defamation and jurisdiction are other legal issues worthy of mention that are looming on the horizon. A recent case between an Australian businessman and Dow Jones emphasizes this. The case involved Mr. Joseph Gutnick and an article that appeared in *Barron's*, which is a weekly financial magazine and a cousin of the *Wall Street Journal*. An October 2000 article, which appeared in print and on Dow Jones's Internet site, claimed that Mr. Gutnick was "the biggest customer" of a convicted money launderer. Dow Jones was sued by Mr. Gutnick in the Australian state of Victoria, which has some very strict laws regarding defamation and libel. The case involved considerable legal wrangling in terms of jurisdiction, whether Australian law was applicable since Dow Jones is a U.S.-based company, and which specific Australian law was applicable. After an initial opinion against Dow Jones and two subsequent higher court appeals in favor of Mr. Gutnick, Dow Jones and other publishers engaged in global e-business activities have been left to wonder how future issues might impact them (Gutnick, 2004). Questions relate to existing court precedents and the issues they address. Are these precedents providing the basis for future legislation? And, of course, there is the ever-present matter of technology and its use always outpacing the law governing its use in general.

As if defamation actions involving civil litigation are not troubling enough, jurisdictional issues have also entailed criminal law as well. One of the most famous cases involved Yahoo and the sale of Nazi memorabilia on one of its auction Web sites. A French court ruled that such activity breached French law against the display of Nazi items. Yahoo took positive steps to remove and ban all such hate paraphernalia from its auction sites, but it has continued to fight jurisdiction of the French ruling in American courts. It did win its case in a U.S. federal court on 1st Amendment and free speech protections, but French civil rights supporters appealed to a U.S. federal appeals court (Sprigman, 2001).

There are other important issues relevant to how different countries address IP and other issues. For example, although Canada and the U.S. follow similar copyright schemes, Canada does not consider copying or downloading music from the Internet for personal noncommercial use to be copyright infringement. Thus, ISPs in Canada are not liable for contributory infringement (Kotlyarevskaya, 2005). On the other hand, laws in Germany, Japan, and the European Union contain provisions concerning ISP liability (Gervais, 2001). Some have suggested that a Canadian system is appropriate for the U.S., whereas others have indicated the opposite (Kotlyarevskaya, 2005).

Differences in trademark law exist as well. For example, the U.S. Congress enacted the "Controlling the Assault of Non-Solicited Pornography and Marketing Act of 2003," which is popularly known as the CAN_SPAM Act. This statute requires e-mail recipients to be able to "opt out" of receiving unwanted commercial e-mail, whereas in Europe commercial e-mailers must obtain consent before sending bulk e-mails, an obvious significant difference for those engaged in e-business.

There are differences in patent laws as well among countries. For example, in the U.S., patents are awarded to the person who invents, whereas in Europe the patent goes to the first to file. Moreover, in the U.S., an inventor is given a 1 year grace period following disclosure to file a patent application, whereas in Europe, no patent is possible if an invention were disclosed in that way prior to filing. Finally, business method patents, which have a strong relationship to e-business activity, have become very popular in the U.S., whereas in Europe the view is that the U.S. awards too many trivial patents (Bray, 2005).

In addition to IP differences among countries, those engaged in e-business must also be aware of the lax or nonexistent enforcement of IP laws in some countries, for example, lax or no enforcement of laws related to downloading digital content. Such an environment only serves to make matters difficult for e-business ventures and could even lead to some organizations refusing to engage in business activity because of that laxness.

Recommendations for E-Businesses

The previous sections of this chapter have provided in depth discussion about trademark, copyright, and patent issues as they can and do relate to e-business. Table 1 also highlights some of the IP issues that we have addressed.

The changing business environment associated with e-commerce today is dynamic, to say the least. Organizations are faced with a myriad of decisions related to business practices,

Table 1. IP issues and e-business

IP Type	Applicable Issues	Legal Cases Referenced
Trademark	Appropriate use of domain names	Sergy Gridasov vs. Google[a]
	Anticybersquatting Consumer Protection Act (ACPA)	Planned Parenthood Federation of America, Inc., vs. Bucci
	Registration of domain names	
	Infringing on others' rights	
Copyright	Digital Millennium Copyright Act (DCMA)	ACM Records vs. Napster, Inc.
	Digital rights media (DRM)	Shetland Times vs. The Shetland News
	Posting of copyrighted material on Web sites	Intellectual Reserve, Inc. vs. Utah Light Ministry, Inc.
	Appropriate and inappropriate linking	Ticketmaster Corp. vs. Tickets. com, Inc.
	ISP liability issues	
Patents	Patents applicable to software	Diamond vs. Diehr
	Business method patents	State Street Bank & Trust, Inc. vs. Signature Financial Group
	Effectiveness of software patents	MercExchange vs. eBay
	Reverse engineering	

Note: [a] Google did not file a lawsuit against Gridasov. Instead, Google filed a complaint with The National Arbitration Forum, a legal alternative to court litigation.

for example, brick and mortar, click and mortar, e-commerce only, and so forth. Confounding the problem is the lack of understanding, perhaps even ignorance, related to e-business and the array of IP laws that can affect those businesses. Indeed, the subject matter can be quite involved, can be replete with legal jargon, and can change as a result of new statutes or court-mandated decisions. This uncertainty suggests that e-businesses need to become fully cognizant of these issues and how best to deal with them. In this section, we offer some suggestions that will be helpful for e-businesses, and may go a long way toward ensuring the proper safeguard of a business' IP assets, while at the same time serving to protect them from infringing others. It should also be noted that the suggestions offered are representative of the issues that e-businesses face every day, and that to address all of them would require much more investigation than is possible in this chapter.

Establish a team to identify a firm's important intellectual capital. Skyrme (1997) suggests that management of intellectual capital to audit and manage intangible assets is important today. IP professionals in organizations must be able to work as part of this team to identify significant intellectual capital, protect it, and transform it into tangible corporate assets. Ultimately, the firm's national/international reputation and position could be safeguarded, and barriers to substitution could be created, thereby preventing imitation by competitors.

Secure the services of the right attorney. Most businesses, e-business or otherwise, realize the importance of appropriate legal counsel, so it is not unusual to find organizations, especially larger ones, with many on staff attorneys or attorneys on retainer as needed. Although these attorneys may be highly appropriate for most corporate needs, they may lack the necessary background in IP law. If a business is considering the development of an e-business model, or is currently engaged in e-business, it is extremely necessary that attorneys with IP knowledge be consulted.

Be sure to include IP attorneys in all e-business discussions, design, and development efforts. The nature of e-business most often involves an organization's knowledge assets that are IP as well. These can take the form of copyrighted digital information, the organization's domain names, trademarks, and software and other patents. It is essential that IP attorneys be consulted regarding what others, such as competitors and customers, may do as a result of accessing an organization's IP information online. At the same time, these same attorneys will assist in determining just what actions this organization can do legally regarding others' similar assets.

Consider appropriate IP training for MIS professionals. Although most IP professionals involved with e-business activity, for example, programmers, Webmasters, and Web designers, are very good technically; they may lack any IP knowledge. Issues such as appropriate and inappropriate linking and use of metatags are common for these individuals, but they may have little to no knowledge about the legal aspects of employing these techniques. This type of training can be very fulfilling to the organization in that it could integrate into all of the organization's training activities, which are most likely tied to many internal processes of the organization.

Ensure the appropriateness of all legal contracts affecting e-business activities. Many e-businesses, especially perhaps smaller ones, may lack technical resources to design, develop, implement, and maintain e-business Web sites. Instead, they may find it much more effective to hire a consultant or an outsourcing vendor to do this work. It is imperative that all duties, responsibilities, and expectations as they pertain to IP assets be thoroughly defined. For example, it is theoretically possible for a company to hire a consultant to develop an e-business application with the expectation that the e-business will be able to use the application. This may be spelled out in the contractual language between the parties. However, unless otherwise specified, the consultant could patent that application and retain ownership of it. At the end of the contract, the e-business could find that it is no longer able to use that application unless it licenses it from the consultant.

Consider cross-licensing agreements with other patent holders. Many organizations, for example, IBM, have a patent family numbering in the thousands. In turn, these companies often consider arrangements with other organizations to allow those organizations to use IBM's patented products in exchange for rights to use or license that organization's patented products. In the end, it can be a win/win matter for both parties. However, it is imperative that any business recognizes the importance of appropriate legal counsel before entering into any such arrangement.

Clarify relationships with ISPs. Many e-businesses will enter relationships with ISPs or other Web-hosting organizations. It is important to recognize that ISPs are, for the most part, shielded from any liability regarding possible copyright infringement that may result from posting of copyrighted material on Web sites or related to e-business activity.

Conclusions, Research Issues, and Trends

The relationship between e-business activity and IP is strong and very much a vibrant issue today. While corporate attorneys may be very knowledgeable about traditional business-related issues such as contracts, they may be less aware of the potential issues and problems arising from the use and misuse of IP assets of their own organizations and that of others as well. Except for isolated examples, IT researchers have generally ignored these topics too. Unfortunately, the role of trademarks, copyrights, and patents as related to e-business activity is too important to ignore anymore.

This chapter has discussed important issues related to the conduct of e-business and the relationship that IP issues, specifically trademarks, copyrights, and patents, play today in this approach to doing business. Generic subject matter relevant to these three forms of IP was discussed, along with specific points relevant to e-business activity today. We have also provided some important recommendations for e-business organizations.

From the standpoint of importance, although all of the issues discussed are significant and relevant to e-business success today, we believe two things may not be considered by e-business organizations, but which are crucial for their success. The first is the nature of appropriate legal advice. The domain of IP law is unique, certainly much different from traditional contract and business law that may be familiar to most corporate attorneys. Therefore, identifying legal counsel knowledgeable in e-business aspects of IP law is crucial. Second is the matter of appropriate training for IT professionals. Although this group is very knowledgeable about the technical aspects of Web design and development, they are often less aware, if aware at all, of the IP issues confronting these IT areas. It is important that they receive appropriate training so as to minimize, if not eliminate, the threats of lawsuits being levied against e-businesses.

The role that IP plays today involving e-business activities is not what many would call mainstream IT research. As an example, many IT researchers have dismissed the importance of software patents for more than 2 decades, even though the business community continues to invest heavily in this for of IP protection (e.g., see Mykytyn & Mykytyn, 2002, for a review of this issue). At the same time, more recent research (Mykytyn et al., 2005) reports that IT academics/faculty are much more amenable to incorporating IP issues into there IT coursework; in fact, that research included follow-up contact with a number of IT academics who participated in the initial phase of the study. Many reported that they had begun to incorporate some IP aspects into their coursework. Notwithstanding this bit of encouraging news, we believe that more is needed by IT researchers today.

This issue of software ownership is an important topic for IT researchers that may or may not be considered. If the issue of software patents is considered part of the equation, it is probable that most IT researchers may not have considered such elements. They have the opportunity to do so.

Another research question concerns economic gains achieved by e-businesses as a result of protecting IP. Are there specific gains that can be attributed to taking protective measures? These gains could come in the form of increased market share, greater number of customers, or more satisfied customers. Related to possible direct financial gains are indirect gains. Should an e-business protect assets through copyright, trademark, and/or patents, what is the indirect effect on the business' competition? The competition could be forced into playing catch-up or even worse. This is a rich research question that could be grounded in organizational theory and behavior, economics, and, of course, IP law.

IT researchers should find the relationship between e-businesses, Web content, and other countries' laws and requirements not only interesting, but critical for research if businesses are going to be able to protect themselves and their IP assets. This is especially relevant in terms of content posted on e-business sites. Here again, IT researchers should find abundant research opportunities with regard to what actions e-businesses take, if any, to deal with these issues and protect themselves.

Additional research should examine IT curricula to see if any additional progress has been made following the work by Mykytyn et al. (2005). It is true that graduates from most IT programs receive considerable coursework in Web development, JAVA, Web design, and the like. It is less certain, however, whether these graduates know anything about the potential legal effects and impacts that their work may have on their organizations.

Along with the proposed research agenda, we believe there are a number of issues that should be categorized as trends. First, the international aspects of e-business will continue to heighten. Today, for example, the U.S. patent laws regarding computer software differ from those of the European Union. In fact, patent law in general between the U.S. and most other countries differs. As noted, the U.S. follows a "first to invent" policy, whereby the first person to invent an invention is awarded a patent. Most other countries follow a "first to file" policy, whereby a person who discloses his/her invention to the public and gains protection is awarded the patent. Issues surrounding which countries' courts have jurisdiction in lawsuits will most likely increase as the overall breadth of this approach to doing business increases. These types of international issues will most likely lead to significant challenges to businesses to identify legal counsel that is knowledgeable of the international environment (Bray, 2005).

We also believe that undergraduate and graduate IT curricula will need to be reexamined for its lack of depth and attention to the legal issues surrounding e-business. Many textbooks on e-business and e-commerce devote little to no detail about IP issues other than perhaps some discussion about how it can be illegal to download music. As we have shown in this chapter, the depth of issues involving trademarks, copyrights, and patents is much greater than that. Model curricula for IT majors will hopefully provide greater attention to these issues in e-business courses such as Web programming, Web development, and e-commerce/e-business.

The creation of laws seems to follow the advancement of technology, that is, the law lags. In particular, with the growing dependence involving e-business, greater attention may be forthcoming in terms of how tort laws may impact this environment. One such tort is defamation, which was addressed briefly. In general, contracts between business-to-business (B2B) partners can address the legal environment involving their relationships. Unfortunately, innocent third parties may be hurt.

Finally, we believe e-business activity throughout the world will continue to increase. With that increase, we see nothing to indicate that the IP environment will diminish in terms of its importance and its impact on businesses, consumers, and governmental bodies.

References

A & M Records, Inc. vs. Napster, Inc., 54 U.S.P.Q.2d 1746 (ND Cal. 2000)

Albert, S. N., Sanders, J. A., & Mazzaro, J. M. (2005). Twentieth survey of white collar crime: Article: Intellectual property crimes. *American Criminal Law Review, 42*, 632-676.

Allison, J. R., & Tiller, E. H. (2003). The business method patent myth. *Berkeley Technology Law Journal, 18*, 987-1084.

Anticybersquatting Consumer Protection Act, 15 U.S.C. 1114(2)(D) (2000).

Biddinger, B. P. (2001). Limiting the business method patent: A comparison and proposed alignment of European, Japanese, and United States patent law. *Fordham Law Review, 69*, 2523-2554.

Blaise, F. (2005). Comment: Game over: Issues arising when copyrighted work is licensed to video game manufacturers. *Albany Law Journal of Science & Technology, 15*, 518-542.

Bray, R. (2005). The European Union software patents directive: What is it? Why is it? Where are we now? *Duke Law & Technology Review, 11*.

Campbell-Kelly, M. (2005). Not all bad: An historical perspective on software patents. *Michigan Telecommunications and Technology Law Review, 11*, 191-248.

Cantzler, C. S. (2000). Comment: State Street: Leading the way to consistency for patentability of computer software. *Colorado Law Review, 71*, 423-461.

Chin, D. (1994). MS, Stac battle it out. (Microsoft Corp.; Stac Electronics). *Computer Dealer News*. Retrieved June 29, 1994, from http://www.findarticles.com/p/articles/mi_m3563/is_n13_v10/ai_16146374

Croman, S. (2005). Note & comment: Where the Netcom yardstick comes up short: Courts should not apply the facts of Netcom as an example of intermediate and transient storage under § 512(a) of the DMCA. *Washington Law Review, 80*, 417-445.

Diamond vs. Diehr, 450 US 175 (1981).

Digital Economy 2003. (2003). Washington, DC: US Department of Commerce, Economics and Statistics Administration. Retrieved October 25, 2005, from https://www.esa.doc.gov/2003.cfm

Digital Millennium Copyright Act, Pub. L. No. 105-304, 112 Stat. 2860 (1998).

Dockins, M. (2005). Comment: internet links: The good, the bad, the tortuous, and a two-part test. *Toledo Law Review, 36*, 367-402.

Dueker, K. S. (1996). Trademark law lost in cyberspace: Trademark protection for internet addresses. *Harvard Journal of Law & Technology, 9*, 483-512.

Field, T. G., Jr. (2000). *Trademarks & business goodwill.* Retrieved September 9, 2005, from http://www.fplc.edu/tfield/trademk.htm

Fitzdam, J. D. (2005). Note: Private enforcement of the digital millennium copyright act: Effective without government intervention. *Cornell Law Review, 90*, 1085-1117.

Gervais, D. (2001). Transmissions of music on the internet: An analysis of the copyright laws of Canada, France, Germany, Japan, the United Kingdom, and the United States. *Vanderbilt Journal of Transnational Law, 34*, 1363-1416.

Ghosh, S., (2002). The merits of ownership; or, how I learned to stop worrying and love intellectual property review essay of Lawrence Lessig, the future of ideas, and Siva Vaidhyanathan, copyrights and copywrongs. *Harvard Journal of Law & Technology, 15*, 454-496.

Graver Tank & Mfg. Co. Vs. Linde Air Prods. Co., 339 U.S. 605 (1950).

Guillot, G. H. (2000) *A guide to proper trademark use, all about trademarks.* Retrieved March 30, 2000, from http://www.ggmark.com/guide.html

GuFN, Z. (2005). MercExchange vs. e-Bay: Should newsgroup postings be considered printed publications as a matter of law in patent litigation? *Golden State University Law Review, 35*, 225-258.

Gutnick vs. Dow Jones. Retrieved September 7, 2005, http://www.fact-index.com/g/gu/gutnick_v__dow_jones.html

Hunter, D. (2005). Culture war. *Texas Law Review, 83*, 1105-1136.

Iannella, R. (2001). Digital rights management (DRM) architectures. *D-Lib Magazine, 7*. Retrieved October 26, 2005. from http://www.dlib.org/dlib/june01/iannella/06iannella.html

Kamarck, M. D. (1999). Detours, misdirections and false starts on the information super highway: The hidden dangers in marketing your Web site. *E-Commerce Law Reports.* Retrieved September 7, 2005.from http://www.rmslaw.com/articles/art89.htm

Koffsky, M. I. (1995). Patent preemption of computer software contracts restricting reverse engineering: The last stand? *Columbia Law Review, 95*, 1160-1187.

Kotlyarevskaya, O. (2005). Annual review 2005: Part II: Entertainment law and new media: XI. Foreign & international law: A note: BMG Canada, Inc. vs. Doe & Society of Composers, Authors & Music Publishers of Canada vs. Canadian Ass'n of Internet Providers: Why the Canadian music compensation system may not work in the United States. *Berkeley Technology Law Journal, 20*, 953-973.

Lipson, J. C. (2001). Financing information technologies: Fairness and function. *Wisconsin Law Review, 2001*(4), 1067-1157.

Mata, F. J., Fuerst, W. L., & Barney, J. B. (1995). Information technology and sustained competitive advantage: A resource-based analysis. *MIS Quarterly, 19*, 487-505.

McCullagh, D., & Homsi, M. (2005, Spring). Leave DRM along: A survey of legislative proposals relating to digital rights management technology and their problems. *Michigan State Law Review,* 317-327.

Merges, R. P. (2000). One hundred years of solicitude: Intellectual property law, 1900-2000. *California Law Review, 88*, 2187-2240.

Merz, J. F., & Pace, N. M. (1994). Trends in patent litigation: The apparent influence of strengthened patents attributable to the Court of Appeals for the Federal Circuit. *Journal of the Patent and Trademark Office Society, 76*, 579-590.

Moffat, V. (2004). Mutant copyrights and backdoor patents: The problem of overlapping intellectual property protection. *Berkeley Technology Law Journal, 19*, 1473-1532.

Mykytyn, P. P. Jr., & Mykytyn K. (2002). Computer software patents: A dilemma in competitive advantage IT research. *Communications of the Association for Information Systems, 8*, 109-130. Retrieved September 7, 2005. from http://cais.isworld.org/articles/8-7/default.asp?View=Journal&x=31&y=5

Mykytyn, P., Mykytyn, K., & Harrison, D. (2005). Integrating intellectual property concepts into IS training: An empirical assessment of relevance-rigor disconnections. *Decision Sciences Journal of Innovative Education, 3*, 1-27.

National Arbitration Forum. (2005). Retrieved August 13, 2005, from http://www.arb-forum. com/domains/decisions/474816.htm

Planned Parenthood Federation of America vs. Bucci, No. 97 Civ. 0629 (KMW), 1997 WL 133313, at 1 (S.D.N.Y. Mar. 24, 1997), aff'd, 152 F.3d 920 (2d Cir. 1998).

Samuelson, P. (1999). Intellectual property and the digital economy: Why the anti-circumvention regulations need to be revised. *Berkeley Technology Law Journal, 14*, (pp. 519-566).

Shetland Times vs. Shetland News. 1997 S.L.T. 669 (Sess. Cas. 1996).

Skyrme, D. J. (1997). *From information management to knowledge management: Are you prepared?* Retrieved December 12, 2005, from http://www.skyrme.com/pubs/on97full. htm

Sprigman, C. (2001). *Why the Hague convention on jurisdiction threatens to strangle e-commerce and internet free speech*. Retrieved August 31, 2005, from http://writ.corporate. findlaw.com/commentary/20010927_sprigman.html

State Street Bank & Trust Co. vs. Signature Financial Group, Inc. 149 F.3d 1368 (Fed. Cir. 1998), cert. denied, 525 U.S. 1093 (1999).

Ticketmaster Corp. vs. Tickets.com, Inc., No. CV99-7654 HLH, 2000 U.S. Dist. LEXIS 4553, at 1 (C.D. Cal. Mar. 27, 2000), 54 U.S.P.Q.2d (BNA) 1344 (C.D. Cal. 2000).

UMG RECORDINGS, INC., et al., Plaintiffs, vs. MP3.COM, INC, 00 Civ. 472 JSR, U.S. District Court for the Southern District of New York, September 6, 2000.

USPTO, United States Patent and Trademark Office, http://www.uspto.gov

15 U.S.C. §§ 1051-1127 (1988 & Supp. IV 1992).

15 U.S.C. §§ 1114(1), 1125(a) (1988 & Supp. IV 1992).

Voet, M. A. (1995). Patent practitioners—don't let GATT get you. *Managing Intellectual Property, 47*, 20-25.

Wiese, W. D. (2000). Death of a myth: The patenting of internet business models after State Street Bank. *Marquette Intellectual Property Law Review, 4*, 17-47.

Chapter IV

E-Business Technologies in E-Market Literature

Nikos Manouselis, Agricultural University of Athens, Greece

Abstract

E-business processes are implemented through existing, as well as novel technologies. This book chapter focuses on the field of electronic markets (e-markets), and studies the technologies and solutions that are applied and proposed in this field. In particular, the chapter reviews e-market literature in order to identify which are the technological trends that have appeared in the e-markets field during the last decade. A conceptual model that allows for the classification of e-market research literature according to a number of technical topics is first introduced. Then, e-market literature is reviewed, and the technologies that seem to be attracting more research attention are identified. Representative contributions are discussed, and directions for future research are indicated. The overall aim of this chapter is to provide a blueprint of the literature related to e-business technologies for e-markets.

Introduction

According to the 2005 report of the United Nations Conference on Trade and Development (UNCTAD, 2005), e-commerce continues to grow in all sectors. In the United States (the largest e-commerce market), e-commerce is still most prominent in manufacturing and wholesale trade, but on the other hand, growth rates are highest in retail trade (B2C) and services. In the United States, the largest global e-commerce market, e-commerce sales have continuously grown during the last years. With a growth rate (24.7%) significantly higher than for total retail trade (4.3%), the share of e-commerce in total retail trade is also growing. The latest available figures indicate that its share has more than doubled (UNCTAD, 2005). Eurostat data (http://epp.eurostat.cec.eu.int/) show that for the European Union (EU), e-commerce sales over the Internet increased from 0.9% in 2002 to 2.2% in 2004. Compilations by the OECD suggest that online sales represent a small but growing share of total sales in most EU member countries, and that there is solid growth in B2C e-commerce (OECD, 2004).

As a result, numerous electronic markets (e-markets) are continuously being deployed. For instance, the European Observatory of e-Markets eMarketServices (http://www.emarket-services.com) has listed, until January 2006, about 905 e-markets from various business sectors. E-markets aim to facilitate information exchange and support activities related to business process management and transactions. They are characterized by a frictionless and very low-cost flow of information between buyers and sellers. Moreover, they allow sellers to reach a wider consumer base, and buyers to have access to a large number of sellers. E-markets are therefore expected to create economic value for buyers, sellers, market intermediaries, and for society as a whole (Bakos, 1998; Grieger, 2003).

In e-markets, proposed technologies and solutions vary from simple online catalogues that provide more information about products to interested customers, to sophisticated collaborative project management and supply-chain-management environments (Dai & Kauffman, 2002b). They address various technical topics, such as architectures, interoperability, services, protocols, data management, and networking. Nevertheless, there has not been, so far, a comprehensive overview of the technologies proposed, the dimensions addressed, or the solutions tested. This chapter aims to cover this aspect by providing a blueprint of research literature and e-business technologies for e-markets.

An attempt to review and classify published research in this field can be an interesting and useful contribution to e-business researchers, managers, and practitioners/implementers. It can answer questions such as the following: which technical topics attract more attention in the field of e-markets? What are the proposed technologies and solutions? What are possible future directions of their development? Within this context, the aim of this chapter is to provide an overview of recent technological contributions in the field of e-markets. More specifically, it reports results from a study of e-market research that has been published during the past decade in scientific journals. The results provide interesting insight about the technologies for e-business processes in e-market environments, and outline implications for practice and research.

The chapter is structured as follows. The "Background" section provides some background on e-markets, as well as an overview of relevant studies. "Methodology" presents the methodology followed in order to identify and classify e-market literature around technical topics.

"Results" presents and discusses the results of the classification and reviews representative contributions. Finally, "Conclusion" provides the conclusions of this study and outlines some implications for related research.

Background

E-Markets

In the influential paper of Malone, Yates, and Benjamin (1987), e-markets have been defined according to the traditional market paradigm: structures that coordinate the flow of materials or services, through supply and demand forces, as well as through external transactions between different individuals and firms. Market forces determine the design, price, quantity, and target delivery schedule for a given product, which will serve as input into another process. The buyer of the good or service compares its many possible sources, and makes a choice based on the best combination of these attributes. Another prevailing definition, which has a more technological focus, was given by Bakos (1991): an electronic marketplace (or electronic market system) is an interorganizational information system that allows the participating buyers and sellers to exchange information about prices and product offerings. As Bakos (1991) notes, this definition of e-markets has a narrower, system-oriented focus in comparison to the more general definition of Malone et al. (1987), which refers to an e-market as a governance mechanism. As Internet became more and more widespread, providing a cheap and easy way for market participants to communicate and exchange information, the term "e-markets" tended to concern the systems described by Bakos (1991). Thus, nowadays, an e-market can be considered as an information system that intends to provide market participants with online services that will facilitate information exchange between them, with the purpose of facilitating their business transactions.

Thus, e-markets can support one or more phases of a transaction process, starting from information finding and ending with after-sales service support (Strader & Shaw, 1997). Different types of e-markets have been identified in the literature. First of all, depending on the nature of transactions they support, e-markets can be classified according to the combination of parties they involve. Therefore, most of the existing e-markets can be classified as business-to-consumer (B2C), business-to-business (B2B), and consumer-to-consumer (C2C) ones. Other, less popular, types also exist, such as government-to-consumer (G2C) and government-to-business (G2B) e-markets (Turban,, King, Lee, & Viehland., 2004).

Depending on their target audience, e-markets can be distinguished as buyer-oriented, seller-oriented, or neutral (Grieger, 2003). Buyer-oriented e-markets mainly aggregate buyers, allowing them to also aggregate their expenditure, reduce administration costs, increase visibility, and facilitate global sourcing. Seller-oriented e-markets concentrate on bringing multiple sellers together into a central catalogue and product information repository, in order to allow them to achieve higher visibility and conduct trade with as many buyers as possible. Moreover, e-markets can be either characterized as vertical or horizontal (Grieger, 2003). Horizontal e-markets cover the needs of a wider audience, offering a broad range of products or services that are related with this audience. On the other hand, vertical e-markets offer a class of products or services that aim to one or more particular industry sectors (Wellman, 2004). E-markets can also be distinguished as open/public and closed/private ones (Grieger, 2003; Wellman, 2004). Stanoevska-Slabeva (1999) identifies, as single or homogeneous e-markets, those that are developed by a single enterprise in order to support online distribution of the enterprises' products. Similarly, multiple or heterogeneous e-markets are those where multiple enterprises participate. Other classifications have also been introduced in the literature. Grieger (2003) presents some of them: e-markets with fixed vs. variable pricing mechanisms; e-markets that support information exchange, negotiation, or settlement of after-sales respectively; e-markets that use an aggregation vs. a matching market mechanism; e-markets that support different business objectives (manufacturing vs. operating inputs, and spot vs. systematic sourcing).

Literature Reviews and Case Study Surveys

One of the first papers reviewing the e-market field has been the one from Bakos (1991). It performed a strategic analysis of e-markets based on economic models of search, and reviewed some characteristic applications that adopted principles from traditional markets theory, and implemented them in an electronic way. This analysis particularly focused on the services that its selected case studies offered, but did not provide much information about the technologies used in each case. In two other studies, Strader and Shaw (1997, 1999) analyzed the impact of e-markets from a transaction cost perspective, and referred to a number of e-market examples. A particular technology-related topic that they identified is the use of widely accepted standards for the description of products and services in an electronic format, so that interoperability between different electronic markets can be accomplished. In a similar manner, an overview of the e-markets' area was presented by Segev, Gebauer, and Faerber (1999). In this study, five representative examples of Internet-based e-markets were reviewed, and common elements and features were outlined. They discussed different policies for admitting new participants, various revenue models, quality of the product catalog, as well as services to support a transaction process. Again, the back-office technologies for these features are not discussed. In the study of Timmers (1998), a review of e-market business models was provided. The author described characteristic business models and referred to representative e-market examples implementing them, without analyzing the supporting technologies.

The paper of Smith, Bailey, and Brynjolfsson (1999) has been, to our knowledge, the first important overview and assessment of the area of online markets. It mainly addressed ways to measure efficiency in online markets, focused on potential sources of price dispersion, and introduced important developments to watch in e-markets. In this review, technology-related topics were not addressed. A very comprehensive literature review in the area of e-markets is the one of Grieger (2003) that focused on the supply chain dimension of e-markets. In this study, the author examined several e-markets, and classified them according to several dimensions. Technical dimensions were not used for this classification. Furthermore, Anandalingam, Day, and Raghavan (2005) presented an introductory survey of essential literature on e-markets. Although several mechanisms and settings have been reviewed, the authors' focus seemed to be more on auctions. Therefore, aspects such as mechanisms to facilitate multi-item auctions or the winner determination auction have been described. Finally, technical topics that concern e-markets have been partially covered in the context of the larger e-commerce literature review from Kauffman and Walden (2001). This study analyzed e-commerce literature on several levels, including a technology one. It addressed several technical topics, such as agent technologies, network infrastructures, and structural standards.

There are also publications that focus on specific segments or industries of e-markets. The study by Kollmann (2000) has focused specifically on the sector of German-language online markets for used cars. It provided a business-oriented evaluation tool for e-markets in the form of a competition analysis matrix, which did not include any technological character-istics. Rosson and Davis (2004) focus on Canadian e-markets, presenting a survey of 13 existing case studies. They discuss characteristics such as the e-market scope (vertical vs. horizontal) and type (sell-side, buy-side, etc.), but do not examine the technologies support-ing the covered e-markets. In Dai and Kauffman (2002b), an analytic framework is used to study and classify business-to-business (B2B) e-markets. In their study, B2B e-markets are also analyzed from a technological perspective, according to the type of e-market functions their services support. Moreover, the role of some B2B e-markets as technology adapters is described, offering some insight to the technologies they offer to e-market participants that allow integration of e-commerce systems, provision of technological standards, and implementation of outsourced services. Holzmueller and Schluechter (2002) also focus on B2B marketplaces, for the country of Germany. They examine the future of German B2B e-markets using a Delphi survey from e-market experts, and they identify how these experts weight the importance of various services that a B2B e-market may offer (e.g., e-mail, EDI, online communication, search possibilities, etc.). In the study of Lenz, Zimmermann, and Heitmann (2002), a survey of 248 European B2B e-markets is carried out. They also exam-ine various e-market services, classifying them into wider categories (such as collaboration services, financial services, shopbots, negotiation, etc.), and examining their current status of development in the European e-markets.

In general, previous studies either focus on the analysis of the literature, or provide a survey of e-market case studies. Only one study (Holzmueller & Schluechter, 2002) was based on the opinion of e-market experts. This difference in employed methods has been also reflected in their results: the studies focusing more on proposed technologies for e-markets have been the ones based on surveys of existing case studies. On the contrary, e-market literature reviews generally adopted an economic or business perspective, neglecting the technology aspects. To our knowledge, there has not been, so far, an overview of e-market literature from the perspective of technology. In our opinion this is an important shortcoming, since new and innovative technologies are usually first proposed and tested in relevant research studies. Therefore, academic literature can be a valuable source for identifying which technologies are proposed, which dimensions have been addressed, or which solutions have been tested in e-markets. We therefore decided to examine e-market literature of the last decade, in order to identify the most important technological trends in the field of e-markets.

Methodology

In order to classify e-market research papers that deal with technical topics, we reviewed relevant classification frameworks. First of all, we reviewed e-commerce research classifications such as the ones of Kauffman and Walden (2001), Urbaczewski, Jessup, and Wheeler (2002), Ngai and Wat (2002), and Turban et al. (2004). We also considered the Information Systems research classifications of Liang and Chen (2003) and Orlikowski and Iacono (2001). Finally, we examined the reference framework that has been engaged by the e-Commerce Working Group of the European Standardization Committee CEN/ISSS to analyze and categorize e-commerce models and architectures (CEN, 2001).

It has been concluded that the framework proposed by Urbaczewski et al. (2002) covers the generic e-market topics with the organizational, economic, technical, and other topic areas. In this light, these topic areas are used to specify our framework. The topics of each area have been appropriately elaborated to cover the characteristics and particularities of the e-market research field. This process led to the development of an overall classification framework for e-market research, which is presented in Figure 1 and described in detail elsewhere (Manouselis, 2005). The focus of this chapter is on technical dimensions, therefore only the topics relevant with technical research have been selected from the framework. These technical topics have been identified in related classification frameworks, and were appropriately refined after the e-market literature review. Table 1 further describes the topics in the technical research area.

Figure 1. A classification framework for e-market research

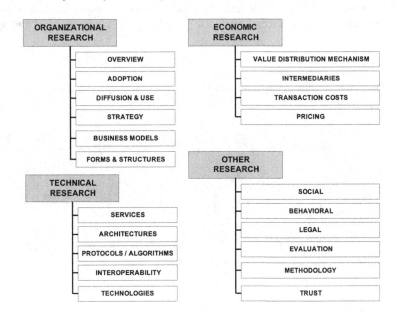

Table 1. Technical research topics

Technical Research	
Architecture	Papers dealing with architectures for e-markets, including modeling e-markets as well as designing/developing infrastructures for e-markets.
Interoperability	Papers that specifically address the interoperability issues of e-markets. Business process modeling (using a common language such as ebXML, 2005) or interoperable product catalogs are issues classified in this category.
Services	Papers that specifically focus on services that e-markets offer.
Protocols / Algorithms	Papers presenting different protocols and algorithms implementing e-market mechanisms, such as value distribution ones.
Technologies	Papers discussing proposed technologies for e-markets, such as the use of Web services or XML, with data management models and techniques used specifically in e-market implementation, and with the network-level implementation of e-markets.

The proposed framework is used for classifying the papers of an e-market literature review. The review is based on a study of publications in scientific journals with a long tradition, as well as journals specifically focusing on e-commerce that have appeared during the late 1990s. It has been carried out by examining 18 journals that were considered as well-accepted publication outlets for e-commerce research. Year 1995 was chosen as a starting date for our review, since our study revealed that e-market papers started appearing systematically in these journals from that year and forth.

The examined journals' contents have been thoroughly reviewed in order to locate papers relevant to e-markets. More specifically, the papers that were initially identified, included in their title, abstract, keywords or full text one or more related keywords such as electronic or online "markets," "marketplaces," "auctions," "exchanges," "negotiations," "trading,"

Figure 2. Distribution of identified e-market papers per examined journal

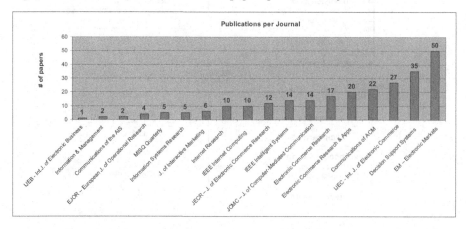

Figure 3. Estimated annual rate of e-market papers per examined journal

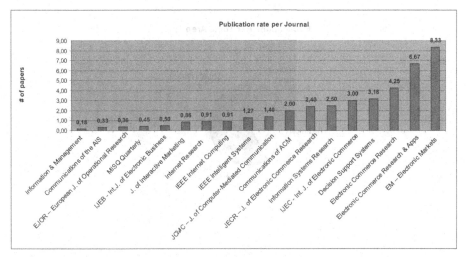

"shop," "mall," and so forth. More than 400 papers have been initially collected in this way. We briefly examined each one of these papers in order to filter out those that were not directly relevant to the field of e-markets, or were considered too generic for the scope of our study. Finally, 248 papers were identified as appropriate.

Figure 2 illustrates the journals covered in this study, ranked according to the number of identified e-market papers. The journal with the highest number of e-market papers is the *Electronic Markets* journal (50 papers). This was expected, since this journal focuses particularly on e-market topics. Second is *Decision Support Systems*, which has published 35 e-market related papers so far (including papers "In Press"). Other journals with a high number of e-market papers are *International Journal of Electronic Commerce* (27 papers), *Communications of the ACM* (22 papers), and *Electronic Commerce Research & Applications* (20 papers). Since several of the specialized e-commerce journals have launched their operation after the Dot.com explosion of 1999, newer journals (such as *Electronic Commerce Research & Applications*) might not have the opportunity to publish, so far, as many e-market papers as more traditional journals (such as *Decision Support Systems*). We further investigated this point by calculating the rate of e-market papers each journal has published per examined year. Figure 3 presents the ranking of journals according to this annual e-market publication rate. Again, *Electronic Markets* seems to be the journal publishing the highest number of e-market papers (about 8 papers per year). We note, though, that two relatively new e-commerce journals follow: these are *Electronic Commerce Research & Applications* (about 7 papers per year) and *Electronic Commerce Research* (about 4 papers per year). Traditional journals also publish e-market research regularly. For instance, *Decision Support Systems* and *International Journal of Electronic Commerce* publish about 3 e-market papers per year.

Figure 4. Distribution of e-market papers per topic area

It has to be noted that the coverage of our review had some limitations. In most cases, we collected all e-market papers that were published in the examined journals from 1995 to 2005. In two particular cases though, *Electronic Markets* and *Information Systems Research*, the review started from later years (1999 and 2002, respectively) since we did not have full access to the older contents of the journals. In addition, there are some high quality journals (such as *Journal of Organizational Computing and Electronic Commerce* and *Harvard Business Review*) that we did not include in this review. The main reason is that at the time of this study, we did not have access to the journals' full contents. Therefore, we could not exhaustively search all issues for published e-market papers. Additionally, focusing on journals that published primarily e-commerce research, we did not extend our review to other publications that may have included some papers about e-markets (such as economic journals). Nevertheless, we consider the list of journals covered rather extensive: it includes 10 out of the 15 most appropriate journals for e-commerce research, and 8 out of the 10 journals for e-commerce research with highest quality, according to the rankings provided by Bharati and Tarasewich (2002). Although this review was not exhaustive, it serves as a comprehensive base for an understanding of e-market research.

Results

Initially, we classified all 248 e-market papers in the four general topic areas that are described in Figure 1. The result of this initial classification is presented in Figure 4. This figure indicates that the highest percentage of examined publications belongs to the Economic and the Technical areas (35% and 30% of the total respectively). Organizational Research also attracts important research interest, since 21% of the published papers cover this area. Finally, about 14% of e-market papers cover Other Research topics. In this chapter, we focus on the 28% of e-market papers (that is, 118 papers) that mainly focus on technical topics.

Figure 5. Distribution of publications per category of the technical area

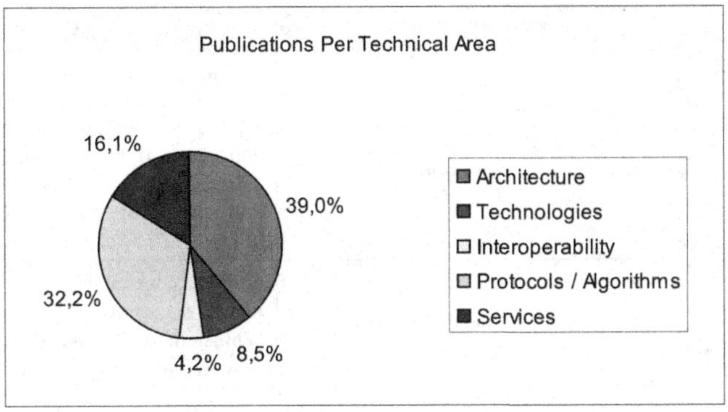

Publications Per Technical Area

16,1%

39,0%

■ Architecture
■ Technologies
□ Interoperability
□ Protocols / Algorithms
■ Services

32,2%

4,2%   8,5%

Figure 5 presents the distribution of these 118 papers according to the topics in the Technical topic area. It is interesting to note that Architectures (with 39% of total Technical Research papers) and Protocols/Algorithms (with 32.2%) monopolize this e-market research area. Topics such as Interoperability (which is identified as a key issue from e-commerce experts, as discovered by Dai & Kauffman, 2002a) and Technologies have been slightly covered. Nevertheless, this can be due to the fact that such papers are published in journals other than the ones examined, as well as the fact that low-level technical solutions are usually covering all e-commerce fields and not e-markets in particular. Finally, e-market Services seem to be attracting an important degree of attention: about 16.1% of Technical Research papers are about Services.

Figure 6 presents the classification of papers covering technical topics per journal examined. The majority of the papers in *Decision Support Systems* (20 out of the 35 e-market papers

Figure 6. Publications related to the technical area, per journal

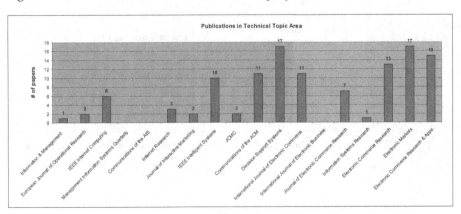

Table 2. Issues, contributions, and representative references in the topic of architecture

Issues	Contributions	Representative References
Models	E-market conceptual models and frameworks	Baghdadi, 2004; Blecker, Abdelkafi, Kreutler, & Kaluza., 2004; Brandtweiner & Scharl, 1999; Gomber & Maurer, 2004; Jaiswal, Kim, & Gini., 2004; Kain, Aparicio, & Singh, 1999; Mandry, Pernul, & Roehm, 2001; Roehm & Pernul, 2000; Wang, 1997; Wicke, 1999
	Designing e-market models	Fontoura, Ionescu, & Minsky, 2005; Geyer, Kuhn, & Schmid, 1997; Hamalainen, Whinston, & Vishik, 1996; Mullen & Breese, 2000
	E-market negotiation mechanisms models	Chiu, Cheung, Hung, Chiu, & Chung, in press; Srivastava & Mohapatra, 2003
	E-market metamodels	Bhargarva, Krishnon, & Mueller, 1997; Lindemann & Schmid, 1999
Infrastructure	Infrastructure design of e-market applications	Collins, Ketter, & Gini, 2002; Fan, Stallaert, & Whinston, 1999; Gates & Nissen, 2001; Harrison & Andrusiewicz, 2004; Jannsen & Sol, 2000; Kaihara, 2003; Karacapilidis & Moraitis, 2000; Karacapilidis & Moraitis, 2001; Liu, Wang, & Teng, 2000; Maamar, Dorion, & Daible, 2001; Teich, Wallenius, Wallenius, & Zaitsev, 1999b; Wang, Tan, & Ren, 2004
	Simulators of e-markets	DiMicco, Maes, & Greenwald, 2003; Kearns & Ortiz, 2003; Praca, Ramos, Vale, & Cordeiro, 2003; Zimmerman, Thomas, Gan, & Murillo-Sanchez, 1999
	Infrastructure for automated matching mechanisms in e-markets	Chkaiban & Sonderby, 2000; Dumas, Benatallah, Russel, & Spork, 2004; Ha & Park, 2001; Lin & Chang, 2001
	Infrastructure for virtual field experiments	Kim, Barua, & Whinston, 2002
	Infrastructure for mediating product catalogs	Lincke & Schmid, 1998
	Auction decision support system infrastructure	Gregg & Walczak, in press
	Infrastructure for mobile e-market services	Kwon, in press
	Infrastructure for supply chain e-markets	Gerber & Klusch, 2002; Gerber, Russ, & Klusch, 2003
	E-market recommendation service infrastructure	Ha, 2002

that are published in this journal), *Electronic Markets* (20 out of the 50 papers), *Electronic Commerce Research & Applications* (16 out of the 20 papers), and *International Journal of Electronic Commerce* (15 out of the 27 papers), are around technical topics. In the following paragraphs, we review the open issues around each technical topic, as well as the representative publications.

Architecture

The technical topic of *architecture* refers to approaches for modeling and developing of e-market architectures. In particular, it concerns the design and development of e-market models, such as conceptual models and frameworks for e-markets, models for negotiation mechanisms in e-markets, as well as metamodels for the analysis or classification of e-market components. Additionally, it concerns the design, specification, and implementation of e-market infrastructures, such as the design of e-market applications, e-market simulators, and e-market tools (matching mechanisms, product catalogs, recommendation services, etc.). These major issues are presented in Table 2. The most important contributions and representative references are also reported.

There are several studies in the e-market literature reporting contributions in the areas presented. First of all, there are contributions presenting conceptual models or frameworks that represent e-market architectural elements. Such is the work of Wang (1997), Kain et al. (1999), Brandtweiner and Scharl (1999), Baghdadi (2004), Wicke (1999), Gomber and Maurer (2004), and Blecker et al. (2004). Models or frameworks for particular types of markets also exist, such as the ones proposed for secure e-markets from Roehm and Pernul (2000), Mandry et al. (2001), and Jaiswal et al. (2004). Apart from viewing e-market architectures in total, such contributions can also focus on architectures of e-market modules. For example, negotiation mechanism architectures can be found modeled in a conceptual way (Chiu et al., in press; Srivastava & Mohapatra, 2003). Other contributions include papers regarding the design of e-market architectures (Fontoura et al., 2005; Geyer et al., 1997; Hamalainen et al., 1996; Mullen & Breese, 2000). An important strand of related work concerns proposed metamodels for describing, analysing, and/or specifying e-markets. Characteristic examples are the papers of Bhargarva et al. (Bhargava, Krishnan, & Mueller,1997) and Lindemann and Schmid (1999).

Another dimension of the e-market architectures area concerns contributions about architectures that are implemented through proposed infrastructures. The most common case is papers presenting the architecture of implemented e-markets (Collins et al., 2002; Fan et al., 1999; Gates & Nissen, 2001; Harrison & Andrusiewicz, 2004; Jannsen & Sol, 2000; Kaihara, 2003; Karacapilidis & Moraitis, 2000; Karacapilidis & Moraitis, 2001; Liu et al., 2000; Maamar et al., 2001; Teich et al., 1999b; Wang et al., 2004). Other infrastructure implementations are also presented, including automated matching mechanisms (Chkaiban & Sonderby, 2000; Dumas et al., 2004; Ha & Park, 2001; Lin & Chang, 2001) as well as other special types of e-market infrastructures. Examples include:

- The e-market infrastructure for virtual field experiments of Kim et al. (2002)
- The infrastructure for mediating e-market catalogs of Lincke and Schmid (1998)

- The infrastructure of an auction decision support system presented by Gregg and Walczak (in press)

- The infrastructure for an e-market with mobile services described by Kwon (in press)

- The infrastructure for supply chain management e-markets that Gerber and Klusch (2002) and Gerber et al. (2003) implemented for trading timber

- The infrastructure for e-market recommendation services that Ha (2002) describes

A class of such contributions with particular interest are e-market simulators. These are infrastructures that allow for simulating e-market participants behaviours in different application domains, such as electric power markets (Praca et al., 2003; Zimmerman et al., 1999), financial markets (Kearns & Ortiz, 2003), and simulators for studying dynamic pricing strategies in markets (DiMicco et al., 2003).

From the review of these contributions, it can be concluded that research in the topic area of e-market architectures has particularly focused on ways of modelling and metamodelling e-markets, as well as in studying the development of various infrastructures related to e-market services. Modelling e-markets can greatly facilitate their analysis and implementation; therefore, additional focus should be given on the use of software-related tools, such as the Unified Modelling Language (UML), and their combination with widely accepted software development approaches, such as the rational unified process (RUP), in order to provide e-market developers with formal tools for the specification of e-market architecture, that can be reused in more than one implementation. In addition, metamodelling of e-markets can help in the identification of their most important components and characteristics, contributing, for instance, to their development and description as independent components or services; for example, according to the emerging paradigm of Web services (Beneventano, Guerra, Magnani, & Vincini, 2004). Another dimension is the use of the e-market metamodels in order to facilitate the users' access to e-markets; for example, by developing Internet-based directories or online recommendation services for e-markets (Manouselis & Costopoulou, 2005a; Manouselis & Costopoulou, 2005b).

Interoperability

Interoperability refers to the ability of different systems to interoperate, that is, to cooperate and exchange information in preagreed, well-defined formats. In e-market literature, interoperability concerns various issues, such as the exchange of business documents in a format that different systems may understand, the description of products in electronic catalogs in an interoperable manner, the use of appropriate technical markup languages such as XML, and the definition of appropriate semantics, as well as the exchange of interoperable messages between systems. These topics, the most important contributions, and representative references are presented in Table 3.

There are a few studies in the e-market literature concerning interoperability issues in e-markets. Such papers cover issues such as interoperable business document exchange

Table 3. Issues, contributions, and representative references in the topic of interoperability

Issues	Contributions	Representative References
Interoperability	Interoperable business document exchange	Glushko, Tenenbaum, & Meltzer., 1999
	E-catalog and product description/ classification interoperability	Baron, Shaw, & Bailey, 2000; Beneventano et al., 2004; Fensel, Ding, Omelayenko, Schulten, Botquin, Brown, & Flett, 2001
	XML language use and semantics	Smith & Poulter, 1999
	Communication/messages semantic interoperability	Vaishnavi & Kuechler, 2003

(Glushko et al., 1999), e-catalog and product description/classification interoperability (Baron et al., 2000; Beneventano et al., 2004; Fensel et al., 2001), XML language use and semantics (Smith & Poulter, 1999), and communication/messages semantic interoperability (Vaishnavi & Kuechler, 2003).

Interoperability is an issue of extreme importance in e-business, and extended work is carried out in standardization bodies and specification groups, such as the European Committee for Standardization CEN (CEN, 2001). More work is required in the field of e-markets, in order to facilitate the reusability of e-business information from different systems, as well as the communication among different systems and technologies. The range of topics includes electronic data interchange (e.g., the Open-EDI reference model ISO/IEC 14662), classification of products (e.g., the UN/CEFACT UNSPSC product and services classification, http://www.unspsc.org/), multilingual electronic catalogues (e.g., BMEcat, http://www.bmecat.org/), e-invoicing (e.g., CEN/ISSS, 2003a), and description of core business processes and messages (e.g., ebXML bpPROC, 2001).

Technologies

This topic refers to particularly applied technologies, as well as issues relevant to networking and data management in e-markets. It concerns the study of technologies such as agent technologies, particular implementations of e-markets, human computer interaction (HCI) issues in e-markets, and networking issues. These issues, the most important contributions, and representative references are presented in Table 4.

There are several studies in the e-market literature reporting contributions in these areas. First of all, there are contributions presenting the application of technologies related with agents in e-markets. Such contributions include reviews of agent technologies in e-markets (Gregg & Walczak, 2003; Maes, 1999; Maes, Guttman, & Moukas, 1999) and studies of e-markets that are enabled from using agent technologies (Crowston & MacInnes, 2001). Other contributions deal with details of implementing particular technical solutions, such as the specifications of the eCo initiative for business documents exchange (Glushko et al.,

Table 4. Issues, contributions, and representative references in the topic of technologies

Issues	Contributions	Representative References
Agent technologies	Agent technologies in e-markets	Gregg & Walczak, 2003; Maes, 1999; Maes et al., 1999
	E-markets enabling agent-oriented queries	Crowston & MacInnes, 2001
Technical implementations	eCo initiative for business documents exchange	Glushko et al., 1999
	Extranet implementation	Angeles, 2001
Interactivity (HCI) technologies	Virtual world environments	Shen et al., 2002
	Multimedia cues use	Vishwanath, 2004
Technical requirements	B2B e-markets	Feldman, 2000
Networking	Network congestion pricing	Henderson et al., 2001

1999) and the HealthTex extranet implementation (Angeles, 2001). Moreover, there are contributions dealing with interactivity technologies in e-markets, such as the development of virtual world environments (Shen, Radakrishnan, & Georganas, 2002) and the use of multimedia cues (Vishwanath, 2004). Some contributions also refer to technical requirements for e-markets, such as Feldman (2000) does for the particular case of B2B e-markets. Finally, a small number of papers concerns networking technologies issues, since such aspects of e-markets are usually covered by specialized publications and do not appear in e-market research. The only indicative example we identified deals with networking congestion and pricing schemes (Henderson, Crowcroft, & Bhatti, 2001).

The small number of purely technical contributions in the e-market area is explained if we consider that these topics are e-commerce wide and not e-market specific, and that the coverage of this review has not included many technical journals. On the other hand, in our opinion, further work is definitely required on technical topics such as the use of Web services for the implementation of e-market services, as well as the exploration of HCI issues concerning e-market environments.

Protocols/Algorithms

This technical topic refers to the design and development of e-market mechanisms and services, implementing various e-market protocols or algorithms. It concerns issues such as the design and development of pricing algorithms, trading algorithms, as well as buyers' decision support algorithms. The issues currently covered in e-market literature are presented in Table 5. The most important contributions and representative references are also reported.

There are several studies in the e-market literature reporting contributions in this area. First of all, there are some contributions that discuss pricing algorithms. These include the works of Zacharia, Evgeniou, Moukas, Boufounos, and Maes (2001) and Deck and Wilson (2002). Moreover, there are some contributions that present algorithms that aim to support the purchase decision process, such as algorithms for auction support systems (Bapna, Goes, & Gupta, 2003; Teich, Wallenius, Wallenius, & Zaitsev, 2001) and algorithms that support recommendation services (Linden, Smith, & York, 2003; Tewari, Youll, & Maes, 2002).

Nevertheless, most contributions fall into the category of trading algorithms. There exist papers that review families of trading algorithms (Sandholm, 2000a; Sandholm, 2000b; Stroebel, 2000; Teich, Wallenius, & Wallenius, 1999a; Teich, Wallenius, Wallenius, & Koppius, 2004), papers that propose methodologies to model algorithms and protocols (Dumas, Governatori, Ter Hofstede, & Oaks, 2002; Stroebel, 2001), as well as novel contributions proposing automatic design of trading algorithms (Cliff, 2003). Most contributions, though, present agent-automated algorithms, including Wellman, Cheng, Reeves, and Lochner (2003a); Wellman, Greenwald, Stone, and Wurman (2003b); Wellman, Wurman, O'Malley, Bangera, Lin, Reeves, and Walsh (2001); Greenwald and Stone (2001); Wurman, Walsh, and Wellman (1998); Sandholm (1999); Ito Hattori, and Shintani (2002); Ono, Nishiyama, and Horiuchi (2003); Yuan and Lin (2004); Deveaux, Paraschiv, and Latourrette (2001);

Table 5. Issues, contributions, and representative references in the topic of protocols/algorithms

Issues	Contributions	Representative References
Pricing algorithms	Pricing algorithm analysis	Deck & Wilson, 2002; Zacharia et al., 2001
Trading algorithms	Review of trading algorithms	Sandholm, 2000a; Sandholm, 2000b; Stroebel, 2000; Teich et al., 1999a; Teich et al., 2004
	Modelling trading algorithms	Dumas et al., 2002; Stroebel, 2001
	Designing automatically trading algorithms	Cliff, 2003
	Agent-automated trading algorithms	Collins et al., 2001; Deveaux et al., 2001; Dumas et al., 2005; Goldman & Kraus, 2004; Greenwald & Stone, 2001; Ito et al., 2002; Kitts & LeBlanc, 2004; Ono et al., 2003; Padovan et al., 2002; Sandholm, 1999; Teuteberg, 2003; Vulkan & Preist, 2003; Wellman et al., 2003a; Wellman et al., 2003b; Wellman et al., 2001; Wurman et al., 1998; Yuan & Lin, 2004
	Examination of nonautomated trading algorithms	Bichler & Kalagnanam, in press; Burmester et al., 2004; Deck & Wilson, 2002; Di Noia et al., 2003; Gerber et al., 2004; Kalagnanam et al., 2001; Seifert et al., 2004; Tallroth, 2004
Decision support algorithms	Auction decision support	Bapna et al., 2003; Teich et al., 2001
	Recommendation	Linden et al., 2003; Tewari et al., 2002

Dumas, Aldred, Governatori, and Ter Hofstede (2005); Goldman and Kraus (2004); Kitts and LeBlanc (2004); Teuteberg (2003); Collins, Bilot, Gini, and Mobasher (2001); Padovan, Sackmann, Eymann, and Pippow (2002); and Vulkan and Preist (2003). Finally, many papers examine algorithms for nonautomated trading environments, although they sometimes engage an automated trading simulation to study these algorithms. Such papers include algorithms on optimal allocation (Seifert et al., 2004), multiattribute auctions (Bichler & Kalagnanam, in press), low price matching (Deck & Wilson, 2002), clearing continuous double auctions (Kalagnanam, Davenport, & Lee, 2001), uncoercible bidding games (Burmester, Magkos, & Chrissikopoulos, 2004), multiquote double auctions (Tallroth, 2004), as well as algorithms for matching buyers and sellers (Di Noia, Di Sciascio, Donini, & Mongiello, 2003; GerberTeich, Wallenius, & Wallenius, 2004).

Extensive work has been carried out in the topic area of algorithms and protocols, and most topics are covered to a satisfactory extent. In addition, this is an area of e-market technologies that has very strong roots in theoretical contributions in the field of e-markets (e.g., game theory and consumer behaviour analysis).

Services

This topic concerns types and categories of services that e-markets offer to their users. These concern descriptions of typical e-market services, analyses of various case studies, as well as studies of the evolution of e-market services in the course of time or for particular business sectors. The major issues currently covered by e-market papers, most important contributions, and representative references are presented in Table 6.

There are several studies in the e-market literature reporting contributions in these areas. First of all, there are contributions that review and classify typical e-market services. These include examination of services in specific e-market business models (Timmers, 1998), e-market services classified by actor role (O'Daniel, 2001), by interaction degree required (Akkermans, 2001), by the type of the e-market (Raisinghani & Hanebeck, 2002) and by the e-market channels engaged (Simons, Steinfield, & Bouwman, 2002).

Moreover, there are contributions presenting specific case studies of services provided by e-markets. Such case studies include mass customization services (Warkentin et al., 2000), product representation services (Koppius et al., 2004), pre- and postpurchase services (Cao & Gruca, 2004), agent-based services (Liang & Huang, 2000; Moukas et al., 2000; Silverman et al., 2001). Other studies concern the services of particular case studies of e-markets, such as real-estate e-market services (Crowston & Wigand, 1999), financial e-market services (Gallaugher & Melville, 2004; Minakakis & Rao, 1999), and software e-market services (Elfatatry & Layzell, 2004).

Finally, there are contributions examining the current status and the future evolution of e-market services. Such contributions include the analysis of services that are offered by B2B e-markets (Raisinghani & Hanebeck, 2002), e-market participants' expectations about B2B market services (Holzmueller & Schluechter, 2002), e-market operators perspective on B2B market services (Holzmueller & Schluechter, 2002; Lenz et al., 2002; Wang & Archer, 2004), as well as the use of trust-related services in e-markets (Palmer et al., 2000).

Table 6. Issues, contributions, and representative references in the topic of services

Issues	Contributions	Representative References
Typical e-market services	Per business model	Timmers, 1998
	Per actor role	O'Daniel, 2001
	Per e-market type	Raisinghani & Hanebeck, 2002; Wang & Archer, 2004
	Per interaction degree	Akkermans, 2001
	Per market channels	Simons et al., 2002
Case study analysis	Mass customization	Warkentin, Bapna, & Sugumaran, 2000
	Product representation	Koppius, van Heck, & Wolters, 2004
	Pre- and postpurchase services	Cao & Gruca, 2004
	Agent-based services	Liang & Huang, 2000; Moukas, Zacharia, Guttman, & Maes, 2000; Silverman, Bachann, & Al-Akharas, 2001
	Real-estate e-markets	Crowston & Wigand, 1999
	Financial services e-markets	Gallaugher & Melville, 2004; Minakakis & Rao, 1999
	Software services e-markets	Elfatatry & Layzell, 2004
Status & evolution of e-market services	Analysis of B2B market services	Raisinghani & Hanebeck, 2002
	Participants expectations about B2B market services	Holzmueller & Schluechter, 2002
	Operators perspective on B2B market services	Holzmueller & Schluechter, 2002; Lenz et al., 2002; Wang & Archer, 2004
	Trust services use	Palmer, Bailey, & Faraj, 2000

The topic area of e-market services is expected to constantly grow, as new services for supporting the phases of a transaction process are introduced. In addition, apart from their apparent consumer orientation, e-markets are also considered as powerful business tools that can facilitate the proper operation of the whole supply chain (Grieger, 2003). Dai and Kauffman (2002b) have provided a very enlightening framework of services that B2B e-markets may offer, which includes (among others) workflow management, collaborative project management, supply chain management, system integration, and compliance with standards.

Conclusion

This chapter aimed to provide an overview of recent technological developments and trends in the field of e-markets. More specifically, it reported results from a review of e-market papers that have been published during the past decade in scientific journals, and that particularly focused on topics related to the application of e-business technologies in e-markets. The review covered 18 journals that publish e-commerce research, and selected the 118 (out of the overall sample of 248) papers that cover some technical topic. Using a classification framework for e-market research, five technical topic areas have been identified: e-market architectures, interoperability, services, protocols/algorithms, and technologies. The most important issues in each topic area have been discussed, and representative contributions have been reviewed. The results of this review provided interesting insight about the current status, as well as the future perspectives, of e-business technologies in e-market research.

In particular, it has been identified that the topic areas attracting more attention in e-market research have been architectures and protocols/algorithms. On the other hand, there seems to be a shortage of research related to more low-level technical topics, such as the ones covered by the technologies and interoperability areas. Our study revealed several directions where future research could be focused. First of all, particular importance should be given to the exploration of models, techniques, and languages for the description of e-market components in terms of Web services (Beneventano et al., 2004), as well as business processes and documents (eBXML, 2005). For this purpose, additional research is required towards the implementation of interoperability specifications and standards. This may, in turn, facilitate the automated business information exchange between e-market systems, and the integration of already existing information in different e-market systems (a topic termed as the *reusability* of business information). A future perspective that attracts more and more attention is the cooperation of e-markets in networks called e-market "federations" (Stanoevska-Slabeva, 1999). Furthermore, international standardization bodies (CEN/ISSS, 2003b) focus on the development of open source solutions for enterprise uses, particularly in the case of small and medium enterprises (SMEs). Another open issue is the further exploration of decision support algorithms, models and systems for e-market buyers and sellers (Manouselis & Costopoulou, 2005b). Finally, the application of novel technologies will allow the deployment of a new generation of e-market services. Examples include the exploration of ambient or virtual e-market environments that will intelligently help the users carry out their transactions (Shen et al., 2002), as well as mobile devices that will allow for on-site customer service (Vrechopoulos, O'Keefe, Doukidis, & Siomkos, 2004) integrated with shopping, working, or living environments of the users.

The analysis presented in this chapter took place in the context of a wider e-market literature review that covered all e-market research topic areas. In this chapter, we particularly focused on the 118 e-market papers of our sample that covered technical topics. There may be some additional papers, outside the coverage of our review that may be addressing e-market technical issues. Therefore, the list of reviewed contributions should be not considered exhaustive. On the contrary, the primary concern of the chapter has been to identify the main contributions related to technical topics, and to serve as an initial roadmap to relevant research. This chapter engages a systematic way for classifying and examining e-market literature; therefore, it could be possibly used as a case study for studying any other topic area of Figure 1. As a matter of fact, we aim to perform such focused studies for the rest of the topic areas in the future. In addition, future work will include covering publications from other important sources, such as key conferences and the "grey" literature of the e-business area, in order to give a more complete picture of technologies and solutions for e-business process management in e-markets.

References

Akkermans, H. (2001). Intelligent e-business: From technology to value. *IEEE Intelligent Systems, Special Issue on Intelligent E-Business, 16*(4), 8-10.

Anandalingam, G., Day, R. W., & Raghavan, S. (2005). The landscape of electronic market design. *Management Science, 51*(3), 316-327.

Angeles, R. (2001). Creating a digital marketspace presence: Lessons in extranet implementation. *Internet Research: Electronic Networking Applications and Policy, 11*(2), 167-184.

Baghdadi, Y. (2004). ABBA: An architecture for deploying business-to-business electronic commerce applications. *Electronic Commerce Research & Applications, 3*, 190-212.

Bakos, Y. (1991). A strategic analysis of electronic marketplaces. *Management Information Systems Quarterly, 15*(3), 295-310.

Bakos, Y. (1998). The emerging role of electronic marketplaces on the Internet. *Communications of the ACM, 41*(8), 35-42.

Bapna, R., Goes, P., & Gupta A. (2003). Replicating online yankee auctions to analyze auctioneers' and bidders' strategies. *Information Systems Research, 14*(3), 244-268.

Baron, J. P., Shaw, M. J., & Bailey, A. D.Jr. (2000). Web-based e-catalog systems in B2B procurement. *Communications of the ACM, 43*(5), 93-100.

Beneventano, D., Guerra, F., Magnani, S., & Vincini, M. (2004). A Web service based framework for the semantic mapping amongst product classification schemas. *Journal of Electronic Commerce Research, 5*(2), 114-127.

Bharati, P., & Tarasewich, P. (2002). Global perceptions of journals publishing e-commerce research. *Communications of the ACM, 45*(5), 21-26.

Bhargava, H. K., Krishnan, R., & Mueller, R. (1997). Decision support on demand: Emerging electronic markets for decision technologies. *Decision Support Systems, 19*, 193-214.

Bichler, M., & Kalagnaman, J. (in press) Configurable offers and winner determination in multi-attribute auction. *European Journal of Operational Research.*

Blecker, T., Abdelkafi, N., Kreutler, G., & Kaluza, B. (2004). Auction-based variety formation and stering for mass customization. *Electronic Markets, Special Issue on Innovative Auction Markets, 14*(3), 232-242.

Brandtweiner, R., & Scharl, A. (1999). An institutional approach to modeling the structure and functionality of brokered electronic markets. *International Journal of Electronic Commerce, 3*(3), 71-88.

Burmester, M., Magkos, E., & Chrissikopoulos, V. (2004). Uncoercible e-bidding games. *Electronic Commerce Research, 4*, 113-125.

Cao, Y., & Gruca, T. S. (2004). The influence of pre- and post-purchase service on prices in the online book market. *Journal of Interactive Marketing, 18*(4), 51-62.

CEN. (2001). *Summaries of some frameworks, architectures and models for electronic commerce*, CWA 14228:2001E, European Committee for Standardization.

CEN/ISSS. (2003a). *Report and recommendations of CEN/ISSS e-invoicing focus group on standards and developments on electronic invoicing relating to VAT directive.* 2001/115/EC, European Committee for Standardization CEN/ISSS.

CEN/ISSS. (2003b). *CEN/ISSS roadmap for addressing key eBusiness standards issues 2003-2005.* eBusiness Standards Focus Group, European Committee for Standardization CEN/ISSS.

Chiu, D. K. W., Cheung, S. C., Hung, P. C. K., Chiu, S. Y. Y., & Chung, A. K. K. (in press) Developing e-negotiation support with a meta-modeling approach in a Web services environment. *Decision Support Systems.*

Chkaiban, G., & Sonderby, M. (2000). AATP: Auction agent transfer protocol. *Electronic Markets, 10*(2), 94-101.

Cliff, D. (2003). Explorations in evolutionary design of online auction market mechanisms. *Electronic Commerce Research & Applications, 2*, 162-175.

Collins, J., Bilot, C., Gini, M., & Mobasher, B. (2001). Decision processes in agent-based automated contracting. *IEEE Internet Computing*, 61-72.

Collins, J., Ketter, W., & Gini, M. (2002). Multi-agent negotiation testbed for contracting tasks with temporal and precedence constraints. *International Journal of Electronic Commerce, 7*(1), 35-57.

Crowston, K., & MacInnes, I. (2001). The effects of market-enabling Internet agents on competition and prices. *Journal of Electronic Commerce Research, 2*(1), 1-22.

Crowston, K., & Wigand, R. T. (1999). Real-estate war in cyberspace: An emerging electronic market?. *Electronic Markets, 9*(1/2), 37-44.

Dai, Q., & Kauffman, R. J. (2002a). B2B e-commerce revisited: Leading perspectives on the key issues and research directions. *Electronic Markets, 12*(2), 67-83.

Dai, Q., & Kauffman, R. J. (2002b). Business models for Internet-based B2B electronic markets. *International Journal of Electronic Commerce, 6*(4), 41-72.

Deck, C. A., & Wilson, B. J. (2002). The effectiveness of low price matching in mitigating the competitive pressure of low friction electronic markets. *Electronic Commerce Research, 2*, 385-398.

Deveaux, L., Paraschiv, C., & Latourrette, M. (2001). Bargaining on an Internet agent-based market: Behavioral vs. optimizing agents. *Electronic Commerce Research, 1*, 371-401.

Di Noia, T., Di Sciascio, E., Donini, F. M., & Mongiello, M. (2004). A system for principled matchmaking in an electronic marketplace. *International Journal of Electronic Commerce, 8*(4), 9-38.

DiMicco, J. M., Maes, P., & Greenwald, A. (2003). Learning curve: A simulation-based approach to dynamic pricing. *Electronic Commerce Research, 3*, 245-276.

Dumas, M., Aldred, L., Governatori, G., & Ter Hofstede, A. H. M. (2005). Probabilistic automated bidding in multiple auctions. *Electronic Commerce Research, 5*, 25-49.

Dumas, M., Benatallah, B., Russel, N., & Spork M. (2004). A configurable matchmaking framework for electronic marketplaces. *Electronic Commerce Research & Applications*, *3*, 95-106.

Dumas, M., Governatori, G., Ter Hofstede, A. H. M., & Oaks, P. (2002). A formal approach to negotiating agents development. *Electronic Commerce Research & Applications*, *1*, 193-207.

ebXML (Electronic Business using eXtensible Markup Language). (2005). Retrieved January 29, 2006, from http://www.ebxml.org/

ebXML bpPROC. (2001). *Catalog of common business processes v1.0.* ebXML Business Process Team, UN/CEFACT and OASIS.

Elfatatry, A., & Layzell, P. (2004). Negotiating in service-oriented environments. *Communications of the ACM*, *47*(8), 103-108.

Fan, M., Stallaert, J., & Whinston, A. B. (1999). The design and development of a financial cybermarket with a Bundline Trading Mechanism. *International Journal of Electronic Commerce*, *4*(1), 5-22.

Feldman, S. (2000). Electronic marketplaces. *IEEE Internet Computing*, *4*(4), 93-95.

Fensel, D., Ding, Y., Omelayenko, B., Schulten, E., Botquin, G., Brown, M., & Flett, A. (2001, July/August). Product data integration in B2B e-commerce. *IEEE Intelligent Systems*, 54-59.

Fontoura, M., Ionescu, M., & Minsky, N. (2005). Decentralized peer-to-peer auctions. *Electronic Commerce Research*, *5*, 7-24.

Gallaugher, J. M., & Wang, Y.-M. (1999). Network externalities and the provision of composite IT goods supporting the e-commerce infrastructure. *Electronic Markets*, *9*(1/2), 14-19.

Gates, W. R., & Nissen, M. E. (2001). Designing agent-based electronic employment markets. *Electronic Commerce Research*, *1*, 239-263.

Gerber, A., & Klusch, M. (2002, January/February). Agent-based integrated services for timber production and sales. *IEEE Intelligent Systems*, 33-39.

Gerber, A., Russ, C., & Klusch, M. (2003). Supply web co-ordination by an agent-based trading network with integrated logistics services. *Electronic Commerce Research & Applications*, *2*, 133-146.

Gerber, C., Teich, J., Wallenius, H., & Wallenius, J. (2004). A simulation and test of OptiMark's electronic matching lorithm and its simple variations for institutional block trading. *Decision Support Systems*, *36*, 235-245.

Geyer, G., Kuhn, C., & Schmid, B. (1997). Designing a market for quantitative knowledge. *International Journal of Electronic Commerce*, *1*(4), 89-108.

Glushko, R. J., Tenenbaum, J. M., & Meltzer, B. (1999). An XML framework for agent-based e-commerce. *Communications of the ACM*, *42*(3), 106-114.

Goldman, C. V., & Kraus, S. (2004). The value of temptation. (2004). *Electronic Commerce Research*, *4*, 415-454.

Gomber, P., & Maurer, K.-O. (2004). Xetra bEST - Intregration of market access intermediaries' requirements into market design. *Electronic Markets, Special Issue on Innovative Auction Markets, 14*(3), 214-222.

Greenwald, A., & Stone, P. (2001). Autonomous bidding agents in the trading agent competition. *IEEE Internet Computing, 5*(2), 52-60.

Gregg, D. G., & Walczak, S. (in press). Auction advisor: An agent-based online-auction decision support system. *Decision Support Systems*.

Gregg, D. G., & Walczak, S. (2003). E-commerce auction agents and online-auction dynamics. *Electronic Markets, 13*(3), 242-250.

Grieger, M. (2003). Electronic marketplaces: A literature review and a call for supply chain management research. *European Journal of Operational Research, 144*, 280-294.

Ha, S. H. (2002, November/December). Helping online customers decide through Web personalization. *IEEE Intelligent Systems*, 34-43.

Ha, S. H., & Park, S. C. (2001, July/August). Matching buyers and suppliers: An intelligent dynamic exchange model. *IEEE Intelligent Systems*, 28-40.

Hamalainen, M., Whinston, A. B., & Vishik, S. (1996). Electronic markets for learning: Education brokerage on the Internet. *Communications of the ACM, 39*(6), 51-58.

Harrison, J. V., & Andrusiewicz, A. (2004). A virtual marketplace for advertising narrowcast over digital signage networks. *Electronic Commerce Research & Applications, 3*, 163-175.

Henderson, T., Crowcroft, J., & Bhatti, S. (2001, September-October). Congestion pricing: Paying your way in communication networks. *IEEE Internet Computing*, 85-89.

Holzmueller, H. H., & Schluechter, J. (2002). Delphi study about the future of B2B marketplaces in Germany. *Electronic Commerce Research & Applications, 1*, 2-19.

ISO/IEC 14662. (2004). *Information technology—open-EDI reference model*. ISO/IEC JTC 1. Retrieved January 29, 2006, from http://www.disa.org/international/is14662.pdf

Ito, T., Hattori, H., & Shintani, T. (2002). A cooperative exchanging mechanism among seller agents for group-based sales. *Electronic Commerce Research & Applications, 1*, 138-149.

Jaiswal, A., Kim, Y., & Gini, M. (2004). Design and implementation of a secure multi-agent marketplace. *Electronic Commerce Research & Applications, 3*, 355-368.

Janssen, M., & Sol, H. G. (2000). Evaluating the role of intermediaries in the electronic value chain. *Internet Research: Electronic Networking Applications and Policy, 10*(5), 406-417.

Kaihara, T. (2003). A study on virtual market model for e-marketplace server. *Electronic Commerce Research & Applications, 2*, 278-285.

Kain, A. K., Aparicio, M., & Singh, M. P. (1999). Agents for process coherence in virtual enterprises. *Communications of the ACM, 42*(3), 62-69.

Kalagnanam, J. R., Davenport, A. J., & Lee, H. S. (2001). Computational aspects of clearing continuous call double auctions with assignment constraints and indivisible demand. *Electronic Commerce Research, 1*, 221-238.

Karacapilidis, N., & Moraitis, P. (2000). Intelligent agents as artificial employees in an electronic market. *Journal of Electronic Commerce Research, 1*(4), 133-142.

Karacapilidis, N., & Moraitis, P. (2001). Building an agent-mediated electronic commerce system with decision analysis features. *Decision Support Systems, 32*, 53-69.

Kauffman, R. J., & Walden, E. A. (2001). Economics and electronic commerce: Survey and directions for research. *International Journal of Electronic Commerce, 5*(4), 5-116.

Kearns, M., & Ortiz, L. (2003). The Penn-Lehman automated trading project. *IEEE Intelligent Systems, Special Issue on Agents and Markets, 18*(6), 22-31.

Kim, B., Barua, A., & Whinston, A.B. (2002). Virtual field experiments for a digital economy: A new research methodology for exploring an information economy. *Decision Support Systems, 32*, 215-231.

Kitts, B., & LeBlanc, B. (2004). Optimal bidding on keyword auctions. *Electronic Markets, Special Issue on Innovative Auction Markets, 14*(3), 186-201.

Kollman, T. (2000). Competitive strategies for electronic marketplaces: A study of German-language trading sites for used cars on the WWW. *Electronic Markets, 10*(2), 102-109.

Koppius, O. R., van Heck, E., & Wolters, M. J. J. (2004). The importance of product representation online: Empirical results and implications for electronic markets. *Decision Support Systems, 38*, 161-169.

Kwon, O. (in press). Multi-agent system approach to context-aware coordinated web services under general market mechanism. *Decision Support Systems*.

Lenz, M., Zimmermann, H.-D., & Heitmann, M. (2002). Strategic partnerships and competitiveness of business-to-business e-marketplaces: Preliminary evidence from Europe. *Electronic Markets, 12*(2), 100-111.

Liang, T. P., & Chen, D.-N. (2003). Evolution of information systems research. In *Proceedings of the Pacific Asian Conference on Information Systems*, Adelaide, Australia (pp. 834-842). Atlanta, GA: Association for Information Systems.

Liang, T.-P., & Huang, J.-S. (2000). A framework for applying intelligent agents to support electronic trading. *Decision Support Systems, 28*, 305-317.

Lin, F.-R., & Chang, K.-Y. (2001, July/August). A multiagent framework for automated online bargaining. *IEEE Intelligent Systems*, 41-47.

Lincke, D.-M., & Schmid, B. (1998). Mediating electronic product catalogs. *Communications of the ACM, 41*(7), 86-88.

Lindemann, M. A., & Schmid, B. F. (1999). Framework for specifying, building, and operating electronic markets. *International Journal of Electronic Commerce, 3*(2), 7-21.

Linden, G., Smith, B., & York, J. (2003, January-February). Amazon.com recommendations: Item-to-item collaborative filtering. *IEEE Internet Computing*, 76-80.

Liu, H., Wang, S., & Teng, F. (2000). Real-time multi-auctions and the agent support. *Journal of Electronic Commerce Research, 1*(4), 143-151.

Maamar, Z., Dorion, E., & Daigle, C. (2001). Toward virtual marketplaces for e-commerce support. *Communications of the ACM, 44*(12), 35-38.

Maes, P (1999). Smart commerce: The future of intelligent agents in cyberspace (keynote speech at Direct Marketing Association Conference, 1998). *Journal of Interactive Marketing, 13*(3), 66-76.

Maes, P., Guttman, R. H., & Moukas, A. G. (1999). Agents that buy and sell. *Communications of the ACM, 42*(3), 81-91.

Malone, T. W., Yates, J., & Benjamin, R. I. (1987). Electronic markets and electronic hierarchies. *Communications of the ACM, 30*(6), 484-497.

Mandry, T., Pernul, G., & Roehm, A. W. (2001). Mobile agents in electronic markets: Opportunities, risks, agent protection. *International Journal of Electronic Commerce, 5*(2), 47-60.

Manouselis, N. (2005). *Electronic markets: Literature review, classification, and identification of open issues* (Tech. Rep.). Athens, Greece: Agricultural University of Athens, Informatics Laboratory. Retrieved January 29, 2006, from http://e-services.aua.gr

Manouselis, N., & Costopoulou, C. (2005b). Designing an Internet-based directory service for e-markets. *Information Services & Use, 25*(2), 95-107.

Manouselis, N., & Costopoulou, C. (2005a). Towards a metadata model for e-markets. In *Proceedings of the 12th Research Symposium on Emerging Electronic Markets (RSEEM 2005)* (pp. 169-184). Amsterdam, Netherlands: Vrije University.

Minakakis, L., & Rao, B. (1999). Competing in online markets: Financial services as a case in point. *Electronic Markets, 9*(4), 263-268.

Moukas, A., Zacharia, G., Guttman, R., & Maes, P. (2000). Agent-mediated electronic commerce: An MIT Media Laboratory perspective. *International Journal of Electronic Commerce, 4*(3), 5-22.

Mullen, T., & Breese, J. (2000). Experiments in designing computational economies for mobile users. *Decision Support Systems, 28*, 21-34.

Ngai, E. W. T., & Wat, F. K. T. (2002). A literature review and classification of electronic commerce research. *Information and Management, 39*, 415-429.

O'Daniel, T. (2001). A value-added model for e-commerce. *Electronic Markets, 11*(1), 37-43.

OECD. (2004). *Information technology outlook.*

Ono, C., Nishiyama, S., & Horiuchi, H. (2003). Reducing complexity in winner determination for combinatorial ascending auctions. *Electronic Commerce Research & Applications, 2*, 176-186.

Orlikowski, W. J., & Iacono, S. (2001). Research commentary: Desperately seeking the IT in IT research—a call to theorizing the IT artifact. *Information Systems Research, 12*(2), 121-134.

Padovan, B., Sackmann, S., Eymann, T., & Pippow, I. (2002). Prototype for an agent-based secure electronic marketplace including reputation-tracking mechanisms. *International Journal of Electronic Commerce, 6*(4), 93-113.

Palmer, J. W., Bailey, J. P., & Faraj, S. (2000). The role of intermediaries in the development of trust on the WWW: The use and prominence of trusted third parties and privacy statements. *Journal of Computer-Mediated Communication, 5*(3).

Praca, I., Ramos, C., Vale, Z., & Cordeiro, M. (2003). MASCEM: A multiagent system that simulates competitive electricity markets. *IEEE Intelligent Systems, Special Issue on Agents and Markets, 18*(6), 54-60.

Raisinghani, M. S., & Hanebeck, H.-C. L. (2002). Rethinking B2B e-marketplaces and mobile commerce: From information to execution. *Journal of Electronic Commerce Research, 3*(2), 86-97.

Roehm, A. W., & Pernul, G. (2000). COPS: A model and infrastructure for secure and fair electronic markets. *Decision Support Systems, 29*, 343-355.

Rosson, P., & Davis, C. (2004). Electronic marketplaces and innovation: The Canadian experience. *International Journal of Information Technology and Management, 3*(1), 41-58.

Sandholm, T. (1999). Automated negotiation. *Communications of the ACM, 42*(3), 84-85.

Sandholm, T. (2000a). Approaches to winner determination in combinatorial auctions. *Decision Support Systems, 28*, 165-176.

Sandholm, T. (2000b). Issues in computational Vickrey auctions. *International Journal of Electronic Commerce, 4*(3), 107-129.

Segev, A., Gebauer, J., & Faerber, F. (1999). Internet-based electronic markets. *Electronic Markets, 9*(3), 138-146.

Seifert, R. W., Thonemann, U. W., & Hausman, W. H. (2004). Optimal procurement strategies for online spot markets. *European Journal of Operational Research, 152*, 781-799.

Shen, X., Radakrishnan, T., & Georganas, N. D. (2002). vCOM: Electronic commerce in a collaborative virtual world. *Electronic Commerce Research & Applications, 1*, 281-300.

Silverman, B. G., Bachann, M., & Al-Akharas, K. (2001, July/August). Do what I mean: Online shopping with a natural language search agent. *IEEE Intelligent Systems*, 48-53.

Simons, L. P. A., Steinfield, C., & Bouwman, H. (2002). Strategic positioning of the Web in a multi-channel market approach. *Internet Research: Electronic Networking Applications and Policy, 12*(4), 339-347.

Smith, H., & Poulter, K. (1999). Share the ontology in XML-based trading architectures. *Communications of the ACM, 42*(3), 110-111.

Smith, M. D., Bailey, J., & Brynjolfsson, E. (1999). Understanding digital markets: Review and assessment. In Brynjolfsson E. & Kahin B. (Eds.), *Understanding the digital economy.* Cambridge, MA: MIT Press.

Srivastava, V., & Mohapatra, P. K. J. (2003). PLAMUN: A platform for multi-user negotiation. *Electronic Commerce Research & Applications, 2*, 339-349.

Stanoevska-Slabeva, K. (1999). The concept of federated electronic markets. In *Proceedings of the 2nd Workshop on Advanced Issues of E-Commerce and Web-Based Information Systems (WECWIS 1999)* (pp. 164-167). Santa Clara: IEEE Computer Society Press.

Strader, T. J., & Shaw, M. J. (1997). Characteristics of electronic markets. *Decision Support Systems, 21*, 185-198.

Strader, T. J., & Shaw, M. J. (1999). Consumer cost differences for traditional and Internet markets. *Internet Research: Electronic Networking Applications and Policy, 9*(2), 89-492.

Stroebel, M. (2001). Design of roles and protocols for electronic negotiations. *Electronic Commerce Research, 1,* 335-353.

Stroebel, M. (2000). On auctions as the negotiation paradigm of rlectronic markets. *Electronic Markets, 10*(1), 39-44.

Tallroth, E. (2004). Continuous trading in thin private value markets: The multiple-quote double auction. *Electronic Markets, Special Issue on Innovative Auction Markets, 14*(3), 223-231.

Teich, J., Wallenius, H., & Wallenius, J. (1999a). Multiple-issue auction and market algorithms for the world wide web. *Decision Support Systems, 26,* 49-66.

Teich, J., Wallenius, H., Wallenius, J., & Koppius, O. R. (2004). Emerging multiple issue e-auctions. *European Journal of Operational Research, 159,* 1-16.

Teich, J., Wallenius, H., Wallenius, J., & Zaitsev, A. (1999b). A multiple unit auction algorithm: Some theory and a Web implementation. *Electronic Markets, 9*(3), 199-205.

Teich, J. E., Wallenius, H., Wallenius, J., & Zaitsev, A. (2001). Designing electronic auctions: An Internet-based hybrid procedure combining aspects of negotiations and auctions. *Electronic Commerce Research, 1,* 301-314.

Teuteberg, F. (2003). Experimental evaluation of a model for multilateral negotiation with fuzzy preferences on an agent-based marketplace. *Electronic Markets, 13*(1), 21-32.

Tewari, G., Youll, J., & Maes, P. (2002). Personalized location-based brokering using an agent-based intermediary architecture. *Decision Support Systems, 34,* 127-137.

Timmers, P. (1998). Business models for electronic markets. *Electronic Markets, 8*(2), 3-8.

Turban, E., King, D., Lee, J., & Viehland, D. (2004). *Electronic commerce: A managerial perspective 2004.* Upper Saddle River NJ: Prentice Hall.

UNCTAD. (2005). *Information economy report 2005* (UNCTAD/SDTE/ECB/2005/1). Geneva: United Nations Conference on Trade and Development.

Urbaczewski, A., Jessup, L. M., & Wheeler, B. (2002). Electronic commerce research: A taxonomy and a synthesis. *Journal of Organisational Computing and Electronic Commerce, 12*(4), 263-305.

Vaishnavi, V. K., & Kuechler, W. L. (2003). An approach to reducing e-commerce coordination costs in evolving markets using a semantic routing protocol. *Journal of Electronic Commerce Research, 4*(3), 113-127.

Vishwanath, A. (2004). An empirical investigation into the use of heuristics and information cues by bidders in online auctions. *Electronic Markets, Special Issue on Innovative Auction Markets, 14*(3), 178-185.

Vrechopoulos, A. P., O'Keefe, R. M., Doukidis, G. I., & Siomkos, G. J. (2004). Virtual store layout: An experimental comparison in the context of grocery retail. *Journal of Retailing, 80*(1), 13-22.

Vulkan, N., & Preist, C. (2003). Automated trading in agent-based markets for communication bandwidth. *International Journal of Electronic Commerce, 7*(4), 119-150.

Wang, H. (1997). A conceptual model for virtual markets. *Information and Management, 32,* 147-161.

Wang, S., & Archer, N. (2004). Strategic choice of electronic marketplace functionalities: A buyer-supplier relationship perspective. *Journal of Computer-Mediated Communication, 10*(1). Retrieved December 6, 2006 from http://jcmc.indiana.edu/vol10/issue1/

Wang, Y., Tan, K.-L., & Ren, J. (2004). PumaMart: A parallel and autonomous agents based internet marketplace. *Electronic Commerce Research & Applications, 3,* 294-310.

Warkentin, M., Bapna, R., & Sugumaran, V. (2000). The role of mass customization in enhancing supply chain relationships in B2C e-commerce markets. *Journal of Electronic Commerce Research, 1*(2), 45-52.

Wellman, M. P. (2004). Online marketplaces. In M. P.Singh (Ed.), *Practical handbook of Internet computing.* Boca Raton FL: CRC Press LLC.

Wellman, M. P., Cheng, S.-F., Reeves, D. M., & Lochner, K. M. (2003a). Trading agents competing: Performance, progress, and market effectiveness. *IEEE Intelligent Systems, Special Issue on Agents and Markets, 18*(6), 48-53.

Wellman, M. P., Greenwald, A., Stone, P., & Wurman, P. R. (2003b). The 2001 trading agent competition. *Electronic Markets, 13*(1), 4-12.

Wellman, M. P., Wurman, P. R., O'Malley, K., Bangera, R., Lin, S., Reeves, D., & Walsh, W. E. (2001, March-April). Designing the market game for a trading agent competition. *IEEE Internet Computing,* 43-51.

Wicke, G. A. (1999). Electronic markets - A key to mobility. *Electronic Markets, Special Issue on Electronic Commerce and Logistics, 9*(3), 162-168.

Wurman, P. R., Walsh, W. E., & Wellman, M. P. (1998). Flexible double auctions for electronic commerce: Theory and implementation. *Decision Support Systems, 24,* 17-27.

Yuan, S.-T., & Lin, Y.-H. (2004). Credit based group negotiation for aggregate sell/buy in e-markets. *Electronic Commerce Research & Applications, 3,* 74-94.

Zacharia, G., Evgeniou, T., Moukas, A., Boufounos, P., & Maes, P. (2001). Economics of dynamic pricing in a reputation brokered agent mediated marketplace. *Electronic Commerce Research, 1,* 85-100.

Zimmerman, R. D., Thomas, R. J., Gan, D., & Murillo-Sanchez, C. (1999). A web-based platform for experimental investigation of electric power auctions. *Decision Support Systems, 24,* 193-205.

Chapter V

E-Commerce Standards:
Transforming Industry Practice

Stephen Hawk, University of Wisconsin-Parkside, USA

Weijun Zheng, University of Wisconsin-Parkside, USA

Abstract

This chapter introduces XML-based e-commerce standards that have emerged within the past decade. The chapter describes the history of e-commerce standards, and then presents representative horizontal and vertical e-commerce standards by detailing their functionality, and how their development has been shaped by various stakeholders. The chapter also describes the potential for these standards to transform B2B practice by providing three industry examples. The chapter finishes by suggesting directions for future research by describing factors that could influence the future of these standards. Due to the central role these standards are likely to play in future e-commerce activity, most firms will at some point need to become aware of their capabilities, their application, and potential impact. This chapter is intended to provide an overview of the situation as it is understood today, and presents likely scenarios for how these standards may progress.

Introduction

E-commerce (electronic-commerce) refers to business over the Internet. The two major forms of e-commerce are business-to-consumer (B2C) and business-to-business (B2B). While B2C caters mostly to consumers, B2B e-commerce refers to one business selling to another business via the Web. According to the Gartner Group, B2B e-commerce is expected to grow from $145 billion in 1999 to more than $7 trillion by 2004, which will represent more than 7% of all sales transactions worldwide.[1] Traditional electronic data interchange (EDI) standards are well developed and are what have been used for decades as the basis for pre-Internet B2B e-commerce. However, it has been widely recognized that traditional EDI will eventually be supplanted by newer Internet-based B2B standards. These standards have only begun to be significantly adopted in select industries the past few years so their impact can be discussed mostly in terms of potential. As a great majority of e-commerce revenue comes from B2B transactions, and most of that comes from transactions carried out via traditional EDI (Knorr, 2002), the newer standards have the potential for becoming a foundation technology for generating a majority of e-commerce revenue in the not-too-distant future.

The mission of this chapter is to introduce these newer e-commerce standards. We begin by describing some basic background and history of e-commerce standards. The chapter then presents representative horizontal and vertical e-commerce standards by detailing their functionality, and how their development has been shaped by various stakeholders (e.g., formal standards bodies, vendors, etc.). The chapter also describes the potential for these standards to transform B2B practice in industries where they are adopted by providing three industry examples. The chapter finishes by suggesting directions for future research by describing factors that could influence the future of these standards. Although we have tried to reduce the technique jargon, there are still a number of basic terms that are necessary in order to discuss these standards, how they have developed, and are beginning to be used.

Background

E-commerce is fundamentally changing both companies' business processes and the value chains in which they operate. Greater automation speeds up business processes and makes them more efficient, promising productivity gains—and greater prosperity—both now and in the future. In order to enable e-commerce, common format conventions, or standards, are fundamental to the success of e-commerce.

A standard is a framework of specifications that has been approved by a recognized standards organization (de jure standard), is accepted as a de facto standard by the industry or is one of the open standards (Hawkins, Mansell, & Skea, 1995). Standards provide a blueprint for the future of industries, offering both stability and neutrality to a set of specifications. By providing a target for development, standards reduce the time and cost needed to develop systems and services, increase market access and acceptance, and reduce administrative and materials overhead. In today's e-commerce, standards have become a strategic tool for delivering innovation, reducing costs, improving the quality of goods and services produced, and opening new business opportunities (Kotok, 2002a, 2002b).

To better understand why standards are crucial to business, consider a relatively simple process: requesting a quote. Typically, the customer requests a product quote by sending its supplier a message with different kinds of specifications. After receiving the message, a supplier could respond by performing three different activities: checking availability of the product in its inventory; sending back the quote to the customer if its inventory matches the specification; and if not, referring the customer to another supplier. These activities are normally carried out by the supplier's own internal systems that are not visible to the customer. Without a clearly defined dialog between trading partners, the electronic exchange of messages for this transaction would be very difficult to accomplish. Similar to this case, many other transactions and information relevant to e-commerce must also be depicted (or "mapped") electronically in ways so that they can be exchanged between companies. There could be multiple companies in collaboration with one another along a supply chain. These companies normally have very different internal systems, but need to share some aspects of their business processes and exchange many different types of business documents as part of their interactions, which makes the electronic exchange of messages even more complex.

Implemented through various technologies, e-commerce standards provide a common language and format that make it possible for all trading partners to develop the processes and systems needed to exchange business information with each other. The development of e-commerce standards, according to CEN/ISSS eBusiness Standards Focus Group, will alleviate concerns about data protection and security, ensure interoperability, lower the cost of entry through free reference implementations, give good guidance, establish a more mainstream e-commerce software market; provide practical guidance by example, and aim for maximal ease of use (Li, 2003). All of these will help to remove some of the major barriers for e-commerce development and transform industry practice.

History of E-Commerce Standards

Today's B2B electronic commerce actually started with traditional electronic data interchange (EDI), the computer-to-computer exchange of business data in a standardized format. Starting from the late 1960s, as businesses began to computerize their internal operations, EDI was developed in an effort to reduce the burden of paperwork, and also as an attempt at implementing the fictional "paperless" office.

Traditional EDI users used leased or dedicated telephone lines or a value-added network (VAN)[2], such as those run by IBM, GE, or AT&T, to carry data exchanges. These lines would then be used to connect participating trading partners who in turn would need to install the VAN's proprietary software to translate and transmit their business documents in EDI formats. Although traditional EDI could result in faster transfer of documents at a lower cost and with fewer errors, it unfortunately was complex and expensive to implement. This, and its use of proprietary communication protocols,[3] effectively blocked most small-to-medium sized enterprises (SMEs) from its advantages (Scala & McGrath, 1993).

In the 1970s, several industries sponsored a shared EDI system that they usually turned over to a third-party network. In some cases, the shared system was developed by the third party for the group of common companies or an industry trade group. In 1975, the Transportation Data Coordinating Committee (TDCC) developed the first set of interindustry EDI standard covering air, motor, ocean, rail, and some banking applications (Berge, 1991).

The milestone of EDI development came in 1985, when X12 was released by the American National Standards Institute (ANSI). X12 was the primary North American standard for defining EDI transactions. Along with ANSI X12, EDIFACT (EDI for administration, commerce, & transport) started out as an international standard through the auspices of the United Nations. Following the implementation of ASC X12 and EDIFACT, EDI became crucial to nearly every industry. In 1997, X12 merged with EDIFACT, the global standard for EDI transactions.[4]

As the Internet became widely used in the 1990s, companies began to realize that EDI could reach well beyond those who could afford the traditional VAN approach. While traditional EDI is still widely used, companies needed a common language through which to exchange structured information between their computer systems over the Internet. HTML, the first generation language of the Internet, is not suited for this task as it defines only the formatting of information, not its meaning. The introduction of the Extensible Markup Language (XML) in 1997 launched a new series of efforts towards redefining languages for diverse industry sectors and business communities.

XML is a data-description standard designed by the World Wide Web Consortium (W3C) to simplify Web-based e-commerce transactions among supply-chain partners. XML itself is neither a language nor syntax, but a formal grammar, meant to build languages and syntaxes that exist in a neutral format (operating system and language independent). This explains its flexibility and strength, but also the proliferation of XML-based specialized languages and applications. XML is well suited to represent both data and documents, and allows specifying a model of documents and a means of validation of those documents against a given model. XML has rapidly become a key technology in two domains: (1) document and content management; (2) data interchange. In the document and content management domain, all EDI communities are working hard to develop new sector-specific languages. In the data interchange area, most tools being developed for messaging, enterprise application integration (EAI), and e-commerce (e.g., RosettaNet, ebXML, SOAP and Web services) are based on XML-encoded data (IDA, 2003). Major IT suppliers and user groups have enthusiastically embraced XML as the way to go in the future. It is expected that XML will soon become the dominant world standard for B2B e-commerce transactions over the Internet.

However, in any business application, XML itself is not the answer. It is only a standard foundation on which answers can be built. There is not just one XML-based standard emerging, but many. Some standards address particular industry sectors, and others that are intended as a basic platform for e-commerce in any industry. In the next section, we will describe several significant initiatives to develop contemporary e-commerce standards. These initiatives are first described by their functionalities. Then, the supporting standard bodies behind each are introduced.

Representative Contemporary
E-Commerce Standards

There are a number of e-commerce standards that have been developed the past few years. They cover a broad range of functionality and represent different approaches for handling interactions. These standards rarely work alone to support Web-based B2B e-commerce transactions. Instead, they exist in a hierarchy of standards from the foundational Internet standard, communication protocols, interaction standards, to data exchange formats (Zhao, Xia, & Shaw, 2005). It is beyond this book chapter's scope and objective to systematically introduce and describe each of these standards. However, it is noted that e-commerce standards generally fit into one of two categories: *vertical* or industry-specific standards that address the unique needs of firms within the industry, and *horizontal* standards that provide more general capabilities that would be useful in a wide variety of industries (Markus, Steinfield, & Wigand, 2003). Examples of vertical standards include RosettaNet, MISMO®, and STAR. Prominent examples of horizontal standards are SOAP, ebXML, and Web services using UDDI and WSDL. This chapter presents several of the well-developed and influential standards with the goal of giving readers an idea of what these standards are attempting to accomplish. The following presents vertical standards, followed by a discussion of horizontal standards.

Vertical Standards

A vertical standard is one that is specific to some kind of activity and/or some industrial sector (Aklouf, Piera, Ameur, & Drias, 2005). As a data-description standard, XML is not enough to handle interapplication communication between a wide range of companies and services. Nothing in XML ensures that the XML documents exchanged by two firms are mutually intelligible; it only provides the rules for how to create a properly structured document.

Since XML itself does not address the semantics of document content, it can be used to describe anything the creator of the document wishes. The problem is how to ensure that others understand what the document's creator intended. One potential solution might be for two trading partners to agree on the same set of XML tags. This, however, would still not be sufficient to address the meaning of data in a document, as the same tag could be interpreted differently by different parties. For example, one firm may use a *"Price"* element to mean *"RetailPrice"* while another firm could use the same element to mean *"WholesalePrice."* Without standardization of semantics, perhaps the best that could be hoped for would be for a business offering Web services to unambiguously explain the meanings of the tags contained its XML documents.

For documents to be understood by the two parties, they must agree on the meaning and organization of the data elements contained in them. While a pair of business partners might agree on the XML documents that are the inputs and outputs of their respective services, and create the mappings between the data used by their internal systems and the XML documents, this approach does not scale well when the number of trading partners increases. New mappings would have to be created for each additional partner.

Vertical standards attempt to address the preceding problem. A vertical standard represents the business knowledge of a specific industry, product, or process, and could:

- Provide a standard dictionary of data elements, their names, meanings, technical representations, and coding standards
- Define the structure of XML documents that will be exchanged
- Define business processes; for instance, what sequence of steps would occur in particular kinds of interactions between parties?

Standardizing industry-specific vocabulary would be a significant step toward semantic interoperability. This would also provide the foundation that would allow the creation of standard business documents for the industry. By addressing these two issues, firms that implement the standard would be able to understand the documents exchanged with each other. This does not mean, however, that both firms would have agreed on when to use any of the documents. For a given business process, for instance, how are these interactions "choreographed"? Defining the choreography for a given process specifies a series of ordered message exchanges and the conditions under which these messages are exchanged. In some cases, the context for using a document may be well understood or simple enough so that it need not be addressed by a vertical standard, while in others the choreography defined in the standard could clarify how two parties would interact with each other via the XML documents.

There are a large number of vertical standards, and it is therefore beyond the scope of this chapter to enumerate them. The following are some representative, well-established vertical standards. Table 1 shows the standards, the industries where they are used, and a basic summary of the issues addressed by each. All of the following standards provide a data dictionary of industry-specific terms and define the structure of documents, but not all define the processes where the documents are used.

Table 1. Representative vertical standards

		Issues Addressed by the Standard		
Standard	**Industry**	**Data Dictionary & XML docs**	**Business Process**	**Other**
AgXML	Oilseed and grain	Yes	Yes	-
CIDX	Chemical	Yes	Yes	Security
MISMO	Mortgage	Yes	No	-
OTA	Travel	Yes	Yes	-
RosettaNet	Semiconductor, IT, and Electronic components	Yes	Yes	Messaging & infrastructure
STAR	Automotive retail	Yes	No	Dealer infrastructure and messaging

Among all the vertical standards, RosettaNet is one of the most extensive and detailed. The core of the RosettaNet standard is the partner interface process (PIP) that defines the sequence of steps required to execute a specific, predefined business process between supply-chain partners as well as the documents that are exchanged during each of the steps. As an example, the "Request Quote" PIP starts with a buyer sending a "product quote request" to a vendor, with two possible responses from the vendor; a quote or a referral to another vendor. For two firms to conduct business using RosettaNet, they both must have implemented one or more PIPs in common. The more PIPs two trading partners have both implemented in common, the more their B2B interactions can be conducted using RosettaNet.

In addition to PIPs, RosettaNet also defines data dictionaries and data guidelines for terms used in PIP documents. The RosettaNet Business Dictionary defines the properties used in basic business activities between trading partners. The RosettaNet Technical Dictionary defines properties for products, components, devices, and services relevant for the supply chains in the IT/electronics industry. Together, these define both business properties and terms found in technical product descriptions that are used across PIP documents.

Finally, the RosettaNet implementation framework (RNIF) provides messaging standards that are common to all of the PIPs. RNIF lays out the basic message structure that is common to all PIP exchanges by defining the envelope that contains RosettaNet messages. This envelope includes the headers required in any PIP document exchange, whereas the XML document defined in a PIP would be the "payload" contained within this envelope. RNIF also sets general standards for how the interactions found in PIPs are carried out. RNIF, for example, specifies a mechanism for reliable messaging based on acknowledgements and supplies choreography models that all PIPs must follow. It also specifies schemas[5] for acknowledgment and exception (error) messages. RNIF makes RosettaNet different from the other vertical standards in that it deals much more extensively with issues that are typically the domain of horizontal standards. After the discussion of horizontal standards in the next section, the discussion will return to a recap of how RosettaNet compares to them.

Finally, one useful feature of RosettaNet is not part of the standard itself, but is included in the RosettaNet Web site. Firms that have implemented a PIP can register themselves with RosettaNet's "Trading Partner Directory," a registry of firms that have implemented each PIP. Their Web site can be searched to locate firms that have implemented a given PIP with the ability to use additional search criteria such as industry and location.

Horizontal Standards

A horizontal standard "is a general set of standards that defines exchange protocols and information formats without referencing any product or service." (Aklouf et al., 2005, p. 71). Horizontal standards have broad applicability and are not tied to the requirements of any particular industry or application. Figure 1 describes a Web-service architecture that is based on a particular horizontal standard: Web services using UDDI and WSDL.[6] It is general enough, however, to describe much of the functionality found in other horizontal standards to provide a useful overview of many issues addressed by these standards.

The two parties shown at the bottom of Figure 1 are the ones that interact with each other to carry out some business process: The service requester interacts with the service provider

Figure 1. Web service oriented architecture[7]

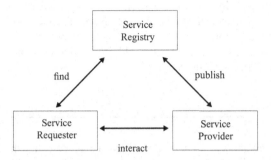

by sending an XML document requesting the service and providing the data needed by the provider. The provider maps this request into the format used by its internal systems, and generates a response in the form of an XML document that is returned to the service requester. But, how does the requester know how to structure the XML document expected by the service provider and what data to provide?

The service registry addresses the problem of knowing how to request a service by enabling prospective requesters to locate and understand requirements for invoking services offered by a provider. A service registry may be hosted by the service provider or a third party. In either case, a horizontal standard can provide a way to describe services and how to invoke them. The service provider creates the service description and the requester uses the description to understand what is needed to invoke the service. Finally, horizontal standards specify how service providers publish their descriptions to a registry, and how service requesters find descriptions therein. This general framework is broadly relevant for interactions related to different industries, and for different products, services, and business processes.

The following provides an overview of the three main horizontal standards included in this chapter: SOAP, ebXML, and Web services.

SOAP

Simple object access protocol (SOAP) provides methods for a program running under one operating system to communicate with a program in the same or another operating system using XML to structure the information exchange (Alexander & Zhang, 2005). SOAP (http://www.w3.org/TR/soap/) was originally developed as a means of invoking remote procedures over the Internet. If used by itself, remote procedure invocation is the function normally performed by a SOAP message. SOAP, however, does not require a SOAP message to contain a remote procedure call. A common use of SOAP is its inclusion in other standards, where its purpose is to provide an envelope for some other type of message instead of invoking a procedure. The envelope in this case would serve as a container for the "payload," where the payload is the real content of the SOAP message, and surrounding SOAP fields contain information used to help the recipient process the payload. The content of a SOAP message may be a UDDI, WSDL, or ebXML message, or transaction data in the form of an XML document. In this case, the SOAP envelope contains information about the message's payload. For instance, it could contain information about the recipient or sender, encoding style, and other information about how to process and interpret the message. In terms of what is shown in Figure 1, SOAP could provide the envelope that contains the "interact," "find," and "publish" interactions.

ebXML

ebXML (http://www.ebxml.org) strengths lie in the area of representing the business process semantics that allow trading partners to understand each other's capabilities and require-ments for engaging in e-commerce. It provides a framework and processes for e-commerce collaborations without defining the specific terms and processes to be used in any particular collaboration between trading partners. It allows for these to be defined, but leaves it to others to do so.

"Core components" are ebXML's means for providing a standard data dictionary. They are intended to be industry-neutral, and contain definitions (individual data elements and ag-gregations of elements) that are relevant across industries. These serve as low-level building blocks that are used throughout ebXML, for instance, when defining ebXML documents. How industry-specific terms are decided upon and standardized are not part of the ebXML standard.

Messaging services in ebXML use another standard, SOAP (simple object access protocol), as an envelope for ebXML messages. As noted earlier, a SOAP message can hold a payload that could be any XML document, such as one that represents a business document. SOAP, therefore, provides an envelope for ebXML messages. ebXML does not simply use SOAP as-is for messaging. SOAP is extensible, and allows for higher-level protocols to add entries to serve their unique purposes. For instance, the MessageHeader element is a required ebXML element added to SOAP message when used to hold an ebXML messages. One of the things it does is to identify the version of ebXML in the current message.

Security of ebXML interactions is provided through a combination of *XML Signature* and *XML Encryption*. XML Signature provides message integrity and authentication informa-tion about the originator of a message. The XML signature defines XML elements that would be embedded in an XML document that would allow the receiver to verify that the message has not been modified from what the sender originally sent. With XML encryp-tion, either part or all of an XML message can be secured through encryption, so that the encrypted portion of the message would not be visible to other parties besides the originator and ultimate recipient.[8]

A strong point of ebXML is its ability to represent semantic information that can be used to assess the compatibility of the processes of prospective trading partners, and for coming to a mutual agreement on how business is to be conducted electronically. Collaboration protocol profile (CPP) and collaboration profile agreements (CPA) are the two main com-ponents that support this.

A CPP allows a firm to express its business processes and business service interface require-ments in a way that can be understood by others. A CPP can be used by prospective trading partners to assess the requirements of and options for conducting business via ebXML. If prospective trading partners determine that their CPPs are compatible, they could develop a collaboration profile agreement to specify exactly how business will be conducted between them. The CPA defines terms and conditions for document exchange as well as all the valid, visible, and enforceable interactions, and how to execute them. A CPA is formed from CPPs of the parties involved, and contains only those elements that are in common. The two parties then negotiate the parameters to produce a final CPA. CPAs serve as the basis for configuring the technical details of conducting e-commerce in ebXML.

ebXML also provides mechanisms for firms to locate each other: the ebXML registry and ebXML repository. Repositories are where data about firms and their processes are stored. In it are stored descriptions of products, services offered, basic firm information, CPP, CPA, core components, predefined messages, and other objects to enable parties to exchange data electronically. Registries store information about items in a repository; it is where relevant repository items and metadata about them can be registered. Registries can be queried to find the location of repository information. The registry information model (ebRIM) provides a high-level blueprint for metadata in the ebXML registry, and any ebXML registry must follow ebRIM.

The general model for how ebXML works is for prospective trading partners to discover each other, and the services and products they offer, using ebXML registries/repositories. Then, based on their CPPs, the firms determine which shared business processes and associated document exchanges need to be used for interacting with each other. Once they decide to collaborate, the firms would agree on contractual terms relating to the processes used, and documents exchanged by creating a CPA. The firms would then exchange information and services in accordance with these agreements.

Web Services Using WSDL, UDDI, and SOAP

Two standards that work together in enabling Web services are Web services Description Language (WSDL) and universal description, discovery, and integration (UDDI). These, in turn, rely on an existing standard, SOAP, as the primary means of sending messages that invoke Web services, and as an envelope for UDDI and WSDL messages (http://www.uddi. org/: http://www.w2.org/TR/wsdl).

WSDL is used to describe services offered by businesses. WSDL uses XML to describe a Web service in a generic way that can be mapped to the capabilities provided by the actual internal systems. WSDL allows for the definition of how to invoke a service, its input requirements, and what, if any, response is provided as a result.

WSDL provides two modes of using Web services; a remote procedure (RPC) style and a document style. With the RPC style, the service corresponds to a remote procedure call. The input requirements define data elements that correspond to the method's input parameters and the response corresponds to the method's output. The RPC style provides a synchronous response that would be appropriate when real-time requirements exist for invoking the service. The document style follows the asynchronous approach found in traditional EDI, ebXML. and RosettaNet. The input and output "documents" normally correspond to business documents that would be exchanged during the business transaction, for example, a purchase order. Processing is asynchronous so this could be used when the initiating firm is not expecting an immediate response.

UDDI provides a registry for businesses to list themselves on the Internet. Its goal is to help companies find each other and assess the interoperability of their systems (Newcomer, 2002). UDDI can be viewed as an online version of a telephone book's white, yellow, and green pages as follows:

- **White pages:** Provide name and contact for the business
- **Yellow pages:** Describes type of business, its location, and products offered
- **Green pages:** Details about the business' processes and how to invoke them; a pointer to the business' WSDL file could be placed here

UDDI registries are hosted by members of the UDDI consortium. Once a potential business partner is found using a UDDI query, details about invoking the desired services would be retrieved. The details of how to invoke the service in a UDDI entry are somewhat general, and can optionally point to a WSDL description of the service. UDDI, however, allows for entries to refer to other types of services such as ebXML or RosettaNet. A firm could offer its Web services and make WSDL descriptions available on its own without using UDDI. UDDI, however, provides a way to make it easier for other firms to locate the firm and understand the services offered.

The typical scenario for service discovery and invocation is as follows. A business would locate potential trading partners using UDDI queries. Based on whatever factors are relevant for making this choice (e.g., location, products offered, Web services offered, etc.), the business would select trading partners and the services to invoke using SOAP. Its systems would then use the WSDL description of the service to configure the translation between its internal processes and the needed messages that are sent and received via SOAP. Finally, the interactions with other businesses would be carried via SOAP message exchanges according to the WSDL description of the service.

WS-Security defines enhancements to SOAP to provide three capabilities: credential exchange, message integrity, and confidentiality. WS-Security delivers a foundation for implementing security functions such as integrity and confidentiality in messages implementing higher-level Web services applications. The WS-Security specifications describe a mechanism for securing Web services message exchanges using a variety of existing security technologies and methodologies.[9]

Summary of Standards

SOAP is a relatively simple standard when compared to Web services and ebXML, as well as being a component in those two standards. Web services and ebXML both provide a number of similar features, but still differ considerably in some of the capabilities included.

Table 2 summaries ebXML and Web services to highlight the similarities and differences between the two standards. Both standards provide a registry with similar capabilities

Table 2. Overview of horizontal e-commerce standards

Standard	ebXML	Web services using WSDL & UDDI
Data dictionary	Core components – defines basic terms in that cross industries	
Use of SOAP for requesting services	SOAP – containing ebXML documents	2 modes of using SOAP: • document-style (asynchronous), or • remote procedure call style (synchronous)
Business process descriptions	CPP – collaboration protocol profile • Provide details of how to invoke a service, where services are defined in the context of a series of process steps. CPA – collaboration protocol agreement • Uses CPPs to develop a mutually feasible agreement	WDSL – Provide details on how to invoke a service and what data to provide
Registries – publish, store, and find business partners and their processes	ebRIM	UDDI

ebXML is the only one to provide some support for defining business terms using its core components. Both protocols use SOAP as envelope for messaging. When it comes to requesting a service, however, Web services provides two options. A request for service under ebXML is similar to Web service's document-style use of SOAP and both are similar to traditional EDI. Web service's RPC style could be useful in situations that require a quick response to a service request.

Another significant difference between ebXML and Web services is how they define and use business process descriptions. WSDL/UDDI and SOAP were originally intended for straightforward transactions found in B2B marketplaces (Havenstein, 2005). WSDL describes how to invoke Web services, but does little to help firms to understand the semantics involved. ebXML, on the other hand, has much greater capability for describing how interactions are choreographed. ebXML can be used to develop mutual understanding, negotiating differences, and agreeing on a mutual process to follow. Web services' view of business processes is restricted to a technical view of what is required to invoke a single process, while ebXML attempts to deal with the semantics of processes requiring a sequence of interactions between parties.

Although Web services' simpler view of process definition might be a deficiency, it could be strength in some cases. SOAP, WSDL, and UDDI address an important problem in a relatively simple, easy-to-implement manner, and this may often be a sufficient solution. Although Web services could be used to handle a series of interactions between parties, it does not address how to represent or set up such agreements. If this is needed, one solution would be if the firms are in an industry where a vertical standard defined the relevant processes. In this case, the horizontal standard's capability to represent business processes and allow for negotiating a trading agreement would be less important. Such capability has the potential to provide value if there is in fact a lot of variation in the services exposed by firms over the Internet. It should be noted, however, that a forthcoming enhancement to WSDL called "Web Services Choreography Description Language" (WS-CDL) will allow Web services to approach ebXML's ability to represent processes as a series of interactions.[10]

The core of vertical standards is the creation of a data dictionary and the definition of standard documents used in particular industries. This feature enables standard documents to be exchanged and interpreted by all firms that have implemented interfaces to the standard. Many vertical standards go beyond this to define processes carried out using the standard documents. In some cases, processes are provided as examples of business interactions; in others an extensive set of processes are defined.

RosettaNet is the most comprehensive of the vertical standards presented herein. RosettaNet also overlaps what ebXML and Web services do in that it defines message structure and generic interaction patterns that apply to any transaction. The fact that RosettaNet was developed prior to the horizontal standards may help explain this; without existing horizontal standards to address these general problems RosettaNet developers chose to incorporate this capability. However, RosettaNet is not in competition with the horizontal e-business standards like ebXML or Web services. It actually benefits from the horizontal standards, as they enable RosettaNet to concentrate its efforts on standardizing e-business processes, by no longer having to develop and maintain infrastructure pieces that can be adopted from horizontal standards like ebXML.

As other e-business standards emerged, RosettaNet has remained flexible and seek convergence where possible. Currently, RosettaNet is in the process of adopting the ebXML Registry and Repository specifications, the ebXML BPSS (business process specification schema), the ebMS (messaging services), and the CPPs (the partner profiles). While ebXML and Web services are relatively new and have few implementations to boast of, RosettaNet's maturity comes from billion of dollars worth of real e-business being conducted by business partners using RosettaNet specifications. This has lead to further RosettaNet adoption in Europe and Asia.

Developing B2B E-Commerce Standards

The development of B2B e-commerce standards has involved many stakeholders' efforts, including companies, industry associations, government agencies, academic institutions, and international organizations, and so forth. Among them, standards developing organizations (SDOs) have played a fundamental role for initiation, facilitation, and implementation of B2B e-commerce standards. These SDOs can produce either horizontal or vertical standards. A brief discussion of both would give the readers a better idea of the landscape of e-commerce SDOs.

Horizontal SDOs

Among the different horizontal SDOs or groups, there are several that are worthy of particular attention in the process of B2B e-commerce standardization. Their ongoing works have or will have tremendous impacts on the development of B2B e-commerce standards. The next table, followed by a brief explanation of each SDO, gives a short list of several representative horizontal B2B e-commerce SDOs and their standard developing work.

UN/CEFACT was established in 1996 by the Economic Commission for Europe (UN/ECE) within the United Nations.[12] Open to participation from member states, intergovernmental organizations, and industry associations, UN/CEFACT also has participation from many private-sector associations work at the policy level and hundreds of private-sector technical experts in UN/CEFACT working groups.

UN/CEFACT's activities, in general, focus on developing and expanding global EDI standards with a network of supporting private and public sector institutions. It publishes the UN/EDIFACT standards that are used internationally. One of UN/CEFACT's milestones

Table 3. Representative horizontal standards bodies and their work

Standard bodies	Standards Developed		
	Framework Standards	Document & Data Standards	Infrastructure Standards
Government Authority Type			
ISO[11]	ebXML		
UN/CEFACT	ebXML	Core components	
X12		Core components	
Consortia Type			
W3C			WSDL: Web-service description language WS-CDL: Web-service choreography description language SOAP: Simple object access protocol
OASIS	ebXML	UBL: Universal business language	UDDI: Universal description, discovery, and integration XACML: Extensible access control markup language
OAG		OAGIS & OAMAS	

Note: United Nations Centre for Facilitation of Procedures and Practices for Administration, Commerce and Transport (UN/CEFACT) (http://www.unece.org/cefact/)

is the launch of ebXML by UN/CEFACT and the Organization for the Advancement of Structured Information Standards (OASIS) in September 1999. After the completion of the first phase of ebXML framework in May 2001, the UN ECE and OASIS split the remaining tasks, with UN/CEFACT responsible for process-related work including business processes and core components and OASIS responsible for infrastructure work including transport, routing and packaging, registry and repository, collaboration-protocol profile and agreement, security, and conformance.

The ANSI Accredited Standards Committee X12

The ANSI Accredited Standards Committee (ASC) X12 (http://www.x12.org) is a membership based not-for-profit standard body chartered in 1979 by the American National Standards Institute (ANSI). ANSI represents the U.S. in the International Organization for Standardization (ISO). ASC X12 memberships are open to "any individual, company, or organization that may be directly and materially affected by ASC X12 activities."[13] Since 1987, Data Interchange Standards Association (DISA) has served as the secretariat for the X12 standards development process.

ANSI itself does not write standards. Instead, ANSI develops the procedures that other standards bodies, such as IEEE, use to develop standards. It also reviews the procedures and processes that these standards-developing bodies use, and in the end approves the standards they develop as ANSI standards. ASC X12 has developed its standard system through different years releases (a complete set of X12 standards), subreleases (republished releases), technical reports and guidelines, as well as workbooks and alphabetic code lists. While it continues to develop and enhance business message standards based on the X12 EDI syntax, ASC X12 now intends to clarify its message design architecture, XML schema syntax, and XML design rules and guidelines with the collaboration of the UN/CEFACT. Both of ANSI X12 and UN/CEFACT recently have agreed to focus all XML subcommittee efforts into the ebXML framework specification development initiative.[14] In addition, ASC X12 and UN/CEFACT jointly developed object oriented EDI (OO-EDI) to meet a mutual goal to provide one global EDI standard.

Organization for the Advancement of Structured Information

OASIS (http://www.oasis-open.org/) is a not-for-profit international consortium founded in 1993. More than 3,000 members of OASIS are venders, users, and specialists of standards-based technologies that represent over 600 organizations and individual members in 100 countries. OASIS has its members themselves (excluding individual members) set the OASIS technical agendas, form technical committees, and vote on the completed works. The National Institute of Standards and Technology (NIST) plays an active role within OASIS.

OASIS produces "worldwide standards for security, Web services, conformance, business transactions, supply chain, public sector, and interoperability within and between marketplaces"[15] through an open, democratic, vendor-neutral process. It is especially active on Web services standards in comparison to the other standard organizations. However, OASIS is more like a standardizer rather than inventors of technology like W3C. The work of OASIS helps to make structured information standards easy to adopt and the products practical to use in the real world, thereby complementing those of the other standard organizations rather than create more. One of the most important works OASIS has done in the e-commerce area is the joint ebXML project with the UN/CEFACT in November 1999. In addition, OASIS now hosts two of the most widely respected information portals on XML and Web services standards: XML.org and Cover Pages.[16] Many organizations, technologists, and business people rely on XML cover pages for daily updates on XML resources and industry initiatives.

World Wide Web Consortium

Created on October 1994, W3C is the main technology standards body for the World-Wide Web (http://www.w3.org/)and the most influential standard body by far in XML related standards. W3C is now hosted by the Laboratory for Computer Science (LCS) at MIT, the French National Institute for Research in Computer Science and Control (INRIA), and Keio University. Membership at W3C is only open to organizations and is not free, but W3C Web site serves as a central location to disseminate the technical specifications written by the consortium, as well as other related information, which is free to all. Today, over 450 members and nearly 70 full-time staff around the world are contributing to the development of W3C specifications and software.[17]

W3C's activities and other work are primarily in four domains: architecture domain, interaction domain, technology and society domain, Web Accessibility Initiative (WAI). Through these activities, W3C provides technical reports, open source software, and services (e.g., validation services). The network protocols that the W3C established with the collaboration of global community include the XML specification and its complementary specifications (often referred to as the "XML Family of Standards"). In addition, XML schemas and resource description format (RDF) have received great attention from the W3C.

Open Applications Group

Open Applications Group (OAG) (http://www.openapplications.org/) is a nonprofit consortium founded in February 1995 by leading enterprise application software developers. To date, the OAG is comprised of nearly 50 members including customer organizations, systems integrators, middleware vendors, as well as application software vendors. Prominent stakeholders, such as AT&T, Microsoft, Compaq, Lucent Technologies, Ford Motors, and so forth, are in OAG's membership.

OAG is the largest publisher of XML-based content for business software interoperability in the world.[18] The OAG builds and publishes the detailed specifications necessary to use the XML content and a common middleware application programming interfaces (APIs) specification.[19] From its first year of existence, OAG continues to release specifications with richer functions, and has done extensive prototyping with XML to successfully validate its applicability for business software, primarily, the open applications group integration specification (OAGIS), and the open applications group common middleware API specification (OAMAS).

Vertical SDOs

Due to their focused and in-depth coverage of standards that are of direct interest to firms within an industry, vertical SDOs are more attractive to firms than industry neutral SDOs. For example, Electronics Industry Data Exchange Group (EIDX) is a vertical e-commerce SDO in the electronics industry, and only 5 out of 46 EIDX members also join ASC X12, the US-based cross-industry e-commerce SDO. Many horizontal SDOs also have industry-focused groups within them in order to motivate firms to participate in the consortium. For instance, ASC X12 has subcommittees working in the insurance, transportation, and health-care industries. The content of standards from horizontal and vertical SDOs may overlap or complement one another. Therefore, collaborations between them are common, especially

Table 4. Industry and their vertical SDOs[20]

Industry	SDOs
Agriculture	AgXML (http://www.agxml.org)
Accounting	XBRL (http://www.xbrl.org)
Automobile	AIAG (http://www.aiag.org)
Automobile retail	STAR(http://www.starstandard.org)
Chemical	CIDX (http://www.cidx.org)
Electronics	EIDX (http://eidx.comptia.org)
Energy	PIDX, PPDM, POSC
Financial–banking	BITS
Financial–insurance	ACORD (http://www.acord.org)
Financial–mortgage	MISMO (http://www.mismo.org)
Financial–real estate	RETS, MITS
Financial	FISD, FIX Protocol (http://www.fixprotocol.org), FPML (http://www.fpml.org), IFX (http://www.ifxforum.org)
Geography	OpenGIS (http://www.opengeospatial.org/ogc)
Healthcare	CDISC (http://www.cdisc.org), HL7 (http://www.hl7.org)
Human Resources	HR-XML (http://www.hr-xml.org)
Legal	Legal XML (http://www.legalxml.org
Marine	EMSA, Maritime
Paper	PapiNet (http://www.papinet.org)
Retail	ARTS (http://www.nrf-arts.org)
Semiconductor, IT, & electronic components	RosettaNet (www.rosettanet.org)
Transportation	LandXML (http://www.landxml.org)
Travel	OTA (http://www.opentravel.org)

for firms engaging across industries transactions. For instance, ebXML proposed by OASIS has gained support from some vertical SDOs such as OTA and RosettaNet. It is also possible that standards from the two camps have significant overlap and therefore compete with each other (Zhao et al., 2005). Table 4 lists several major vertical SDOs.

The standards-developing approaches used by the SDOs are either *de jure* or *de facto*. Traditional standards development organizations (ISO, IEEE, etc.), scientific or professional societies, trade associations, or industrial standard organizations that can have a liaison with formal official bodies, establish *de jure* standards by their legal authority, and as such, face no challenges in the marketplace. They usually serve coordinating and distributing functions that the paying-members of the organization manage. They facilitate the development of standards, but volunteers do the bulk of the work, and no royalties are paid. In contrast, vertical industry groups or consortia, usually formed in response to intense competition among the largest companies, primarily rely on participants' voluntary consensus that later on emerge as industry *de facto* standards (Toth, 1996). These SDOs can charge fees to members to fund their standard development activities. In order to permit smaller companies to participate, the rates usually vary according to companies' revenue level. During the past few years, many industries have recognized the importance of developing common B2B e-commerce standards to facilitate information sharing in the value chain. A great number of industry-led SDOs or "forums," therefore, have emerged for industry participants to collaboratively develop e-commerce standards (Mähönen, 1999).

Unfortunately, the B2B e-commerce standard landscape has become much more complex and confusing today due to that many standards groups or bodies are involved in the process of B2B e-commerce standardization. The need for common B2B e-commerce standards had long been recognized by many industries and governments. However, the current situation has a long way to go before convergence on common standards occurs.

Transforming the Industry with E-Commerce Standards

The changes that new e-commerce standards have brought about in the practices of industries are broad and deep. Although starting slowly, the new e-commerce standards are emerging in and across various industries. Both horizontal B2B standards such as ebXML, and vertical standards such as RosettaNet are finding their ways into the practices in a number of industries.

Case 1: Automotive Industry

The automotive industry is one of the industries that ebXML has attracted significant attention from. Beginning in April of 2004, General Motors began to replace its traditional EDI with a messaging services based on ebXML.[21] GM will support traditional EDI, but plans to migrate to ebXML through EDI services provide by Covisint (Industrial Distribution,

2002). The approach towards providing both EDI and ebXML called "Covisint Connect" was developed by an industry consortium that included General Motors, DaimlerChrysler, Delphi, Ford Motor Company, and Johnson Controls.[22] Covisint Connect was designed with automotive specific functionality to simplify and improve communications between companies in the industry. It provides a direct replacement for current EDI methods and a foundation for the exchange of XML documents utilizing ebXML. Covisint Connect includes features specifically designed to enable smaller companies, even those not currently using EDI, to connect to their customers and suppliers.[23]

The migration from their current EDI provider to Covisint Connect will involve more than 6,000 GM suppliers. During the transition to Internet-based ebXML, Covisint will continue to route EDI messages to and from the prior value-added network of those suppliers who have yet to migrate to Covisint Connect. In addition to being based on ebXML, Covisint Connect will use Open Application Group's (OAG) standards for document content. Not only will this reduce the cost of supporting and operating its EDI systems, it will allow GM to enable a larger number of (mostly smaller) suppliers to use it who currently do not use EDI. Other automakers in the consortium and their suppliers will follow suit and migrate towards ebXML for supplier interactions (Meehan, 2001).

Automakers also have begun using ebXML to interact with its dealerships. One estimate suggests that EDI costs will be cut in half as a result of replacing traditional EDI with ebXML (Sullivan & Babcock, 2004). Cost savings will accrue both to dealerships and automakers.

Although these efforts are still underway, the automotive industry is among the more advanced industries in its migration from traditional EDI to newer e-commerce standards. The benefits are twofold. First, the estimated cost of using ebXML is substantially less than traditional EDI in dealing with suppliers who currently use EDI (Sullivan & Babcock, 2004). Second, due to reduced cost and the ease of set up and operation, the industry is able to switch a number of smaller suppliers to using ebXML that heretofore were not EDI-capable. Thus, ebXML allows the auto industry to extend the benefits from EDI to a larger number of suppliers (e.g., greater responsiveness and reduced cost of transacting business).

Case 2: Electronics Industry

As a vertical standard, RosettaNet has certainly established a reputation in the global high-technology industry for bringing businesses closer together. The global consortium now involves more than 500 of the world's leading electronics components, information technology, logistics, semiconductor manufacturing, and telecommunications companies.[24] Some giant players, such as Intel, Nokia, Sony, and Cisco Systems, have been particularly bullish on RosettaNet's developments and advocate the implementation of RosettaNet for the electronic industry. Not only have these companies lent highly placed executives to the consortium, they have also shown enough confidence in RosettaNet to actually rip out much of its EDI connections in deference to RosettaNet PIPs. Intel, for instance, conducts more than 30,000 RosettaNet-based transactions per month, with more than 90 customers and suppliers who are based in 17 countries.[25]

In the electronic industry, those who have started using RosettaNet standard primarily for supply-chain processes, such as price changes, catalog updates, and product introductions, have reported efficiencies, even if they are using it only on a limited basis. Implementing XML-based RosettaNet standards allows the use of the Internet as a low-cost transmission medium while supporting much higher transaction volumes and performance scalability than traditional Web-based tools. For instance:

- 3Com has begun using a catalog-update PIP with reseller CompUSA to speed up the introduction of new products. Typically, if 3Com has a new product it wants its distributors and resellers to put into their catalogs, it communicates this by phone, fax, or e-mail. With the PIP for product catalogs, it can send single product introductions automatically, cutting down the rate of inaccuracy and the process time from several weeks to hours (Medina, 2000).

- Arrow Electronics has also started using a PIP from RosettaNet. The PIP significantly reduces the time it takes to change product orders. Traditionally, Arrow would accumulate change orders throughout the day in its inventory-management system and then submit them overnight through an EDI transmission. The next day, the customer would check its sales order-entry system to see if the product was available and then respond that evening. The process could take anywhere from 36 to 48 hours. With a PIP, the purchase-order change happens immediately (Medina, 2000).

- Shinko's collaboration with Intel previously required a multilevel, mostly manual procurement process involving spreadsheets, e-mail, manual paperwork, and costly faxes between the U.S. and Japan. This process required a lot of exception management, and information regarding work-in-process, procurement, and settlement was exchanged through various manual and semi-manual methods that required a great deal of effort. Figure 2 illustrates the old process and the new process under RosettaNet. The most obvious benefit for Shinko in making this change was the elimination of substantial faxing costs between the U.S. and Japan. Shinko was able to achieve a 50% reduction in manual workload, and at the same time establish a 100% error-free process environment. In addition, order management throughput time was reduced from 24 hours to less than 1 hour.

However, the benefits of RosettaNet implementation go beyond the stated numbers. In the collaboration of Intel and Shinko, for instance, Intel has not included the value of additional tasks that employees can now perform with the time available as a result of implementing RosettaNet. Also, the benefits of extending supply-chain visibility into the entire business environment are just beginning to be understood. "The promise of increased supply chain visibility is extremely compelling," explains Brown. VP at Intel Manufacturing Group, "Making business decisions with good, hard data from the entire business environment instead of just local ERP systems allows a business to anticipate changes in the business climate much sooner and to respond to those changes with greater agility."[27]

RosettaNet has taken a leadership role in driving global e-business process standards for its partners. From 2000, when the first set of RosettaNet PIPs was released, the number of companies adopting RosettaNet grew rapidly. In 2002, the total number of distinct trading partners using RosettaNet to trade with board members grew by 207%. In Asia, millions of

Figure 2. Process changes in Shinko's order management[26]

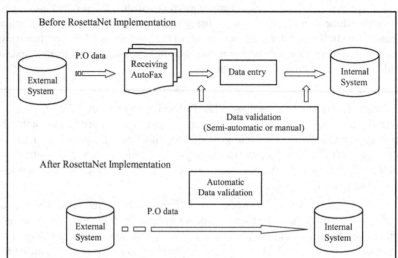

dollars from government funds are used to promote RosettaNet implementations and projects because it is believed that the use of the RosettaNet could simplify the coordination of the fragmented high-tech outsourcing process in Asia and reduce high-inventory expense and production stoppages (McFarlan & Belokhvostova, 2004). The success of RosettaNet has also caused several industry organizations to adopt the RosettaNet messaging specification as an industry standard. The Chemical Industry Data Exchange has defined the CIDX protocol, which is based on RNIF1.1, and the American Petroleum Industry has defined the Petroleum Industry Data Exchange (PIDX),which is based on RNIF2.0 specifications. "Looking ahead, RosettaNet will continue to focus on the creation and adoption of standards and services driven by its members as well as expand into adjacent industries, such as logistics, consumer electronics and aerospace."[28]

Case 3: Mortgage Industry

The home mortgage industry is highly fragmented, with most processes requiring the efforts of more than one organization. Example processes are loan origination and underwriting, loan closing, mortgage recording, loan servicing, and sales of mortgages to secondary investors. An X12 standard developed for this industry did not achieve much success for a number of reasons; chief among them was that the bureaucracy involved in the X12 effort produced a standard that was not specific enough to their industry (Cooley, 2005). The Mortgage Industry Standards Maintenance Organization (MISMO® Inc.) was formed in 1999 to develop, promote, and maintain XML-based e-commerce standards for the mortgage industry. More than 100 companies and 600 individuals are involved in the MISMO standards setting process, with membership in MISMO being voluntary and open to all. MISMO uses workgroups to concentrate on the various aspects of the mortgage industry's value chain.

An important motivation for developing e-commerce standards for this industry is the high cost of many processes wherein a good proportion of those costs come from data collection and data entry. The costs of underwriting and closing a loan, for example, run between $800 and $1,000. Estimates indicate that more than one third of the loan origination effort involves collecting and entering data and correcting errors. Every time the paperwork for a loan application moves between parties, much of the data needs to be reentered into different systems with additional effort to detect and correct errors (Story, 2003). MISMO developed standard XML documents for the mortgage industry with the intent of solving this problem by allowing a given XML document to move from step to step and between organizations without the need for reentry.

MISMO standards include a data dictionary that identifies the names, meaning, representation, and coding information for elements. MISMO standards also define a number of documents that use these elements such as the mortgage application, underwriting, credit report, and mortgage insurance application. These two components are standard content of any vertical standard. A feature unique to MISMO is embedding these business-oriented XML documents within what is termed a "SMART™ Document" as shown in Figure 3.

Besides the data they contain, SMART™ documents use XHTML to embed formatting information so that the document itself can be displayed within a Web browser. A SMART document can be "what the buyer sees and signs," and serves as a data entry form that encapsulates the XML document. This data can then serve as input to software that processes it "lights out," or can be forwarded to the next step for further processing, which could be in a different firm. The document contains a record of the cumulative changes that come from the different steps. The sequence of these changes and any needed electronic signatures are contained within the SMART™ document itself. The entire SMART™ document is embedded in an envelope with a tamper-evident seal. This reduces the need to reenter the data when documents go from step to step or between organizations. Besides greatly lowering the costs of processing and reducing errors that come from duplicate data entry,

Figure 3. SMART Doc™ structure [29]

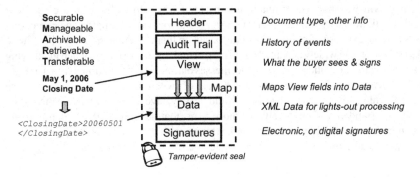

the use of SMART™ document can speed up the entire process since documents can move quickly from one step to the next.

MISMO standards have become well enough established that software for this industry has begun to be certified as to whether it meets MISMO standards. Additionally, there may be competitive pressure for software firms to integrate MISMO standards into their products so that not only could their systems support the internal processes of a customer, they would allow a firm to easily exchange documents electronically with others. Use of MISMO has considerably reduced costs for firms that adopt it, and provide improved service to customers in the form of faster response time. If use of MISMO becomes widespread enough, the whole home mortgage industry could be radically transformed. Not too long ago, this industry made very little use of electronic communications between firms. The long-term vision is for the whole value chain to be totally carried out electronically using the MISMO standard. The impacts on the industry are as yet difficult to predict, as it could both have the result of leveling the playing field, which would be helpful to smaller firms, while also allowing for a concentration of data in the hands of larger firms, which would facilitate consolidation in the industry among those firms (Markus et al., 2003)

One of the future directions for MISMO are to offer users the option to interface with MISMO using PDF documents and to integrate with Web services. Currently, MISMO uses SMART doc and other lower level protocols such as HTTPS and FTP for transferring data between firms. Efforts are underway to provide interfaces to MISMO-based systems via Web services, described in WSDL whereby a firm could invoke a Web service, and receive a SMART™ document in response.

Closing Comments

The synergy or interoperability of applications from different vendors enabled by e-commerce standards allows the industries to create more customizable, advanced, and powerful systems. However, partly due to the diverse and broad scope that e-commerce standards have, little is known about the process of e-commerce standardization. Given the literature addressed in the chapter, we will offer suggestions for further investigation on the emergence of new e-commerce standards.

For instance, which standards are finally finding their way into widespread use vs. those that are still in limited use, and why? Given the large number of overlapping and competing standards and the expense of building systems based on them, understanding the likelihood of a standard becoming widely accepted could help in making a wise choice when identifying the best standard for an application. Many businesses that engage in traditional forms of EDI, such as X12, have yet to be convinced of the benefit of switching to the newer e-commerce standards. An interesting research question would be why have they not yet made the switch to these newer standards? Conversely, for those firms that have made the switch to using newer standards, why did they choose to make this transition, what factors influenced their choice of standard(s), and what lessons can be learned from their experiences?

A different area of examination would be the organizational and industry transformations that have resulted or could result from e-commerce standards adoption. What are the impacts of standards adoption on the operations and effectiveness of businesses? What organizational changes were necessary in order to achieve these impacts? Since e-commerce standards would cost less to use than traditional EDI, they should increase the participation in B2B e-commerce by SMEs. The broader functionality included in these standards over traditional EDI provides additional opportunities for altering how businesses interact. The examples reported earlier provide some evidence about this in selected industries. However, a more systematic cross-industry investigation would be useful in this regard.

Finally, examining the standards-setting environment could be useful. Developing an understanding of the dynamics of how standards groups, vendors, and other players interact to shape standards and influence their adoption could help in devising strategies that companies could apply to coping with standard bodies, as well as the potential development direction of e-commerce standards themselves.

Can an ultimate standard for e-commerce be reached in the same way that X12 and EDIFACT have dominated traditional EDI? Achieving a single dominant standard seems unlikely since these newer standards collectively cover much more ground, with no one standard being comprehensive. In certain areas of functionality, however, emergence of stable winners should do much to convince firms that are sitting on the standards sideline to finally get into the game. This in turn would provide incentive for other firms to do the same.

One factor that would facilitate a standard's adoption would be the availability of software that supports it. This could take the form of either a software vendor enhancing an existing application package, such as ERP, to provide a Web service interface according to the standard, or by creating middleware that translates between existing internal systems to a Web interface according to the standard. The availability of software of this kind should reduce the cost and effort of adopting a standard and thus should accelerate its adoption. However, software vendors may be unlikely to invest in creating this kind of software unless there already is a good market for it. Given this, it may take a while for a critical mass of firms to adopt a standard before it begins to be well supported by the offerings of software vendors. Once a standard achieves both a critical mass of users and software products that support it, a likely scenario would be for the standard to experience a surge of firms adopting it. This, of course, begs the question of how a standard gets to this point. Except for SOAP perhaps, none of the standards are yet there. Some possible scenarios for the future of the standards are as follows:

- SOAP already is widely used and is used in conjunction with a number of other standards. No matter which standards gain acceptance, SOAP will likely play a role.

- ebXML is being promoted by standards bodies that brought us traditional EDI. It is the chosen successor to X12 and EDIFACT. However, it is more complicated than other standards. While the capability for setting up trading agreements using CPPs and CPAs is appealing and potentially powerful, it may prove too difficult for many firms to implement. The ebXML standard has been developed in a top-down manner by standards-bodies, while the actual demand for the whole set of standards is not clear. If industry-specific document standards and standardized CPPs emerge (similar to what has happened in the automotive industry) this would simplify the use of CPPs and CPAs by providing some degree of uniformity across businesses within the industry. This could make these components become similar to RosettaNet's PIPs in the electronics industry.

- The combination of UDDI, WSDL, and SOAP is likely to continue gaining acceptance. It is relatively simple and straightforward when compared to ebXML. SOAP already enjoys relatively wide adoption. UDDI may become widely used beyond WSDL and SOAP-based Web services. It is flexible enough to serve as a registry for other types of Web services, and is therefore in a good position to become the most widely used registry standard. WSDL and SOAP are oriented towards simpler marketplace transactions and may not receive much direct competition here from ebXML.

- RosettaNet is driven by a consortium of firms that are its potential adopters, so it therefore is tailored to their needs. RosettaNet is on the way to becoming widely adopted. Although many of the vertical standards address some of the issues encompassed in horizontal standards, RosettaNet has gone much further than others in this regard. When RosettaNet was developed, there was an absence of horizontal standards that resulted in horizontal components becoming part of this standard. Since its formation, a number of viable horizontal XML standards have appeared and are gaining some acceptance. In the long run, it is likely that the traditional components of vertical standards will remain at the core of RosettaNet. The horizontal components, however, will likely be supplemented by, and perhaps replaced by, other horizontal standards. Aside from the costs transitioning to different horizontal standards, there would not be much reason to incur the costs of maintaining RosettaNet's separate horizontal components unless they address important needs of this industry much better than the other horizontal standards. At this point, it is not clear that this is the case.

- A wide variety of vertical standards have emerged that address the unique needs of their respective industries. Some of these, such as MISMO, are also beginning to see significant implementation and use. It appears, however, that these standards have been developed without much attempt to rely on other horizontal standards to provide a framework for their use. Perhaps the emphasis was to develop the highest value vertical components (data dictionary and standard documents) while providing some horizontal capabilities sufficient for creating functional solutions. As firms gain experience with the vertical standards and as horizontal standards mature, will there be a greater convergence of the two types of standards? In many cases, Web services and ebXML should provide added-value functionality not present in the vertical standards. Over time, therefore, one would expect vertical standards to be extended to specify how their vertical components could be implemented using the capabilities of other horizontal standards. One example of this that was mentioned earlier is efforts to extend MISMO so that interfaces to it could be exposed via Web services.

In conclusion, few businesses have much real experience applying the new e-commerce standards. Others are either in the investigation or experimental phases of standards adoptions. Many others, of course, have yet to seriously consider them or perhaps are only vaguely aware of them. The ultimate usefulness and applicability of these standards, therefore, is hard to predict, and the standards themselves will continue to evolve as businesses gain more experience with them. Due to the central role these standards are likely to play in future e-commerce activity, most firms, especially those already engaged in e-commerce, will at some point need to become aware of their capabilities, their application, and potential impact. This chapter provides an overview of the situation as it is understood today, with some attempt to suggest likely scenarios for how things may progress.

References

Aklouf, Y., Pierra, G., Ameur, Y., & Drias, H. (2005). PLIB ontology: A mature solution for products characterization in B2B electronic commerce. *Journal of IT Standards & Standardization Research, 3*(2), 66-81.

Alexander, D., & Zhang, D. (2005). A comparative study of SOAP and DCOM. *Journal of Systems and Software, 76*(2), 157-169.

Berge, J. (1991). *The EDIFACT standards.* Manchester, UK: NCC Blackwell.

Champion, M., Ferris, C., Newcomer, E., & Orchard, D. (2002, November 14). *Web services architecture* (W3C working draft). World Wide Web Consortium. Retrieved February 28, 2006, from http://www.w3.org/TR/2002/WD-ws-arch-20021114/.

Cooley, S. (2005). The jury is in: MISMO is a win. *Mortgage Banking, 66*(3), 109-110.

Havenstein, H. (2005). Registry demand grows. *Computerworld, 39*(13), 10.

Hawkins, R., Mansell, R., & Skea, J. (1995). *Standards, innovation and competitiveness: The politics and economics of standards in natural and technical environment.* Brookfield, VT: Edward Elgar,.

IDA (Interchange of Data between Administrations). (2003). *Evaluation of XML frameworks.* XML based business frameworks serials. Retrieved March 6, 2006, from http://europa. eu.int/idabc/en/document/1564/5587

Industrial Distribution (no author). (2002). Covisint adopts XML standards. *Industrial Distribution, 91*(3), 28-29.

Knorr, E. (2002). ebXML: A B2B standard on hold. *ZDNet,* March 15, 2002. Retrieved March 6, 2006, from http://techupdate.zdnet.com/techupdate/stories/main/0,14179,2865508,00. html

Kotok, A. (2002a, February). Standards-based methodology for U.S. e-government initiatives. *Data Interchange Standards Association (DISA) white paper.* Retrieved March 5, 2006, from http://www.disa.org/pdfs/white_paper02.pdf

Kotok, A. (2002b, June). Utility deregulation requires effective e-business atandards. *Data Interchange Standards Association (DISA) white paper.* Retrieved March 6, 2006, from http://www.disa.org/pdfs/white_paper03.pdf

Li, M. (2003, July 3). CEN/ISSS report and recommendations on key eBusiness standards issues 2003-2005. *CEN/ISSS eBusiness Standards Focus Group.* Retrieved March 6, 2006, from http://www.eeurope-standards.org/Docs/Roadmap.pdf

Mähönen, P. (1999). Chapter III: The standardization process in IT—too slow or too fast? In K. Jakobs (Ed.), *Information technology atandards and atandardization: A global perspective.* Hershey, PA: Idea Group Publishing.

Markus, M., Steinfield, C., & Wigand, R. (2003). The evolution of vertical IS standards: Electronic interchange standards in the US home mortgage industry. In *Proceedings of the Workshop on Standard Making: A Critical Research Frontier for Information Systems MISQ Special Issue Workshop.* Retrieved March 6, 2006, from http://www.si.umich.edu/misq-stds/proceedings/130_80-91.pdf

McFarlan, F., & Belokhvostova, V. (2004, October). RosettaNet and ebXML: Betting on the right e-commerce standard. *Harvard Business School Case, 9-305-006.*

McFarlan, F., & Mähönen, P. (1999). Chapter III: The standardization process in IT—too slow or too fast? In K. Jakobs (Ed.), *Information technology standards and standardization: A global perspective.* Hershey, PA: Idea Group Publishing.

Medina, H. (2000). The paradox of Rosettanet. *Line 56: The E-business Executive Daily,* September, 2000. Retrieved September 14, 2005, from http://www.line56.com/articles/default.asp?NewsID=1257

Meehan, M. (2001). Covisint exchange vows it will support ebXML Automakers' marketplace deems standard to be critical to open, global e-commerce. *Computerworld, 35*(23), 16.

Newcomer, E. (2002). *Understanding Web services: XML, WSDL, SOAP, and UDDI.* Boston: Addison-Wesley Professional.

Scala, S., & McGrath, R. (1999). Advantages and disadvantages of electronic data interchange: An industry perspective. *Information and Management, 25*(2), 85-91.

Story, C. (2003). A smart alternative. *Mortgage Banking, 63*(6), 71-79.

Sullivan, L, & Babcock, C. (2004, March 1). Driving standards. *Information Week,* (978), 22-23.

Toth, B. (1996). Putting the U.S. standardization system into perspective. *StandardView, 4*(4), 160-178.

Zhao, K, Xia, M., & Shaw, M. (2005). Vertical e-commerce standards and standards developing organizations: A conceptual framework. *Electronic Markets, 15*(4), 289-300.

Endnotes

[1] Cited from http://computing-dictionary.thefreedictionary.com/B2B+e-commerce (accessible through March 3, 2006)

[2] A VAN was a system whereby a third party (the VAN provider) leased lines from local telecommunications providers, often enhancing them with elements such as error detection.

[3] A protocol is the special set of rules that end points in a telecommunication connection use when they communicate.

4   AXC X12 Web site: http://www.x12.org/x12org/about/faqs.cfm#a1 http://www.x12.org/x12org/about/faqs.cfm#a1

5   XML schemas express shared vocabularies and allow machines to carry out rules made by people

6   "Web services" can be used generically to refer to any service exposed via some interface over the Web. "Web services," however, normally refers to a specific standard based on SOAP, WSDL and UDDI.

7   Adapted from Champion et al. (2002)

8   http://www.w3.org/Signature/

9   http://xml.coverpages.org/ws-security.html

10   Source: World Wide Web Consortium (http://xml.coverpages.org/ni2004-12-29-a.html)

11   International Standards Organization (http://www.iso.org/iso/en/ISOOnline.frontpage)

12   Source: UN/CEFACT site (http://www.unece.org/cefact/)

13   Source: ANSI Web site (http://www.ansi.org/)

14   As of today, four ebXML specifications have been approved by ISO as the ISO 15000 (1~4): 2004 serial standards.

15   Source: OASIS Web site (http://www.oasis-open.org/home/index.php)

16   Web sites: http://www.xml.org and http://xml.coverpages.org

17   Source: W3C Web site (http://www.w3.org/)

18   Source: OAG Web site (http://www.openapplications.org/)

19   Middleware is a class of software technologies designed to help manage the complexity and heterogeneity inherent in distributed systems. It is defined as a layer of software above the operating system but below the application program that provides a common programming abstraction across a distributed system.

20   Cited from Zhao et al. (2005)

21   Cited from http://www.covisint.com/migration/gm/ (accessed through 03/03/2006)

22   Cited from http://www.informationweek.com/showArticle.jhtml?articleID=16700279 (accessed through 03/03/2006)

23   Cited from www.covisint.com (accessed through 03/03/2006)

24   Source: www.rosettanet.org

25   Intel News Release, "Intel Uses RosettaNet e-Business Technology Standards," from http://www.intel.com/pressroom/archive/releases/20021210comp.htm (accessible through March 6, 2006)

26   Same as endnote 27

27   "Intel and Shinko use RosettaNet standards to build forecast-to-cash procurement process," cited from: http://www.rosettanet.org/RosettaNet/Doc/0/FSG4VFM-C6RA4B47H0FJB0NNPED/IntelShinkoROICaseStudy.pdf (accessible through March 6, 2006)

[28] RosettaNet Annual Summary Report 2002-2003. (2003). Cited from http://www.rosettanet.org/rosettanet/Doc/0/6CA862VN341KH1QV5ASQEEBM31/RosettaNet+Annual+Sumary6-2-03.pdf (accessible through March 6, 2006)

[29] Adapted from http://www.efscouncil.org/EFSCconference/documents/Gardner-eMortgageOverview.pdf

Chapter VI

Interoperability on the Road to Enhance Government-to-Business

Giorgos Laskaridis, University of Athens, Greece

Penelope Markellou, University of Patras, Greece

Angeliki Panayiotaki, University of Patras, Greece

Athanasios Tsakalidis, University of Patras, Greece

Abstract

This chapter is initiated by the continuously growing governments' effort to transform their traditional profile to a digital one, worldwide, by adopting e-government models using the ICT and the Web. The chapter deals with interoperability, which appears as the mean for accomplishing the interlinking of information, systems, and applications, not only within governments, but also in their interaction with citizens, enterprises, and public sectors. The chapter highlights the critical issue of interoperability, investigating the way it can be incorporated into e-government domain in order to provide efficient and effective e-services. It also describes the issues, tasks, and steps that are connected with interoperability in the enterprise environment, introducing and analysing a generic interoperability platform (CCIGOV platform). Finally, it illustrates future trends in the field and, thus, suggests directions of future work/research.

Introduction

Over the last decade, we have witnessed the rapid evolution of the World Wide Web. This development allowed millions of people all over the world to access, share, interchange, and publish information. At the same time, public and private sector organisations are implementing operational and interactive Web-based applications that are accessible to any user with a computer, a Web browser, and a connection to the Internet. These potentials impact all dimensions of our daily life. New Web sites are launched constantly, providing electronic services (e-services), services addressed to different target groups of users (citizens and enterprises) through Internet.

E-government may ease the functionality of enterprises, aiming at facilitating the daily citizens' obligations. During this decade, many researchers study many different aspects of how e-government may decrease the need of bureaucracy. The researchers deal with interesting, yet difficult ventures to come up with common policies that are able to be applied worldwide. Many results, directions of how e-government may facilitate citizens and enterprise transactions within the public sector, conclude that an interoperability framework must be defined. Interoperability means the ability of ICT systems and of the business processes they support to exchange data and to enable the sharing of information and knowledge.

An interoperability framework can be defined as a set of standards and guidelines that describes the way in which organizations have agreed, or should agree, to interact with each other. An interoperability framework is, therefore, not a static document, and may have to be adapted over time as technologies, standards, and administrative requirements change (IDABC, 2004).

There is a growing awareness that the interoperability of national public ICT infrastructures is a precondition for a more service-oriented and competitive public sector. Ever since the adoption of the Interoperability Decision[1] of the European Council and the European Parliament in July 1999, the European Commission has focused on the pan-European dimension of e-government, and on the interoperability requirements for its implementation.

Interoperable systems working in a seamless and coherent way across the public sector hold the key to providing better services, tailored to the needs of the citizen and business and at a lower cost. Three aspects of interoperability need to be considered: organizational, semantic, and technical interoperability (Lueders, 2005).

Moreover, an essential requirement for the exchange of information is a single language that enables the description of the meaning and structure of the underlying data, that is, a mark-up language. In the context of current technologies and market developments, this mark-up language is XML. XML offers a common metalanguage and terminology to develop means for system and data integration and for gradual transfer to more consistent formats in information assets (Salminen, 2005).

Interoperability aspects presented in this chapter aim to lead the way of e-government helping private sector (enterprises, vendors, etc.), with e-business development being the ultimate scope. There are a lot of steps during the lifecycle of an enterprise or during the daily routine of an enterprise that demand interaction with the public sector. The level of physical interaction can be scaled and ranked; however, it cannot be minimised without the help of e-government.

Enterprises may form different legal entities and may follow alternate business models, but the majority of them follow a certain path at their daily workflow. Advancing e-government at each step of this path will certainly facilitate enterprises' functionality as well as will provide better background for e-commerce.

The steps met during enterprises' workflow that demand interaction with the public sector may be categorized by:

- The kind of service needed (e.g., issue of certificate, payment transaction)
- The quality of data needed (e.g., economic data, construction data)
- The public sector addressed to (e.g., Ministry of Finance, Ministry of Internal Affairs, Municipality)

In most cases, the demanding interaction leads to a combination of two or more distinct categories. Public sector must exchange data directly and not through the enterprises (indirectly). Under this framework, the interoperability aspect leads the way of e-government to e-business.

This chapter aims to investigate how interoperability can be incorporated in the e-government domain in order to facilitate e-business. We describe the issues, tasks, and steps that are connected with interoperability in the enterprise environment, depict the technical dimensions that arise, propose solutions when possible, and discuss the effectiveness of interoperability. In order to support the issues addressed through this chapter, we present a case study, a generic, standardised interoperable platform (CCIGOV platform). Moreover, our goal is to illustrate the future trends in the field and, this way, suggest directions that may produce new scientific results.

Background

The new Web sites that are launched constantly providing e-services, services to different target groups of citizens, and enterprises accessible through Internet, suspend bureaucracy procedures demanding personal contact of the users and loads of paper-based forms to be filled in. This "e-" prefix has been applied to a vast number of domains and applications such as e-commerce, e-business, e-learning, e-health, e-banking, e-marketing, and so forth, flavouring the respective domains with e-services.

In this context, many governments worldwide have realised that their information resources are not only of value in themselves. They are valuable economic assets, the fuel of the knowledge economy. By making sure the information they hold can be readily located and passed between the public and private sectors, taking account of privacy and security obligations, it will help to make the most of this asset, thereby driving and stimulating national and international economy. In order to take advantage of their assets, more and more governments have taken advantage of information and communication technologies (ICT) and the continuing expansion of the Web, and have started e-government strategies to renew the public sector and eliminate existing bureaucracy and therefore reduce costs (Riedl, 2003, Tambouris, Gorilas, & Boukis, 2001).

Although countries worldwide are different culturally, politically, and in population and education, they all have one thing in common, they all realise that their national investment in IT provides enormous opportunities for making the transformation of their government into a citizen-centred e-government (GFRIG, 2003). Although the literature relating to this area proliferates, the definition and the various models of e-government are still unclear among researchers and practitioners of public administration. According to E-governance Institute (2004) *"E-governance involves new channels for accessing government, new styles of leadership, new methods of transacting business, and new systems for organizing and delivering information and services. Its potential for enhancing the governing process is immeasurable."* Another quite broad definition, which incorporates its four key dimensions that reflect the functions of government, that is, e-services, e-democracy, e-commerce, and e-management, is the following *"E-government is the use of information technology to support government operations, engage citizens, and provide government services"* (Dawes, 2002).

E-government goes by different names in different countries; for example, in Australia it is called "government online," in Hong Kong it is called "electronic service delivery," and in India as well as in the UK it is called "electronic government." All these terms refer to the same thing, providing government services and information using the Web (Abramson & Means, 2001; Bacon, Wesling, Casey, & Wodinsky, 2002; Scherlis & Eisenberg, 2003).

It is obvious that governments and governmental institutions and agencies are the most complicated organizations in society, providing the legal, political, and economic infrastructure to support the daily needs of citizens and businesses (Bouguettaya, Rezgui, Medjahed, & Ouzzani, 2004). In their transition from the traditional operation and interoperation to the electronic one, the Web can be considered the key vehicle for the implementation and achievement of this scope. In this framework, governments across the world are grappling today with how to use electronic technologies to improve services to citizens, increase efficiency (including reducing inefficiencies due to redundant and overlapping government agency activities, investments, duplicative reporting requirements, among others), and streamline traditional paper processes. A research survey was recently conducted, in the USA by the Council for Excellence on Government, that involved random telephone interviews with 1,000 adults in the USA, and with 2,000 Internet users from several countries: Australia, Canada, Hong Kong, India, Singapore, and 17 European nations (Bose, 2004). The results suggest that international Internet users often have views of e-government that are similar to those of US Internet users. When people were asked to report their experience with specific types of e-government, informational services garnered the most responses; however, many people thought that they would be very interested in using e-government for transactional services. The majority of the Internet users in each country thought that their government is doing a good or excellent job developing online resources that allow them access to information and conduct online transactions with the government (Bose, 2004).

The types of e-government are categorised based on the following four citizen-centred groups for the delivery of governmental e-services:

- **Individuals/citizens:** Government-to-citizens (G2C), building easy to find, easy to use, one-stop points-of-service that makes it easy for citizens to access high-quality government services. Using the Web for accessing services organised by the needs of citizens such as benefits, loans, recreational sites, educational material, social services, and filing taxes.

- **Businesses:** Government-to-business (G2B), reducing government's burden on businesses by eliminating redundant collection of data and better leveraging e-business technologies for communication. Using the Web for accessing services in different areas such as regulation, economic development, trade, permits/licenses, grants/loans, and asset management.

- **Intergovernmental:** Government-to-government (G2G), making it easier for states and localities to meet reporting requirements and participate as full partners with the federal government in citizen services by sharing and integrating federal, state, and local data, while enabling better performance measurement, especially for grants. Other levels of government are anticipated to see significant administrative savings and be able to improve programme delivery because more accurate data is made available and shared across agencies and levels in a timely fashion.

- **Intragovernmental:** Internal efficiency and effectiveness, adopting commercial best practices in government operation in areas such as supply-chain management, financial management, and knowledge management. Agencies must be able to improve effectiveness and efficiency, eliminating delays in processing and improving employee satisfaction and retention. This category has recently been identified as government-to-employees (G2E) (Ndou, 2004).

E-government also focuses on minimising the burden on businesses, public, and government when obtaining services online by providing a secure infrastructure for online transactions, eliminating the need for separate processes for the verification of identity and electronic signatures (Riedl, 2001).

Several models have been proposed that outline stages of maturity as businesses embrace more of the capabilities of the WWW. Most e-commerce or e-business models outline three or four stages, starting with net presence and often moving through to a stage incorporating elements such as a rich array of information, the full provision and payment of services, or interaction with customers. Government departments often provide different types of services than commercial businesses, and frequently without payment. It is therefore probably inappropriate to extrapolate e-business models to the government sector (Shackleton, Fisher, & Dawson, 2004).

Recently, attempts have been made to establish models of e-government. Riley (2001) outlines a model containing three progressive stages: e-government, e-governance, and e-democracy. In this model, governments move from net presence (e-government), through to service provision and representative democracy (e-governance), to a final stage of e-democracy. Stamoulis, Gouscos, Georgiadis, and Martakos (2001) offer an alternative, suggesting governments and their agencies mature in various spaces rather than in distinct stages. Building on Angehrn's (1997) work, they outline four spaces for a government revenue agency: virtual information space, virtual communication space, virtual transaction space, virtual distribution space (Stamoulis et al., 2001). Markellou, Panayiotaki, and Tsakalidis

(2003) propose that for the implementation and successful operation of e-government, the proper design, which will be the basis in order to receive a series of strategic, administrative, and operational benefits, is necessary. The application of e-government in the public domain can be gradually performed in 14 levels, easing the adjustment of the traditional governmental model to the electronic one. Depending on the maturity and the resources of each governmental authority, the authority is level categorised, and the bottom levels may gradually be applied. This allows the unobstructed flow of information from/to the public sector, and gives the possibility not only to the citizens, but also to the enterprises (private sector) to acquire better access in the services that state provides.

Barriers to efficient service provision arising from the way government is organised are no longer acceptable. The public and their political representatives now expect public administration to be as efficient and effective in achieving its goals as the enterprise sector. To do this entails both new ways of working, back-office transformation, and better use of ICTs. Furthermore, just as the public can transact business with enterprises over the Internet (e.g., reserve airline tickets, purchase books, etc.) they now expect to be able to carry out similar transactions as seamlessly and as easily with public administration. This requires government to provide both information and services that are developed from a :customer-centric" viewpoint (Commission of the European Communities, 2003).

This combination of the use of advanced ICTs, especially the Internet, in the support of new ways of working in public administration, together with the enhanced provision of information and interactive services accessible over different channels, is the foundation of e-government. The challenge here is to "rewrite the rules" for how public administration works internally, interacts with its customers, and uses ICTs, not only to increase productivity by making business transactions easier to carry out, but also to address issues of social inclusion and the digital divide. For this to happen, not only should technology ensure the communication and sharing of information, but also administrative processes should be reorganized and be able to cooperate.

However, the reality today is the emergence of "islands" of e-government that are frequently unable to interoperate due to fragmentation resulting from uncoordinated efforts in developing the services at all levels of public administration.

By joining up administrative processes, everyone, whether in the public or enterprise sectors, could achieve a significant increase in efficiency and lower the cost of operations. Interoperability is essential for this "joining up" of public administration, to share and reuse administrative information, and to provide services and information over multiple channels. In essence, interoperability is a fundamental requirement, from both economic and technical perspectives, for the development of efficient and effective e-government services at both the national and international levels, including the regional and local ones.

According to IDABC (2004), three aspects of interoperability need to be considered:

- **Organisational interoperability:** This aspect of interoperability is concerned with defining business goals, modelling business processes, and bringing about the collaboration of administrations that wish to exchange information and may have different internal structures and processes. Moreover, organisational interoperability aims at addressing the requirements of the user community by making services available, easily identifiable, accessible, and user-oriented.

- **Semantic interoperability:** This aspect of interoperability is concerned with ensuring that the precise meaning of exchanged information is understandable by any other application that was not initially developed for this purpose. Semantic interoperability enables systems to combine received information with other information resources, and to process it in a meaningful manner. Semantic interoperability is therefore a prerequisite for the front-end multilingual delivery of services to the user.

- **Technical interoperability:** This aspect of interoperability covers the technical issues of linking computer systems and services. It includes key aspects such as open interfaces, interconnection services, data integration and middleware, data presentation and exchange, accessibility, and security services.

In multicultural environments like in the European Union, public administration is a complex network of organizations, people, languages, information systems, information structures, rules, processes, and practices. Effective utilization of ICT requires explicit rules for communication and means for the integration of heterogeneous systems and information resources. XML is a tool for the purpose (Salminen, 2005).

Extensible Markup Language, shortened XML (Bray, Paoli, Sperberg-McQueen, Maler, Yergeau, & Cowan, 2004), consists of a set of rules for defining and representing information as *XML documents*, where information structures are indicated by explicit markup. The markup vocabulary and the structures specified for a particular domain create an *XML application*, a formal language for representing information of the domain.

XML was developed from the Standard Generalized Markup Language (SGML) (Goldfarb, 1990) for supporting the management of heterogeneous information resources of the Internet, and to facilitate communication between various software applications. Compared to SGML, the number of rules in XML is clearly smaller, and its character set and resource identification mechanisms are planned for use on the Internet, for representing information content written in all natural languages of the world. The simplicity of XML has encouraged active development work around XML, including both software development and development of XML applications and related languages. Where SGML has been primarily in use as a format for documents intended for human readers, for example, in the form of HTML documents, the use of XML has extended towards data interchange between software applications. In public administration, likewise in other domains, the use of XML can be divided into two major categories: the format for data interchange and the format for information assets. The information assets can be further divided into documents and metadata.

According to Booth, Haas, McCabe, Newcomer, Champion, Ferris, and Orchard (2004), a Web service is a software system designed to support interoperable machine-to-machine interaction over a network. It has an interface described in a machine-processable format (specifically WSDL). Other systems interact with the Web service in a manner prescribed by its description using SOAP messages, typically conveyed using HTTP with an XML serialization in conjunction with other Web-related standards.

A Web service is a software system, identified by a URL, whose public interfaces and bindings are defined and described using XML. Its definition can be discovered by other software

Figure 1. The Web service model

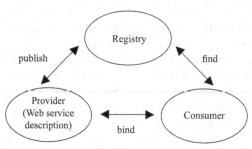

systems. These systems may then interact with the Web service in a manner prescribed by its definition, using XML-based messages conveyed by Internet protocols.

This definition has been published by the World Wide Web consortium (W3C) in the Web services architecture document (Booth et al., 2004). The Web service model consists of three entities: the service provider, the service registry, and the service consumer. Other models, such as a peer-to-peer structure, also exist. Figure 1 shows a graphical representation of the traditional Web service model (Dustdar & Schreiner, 2005).

The service provider creates or simply offers the Web service. The service provider needs to describe the Web service in a standard format, which in turn is XML, and publish it in a central service registry. The service registry contains additional information about the service provider, such as address and contact of the providing company, and technical details about the service. The service consumer retrieves the information from the registry and uses the service description obtained to bind to and invoke the Web service. The appropriate methods are depicted in Figure 1 by the keywords "publish," "bind," and "find." In order to achieve communication among applications running on different platforms and written in different programming languages, standards are needed for each of these operations.

Web services architecture is loosely coupled, service oriented. The Web Service Description Language (WSDL) (Christensen, Curbera, Meredith, & Weerawarana, 2001) uses the XML format to describe the methods provided by a Web service, including input and output parameters, data types, and the transport protocol, which is typically HTTP, to be used. The universal description discovery and integration standard UDDI suggests means to publish details about a service provider, the services that are stored, and the opportunity for service consumers to find service providers and Web service details. Besides UDDI, other standards have been developed as well. The simple object access protocol, SOAP, is used for XML-formatted information exchange among the entities involved in the Web service model. SOAP version 1.2 (SOAP) is a lightweight protocol intended for exchanging structured information in a decentralized, distributed environment (Gudgin, Hadley, Mendelsohn, Moreau, & Nielsen, 2003). It uses XML technologies to define an extensible messaging framework providing a message construct that can be exchanged over a variety of underlying protocols. The framework has been designed to be independent of any particular programming model and other implementation specific semantics.

Nowadays, there is an active and constant trend worldwide to conclude to standards on interoperability framework and on Web services. In Europe, the European Commission has recently adopted the Interoperable Delivery of European eGovernment Services to public Administrations, Business and Citizens (IDABC) programme (http://europa.eu.int/idabc), in order to use the opportunities offered by ICTs to encourage and support the delivery of cross-border public-sector services to citizens and enterprises in Europe, to improve efficiency and collaboration between European public administrations, and to contribute to making Europe an attractive place to live, work, and invest. Especially, the British government has collaborated to conclude an e-government interoperability framework (e-GIF) (http://www.govtalk.gov.uk/schemasstandards/egif.asp). The e-GIF defines the technical policies and specifications governing information flows across government and the public sector. These cover interconnectivity, data integration, e-services access, and content management.

Web Services Interoperability Organisation (WS-I) (http://www.ws-i.org) is an open industry organisation chartered to promote Web services interoperability across platforms, operating systems, and programming languages. The organisation's diverse community of Web services leaders helps customers to develop interoperable Web services by providing guidance, recommended practices, and supporting resources. All companies interested in promoting Web services interoperability are encouraged to join the effort. Specifically, WS-I creates, promotes, and supports generic protocols for the interoperable exchange of messages between Web services. In this context, "generic protocols" are protocols that are independent of any action indicated by a message, other than those actions necessary for its secure, reliable, and efficient delivery, and "interoperable" means suitable for multiple operating systems and multiple programming languages. Last, but not least, there is the World Wide Web Consortium (W3C) (http://www.w3c.org), which develops interoperable technologies (specifications, guidelines, software, and tools) to lead the Web to its full potential.

Case Study: CCIGov Platform

The scope of the case study presented in this section is to investigate the methodology to develop a generic, standardised, interoperable platform (CCIGOV platform) able to model and manage administrative business-related processes and content. This can be achieved using a Web service oriented architecture (SOA) and a Web service orchestration paradigm, in order to follow a one-stop approach where Chambers of Commerce and Industry (CCIs) act as trans-European liaisons (intermediaries) between the government and businesses, that is, introduce a new government model.

The CCIGov platform could be used by governmental organisations (GOs) and CCIs to create and develop common, multilingual, multiplatform, trans-European e-services in a uniform and standardised way; thus, enabling process transparency and facilitating mobility of services and goods in the internal market.

CCIs are associations of enterprises, industrial and commercial, representing the business environment to local, regional, and national government worldwide. In EC member states, the majority of CCIs are public (governmental) authorities in which businesses are obliged to be registered. Thus, CCIs offer various obligatory services to their members, businesses, such as certificates based on legal information in a Chamber's registry, ATA carnets, certificates of origin, export licences, and so forth. Their institutional role is to advise the government, to support local businesses, to offer services, support internal trade and business development, as well as to support and advise on trans-national business issues. Thus, CCIs are governmental organisations that are currently involved in many business-related processes.

Service-oriented architecture (SOA) is an architectural style, based on the notion of services that are independent but cooperating building blocks to develop distributed applications (Channabasavaiah, Holley, & Tuggle, 2004). The SOA model isolates aspects of an application so that, as technology changes, services (components) can be independently updated, limiting the impact of changes and updates to a manageable scope. Managing change is an important benefit of leveraging component architectures and models. Today there are many collaboration techniques, but they vary from one case to another, and are often owner solutions or systems that collaborate without any vision or architecture. A shift towards a service-oriented approach not only standardizes interactions, but also allows for more flexibility in the process. The complete value chain within an organization is divided into small modular functional units, or services. A service-oriented architecture thus has to focus on how services are described and organized to support their dynamic, automated discovery and use. Today, Web service is a powerful technology for implementing operational solutions based on SOA (Castellano, Pastore, Arcieri, Summo, & Bellone de Grecis, 2005).

Web service orchestration describes how Web services can interact with each other at the message level, including the business logic and execution order of the interactions. These interactions may span applications and/or organizations, and result in a long-lived, transactional, multistep process model (Peltz, 2003).

Traditional Approach

At present, legislation in force requires companies to carry out a number of bureaucratic procedures in order to be able to practice their activity. Common denominator for most of those procedures is the fact that the company acts as information mediator. That means that the company has to submit, to governmental authorities, various documents issued by other governmental authorities, or it has to submit the same documents to more than one of those authorities.

The emerging problems are many. The company, for its entire lifecycle, has the care and the responsibility to issue, update, and keep those documents, with a considerable resource cost. For many countries, where the specific phenomenon is more extended, the damage for the national economy is important. That is provoked due to the fact that many foreign enterprises, wishing to investigate other countries, avoid messing with sophisticated bureaucratic procedures demanding significant resources (time, money, and manpower).

We can note three relevant major procedures of this kind, which are the following:

- **Activity initialisation:** It is probably the worst case of the procedures we are discussing. The business has to react with a number of national and/or international GOs, BRGOs (business registration GOs), and CCIs, in order to submit an important number of documents. Many of those documents are issued from some of those authorities and must be submitted to others. A common part of the procedure for a business activity initialisation, for many countries, is the following: The business (Business 1) representative is obliged to visit the national BRGO, in person, in order to get a business registration number. With this information available, the representative visits the national CCI (NCCI) to register and get the approval for the business initialisation. In sequence, he has to go to the local tax office (FGO) in person to get a tax registration number, and finally to return to the NCCI to inform it of this number and associate it with Business 1.

- **Activity termination:** In this case, we have again an identical scenario. The business representative goes with the suitable documentation to the NCCI, gets an approval and, in sequence, he goes to the tax office (FGO). After the record of the termination data to the tax authority database, the representative of the inactive business has to return to the NCCI to notify them of the termination of the procedure. It is a very common fact that this last step is omitted, as the representatives are often tired of the bureaucracy.

- **Participation to public procurements:** The public procurement legislation usually asks all participating companies to submit, with their proposal, a number of documents that approve their legal and tax-clearance status. Those documents are issued by GOs (legislation GO–LGO and Tax Office GO–FGO) and are submitted also to GOs. This practice leads many times to problems, since the paper documents may be outdated at the time they are used.

There are a lot of other relevant cases, involving business with GOs. In each country we can find especially poorly designed procedures that ignore the fact that the government is a complete structure, and each GO acts as an individual authority. We can find such cases in the field of social security, justice and, in general, in the majority of governmental procedures. Figure 2 shows the mess of those procedures, which are usually implemented by the interested parties in person.

Figure 2. CCI-GOs traditional information exchange

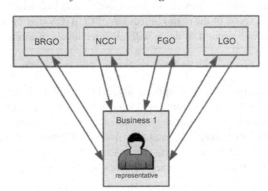

The existing bureaucracy embraces, indirectly, citizens, enterprises, and public sectors to function and complete their daily tasks, especially when dealing with public services. The current functionality model of public sector inserts many difficulties in the operation of enterprises. The main problems that are often compounded are:

- Failures in communication
- Need for shared data and information
- Difficulty in accessing the right information (either identifying the source or the qualitative attributes of the information)
- Collection of large amounts of data over time
- Incompatible data formats
- Data missing or obsolete data
- Metadata (information describing data) is not universally acceptable
- Inconsistent data policies and practices (especially technological ones) across organisations

Interoperable Approach

The CCIGOV platform aims to provide a standardized and flexible environment that will enable GOs (including CCIs) to jointly establish and deliver common e-government services to international businesses. Such joint delivery of common services involves the participation and collaboration of various GOs in terms of:

- Existing IT systems
- Human interaction
- Predefined processes and workflows

Thus, interoperability at all levels among GOs is a prerequisite to deliver common e-services and, for this reason, it is one of the major objectives of CCIGOV platform. The investigated platform is an ambitious attempt to delve with all three levels of interoperability, defined by IDABC (2004):

- As regards **organisational interoperability**, the CCIGOV platform aims at deploying Web service oriented architecture (SOA) and Web service orchestration paradigm in order to enable GOs all over Europe to model and manage/streamline individual business-related administrative processes (involving both human actors and IT systems) and information architectures, with the aim to deliver pan-European, cross-border, multilingual, multiplatform, common services in a transparent way for the end user.
- As regards **semantic interoperability**, the CCIGOV platform aims at establishing a common semantic framework, using metadata, enabling GOs to exchange standardised

information and content that is understood by all the involved human or systemic actors.

- As regards **technical interoperability**, the CCIGOV platform aims at interlinking existing GOs IT systems and infrastructures located in the same or in different countries, by defining and using open interfaces, standards, and protocols.

At this section, the CCIGOV platform will be investigated firstly at national level and secondly at international (pan-European) level. The assumptions taken into consideration are the following:

- A CCI maintains an IT system where it records information on commercial and industrial companies activated at CCI's domain (at national level). The information recorded on each company contains general information and can (but does not yet) record information on legislative documents and financial data on the company.
- The CCI's IT system includes a portal accessible to its target group (commercial and industrial companies). The portal provides security as it provides authentication of the user through a unique login/password combination. Moreover, it provides online fill-in forms and requests.
- Three GOs are involved per country: (a) a tax office GO (FGO), which maintains an IT system where financial data of citizens and companies are constantly updated, (b) a legislation GO (LGO), which maintains an IT system with all the legislation on companies, and (c) a business registration GO (BRGO), which maintains an IT system with the companies' registry in order to record their corporate name and validate its uniqueness.

The CCIGOV platform will provide several Web services for the data exchange between two parties. The Web services provided will be the following:

- **Financial Web service:** The national CCI (NCCI) will send an XML message, containing unique information on a certain company (Business 1), to FGO requesting certain financial data on Business 1. The FGO, through the same Web service, will respond to NCCI through an XML message where the unknown financial data will be provided and selectively stored at NCCI's database. The financial data can be either storable (e.g., tax registration number) or information that does not need to be stored (e.g., financial certificate).
- **Legislative Web service:** The NCCI will send an XML message, containing unique information on a certain company (Business 1), to LGO requesting certain legislative data on Business 1. The LGO, through the same Web service, will respond to NCCI through an XML message where the unknown legislative data will be provided and selectively stored at NCCI's database.
- **Registration Web service:** The NCCI will send an XML message, containing unique information on a certain company (Business 1), to BRGO requesting the validation on corporate name of Business 1. The BRGO, through the same Web service, will respond

Figure 3. CCI—GOs Web services exchange at national level

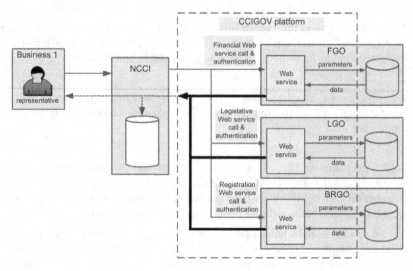

to NCCI through an XML message where Boolean information on the corporate name will be provided and selectively stored at NCCI's database.

All three Web services will contain information on the authentication of the GO (including NCCI) in order for the receiver to validate the requester is authorised to receive confidential information on Business 1. Moreover, the Web services will contain input and output parameters, filled in with the requested and the received information, respectively.

Figure 3 illustrates the proposed exchange of messages among the involved parties at national level.

The CCIGOV platform will try to provide the following services in an interoperable manner:

- **Activity initialisation:** When Business 1 wishes to initialise its activity, its representative enters NCCI portal and fills in the respective registration form. CCIGOV platform will be triggered for NCCI to collect the respective unknown financial and registration data *simultaneously* (business registration number from BRGO and tax registration number from FGO). When both Web services are successfully terminated, NCCI holds the necessary data associated with Business 1, sends a verification message that the registration is successfully completed, and the activation of Business 1 can be finalised.

- **Activity termination:** When Business 1 wishes to terminate its activity, its representative enters NCCI portal and fills in the respective termination form. CCIGOV platform will be triggered only for the financial Web service, in order for NCCI to send to LGO the termination request along with Business 1 identification information (tax registration number). LGO processes the request, disjoins Business 1 from its tax registration number, and returns to NCCI a clearance to proceed. When the Web service is successfully terminated, the termination of Business 1's activity is finalised, and its representative may print the respective certificate through NCCI's portal.

- **Participation to public procurements:** When Business 1 wishes to participate in a public procurement, its representative enters NCCI portal and fills in the respective form–request. CCIGOV platform will be triggered for NCCI to collect the respective legal and tax clearance status; therefore, initiating, *simultaneously*, financial and legislative Web services containing Business 1 identification information (tax registration number and corporate name). When both Web services are successfully terminated, NCCI holds the necessary legal and tax clearance data associated with Business 1, and provides to its representative the specific certificates in valid format through its portal.

When dealing with the international (pan-European) level, there are many situations where businesses wish to initiate any of the previously mentioned services at another country (e.g., initialise/terminate a branch office's activity abroad and participate in public procurements abroad). When this is the case, CCIGOV platform enables companies to access the other country's NCCI, which consequently accesses a companies' native NCCI, and proceed with the request of relevent information. Therefore, in an interoperable approach, CCIs are the information mediators, not companies themselves.

Evaluation

The CCIGOV platform implements the main interoperability goal for the public sector: the one-stop point-of-service that makes it easy for citizens to access high-quality government services. Businesses, in our case, have to deal with a variety of governmental authorities through a single "provider" that can be the national CCI (NCCI), a governmental authority as well. There are a lot of arising benefits implementing this approach. The most significant benefits are:

- **Improvement and simplification:** The specific procedures referring businesses are very complex and bureaucratic today. With the new approach, business representatives have to deal mostly electronically with only one governmental authority, and let it do the "dirty" work in the background.
- **Acceleration:** Since there is no need for a considerable number of in-person visits to various authorities, it is obvious that the whole procedure will become faster. ICTs offer great capabilities that guarantee the rapid completion of the procedure.
- **Cost effective:** The cost is reduced for both businesses and involving authorities, and refers to manpower and paperwork costs.

- **Utilization of technology:** The various authorities' technological infrastructure is upgraded and used more effectively for the public service.

- **Reliability:** The interchanged data are accurate and up-to-date. Furthermore, there is no chance for someone to misrepresent or fake the required documents/certificates.

- **Less paperwork:** The need for submitting a lot of paper documents more than once is reduced significantly.

- **Monitoring:** All procedures can be monitored. That means that it is possible to track the evaluation of a case and also to detect problems and omissions. This capability is also very important for statistical reasons.

Recommendations

Nowadays, more and more governments all over the world are trying to change their traditional profile to an electronic one. E-government aims at improving the government-to-citizen (G2C) and government-to-business (G2B) relationships by enhanced service provision on a 24/7 basis. The ease and speed with which the transactions can be carried out over the Web has been the key driving force in the rapid growth of e-government domain. Especially for businesses, the provided Web applications can make governmental information easily accessed, and can improve, significantly, the interaction with government at all levels (local, regional, state, and federal).

In this framework, one of the most vital goals is to create the proper environment where businesses will meet information society targets. Therefore, the enterprises will apply e-business platforms (ERP, CRM, etc.), use networks, promote e-commerce and e-marketing, automate transactions with local administrations and government and, finally, offer improved services to their customers. The advantages for the businesses will include faster access to information, tenders, and legislation; simple electronic data interchange capabilities with public administration; more efficient and cross-departmental processes; and so forth. On the other hand, administration will profit from the service quality, customer orientation, acceleration, and simplification of processes; cost savings through greater efficiency; transparency; and so forth.

Under this scope, international organisations on e-government and interoperability standards should cooperate along with governments in order to reach a commonly accepted e-government model. This model should deal with, among others, the definition of a commonly accepted messages' language, in order for the Web services to encode/decode their parameters and the GO's authentication information. Additionally, the model should deal with the hosting of one or more services registries to ease the functionality of Web services worldwide. A third trusted party (TTP) can act as a moderator between all involving GOs, including CCIs, and act as a service registry. It can host the participating GOs' registries with their data, parameters, and authentication information. A TTP can also offer timestamp services, where the procedures that take place are time critical. Finally, it can be assigned the responsibility of monitoring the evaluation of the cases.

The new e-government model will probably arise the need for governments' business process reengineering (BPR). BPR is essential for GOs to loose their self-centred character, and for citizens and businesses to become the main core of e-government, as they will initiate the e-services, thus benefiting from them at the most.

The CCISGOV platform is studied in such a way that GOs, other than the ones presented, can easily adopt its mechanism, and provide Web services to businesses (e.g., social security GOs), expanding the e-services provided to businesses and consolidating CCIs as intermediaries.

Thus, platforms, such the CCIGOV one, can easily be adopted, and the businesses eventually profit as they will save time, manpower, and cost when interacting with GOs.

Future Trends

According to Layne and Lee (2001), e-government progresses towards higher levels of integration and interoperability among and between government levels and branches. Interoperability, in essence, leads to extensive information sharing among and between governmental entities. However, the obstacles that prevent a rapid progress in that direction are not merely technical. In fact, the technology side may prove the least difficult to address, while the organizational, legal, political, and social aspects may prove much more of a challenge.

Work must be done to define and agree upon government sector-specific semantics and on the alignment of business processes. Many e-government services exist, such as taxation functions and social services, that require government agreement on their own semantics and processes. Likewise, there are, frequently, additional public sector requirements in general business processes, such as procurement that are not found in the private sector, for example, specific competitive bidding requirements and/or specific approval approaches. For e-government, business process alignment, in many cases, requires an alignment of laws, regulations, and so forth, something that the European Union, with its single market approach, can leverage (Lueders, 2005).

A major contributor to interoperability is voluntary open standards development plus voluntary open standards adoption. Open standards development, without significant adoption of the resultant standards, does nothing in the effort to achieve interoperability. Standards, like software, must evolve to take advantage of technology advances. Best-of breed solutions, evaluated on a best value for money basis, that are continually updated and have software support to meet customer standards-compatibility expectations, are the best approach to achieve and ensure ongoing interoperability.

XML offers a rich variety of possibilities, but its adoption in public sectors requires extensive collaboration in standardization. Work is needed at all levels: international, national, and local. International agreements are needed to avoid extra work and to facilitate international communication. At the national level, work on the international level should be considered as a potential basis for the national recommendations or standards. The amount of efforts needed for standardization in a particular organizational environment is highly dependent on the availability of well-documented base standards. On the other hand, the base standards describing the real world never should be considered totally stable. For example, the set of country codes standardized by the International Organization for Standardization (ISO) and also used in XML to refer to countries needs continuous maintenance, due to geopolitical changes.

Many different standards have been proposed and various approaches have been taken to create a widely accepted and usable way for developing Web services. With WSDL, Web services may be described in a way according to their functionalities. According to Dustdar and Schreiner (2005), QoS and semantic descriptions have been proposed to extend the current WSDL standard, but have not yet found overall acceptance. UDDI and other registry based data models have been implemented, but are not widely used, and in the case of dynamic service discovery, it does not yet meet requirements.

The work needed for local level standardization in a particular organizational environment depends not only on the availability of base standards and recommendations, but also on the type of XML usage. In using XML, for example, for data exchange between software systems, the solution may be a technical implementation. Even though the human users of the systems may participate in the design as user need experts, they do not need knowledge about the implementation details. On the other hand, adopting XML as a format for documents, understanding the changes needed in production processes and capabilities offered by the new solutions usually requires at least some knowledge about XML and about the approach of structured documents.

Continuous changes in specifications and software cause problems to all kinds of XML standardization. One of the hardest challenges is the vulnerability of the Internet. The lack of trust in the technology and people involved is causing a disappearance of people from the Internet community. In the insecure Internet environment, well-planned services may remain without users. Therefore, alternative and more trustworthy network solutions have to be considered for e-government.

E-government services delivery requires interoperability both within and across organizational and administrative boundaries. However, this sharing of information should comply with personal data protection principles, laws, and regulations and generally involves the following tasks: digital data collection, data storage, data processing, data transfer, and data share. This, in its turn, affects the way e-government architectures will be designed and implemented (Riedl, 2003).

Moreover, several issues related to privacy should be addressed. The threats on user privacy in an electronic environment are so many that a single solution does not exist. The future challenges and research in the direction of delivering e-services without jeopardising, but in fact protecting, privacy relate to standards support, intelligible disclosure of data, disclosure of methods, provision of organizational and technical means for users to modify their user model entries, user model servers that support a number of anonymization methods, and adapting user-modelling methods to privacy preferences and legislation (Markellos, Markellou, Rigou, Sirmakessis, & Tsakalidis, 2004, Teltzrow & Kobsa, 2004).

Another key aspect of interoperability relates to secure interconnection and intercommunication (McIntyre, Taylor, & McCabe, 2004). This does not address only the advances in cryptography and protocols for secure Internet communication (e.g., SSL, S-HTTP, etc.) that significantly contributed to securing information transfers within e-government infrastructures (Bouguettaya et al., 2004). It also encompasses a whole range of policies, legal processes, and operational guidelines. Specifically, the ability to share information and process over a secure environment involves publication, support, maintenance, ownership, and access.

Conclusion

E-government has the potential to change public administrations' organization, operation, and interoperation, and in this way to facilitate the interaction with citizens and businesses. The transition from the traditional model of governance to the digital one involves not only technological, but also organizational, economic, social, legal, and democratic dimensions. Furthermore, a number of challenges and risks have been identified and should be solved from both sides, government (e.g., complexity, poor IT infrastructure, human resources and financial constraints, legal issues, etc.) and users (e.g., lack of familiarity and trust, digital gap, etc.).

In this chapter, we emphasized that the interoperability aspect comprises one of the most crucial barriers that e-government should overcome. This requirement relates to local and regional public administrations, enterprise sector, and it also goes beyond the national borders and involves other countries' administrations. Moreover, the interoperability of ICT systems and applications, the sharing and reuse of information and services, the interlinking of various administrative processes, within and between sectors, are essential factors for the delivery of high quality, innovative, seamless, and customer-centric e-government services.

Under this framework, we presented our approach to developing CCIGOV platform. This can model and manage administrative business-related processes and content using Web service oriented architecture and a Web service orchestration paradigm, and follow a one-stop approach, benefiting from CCIs' exploitation. It comprises an effort to deal with the three levels of interoperability, that is, organisational, semantic, and technical. Specifically, it provides financial, legislative, and registration Web services. The benefits from the adoption of this model include, among others: significant time, cost as well as manpower saving, greater convenience, better accessibility, more choices, faster delivery, and so forth Finally, this initiative needs more work in order to gradually integrate all the administrative tasks and processes that businesses want to complete in their interaction with the governmental organizations.

References

Abramson, M. A., & Means, G. E. (Eds.) (2001). *E-government 2001*. Lanham, MD: Rowman and Littlefield.

Angehrn, A. (1997). Designing mature Internet business strategies: The ICDT model. *European Management Journal, 15*(4), 361-368.

Bacon, K., Wesling, C., Casey, J., & Wodinsky, J. (2002). *E-government: The blue print*. New York: John Wiley & Sons Ltd.

Booth, D., Haas, H., McCabe, F., Newcomer, E., Champion, M., Ferris, C., & Orchard, D. (2004, February 11). *Web services architecture* (W3C working group note). Retrieved September 12, 2005, from http://www.w3.org/TR/ws-arch/

Bose, R. (2004). E-government: Infrastructure and technologies for education and training. *Electronic Government, 1*(4), 349–361.

Bouguettaya, A., Rezgui, A., Medjahed, B., & Ouzzani, M. (2004). Internet computing support for digital government. In M. P. Singh (Ed.), *Practical handbook of Internet computing.* CRC Press. Retrieved September 10, 2005, from http://www-personal. engin.umd.umich.edu/~brahim/mypublications/chapter_singh.pdf

Bray, T., Paoli, J., Sperberg-McQueen, C. M., Maler, E., Yergeau, F., & Cowan, J. (2004). *Extensible markup language (XML) 1.1.* W3C recommendation 04 February 2004. Retrieved September 11, 2005, from http://www.w3.org/TR/xml11/

Castellano, M., Pastore, N., Arcieri, F., Summo, V., & Bellone de Grecis, G. (2005). An e-government cooperative framework for government agencies. In *Proceedings of the 38th Hawaii International Conference on System Sciences (HICSS)* (Vol. 5, p. 121c).

Channabasavaiah, K., Holley, K., & Tuggle, Jr., E. M. (2004). *Migrating to a service-oriented architecture.* IBM. Retrieved September 12, 2005, from http://www-106.ibm. com/developerworks/webservices/library/wsmigratesoa/

Christensen, E., Curbera, F., Meredith, G., & Weerawarana, S. (2001, March 15). *Web services description language (WSDL) 1.1 (*W3C note). Retrieved September 12, 2005, from http://www.w3.org/TR/wsdl

Commission of the European Communities. (2003). *Linking up Europe: The importance of interoperability for egovernment services.* Commission Staff Working Paper, Enterprise Directorate General. Retrieved September 10, 2005, from http://www.csi.map. es/csi/pdf/interoperabilidad_1675.pdf

Dawes, S. (2002). *The future of e-government.* Center for Technology in Government, University at Albany/SUNY. Retrieved December 21, 2005, from http://www.ctg.albany. edu/publications/reports/future_of_egov/future_of_egov.pdf

Dustdar, S., & Schreiner, W. (2005). A survey on Web services composition. *International Journal of Web and Grid Services, 1*(1), 1-30.

E-governance Institute. (2004). *Concepts and principles of e-governance.* Rutgers University's National Center for Public Productivity. Retrieved December 21, 2005, from http://www.andromeda.rutgers.edu/~egovinst/Website/institutepg.htm

GFRIG. (2003). *E-government is crucial to create citizen-centred governance.* Global Forum on Re-Inventing Government. Retrieved September 10, 2005, from http://europa. eu.int/idabc/en/document/1769/327

Goldfarb, C. F. (1990). *The SGML handbook.* Oxford, UK: Oxford University Press.

Gudgin, M., Hadley, M., Mendelsohn, N., Moreau, J.-J., & Nielsen, H.-F., (2003, June 24). *SOAP version 1.2 Part 1: Messaging framework* (W3C recommendation). Retrieved September 11, 2005, from http://www.w3.org/TR/soap12-part1/

IDABC. (2004). *European interoperability framework for pan-European e-government services*. Luxembourg: Office for Official Publications of the European Communities. Retrieved September 10, 2005, from http://europa.eu.int/idabc/en/chapter/5845

Layne, K., & Lee, J. (2001). Developing fully functional e-government: A four-stage model. *Government Information Quarterly, 18*, 122-136.

Lueders, H. (2005, February 23-25). Interoperability and open standards for e-government services. In *Proceedings of the 1ˢᵗ International Conference on Interoperability of Enterprise Software and Applications (eGOV INTEROP'05)*, Geneva, Switzerland. Retrieved September 12, 2005, from http://www.softwarechoice.org/download_files/eGovinterop05_paper.pdf

Markellos, K., Markellou, P., Rigou, M., Sirmakessis, S., & Tsakalidis, A. (2004, April 14-16). Web personalization and the privacy concern. In *Proceedings of the 7ᵗʰ ETHI-COMP International Conference on the Social and Ethical Impacts of Information and Communication Technologies, Challenges for the Citizen of the Information Society*, Syros, Greece.

Markellou, P., Panayiotaki, A., & Tsakalidis, A. (2003, June 3-6). E-government and applications levels: Technology at citizen service. In *Proceedings of IADIS International Conference, e-Society 2003*, Lisbon, Portugal (Vol. 2, pp. 849-854).

McIntyre, M., Taylor, G., & McCabe, C. (2004). *Open in Europe. The importance of open source software and open standards to interoperability in Europe*. Open Forum Europe. Retrieved September 15, 2005, from http://xml.coverpages.org/OpenIreland-OS.pdf

Ndou, V. (2004). E-government for developing countries: Opportunities and challenges. *Electronic Journal on Information Systems in Developing Countries (EJISDC), 18*(1), 1-24.

Peltz, C. (2003). Web services orchestration and choreography. *Computer, 36*(10), 46-52.

Riedl, R. (2001, May 22-24). Knowledge management for interstate e-government. In *Proceedings of the Workshop on Knowledge Management in Electronic Government (KMGov)*, Siena, Italy. Retrieved September 11, 2005, from http://www.ifi.unizh.ch/egov/Sienanew.pdf

Riedl, R. (2003). Design principles for e-government services. In *Proceedings of the eGov Day*, Vienna, Austria. Retrieved September 10, 2005, from http://www.ifi.unizh.ch/egov/Wien03.pdf

Riley, T. B. (2001). *Electronic governance and electronic democracy: Living and working in the connected world*. Paper presented at the Commonwealth Heads of Government Meeting, Brisbane, Australia. Retrieved September 10, 2005, from http://www.electronicgov.net/pubs/research_papers/index.shtml

Salminen, A. (2005). Building digital government by XML. In *Proceedings of the 38ᵗʰ Hawaii International Conference on System Sciences (HICSS)* (Vol. 5, p. 122b).

Scherlis, W. L., & Eisenberg, J. (2003). IT research, innovation, and e-government. *Communications of the ACM, 46*(1), 67-68.

Shackleton, P., Fisher, J., & Dawson, L. (2004). Evolution of local government e-services: The applicability of e-business maturity models. In *Proceedings of the 37th Hawaii International Conference on System Sciences (HICSS)* (Vol. 5, p. 50120b).

Stamoulis, D., Gouscos, D., Georgiadis, P., & Martakos, D. (2001). Revisiting public information management for effective e-government services. *Information Management & Computer Security*, *9*(4), 146-153.

Tambouris, E., Gorilas, S., & Boukis, G. (2001). Investigation of electronic government. In *Proceedings of the 8th Panhellenic Conference on Informatics* (Vol. 2, pp. 367-376). Retrieved September 13, 2005, from http://www.egov-project.org/egovsite/tambouris_panhellenic.pdf

Teltzrow, M., & Kobsa, A. (2004). Impacts of user privacy preferences on personalized systems: A comparative study. In C.-M Karat & J. Karat (Eds.), *Designing personalized user experiences for e-commerce*. Dordrecht, The Netherlands: Kluwer Academic Publishers. Retrieved September 15, 2005, from http://www.ics.uci.edu/~kobsa/papers/2004-PersUXinECom-kobsa.pdf

Endnote

[1]   1720/1999/EC: Decision of the European Parliament and of the Council of 12 July 1999 to adopt a series of actions and measures in order to ensure interoperability of, and access to, trans-European networks for the electronic interchange of data between administrations (IDA).

Section II

Mobile Computing

Chapter VII

A Brief Overview of Wireless Systems and Standards

Sundar G. Sankaran, Atheros Communications, USA

Abstract

This chapter provides a brief overview of wireless systems and standards. The evolution of wireless systems from voice-centric circuit-switched systems to data-centric packet-switched systems is discussed. The first- and second-generation wireless systems were designed primarily for voice service. The data rate supported by these systems is very limited. The 2.5G systems were developed to retrofit second-generation systems to support higher data rate applications. The third-generation systems are designed to meet the demands of the Internet era. A wide range of IP-based services is provided using these systems. IEEE 802.16 standard-based systems, commonly referred to as WiMAX, are being proposed as an alternative to third-generation systems for carrying data traffic. Popular wireless LAN and wireless PAN standards are also discussed.

Introduction

Wireless systems have been around for over a century. Guglielmo Marconi successfully transmitted Morse code from Cornwall, England to St-John's, Canada in 1901. The wireless technology has come a long way since then. The proliferation of Internet in every aspect of life resulted in rapid convergence of computing and communication industries fueling an explosive growth of wireless communication in the mid-1990s. Now, mobile computing—the use of a portable computing device capable of wireless networking—is a reality. For example, today's PDAs and cell phones have the capability for Internet surfing. Consequently, one can use the PDAs and cell phones to do everything from stock trading to finding driving directions. WiFi enabled laptops allow the users to connect to Internet from WiFi hotspots, which are becoming ubiquitous. Emerging standards such as WiMAX aim to provide high-speed wireless data access from anywhere at anytime. This chapter describes various wireless standards that have made mobile computing a reality.

First- and Second-Generation Cellular Systems

The first-generation cellular systems, developed in the late 1970s, use analog modulation techniques. These systems are designed primarily to carry analog speech. Very low-rate data transmission is possible in these systems. The advance mobile phone service (AMPS) system, developed by AT&T Bell Labs, is an example of first-generation wireless systems. A good fraction of cellular systems currently deployed around the world are based on AMPS. For example, AMPS is still being used in some rural parts of the U.S.

Starting in the early 1990s, wireless operators started deploying second-generation cellular systems that use digital modulation (Yacoub, 2001). The second-generation systems use advanced digital-signal-processing algorithms to process signals. The transition to digital from analog allowed the second-generation cellular systems to offer higher capacity[1] than the first-generation analog systems. The second-generation systems offer services such as text messaging, also known as short message service (SMS), and circuit switched data (CSD), in addition to legacy voice service.

Some of the popular second-generation cellular systems include global system mobile (GSM), interim standard 136 (IS-136), and interim standard 95 (IS-95). The GSM system (Mouly, 1992) was originally designed and deployed in Europe to solve the fragmentation problems[2] of the first cellular systems in Europe. Now, GSM is the most widely deployed wireless system in the world, with deployments in Europe, Asia, Australia, South America, and some parts of the U.S. IS-136, the American counterpart of GSM, is a digital evolution of the first-generation AMPS system. It is often, albeit imprecisely, referred to as the TDMA standard since it uses time division multiple access (TDMA) air interface. However, it should be noted that many other standards, including GSM, use TDMA. The IS-136 systems are widely deployed in North America. IS-95, pioneered by Qualcomm, is the popular second-generation system based on code division multiple access (CDMA). It is also known as *cdmaOne*. These systems are in wide use in North America, South Korea, India, and China.

The second-generation cellular systems were rolled out before the dawn of the Internet era. Consequently, these systems are not efficient in carrying data: these systems transfer data with circuit switching, which is not as efficient as packet switching, used by systems of later generation. Furthermore, the data rate provided by these systems is very limited. For example, GSM systems provide a maximum data rate of 14.4 kbps.

Evolution from Second Generation to 2.5G

New 2.5G technologies were developed in an effort to retrofit the second-generation systems to be able to support the higher data rates that are required by modern Internet applications. These technologies enable cellular service providers to support features such as Web browsing, e-mail, mobile commerce (m-commerce), and location-based mobile services using existing second-generation infrastructure, with minimal hardware and software upgrades to base stations and handsets.

The popular 2.5G systems include high speed circuit switched data (HSCSD), general packet radio service (GPRS), and enhanced data rates for GSM evolution (EDGE) (Halonen, Romero, & Melero, 2003). HSCSD is a 2.5G upgrade to GSM. It needs just a software upgrade at the base stations. With this upgrade, the maximum data rate per user can be increased to 57.6 kbps. However, the data transfer is still done with circuit switching. GPRS is a 2.5G upgrade to both GSM and IS-136. These systems use packet switching and provide access to the Internet at a maximum data rate of 171.2 kbps. EDGE is a more advanced upgrade, requiring addition of new hardware and software at the existing base stations, to both GSM and IS-136. The EDGE systems can provide a maximum per user data rate of 384 kbps.[3]

The cellular systems belonging to 2.5G and above support a new Web browsing format language called wireless application protocol (WAP). This language was designed to meet the challenges of Web browsing from a wireless handset, which usually has small displays and limited memory. The wireless devices usually run WAP-based microbrowsers. These browsers allow the users to access the Web using one hand without requiring a keyboard.

Third-Generation Cellular Systems

The third-generation cellular systems (Mandyam & Lai, 2002) aim to provide a wide range of Internet protocol (IP) based services, along with voice and data services, using a single handset, whether driving, walking, or standing still in an office setting. The key attributes of third-generation systems include 144 kbps or higher data rate in high mobility (vehicular) traffic, 384 kbps for pedestrian traffic, 2 Mbps or higher for indoor traffic, and *capability to determine geographic position of mobiles and report it to both the network and the mobile terminal.* Some of the third-generation wireless standards include CDMA2000 and universal mobile telecommunication system (UMTS, also known as W-CDMA) (3GPP2 Web site, n.d.; UMTS Forum Web site, n.d.). CDMA2000 is the 3G evolution of IS-95, while W-CDMA is the 3G evolution of GSM and IS-136.

Figure 1. Evolution of wireless standards

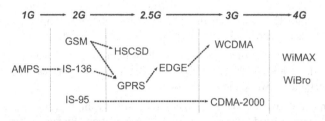

The CDMA2000 family of standards includes CDMA2000 1xRTT (also known as 1xRTT), CDMA2000 1xEV-DO (often referred to as EV-DO), and CDMA2000 1xEV-DV (also known as EV-DV). The 1xRTT (short for single-carrier radio transmission technology) systems provide data rates up to 144 kbps, while the latest generation of EV-DO (short for evolution data optimized) systems are capable of providing data rates up to 3.1 Mbps. 1xRTT and EV-DO have been rolled out in the U.S. by Verizon and Sprint. The EV-DV (short for evolution data voice) supports both voice and data users simultaneously. Due to lack of interest by carriers, the EV-DV development is currently on hold.

UMTS is the European and Japanese counterpart of CDMA2000. The UMTS system has been deployed in Japan by NTT DoCoMo. An evolution of UMTS known as high speed downlink packet access (HSDPA) has been rolled out in the U.S. by Cingular.

Wireless Local Area Networks

Wireless local area networks (WLAN) are rapidly replacing wires within homes and offices. The most common wireless LANs are based on the IEEE 802.11 standard (Gast, 2005; Wi-Fi Web site, n.d.). They are commonly referred to as WiFi networks. The phenomenal growth of Internet combined with increased use of portable, laptop computers also contributed to the rapid acceptance of WLANs. Some of the other factors that can be attributed to their widespread adaptation are their low cost and the ease of installation. They can be easily deployed by individuals within buildings without a license (since these devices usually operate in license-free band).

The original 802.11 standard, adopted in 1997, provided data rates up to 2 Mbps. Higher data rate enhancements to 802.11, commonly referred to as 802.11a, 802.11b, and 802.11g, emerged later. The 802.11b system operates in the 2.4 GHz band and provides data rates up to 11 Mbps. One of the drawbacks of 802.11b is its limited capacity due to the limited bandwidth availability in the 2.4 GHz band. This capacity limitation restricted the use of WLANs in office environments, where higher capacity is usually needed. Furthermore, the 2.4 GHz is already "crowded" with other devices such as cordless phones, Bluetooth, and microwaves. These drawbacks were mitigated with the emergence of 802.11a devices, which operate in the 5 GHz band and provide data rates up to 54 Mbps. The wider bandwidth available in the 5 GHz band allows using 802.11a based WLANs in office environments. The 802.11g standard, adopted in 2003, provides data rates up to 54 Mbps in the 2.4 GHz band. The emerging 802.11n standard promises data rates up to 600 Mbps. The 802.11n draft compliant products are expected to reach the market in the second half of 2006.

WiFi has proven to be a way of providing reliable in-building wireless access. The cellular phone manufacturers are launching dual mode GSM/WiFi devices that can make and receive calls on both cellular network and enterprise WLAN.

The European counterpart of WiFi is HiperLAN (short for high performance radio local area network), standardized by European Telecommunications Standards Institute (ETSI). HiperLANs have similar physical layer as Wi-Fi and are used chiefly in Europe.

Wireless Metropolitan Area Network

Wireless metropolitan area networks (WMAN) aim to provide always on broadband access to Internet at anytime from anywhere. The most successful wireless MAN technology is based on the IEEE 802.16 standard, which is often referred to as WiMAX networks (Ohrtman, 2005; WiMAX Forum Web site, n.d.). WiMAX is an alternative to third-generation cellular systems to provide broadband connections over long distances, and it is considered to be a fourth-generation technology. While the third-generation systems support both circuit and packet switching, the fourth-generation systems support packet switching only. The first-generation WiMAX products are expected to support data rates up to 40 Mbps per channel at vehicular speeds.

High performance radio metropolitan area network (HiperMAN) is the European alternative to WiMAX. Korea adopted a flavor of WiMAX known as wireless broadband (WiBro) as its wireless MAN standard.

Wireless Personal Area Networks

Wireless personal area networks (WPANs) are designed to replace the wires that connect devices to one another (such as printer cables, headphone cables, cables that run from personal computers to mouse, cables that run from set-top boxes). Bluetooth (Bluetooth Web site, n.d.) is the most widely embraced WPAN standard. It operates in the 2.4 GHz unlicensed band and provides short-range communication within a nominal range of 10 meters. Many laptops and cell phones currently support Bluetooth connections. Some car manufacturers, including Acura and BMW, are installing Bluetooth in cars. The latest Bluetooth devices consume extremely low power and provide reliable communication at data rates up to 2.1 Mbps.

ZigBee (ZigBee Web site, n.d.) is another competing technology for wireless PAN. ZigBee devices are expected to be cheaper and simpler than Bluetooth devices. The target applications for ZigBee include general-purpose, inexpensive, self-organizing mesh network that can be shared by medical devices, smoke and intruder alarms, and building and home automation.

Conclusion

The wireless revolution is just beginning. The confluence of communication and computing has created many new applications for wireless systems. The throughput, capacity, and range of wireless systems are constantly being improved. This chapter summarized the evolution that has happened over the last 2 decades.

The first- and second-generation systems were primarily designed for voice applications. The 2.5G systems were designed to be retrofit to 2G systems to support data. The third-generation systems were designed to support both voice and data, while the evolving fourth-generation systems are being designed to support primarily data. The WLAN system based on WiFi has seen tremendous growth and success over the last 5 years.

References

Bluetooth Web site. (n.d.). Retrieved February, 2006 from http://www.bluetooth.com

Gast, M. (2005). *802.11 Wireless networks: The definitive guide* (2nd ed.). Sebastapol: O'Reilly Media, Inc.

Halonen, T., Romero J., & Melero J. (2003). *GSM, GPRS, and EDGE performance: Evolution towards 3G/UMTS*. West Sussex: John Wiley & Sons.

Mandyam, G., & Lai J. (2002). *Third generation CDMA systems for enhanced data services*. San Diego: Academic Press.

Mouly, M., & Pautet, M. (1992). The *GSM system for mobile communications*. Palaiseau: Telecom Publishing.

Ohrtman, F. (2005). *WiMAX handbook*. New York: McGraw Hill Professional.

3GPP2 Web site. (n.d.). Retrieved February 2006 from http://www.3gpp2.org

UMTS-Forum Web site. (n.d.). Retrieved February 2006 from http://www.umts-forum. org

Wi-Fi Web site. (n.d.). Retrieved February 2006 from http://wi-fi.org

WiMAX FORUM Web site. (n.d.). Retrieved February 2006 from http://www.wimaxforum.org

Yacoub, M. (2001). *Wireless technology: Protocols, standards, and techniques*. Boca Raton: CRC Press.

ZigBee Web site. (n.d.). Retrieved February 2006 from http://www.zigbee.org

Endnotes

[1]   Capacity is the number of active users that can be supported at the same time.

[2]   Before GSM deployment, different parts of Europe used different cellular standards and it was not possible to use the same handset everywhere.

[3]   This is the maximum data rate per GSM channel. By combining many GSM channels together, it is possible to achieve data rates up to several megabits per second.

Appendix: Glossary

1xRTT	Single Carrier Radio Transmission Technology
AMPS	Advance Mobile Phone Service
CDMA	Code Division Multiple Access
CSD	Circuit Switched Data
EDGE	Enhanced Data Rates for GSM Evolution
EV-DO	Evolution Data Optimized
EV-DV	Evolution Data Voice
GPRS	General Packet Data Service
GSM	Global System Mobile
HiperLAN	High Performance Radio Local Area Network
HSCSD	High Speed Circuit Switched Data
HSDPA	High Speed Downlink Packet Access
IP	Internet Protocol
IS-136	Interim Standard 136
IS-95	Interim Standard 95
PSD	Packet Switched Data
SMS	Short Message Service
TDMA	Time Division Multiple Access
UMTS	Universal Mobile Telecommunication System
WAP	Wireless Application Protocol
WAP	Wireless Application Protocol
WiFi	Wireless Fidelity
WiMAX	Worldwide Interoperability for Microwave Access
WiBRO	Wireless Broadband
WLAN	Wireless Local Area Network
WPAN	Wireless Personal Area Network
WMAN	Wireless Metropolitan Area Network

Chapter VIII

Wireless Networks Based on WiFi and Related Technologies

Rajendra V. Boppana, University of Texas at San Antonio, USA

Suresh Chalasani, University of Wisconsin-Parkside, USA

Abstract

Multihop wireless networks based on WiFi technology offer flexible and inexpensive networking possibilities. Applications of multihop wireless networks range from personal networks within consumer homes to citywide departmental networks to wide-area vehicular ad hoc networks. In this chapter, we focus on multihop ad hoc networks with communication among user devices and access points, where available, without the restriction that the user devices need to be within the radio range of access points. We first describe pure WiFi networks and their limitations. Next we discuss mixed networks based on WiFi and other wired and wireless technologies to provide robust city-scale networks. This chapter also explores security issues and vulnerabilities of wireless networks. An emerging application of WiFi ad hoc networks-RFID (radio frequency identification) networks based on the WiFi technology for warehouses and large retail stores-is presented. This chapter also presents another emerging application of WiFi-based networks: vehicular ad hoc networks for automobiles.

Introduction

Cellular and WiFi (wireless fidelity) are currently the most popular and actively pursued wireless technologies for consumer and business use. A cellular network consists of several base stations, each covering a small geographical region. Together the base stations cover a wide region such as a city. To be useful, the entire region of interest must be covered without gaps by these base stations. This requires billions of dollars of investment in network infrastructure consisting of wireless spectrum and base stations. An entirely different type of wireless network is made possible by the wireless fidelity (WiFi) technology. This technology (based on the IEEE 802.11 standard (IEEE Computer Society LAN/MAN Standards Committee, 1999)) enables wireless communication on an ad hoc basis. In the simplest configuration, a wireless access point (denoted, *hotspot*) can be used to share an Internet connection among several tens of users in a small area such as a conference room or a coffee shop. The network connectivity is limited to the radio range (about 50 meters) of the hotspots, and communication among users must go through the access point. Such networks, called wireless local area networks (WLANs), are already extensively used by businesses and academic campuses. In this chapter, we focus on multihop ad hoc networks with communication among user devices and access points, where available, without the restriction that the user devices need to be within the radio range of access points.

The WiFi technology is inexpensive due to two factors: (a) the use of free, unlicensed radio spectrum at 2.4 GHz and 5.8 GHz bands obviates heavy investment in private, dedicated radio spectrum, and (b) the widespread use of WiFi equipped PDAs, laptops, and even phones provides significant business opportunities and justification for deploying ad hoc WiFi networks. Since all WiFi devices must comply with the IEEE standard, WiFi products from multiple vendors can be mixed and matched for seamless operation. This has driven the cost of individual WiFi devices low, which in turn, made deployment of WiFi-based networks covering medium to large areas an attractive and, even necessary, business investment.

In this chapter, we describe various trends in the design and deployment of wireless networks based on WiFi and other technologies (Gast, 2005; Macker & Corson, 1998; Murthy & Manoj, 2004). The rest of the chapter is organized as follows. The section "Ad Hoc Wireless Networks" describes pure WiFi networks and their limitations. "Mixed Wireless Networks" describes mixed networks based on WiFi and other wired and wireless technologies to provide robust city-scale networks. "Security in Wireless Networks" describes security issues and vulnerabilities of wireless networks. "RFID Wireless Networks" describes an emerging application of WiFi ad hoc networks: RFID (radio frequency identification) networks based on the WiFi technology for warehouses and large retail stores. "Vehicular Ad Hoc Networks" describes another emerging application of WiFi-based networks: vehicular ad hoc networks for automobiles. The "Summary" section summarizes the chapter.

Ad Hoc Wireless Networks

An ad hoc wireless network is an impromptu network formed by several wireless devices, such as PDAs, laptops, and phones, without relying on an existing network infrastructure

Figure 1. Throughput of a wireless ad hoc network with stationary nodes. The vertical bars indicate throughputs over 1-second intervals. The horizontal line indicates the throughput averaged thus far. The ad hoc network is built using off-the-shelf Linksys 54G routers reprogrammed with Linux operating system. Ad hoc on demand distance vector (AODV) routing protocol is used to discover and maintain routes.

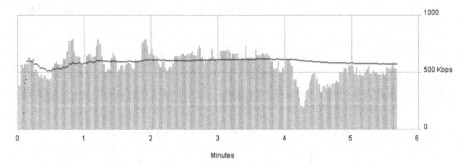

(Perkins, 2000). These devices (denoted as nodes) may be mobile and use a common wireless technology such as WiFi. To facilitate communication among the nodes that are not directly in the radio range of one another, the other nodes act as intermediate routers, just like routers in the Internet. Such networks are useful in military combat situations, where a group of soldiers must be connected to exchange information, or in emergency rescue operations, where there is no network infrastructure or the existing infrastructure has been destroyed. Because of frequent topology changes due to node mobility and due to wireless interference, the existing networking software used for the Internet is not suitable for these ad hoc networks. Consequently, extensive research on routing protocols and transport protocols has been conducted to make ad hoc networks suitable for general-purpose use.

Routing protocols are broadly classified into proactive and reactive protocols. A proactive protocol keeps track of all possible routes within the ad hoc network, and disseminates routing information with others, periodically, or whenever network topology changes significantly. On the other hand, reactive or on-demand routing protocols learn and maintain active routes only. When a new route is needed for a new connection, source of the connection broadcasts, network-wide, a route request (RREQ). The intended destination responds by a route reply (RREP) containing the path information. This process is called route discovery. To minimize the number of transmissions and speedup route discovery, the intermediate nodes that have the requested route may respond to a RREQ.

The two most commonly used transport protocols are user datagram (UDP) and transmission control (TCP) protocols. For compatibility reasons, an ad hoc wireless network must support these protocols. However, TCP is tuned for use on wired networks and does not work well for multihop wireless networks.

Despite several years of research, the performance of current multihop wireless networks is unpredictable. To illustrate the performance issue, we present in Figure 1 the overall network throughput of an 8-node ad hoc network with 7 constant bit rate (CBR) connections, representative of voice over IP traffic, over UDP transport layer (Boppana, 2006). Even though nodes are stationary, the performance varies widely with time, owing to noise and interference caused by transmissions in the network.

Mobility makes it harder to sustain performance in an ad hoc wireless network. To illustrate the performance issues further, we simulated a 50-node mobile ad hoc network in a 1,000 m x 1,000 m field using the ns-2 network simulator (Fall & Varadhan, 1997). Each node has a transmission range of 250 m and nodes move in random directions with an average

Figure 2. Capacity of a single transport-layer connection in a simulated ad hoc network. Owing to the nature of shared transmission space, the capacity of a connection varies inversely proportional to the number of hops from sender to receiver.

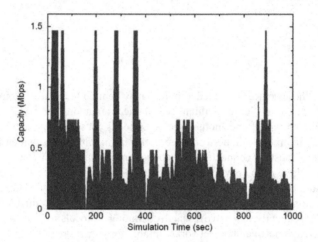

Figure 3. Packet delivery rates of various ad hoc network routing protocols

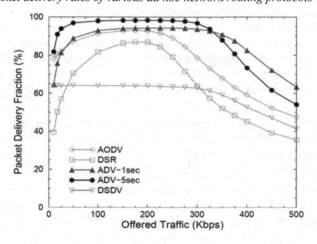

speed of 10 m/s (22.5 miles/hour) and a top speed of 20 m/s. We used a 2 Mbps channel rate for easier analysis. (The current WiFi technology provides various channel rates ranging from 1 Mbps to 54 Mbps, though in practice, the higher rates are used only when the communication nodes are close to each other.)

First, we illustrate the available bandwidth (BW) for a connection without taking any contention or interference for wireless channels (Dyer, 2002). The available BW is based on the number of hops required to reach from a specified source node to its destination node.

Next, we present performance of this network under CBR traffic load. We varied the load from very low to very high, gradually, and measured the performance of the network. We simulated four recent routing protocols: destination sequenced distance vector (DSDV) (Perkins, 2000), adaptive distance vector (ADV) (Boppana & Konduru, 2001), ad hoc on demand distance vector (AODV) (Perkins, Belding-Royer, & Das, 2003), and dynamic source routing (DSR) (Johnson, Maltz, & Hu, 2003). The delivery rate (fraction of injected packets that are delivered to destinations) for this network with various routing protocols is indicated in Figure 3. DSDV and ADV are proactive routing protocols and AODV and DSR are on demand routing protocols. Two variants of ADV are shown based on the amount of time a packet is buffered within a node when there is no route. It is clear that the ability of a mobile ad hoc network to deliver depends greatly on the traffic load, type of routing protocol used, and choice of parameter values (such as buffer time).

Despite these performance issues, ad hoc networks are likely to be the dominant form of local area networks used in future for several reasons.

- Technology developments will make the basic WiFi protocol robust and improve nominal speeds further (Varshney, 2003). Recently, evolving WiFi technology based on MIMO antennas is shown to sustain higher data rates than a fast ethernet.

- Extensive ongoing research on networking software will result in better routing and transport protocols that will exhibit better performance characteristics (Boppana & Zheng, 2005; Desilva, 2004; Dyer, 2002).

- There are no alternatives to mobile ad hoc networks for military combat situations. In fact, Department of Defense (DoD) is one of the early and largest funding agencies for research in this area.

- Wireless networks streaming audio and video will be ubiquitous in consumer homes. Ad hoc networks are particularly attractive because they require no new wiring and satisfy location and space constraints easily (IEEE CCNC, 2006). Already, many consumers with high-speed broadband access have a WiFi-based network (in infrastructure mode using one access point or in multihop mode using additional WiFi extender devices) connecting multiple laptops wirelessly within their homes. Apple's Airport Express is a commercial product designed to stream audio over WiFi channels. The newer WiFi technology based on IEEE 802.11n or the ultra wideband (UWB) wireless technology will likely be used for high-resolution video streaming due to higher BW offered by this technology. However, UWB will be used to complement WiFi networks rather than replace them.

- WiFi based ad hoc networks are the starting point to other types of networks, such as RFID networks and vehicular ad hoc networks (VANETs) (IEEE CCNC, 2005).

In the next two sections, we address twin deficiencies of ad hoc networks: predictable performance and security. First, we describe how to make the performance of WiFi networks robust, and then how to address some of the security issues that require attention in wireless networks.

Mixed Wireless Networks

Given the weaknesses of ad hoc wireless networks, the area covered by them tends to be small. Instead, mixed networks consisting of fixed infrastructure nodes and mobile user nodes are suitable for a medium-range network spanning, for example, a metropolitan area (Boppana & Zheng, 2005). Point-to-point wired, cellular, or WiMAX (based on the IEEE 802.16 standard (IEEE 802.16, 2004) for metropolitan area wireless networks) wireless links among fixed nodes and wireless links for all nodes can be used for connectivity. These networks take advantage of reliability and high bandwidth of wired infrastructure backbone, and flexibility and low cost of wireless links using ad hoc networking concepts. Because these networks make use of ad hoc networking, there is no need for fixed nodes to cover all the desired area. If a fixed node is unavailable as a neighbor, a mobile node can send its data through other mobile nodes to the destination or to the nearest fixed node.

Figure 4. A mixed network with mobile user and fixed infrastructure nodes, denoted by circles and diamonds, respectively. The infrastructure nodes are interconnected by point-to-point links, denoted by dashed lines, for infrastructure support and to provide multiple paths. All nodes are capable of using a common wireless technology, such as WiFi. The radio range of infrastructure nodes is indicated by a circular shaded region.

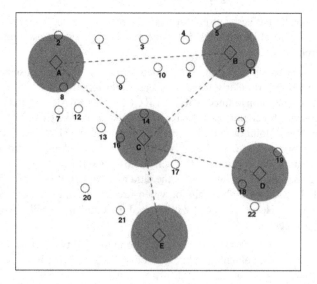

We illustrate this with an example network shown in Figure 4. This network has several mobile nodes that can communicate only via WiFi links and several relatively stationary nodes (denoted, infrastructure nodes) with point-to-point (p2p) links among them. A network of this type can provide multiple paths among user nodes. For example, node 8 in the upper left portion of the network can go through 12 and 13 or A and C to reach node 16. Ad hoc routing is used in cases when a user node is not near an infrastructure node. For example, node 10 can reach node 4 via node 6.

With the advent of new technologies, it is feasible to design such mixed networks. The WiFi is a popular short haul (for distances less than 300 m) wireless link protocol. The fixed infrastructure nodes and p2p links among them are not difficult to set up. The p2p links can be wired links or long-haul wireless links. For example, the new IEEE 802.16 (IEEE 802.16, 2004) is an example of long-haul (for distances less than 10 Km) wireless link protocols. The infrastructure nodes can be already-existing fixed nodes connected via p2p links (for example, access points connected to the Internet), or semi-permanent nodes that remain stationary for a few hours and have p2p links implemented using a different wireless technology. More importantly, elaborate design and implementation to ensure complete geographical coverage by fixed nodes is not necessary, since gaps in the coverage can be managed using ad hoc networking, provided there is enough node density.

To see the performance benefits of mixed networks, we simulated a 60-node network in a 1,500 m X 1,500 m field. We used the Glomosim network simulator (Zeng, Bagrodia, & Gerla, 1998). There are 0, 4, or 9 fixed nodes, and the remaining nodes are mobile with speeds ranging from 1 to 29 m/s. The nominal WiFi link speed is 2 Mbps, and p2p links are full-duplex 2 Mbps. The fixed nodes are placed in a grid pattern, and only adjacent fixed nodes are connected to each other by a p2p link. We used ADV and AODV as the routing protocols for the pure ad hoc network (the network with 0 fixed nodes), and ADV static (ADVS), modified version of ADV to take advantage of p2p links where possible, for the other two networks. ADVSnF indicates the performance of mixed network with n fixed

Figure 5. Performance of 60-node mixed and pure ad hoc networks

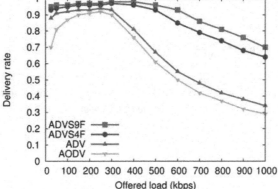

nodes. The delivery rates are given in Figure 5. (See Boppana & Zheng, 2005 for more information.)

Adding a few p2p links (12 links with 9 fixed nodes) improves the delivery rate and overall performance of the network significantly. It is even more illustrative to see the delivery rate, throughput, and packet latencies of a 1,000-node network in a 6 Km × 6 Km area. There are 0, 9, or 25 fixed nodes placed in a grid pattern with only adjacent fixed nodes connected by p2p links. The network with 0 fixed nodes denotes the pure ad hoc network.

These results clearly illustrate the performance benefits of using different link technologies in a mostly WiFi based ad hoc network. They also offer unique business opportunities (Markoff, 2006).

- Mixed networks are easy to set up since the number of stationary nodes required is small (2.5% in the 1,000-node network example). Owing to the use of ad hoc networking concepts, they are not likely to suffer the irksome gaps that are common in cellular networks. In fact, the existing cellular networks can be improved using these techniques. Several cellular networking companies are actively pursuing this type of networks to complement cellular networks.

- They lower the cost of setting up a metropolitan area network to the extent that citywide organizations, such as municipal government agencies or delivery service companies, can set up their own mixed network to provide wireless broadband access without having a telecom company as the carrier.

Figure 6. Delivery rates of 1,000-node mixed networks

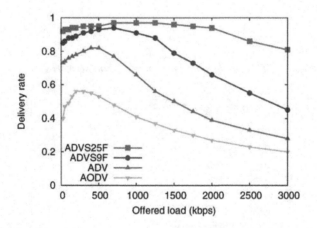

Figure 7. Throughput of 1,000-node mixed networks

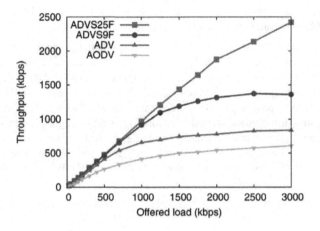

Figure 8. Packet latencies for 1,000-node mixed networks

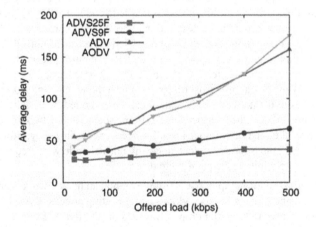

Security in Wireless Networks

Besides performance, security is an important issue in wireless ad hoc networks. The traditional security issues on the Internet are keeping data confidential and unaltered. The most common solution is to encrypt the data by the source application and decrypt it by the destination application (Schneier, 1996). Intermediate nodes cannot examine the contents and cannot alter it without being detected by the destination. Since only some applications need it, this is implemented as an end-to-end solution (that is, the host computers or applications at both ends of a connection invoke and manage the security features). These techniques are also applicable to secure data communication on wireless networks.

In this section, we address a different type of security problem: crippling the network with false route information (Hu, Perrig, & Johnson, 2002; Marti, Giuli, Lai, & Baker, 2000; Zhou & Haas, 1999;). These attacks are on the control traffic rather than data traffic. Wireless networks are more susceptible to this type of attack than wired networks for two reasons: (a) physical access to a network port is not necessary with wireless networks, (b) peer dissemination of routing information and network topology leads to highly leveraged, hard to detect hacker attacks on wireless networks. The issue of unauthorized access to network can be addressed using wireless link-level encryption and decryption (wireless protected access or WPA) and server-based authentication (Varshney, 2003). We describe the second issue in detail.

The attacks on control traffic or routing protocol can be classified into two categories.

- Denial of service (DoS) or resource consuming attack
- Falsifying routes and dropping/delaying data packets

We first describe the impact of the DoS attack. In a routing protocol such as AODV, route discoveries depend on network-wide dissemination (called flooding) of RREQ control packets from a source node seeking route to its destination node. A RREQ broadcasted by a source is rebroadcasted by its neighbors to their neighbors. This is repeated until the destination receives a copy of this RREQ and responds with an RREP control packet that establishes the route between source and destination. A single RREQ broadcasted by a source node results in up to (n-1) additional broadcast transmissions in the wireless network, where n is the number of nodes in the network. This feature can be exploited by a malicious node to launch highly leveraged denial-of-service attacks in mobile ad hoc networks. These malicious nodes behave like the normal nodes in all aspects except that they initiate frequent control packet floods. This is hard to detect since any normal node with frequently broken routes could legitimately initiate frequent route discoveries.

Figure 9 shows the loss of throughput in a 100-node mobile ad hoc network with AODV as the routing protocol and one malicious node initiating routing attacks. Even 1 RREQ/s by the malicious node causes measurable drop in throughput (Desilva & Boppana 2005).

Fortunately, a simple and inexpensive solution to this problem exists. Using statistical profiling of control activity of other nodes, each node can independently determine over-active nodes and effectively shut them off from causing permanent damage to network performance (Desilva & Boppana 2005). With this solution implemented, the performance of the network under attack is shown in Figure 10. Regardless of the attack rate, the normal network throughput is sustained.

The other type of security attack on routing protocol is based on falsifying routes by the malicious node in order to place itself in the path of an active route. This often involves the malicious node claiming a better route than any other node to reach a destination. Data packets received on this route are dropped or delayed arbitrarily by the malicious node.

Figure 9. Loss of throughput with bogus route discoveries by a malicious node in a 100-node mobile ad hoc network. The offered CBR load to network is kept constant at 300, 400, or 500 Kbps, and the throughput achieved is measured as a function of attack rate by the malicious node. The attack rate of zero RREQs/second denotes the normal network.

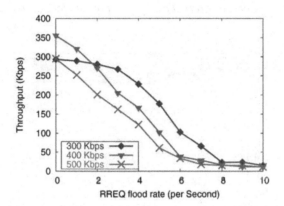

Figure 10. Effectiveness of statistical profiling in the example ad hoc network under DoS attack

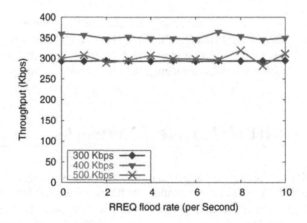

This type of attack is called the blackhole attack. The impact of such attacks can be severe on network performance.

Figure 11 illustrates the impact of a blackhole attack by five malicious nodes in a 100-node network with AODV routing protocol. The malicious nodes send false RREPs in response to 1% of RREQs they hear. The detection of such an attack is expensive.

Figure 11. Impact of blackhole attack over time n a 100-node mobile ad hoc network. There are five malicious nodes sending false RREPs to 1% of RREQs they hear. The attack starts at 200 seconds and stops at 800 seconds. The traffic load is 200 Kbps. The two thick lines (at 200 and 800-second periods) indicate the start and end of the attack. Vertical bars indicate delivery rates for 5-second periods. The jagged horizontal line indicates the average network throughput from the most recent event—start of simulation, start of attack, or end of attack.

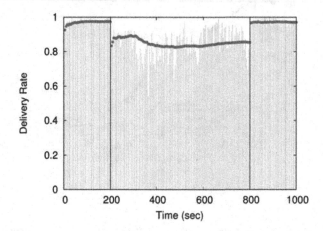

The proposed solutions to mitigate such attacks use hashing and symmetric cryptographic techniques (Hu et al. 2002; Zhou & Haas 1999). This makes the solution even more expensive than the attack itself since each control packet must be verified. Further research is needed to develop efficient solutions to these damaging, but low frequency attacks.

RFID Wireless Networks

Several organizations, including Wal-Mart and Proctor & Gamble (P&G), are currently testing and deploying radio frequency identification (RFID) technology in their supply chains. In addition, the Department of Defense has mandated that its suppliers tag their products at the pallet level using RFID tags. The potential advantages of RFID technology in the supply chain are numerous. RFID technology has the ability to provide up-to-the-minute information on sales of items, and thus can give an accurate picture of the inventory levels. This accuracy may lead to reduction in inventory levels, thus causing a reduction in inventory costs. RFID technology at the pallet level has the potential to automate the distribution of goods in the supply chain between manufacturing plants, warehouses, and retail stores of different organizations, which in turn might reduce labor costs. RFID tags allow companies to identify all items, thus cutting down losses from lost or misplaced inventory.

For the purposes of this section, we assume the supply chain is comprised of the manufacturer, distributor, retailer, and the consumer. As an item with an RFID tag moves from one location to another location in the supply chain, it may be read at several different locations in the supply chain. We define an *RFID transaction* to be an event that corresponds to the reading of an RFID tag by an RFID reader. Each RFID transaction generates data including the RFID tag (EPC), the reader id, and other relevant pieces of information.

The transition of an item with an RFID tag from the manufacturer to the consumer is depicted in Figure 12. In this paper, we assume that the RFID tags are applied at the item, case, and pallet level. For some items, this hierarchy-items in cases and cases in pallets-may not be applicable, and for some items this hierarchy may need to be changed. However, the discussion in this chapter can be readily extended to other hierarchies. As an item is manufactured, an RFID tag is placed on the item, which generates the item creation RFID transaction at the manufacturing facility. Placing an item into a case, placing the case into a pallet, as well as loading a pallet into a delivery truck generate different RFID transactions at the manufacturing facility. At the distributor's warehouse, placing the pallet into a warehouse shelf, and loading the pallet onto a delivery truck (to be delivered to the retail store) generate RFID transactions. In a retail store, events such as shelf replenishment, movement of an item from one shelf to another (possibly because of item misplacement), and sale of an item generate RFID transactions. At the consumer's home, a futuristic model suggests that the consumer's refrigerator (or the storage area if the item does not need to be refrigerated) will be equipped with an RFID tag reader; this results in RFID transactions being generated when an item is placed in the refrigerator and when an item is taken out of the refrigerator, these events possibly triggering a refrigerator replenishment RFID transaction. For more information on RFID transactions and RFID tag reader designs, the reader is referred to Chalasani and Sounderpandian (2004) and Chalasani, Boppana, and Sounderpandian (2005). In each of the facilities (manufacturing facility, the distributor's warehouse, the retail store, and the consumer's home) the tag readers are interconnected, as

Figure 12. Transition of an item from the manufacturer to the consumer in the supply chain and the relevant RFID transactions

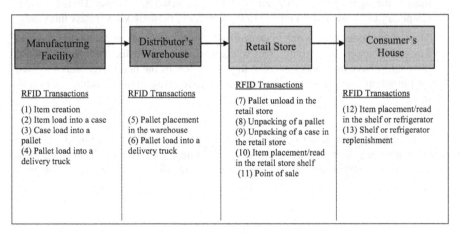

RFID Transactions	RFID Transactions	RFID Transactions	RFID Transactions

Manufacturing Facility → Distributor's Warehouse → Retail Store → Consumer's House

RFID Transactions

(1) Item creation
(2) Item load into a case
(3) Case load into a pallet
(4) Pallet load into a delivery truck

RFID Transactions

(5) Pallet placement in the warehouse
(6) Pallet load into a delivery truck

RFID Transactions

(7) Pallet unload in the retail store
(8) Unpacking of a pallet
(9) Unpacking of a case in the retail store
(10) Item placement/read in the retail store shelf
(11) Point of sale

RFID Transactions

(12) Item placement/read in the shelf or refrigerator
(13) Shelf or refrigerator replenishment

Figure 13. An RFID ad hoc tag reader network; ovals represent tag readers, while squares indicate the RFID tags on items, cases or pallets

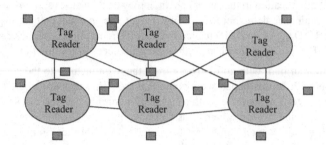

shown in Figure 13. Given the current advances and adaptation trends, the Wi-Fi is likely to be the dominating and economical wireless technology for intertag reader communication. Though there are no commercial implementations, intertag reader network will alleviate communication and performance load on the back-office computer system. In this section, we explore two representative designs of RFID tag reader networks (or simply RFID networks) (Passmore, 2004; RFID.com, 2006).

One may use wired Ethernet (wired) links or wireless links to set up RFID networks. Instead, using only wired or wireless links, mixing both technologies may be advantageous. Combining wired and wireless network technologies to interconnect tag readers (denoted, nodes) provides the benefits of wired network robustness and low-maintenance costs with the flexibility of wireless network for adapting to changing needs. In this type of network, all nodes have wireless capability to communicate among themselves. In addition, some of the nodes have Ethernet connections. There are two possible scenarios.

- Most of the nodes have both wireless and Ethernet connectivity, while the remaining nodes communicate via wireless links only. This scenario models the situation where most of the tag readers are stationary and interconnected by Ethernet. There are a few temporary tag readers that connect to the tag reader network via wireless links only.

- Most of the nodes have wireless capability only and the other nodes have both wireless and Ethernet connectivity. This scenario models the situation where most of the tag readers have only wireless capability and a few of the nodes are interconnected by a different technology and link type to improve connection reliability and performance.

We simulated both types of networks using the Glomosim simulator. We used 81 nodes arranged in a 9 × 9 grid in a 1-sq.-Km field, as shown in Figure 14. The distance between adjacent nodes was 100 meters, and wireless radio transmission range was 125 m. The traffic load consisted of 500-byte packets generated at constant bit rate (CBR). All nodes were stationary for the duration of the simulation (600 seconds). All wired connections were in a near neighbor mesh pattern, in which each node was connected to its adjacent nodes in the grid. The maximum link speed was 2 Mbps (million bits/second) for both wired and wireless links. Though these rates are not representative of what is currently available, the simulation results will be helpful in understanding performance degradation with wireless links in Scenario A and performance improvement with wired links in Scenario B. We used uniform traffic pattern in which each node sends data to all the other nodes with equal probability. We varied the offered load to the network by varying the time between consecutive packets generated by nodes.

For Scenario A, we compared the performance of two networks: one with all wired connections, and another with 9 of the nodes (indicated in black in Figure 14) spaced evenly in the grid pattern with only wireless connectivity. Static routes are used since most of the nodes are wired and mobility is not a practical option. Figure 15 gives the performance impact of wireless vs. wired connections. Up to certain loads, the 9 nodes with only wireless links do as well as they would with wired connections. Beyond that, the wireless transmission interference (interference range is 2-3 times that of valid reception range) limits achievable throughput. For the data we present, loads up to 4 packets/second/node (20 Kbps/node) can be handled by the nodes with wireless links.

For Scenario B, we simulated three different network configurations: no wired links (denoted, 0f), wired links among 4 nodes (denoted in blue in Figure 14) that form an equidistant 2x2 grid (4f), and wired links among 9 nodes (black nodes in Figure 14) that form a 3x3 grid (9f). Though the nodes are stationary during the simulation, the primary reason for using an

Figure 14. Layout of RFID tag reader network. Adjacent nodes are separated by 100 m. The size of the field is 1 Km × 1 Km. Black (dark shade) nodes are the 9 wireless nodes in Scenario A and 9 nodes with wired connections among them in Scenario B. Light shade nodes are the 4 nodes with wired connections among them in the Scenario B.

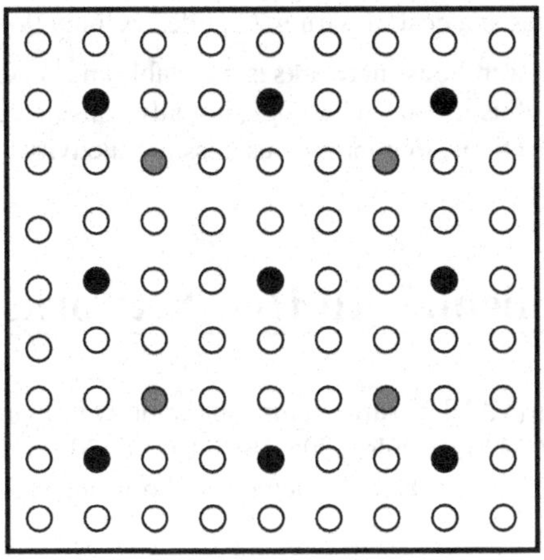

Figure 15.   Impact of wireless links in an all-wired network; throughputs of nine nodes placed in a 3 × 3 grid pattern are examined

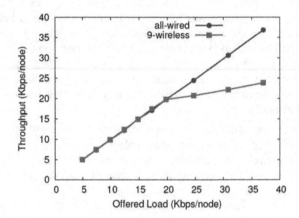

all-wireless or mostly wireless network is the flexibility of relocating tag readers as needed; to adapt to such network topology changes, a dynamic ad hoc routing protocol must be used. In the two configurations with static links, 4 or 12 wired links with 2-Mb/s data rate are used. Figure 16 shows the throughputs of these three networks. While adding 4 wired links to an all wireless network provides about 20% improvement in peak throughput, 12 wired links provide as much as 67% improvement. Since most of the nodes are wireless only, the network is very flexible.

It is noteworthy that the results for Scenario B are not directly comparable to those for Scenario A since we used static routes in the latter case. For comparison purposes, we simulated the two, wired networks with no static routes and ADV as the dynamic routing protocol. While the all-wired network is not affected, the performance of 9-wireless nodes case is reduced to about 12 Kbps/node, about 140% higher than that of the 9f case in Scenario B. But this performance comes at a cost of wiring 72 nodes vs. only 9.

Using WiFi technology for warehouse networks is inevitable and beneficial. RFID networks represent good examples of using the technology, initially considered suitable for military and emergency civil applications, to improve business productivity.

Vehicular Ad Hoc Networks

Vehicular ad hoc networks (VANETs) are exciting and rapidly growing examples of ad hoc networking in practice (ACM Sigmobile, 2005; IEEE CCNC, 2005). The US FCC allocated 75 MHz of spectrum in the 5.8-GHz band for dedicated short-range communication (DSRC)

Figure 16. Impact of wired links in an all-wireless network

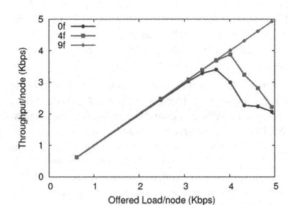

in VANETs (FCC, 2003). A new wireless standard, wireless access for vehicular environments (WAVE), denoted IEEE 802.11p and based on WiFi, is being developed. Compared
to the ad hoc networks described earlier, there are significant differences in the use and
demands placed on VANETs.

Two types of networking concepts will be used to network moving vehicles: (a) One-hop
wireless connectivity from a vehicle to a roadside wireless access point (V2R) and (b) multihop
connectivity among vehicles (V2V). V2R connectivity is similar to Internet connectivity
using WiFi hotspots with mobility added. V2V connectivity will use ad hoc networking concepts similar to mixed networks described earlier. Since vehicular movement is predictable,
VANETs can be designed to perform reliably and efficiently under network overload.

VANETs will be used to improve driver safety in addition to providing Internet connectivity
to users. Consequently, VANETs will be required to support two classes of applications:
safety and nonsafety applications. Emergency road conditions, medical facility location,
and passage of emergency vehicles, such as ambulances, fire trucks, and police cars, are
examples of safety applications. Access to Internet, streaming multimedia to consumers
in vehicles, road congestion advisory, and information of nearby service facilities, such as
restaurants and stores, are examples of nonsafety applications. To accommodate both types
of applications, multiple channels, with some of them dedicated for safety applications and
the others for applications in the order of priority, will be used. In contrast, WiFi is designed
to use one channel for connectivity; multiple radios need to be used for multichannel operation in MANETs and hotspot networks.

VANETs differ from MANETs in terms of energy constraints and security. Since the radios
will be powered by the batteries and engines in vehicles, there will be few energy constraints.
On the other hand, security and disruption to network connectivity will be more problematic
compared to MANETs. Security is more problematic since hackers with unlimited power and

without the need to physical access to a network port can launch the type of attacks currently used on the Internet more easily. Also, since VANETs use wireless links, which have less BW than the wired links used for the Internet, denial-of-service attacks can be devastating. Also, lack of energy constraints mean radios can use high power levels for transmissions (intentionally or inadvertently), which will cause excessive radio interference and reduce V2V network performance.

VANETs provide significant new business opportunities for high-technology companies, service providers, and local businesses. There are significant impediments as well. Involvement of the automobile industry will slow down the process of developing and deploying new technologies for VANETs. A good example is the audio system offered in new automobiles. While the audio players in the consumer market advanced considerably, most manufacturers continue to offer 20-year-old technology as standard equipment, and do not provide any option to connect user equipment. Owing to the intended use of VANETs, there will be significant regulatory constraints by federal, state, and local government agencies.

Summary

Multihop wireless networks based on WiFi technology offer flexible and inexpensive networking possibilities for various purposes ranging from personal networks within consumer homes to citywide departmental networks to wide area vehicular ad hoc networks. While the business significance of citywide ad hoc networks may not be clear in developed countries, these networks will play a crucial role in reaching consumers in rural areas in developing countries. RFID networks improve the efficiency and productivity in the areas of manufacturing and distribution. The biggest and most profitable area for business opportunities may very well be vehicular ad hoc networks. Though the potential of wireless networks seems limitless, the technology available today does not provide dependable network performance of reliability. Extensive research is being conducted on improving the network software and hardware. The future wireless standards, such as IEEE 802.11n, which uses advanced MIMO antennas and new routing and transport protocols, will facilitate designing ad hoc networks that will be suitable for consumer use.

Acknowledgments

Rajendra Boppana's research was partially supported by NSF grants EIA-0117255 and AIA grant F30602-02-1-0001. Suresh Chalasani's research was supported in part by summer research grants awarded by the University of Wisconsin system.

References

ACM Sigmobile. (2005). *ACM International Workshop on Vehicular Ad Hoc Networks*. New York: ACM Press.

Boppana, R. V. (2006). *On setting up a WiFi ad hoc network testbed*. Retrieved December 2006, from http://www.cs.utsa.edu/faculty/boppana/projects

Boppana, R. V., & Konduru, S. P. (2001). An adaptive distance vector routing algorithm for mobile, ad hoc networks. In *Proceedings of IEEE Infocom*. IEEE.

Boppana, R. V., & Zheng, Z. (2005). *Designing ad hoc networks with limited infrastructure support*. Presented at the IEEE Consumer Communication and Networking Conference (CCNC). IEEE.

Passmore, D. (2004). RFID: Network implications, *Business Communications Review*. Retrieved December 2006, from http://www.bcr.com/bcrmag/2004/11/p16.php

Chalasani, S., Boppana, R. V., & Sounderpandian, J. (2005). RFID tag reader designs for retail store applications. In *Proceedings of the 11th Americas Conference on Information Systems (AMCIS)*. Association for Information Systems.

Chalasani, S. & Sounderpandian, J. (2004). RFID for retail store information systems. In *Proceedings of the 10th Americas Conference on Information Systems (AMCIS 2004)*. Association for Information Systems.

Desliva, S. A. (2004). *Techniques to mitigate traffic overload and protocol inefficiencies in mobile ad hoc networks*. PhD dissertation, CS Department, University of Texas at San Antonio.

Desilva, S. & Boppana, R. V. (2005, March). *Mitigating malicious control packet floods in ad hoc networks*. Presented at the IEEE Wireless Communications and Networking Conference.

Dyer, T. D. (2002). *Design and analysis of adaptive routing and transport protocols for mobile ad hoc networks*. PhD dissertation, CS Department, University of Texas at San Antonio.

Fall, F. & Varadhan, K. (1997, November). *NS notes and documentation*. The VINT Project, UC Berkeley, LBL, USC/ISI, and Xerox PARC. Retrieved from http://www-mash.cs.berkeley.edu/ns

Federal Communications Commission. (2003, December 17). *Amendment of the Commission's Rules Regarding Dedicated Short-Range Communication Services in the 5.850-5.925 GHz Band*. FCC 03-324.

Gast, M, (2005). *802.11 wireless networks: The definitive guide* (2nd ed.). O'Reilly Media, Inc.

Hu, Y.-C., Perrig, A., & Johnson, D. B. (2002). Ariadne: A secure on-demand routing protocol for ad hoc networks. In *Proceedings of the 8th ACM International Conference on Mobile Computing and Networking*. New York: ACM Press.

IEEE CCNC. (2005). *The automobile as a network interface.* Presented at the Technology Application Panel, Session 3, IEEE Consumer Communications and Networking Conference.

IEEE CCNC. (2006). *Proceedings of the IEEE Consumer Communication and Networking Conference 2004-2006.* IEEE.

IEEE Computer Society LAN/MAN Standards Committee. (1999). *Part 11: Wireless LAN, medium access control (MAC) and physical layer (PHY) specifications* (Standard ANSI/IEEE 802.11).

IEEE 802.16 Working Group on Broadband Wireless Access Standards. (2004). *IEEE 802.16 standard: WirelessMAN standard for broadband wireless metropolitan area networks* (Standard ANSI/IEEE 802.16).

Johnson, D., Maltz, D., & Hu, Y. (2003). *The dynamic source routing protocol for mobile ad hoc networks.* IETF MANET Working Group, Internet Draft 2003.

Macker, J. P., & Scott Corson, M. (1998). Mobile ad hoc networking and the IETF. *ACM Mobile Computing and Communications Review, 2*(1). New York: ACM Press.

Markoff, J. (2006, February 6). Venture for sharing Wi-Fi draws big-name backers. *New York Times.* Retrieved December 2006 from http://www.nytimes.com/2006/02/06/technology/06mesh.html

Marti, S., Giuli, T., Lai, K., & Baker, M. (2000). Mitigating routing misbehavior in mobile ad hoc networks. In *Proceedings of ACM/IEEE International Conference on Mobile Computing and Networking* (pp. 255-265). New York: ACM Press.

Perkins, C. E. (2000). *Ad hoc networking.* Boston: Addison Wesley.

Perkins, C. E., Belding-Royer, E. M., & Das, S. R. (2003, July). *Ad hoc on demand distance vector (AODV) routing* (RFC 3561). IETF.

RFID-101.com. (2006). *Online guide to RFID technology and products.* Retrieved from http://www.rfid-101.com

Schneier, B. (1996). *Applied cryptography* (2nd ed.). New York: John Wiley & Sons.

Siva Rama Murthy, C., & Manoj, B. S. (2004). *Ad hoc wireless networks: Architectures and protocols.* Prentice Hall.

Varshney, U. (2003). The status and future of 802.11-based WLANs. *IEEE Computer, 36*(6), 102-105.

Zeng, X., Bagrodia, R., & Gerla, M. (1998). Glomosim: A library for parallel simulation of large-scale wireless networks. In *Workshop on parallel and distributed simulation* (pp. 154–161). IEEE.

Zhou, L., & Haas, Z. J.. (1999). Securing ad hoc networks. *IEEE Network Magazine, 13*(6).

Chapter IX

Consumers' Preferences and Attitudes Toward Mobile Office Use:
A Technology Trade-Off Research Agenda

Xin Luo, Virginia State University, USA

Merrill Warkentin, Mississippi State University, USA

Abstract

Consumer preferences, attitudes, and behavior concerning product choice can be of vital importance in the development process and implementation of innovative products or services. The mobile office (MO) is becoming achievable in the business-to-employee (B2E) arena as more work is completed outside the office and the fixed office boundaries extend well beyond the spectrum of the desktop. Potential MO providers (e.g., employers) will encounter adoption resistance as users experience uncertainty. This paper investigates the critical factors in the decision models of consumers when evaluating the acceptance and intention to use MO. It will provide research guidelines for MO designers and developers, IT/IS managers, and IS researchers.

Background

Mobile business (m-business, also known as mobile commerce or m-commerce), an emerging extension of electronic business, has received considerable interest among IS researchers, developers, service providers, and end users. Varshney and Vetter (2002) anticipate that the next phase of e-business will be in the area of m-business with the widespread deployment of wireless technologies. Mobile services have penetrated many leading-edge personal markets such as mobile SMS, mobile games, mobile handset icons, and ring tones. Wireless computing is now becoming widely deployed in the business arena as managers have appreciated the significant added strategic value of having instant access to business information that can enhance work productivity, efficiency, and decision-making, ultimately leading to competitive advantage for the firm. Businesses that cater to consumers' preferences and needs and that capitalize on expanding opportunities, which arise with new technologies, can sustain competitive advantages in today's fiercely competitive marketplace. Deployment of mobile technology infrastructure, along with mobile devices, enables employee mobility and mobility of IT functions. This is transforming businesses processes by enhancing communication, information access, and business transactions from any device anywhere and anytime. Performance benefits from wireless technology adoption are being realized in the business-to-employee (B2E) domain as corporations seek to achieve their business goals by growing their capabilities.

The rapid development of innovative mobile technologies, along with better integration with the existing network infrastructure, presents new challenges for the enterprise. Thanks to existing wireless technologies, such as 2G and 2.5/2.75G, which introduced GPRS (general packet radio service) and EDGE (enhanced data rates for global evolution), new business opportunities are emerging through new value-added services. 3G services are beginning to receive acceptance in such Asian countries as China, South Korea, and Japan. The technological trend and challenge that mobile users are facing is how to better integrate between wireless services, as 3G technologies are being increasingly revamped and further evolved. For the 3G-based CDMA evolutions, handsets will support CDMA, CDMA 1xRTT, and CDMA 1xEV-DO with three kinds of spectrum including 850/1, 900/2, and 100MHz. For the GSM evolution, handsets will support GSM, GPRS, EDGE, and WCDMA, operating in five bands (850/900/1 800/1 900/2 100MHz). In the near future, 4G will surface as a collection of services combining existing technologies, such as 3G and WiFi, with other types of wireless technologies including WiMAX and future evolutions of 3G. 4G will be featured by high usability anytime, anywhere, and with any technology; support for multimedia services at low transmission cost; personalization; and integrated services. As such, 4G will be less disruptive and more widely accepted if the promise is delivered upon. It is expected that 4G networks will be all-IP-based heterogeneous networks that allow users to switch any system at any time and anywhere. 4G systems will not only support data telecommunication services, but also multimedia services. And users in widely diverse locations will use the services, as users can use multiple services from any service provider at the same time. Though 4G mobile technologies may offer even greater opportunities, the gradual maturation and deployment of 3G technologies makes MO become an achievable goal as more work is completed outside the office and the fixed office boundaries extend well beyond the desktop.

There is considerable prior IS research about m-business and wireless technologies (Featherman & Pavlou, 2003; Kleijnen & Ruyter, 2003; Liang & Wei, 2004; Muthaiyah & Ehsan, 2004; Suoranta & Mattila, 2004; Varshney & Vetter, 2002; Zellweger, 1997). However, these research studies have mainly shed light on areas, such as technology acceptance and penetration, as well as technology trends and issues, leaving the domain of consumer preferences and attitudes towards the adoption of innovative products, specifically MO, relatively unexplored. More research is needed to explore the factors that constitute ultimate MO adoption and use, as well as the relative importance of these factors for further diffusion of innovation. In consideration of this objective, we investigate the critical factors in the decision models of consumers when evaluating the acceptance and intention to use MO. Further, we provide research guidelines for MO designers and developers, IT/IS managers, and IS researchers.

Introduction: Mobile Office Technology

Most traditional business applications are developed and deployed for use within fixed office boundaries–using hardware that is not mobile. This confinement results in a wide range of limitations and difficulties if employees cannot access needed information whenever and wherever they want, causing postponement in responding to *customer requests, dissemination of inaccurate information, and delivering lower-quality work output* (Intel, 2004a). Advancements in wireless technologies have triggered a proliferation of mobile devices and broadened the spectrum of solutions for new business applications and services. In the post-2G era, where the business mobile information environment is comparatively dynamic, traditional mobile voice services cannot adequately meet customers' business requirements. 3G networks' throughputs are fairly equivalent to the early DSL networks that revolutionized the home office (Gruman, 2005; Varshney & Vetter, 2002). Notably, according to Gruman (2005), 3G will reduce the expectation gap and delivery gap between wireless and wired connections. For businesses, there is increasing demand for mobile access to multifunctional services that can enhance communication and collaboration as well as management of business information. Liang and Wei (2004), Muthaiyah and Ehsan (2004), and Gruman (2005) indicate that emerging 3G technologies, such as CDMA-based EvDO (evolution, data optimized) and GSM-based UMTS (universal mobile telecommunications system), and HSDPA (high-speed downlink packet access), have the potential to revolutionize MO users using notebook computers and handsets over the high-speed wide area network (WAN).

Due to the dynamic nature of today's business environment, employees are spending less time fixed to their desks and more time in collaborative work meetings, telecommuting, and working in remote locations to accomplish their job objectives. Unlike a fixed office where employees are restricted in a limited environment, MO, including *on the road, at home, and at work* (Cisco, 2002; Gruman, 2005; IBM, 2004; Intel, 2004a, 2004b; North-Smith, 2002), expands the reach of the office environment and provides employees with access to their information, applications/services, and teams, in an anytime and anywhere model, thereby eliminating the obstacles of fixed office boundaries. As more work is completed outside the office and as office boundaries extend well beyond the spectrum of desktop computing, many of the solid business benefits from wireless technology adoption are being realized in the B2E domain. According to Kleijnen and Ruyter (2003), MO has great potential to become one of the most widely utilized m-business solutions with the global user base potentially exceeding 100 million in 2004. It can beef up productivity for employees, since having real-time access to business information is key to increasing productivity and corporate profitability as a whole. The congruence of the findings of Kleijnen and Ruyter (2003), Cisco (2002), IBM (2004), North-Smith (2002), Liang and Wei (2004), Gruman (2005), and Muthaiyah and Ehsan (2004) is that unique MO services, thanks to the revolutionarily enhanced 3G technologies, consist of *accelerating mobile communication and collaboration services* (e-mail, e-fax, unified messaging, groupware messaging), *mobile business information management services* (real-time calendar events, address books, to-do task lists, calculator, word processor), and *mobile information access services* (access to CRM, access to corporate files and corporate databases via secure mobile portal, access to external business information services). These process facilitation services are increasingly becoming incorporated in a mobile corporate portal that is a combination of hardware and software with integrated network development, timely information management, and seamless security mechanisms to enable communications between wireless networks and devices.

Being able to create new expectations among business users who want to constantly maintain work sessions without disruption and disconnection *on the road, at home, or at work*, the emerging deployment of the 3G-powered MO initiatives will greatly transform and improve the way employees work and communicate with colleagues, customers, suppliers, and vendors. These improvements also contribute to rapid responsiveness, decreased costs, improved productivity and work efficiency, and better work/life balance in terms of more flexibility and choices. Managers, however, must understand whether and how MO would be accepted and ultimately adopted by employees/users in order to help companies achieve organizational objectives and obtain competitive advantage. Also, potential providers of MO will encounter a high uncertainty about consumers' acceptance and intention to use. A lack of studies directly investigating the adoption and diffusion patterns of MO is to be expected due to the newness of the MO initiatives *per se*. Employee/user behavior in the MO context also has remained rather uncharted territory, which leads to an important topic for further research within the MIS discipline.

Theoretical Foundation

The theoretical framework of this chapter is grounded in the innovation diffusion theory (IDT) and perceived characteristics of innovating (PCI). Despite the fact that there is little empirical research conducted on MO, there is a plethora of adoption theories and models that investigate and capture user behavior characteristics. In IS research area, the landmark is the technology acceptance model (TAM), proposed by Davis (1989) and Davis (1993), that identified ease-of-use (EOU) and usefulness as the two key determinants influencing user adoption. However, Plouffe et al. (Plouffe, Hulland, & Vandenbosch, 2001) indicate that TAM's parsimony makes individual responses to new technologies differ depending on the context. In a bid to integrate the main user acceptance models, Venkatesh, Morris, Davis, and Davis (2003) formulated the unified theory of acceptance and use of technology (UTAUT), which exhibits significantly enhanced predictive value for adoption intention, with an adjusted R square of approximately 70%. Yet, one weakness of the UTAUT model is that the empirical base did not include e-commerce or m-commerce technologies, which Venkatesh et al. (2003) identified as needing further investigation and testing. Consistent with Plouffe et al. (2001), Kleijnen and Ruyter (2003) argue that the narrow focus of the adoption concepts hinders us from identifying other potential drivers of m-commerce adoption. User acceptance of m-commerce-oriented MO can be identified as a technology adoption. Following the recommendation of Kleijnen and Ruyter (2003), we thus focus on the adoption process in search of valuable insights for building a theoretical framework for critical success factors of MO.

In the domain of adoption process, innovation, and diffusion (ID) is extensively researched and is "*perhaps one of the most widely researched and best documented social phenomena*" (Mahajan & Peterson, 1985). In ID research, IDT, proposed by Rogers (1995), is the most acceptable and reliable framework that has been fairly widely validated in sociology, psychology, and communications as well as IS to explain user adoption of technical innovations. According to Rogers (1995), innovation is "*an idea perceived as new by the individual*" and diffusion is "*the process by which an innovation spreads*." As a consequence, diffusion processes result in the acceptance or penetration of a new idea, behavior, or physical innovation (Rogers, 1995). To make an innovation successful, Rogers' IDT has identified five critical characteristics: relative advantage, compatibility, complexity, communicability, and trialability. Further, Moore and Benbasat (1991) expanded IDT by proposing perceived characteristics of innovating (PCI) in which three additional constructs, including voluntariness, image, and result demonstrability, were identified for ID research. As the key antecedents to technology adoption decision (Plouffe et al., 2001), these PCI factors, along with the additional constructs resided in MO context, must be explored and explained.

- **Relative advantage (perceived usefulness):** The degree to which an innovation is perceived as being better than its precursor (Moore & Benbasat, 1991; Rogers, 1995; Venkatesh et al., 2003). This construct, particularly in MO study, contains issues such as usability and availability. Here, usability relates to enhanced 3G network throughput for wireless business applications or services and application design to deliver the right information to the right users; availability relates to assured network that is reliable in the wireless network in terms of seamless service coverage and handy mobile access.

- **Compatibility:** The degree to which an innovation is perceived as being consistent with the existing values, needs, and past experiences of potential adopters (Moore & Benbasat, 1991; Rogers, 1995; Venkatesh et al., 2003). This relates to the issue of relevance of technology (Wang & Butler, 2003) and interoperability, as well as integration in terms of open standard, of the MO environment with mainline business and office support systems.

- **Complexity**, also referred to as perceived ease-of-use (PEOU), is the degree to which an innovation is perceived as being difficult to use (Davis, 1989, 1993; Moore & Benbasat, 1991; Rogers, 1995; Venkatesh et al., 2003). This can relate to ease of accessing business information, the amount of effort it takes to comprehend the functionality of mobile devices and programs, and how easy it is to retrieve and send information in 3G networks.

- **Communicability:** The extent to which the innovation lends itself for communication, particularly the extent to which the use of the innovation is observable by others (Moore & Benbasat, 1991; Rogers, 1995; Venkatesh et al., 2003). This relates to social influence (also known as "social norm"), since use of an innovation is often influenced by a social context, including supervisors, peers, and others that are highly regarded (Karahanna & Straub, 1999; Kleijnen & Ruyter, 2003). Users might perceive the need to use MO services to achieve work objectives with job-related participants.

- **Image:** The degree to which use of an innovation is perceived to enhance one's image or status in one's social system (Moore & Benbasat, 1991; Rogers, 1995; Venkatesh et al., 2003). According to Plouffe et al. (2001), it signifies the extent to which a user believes an innovation will add social prestige or status.

- **Result demonstrability (RD):** The tangibility of the results of using the innovation, including their observability and communicability (Moore & Benbasat, 1991; Rogers, 1995; Venkatesh et al., 2003). This relates to visibility, which Wang and Butler (2003) consider as the degree to which change is apparent to users. The more visible and more accessible technology changes are, the more likely individual users are to be aware of them and, therefore, more likely to carefully evaluate them. This is in line with Zaltman, Duncan, and Holbek (1973), and Moore and Benbasat (1991) that *"the more amenable to demonstration the innovation is and the more its advantages are, the more likely it is to be adopted."*

Additionally, we propose that *perceived risk* (PR) and *perceived security* (PS) be included into the ID taxonomy for wireless computing. Despite significantly improved technical advancements in 3G security mechanisms, MO users might still be concerned about sensitive information transmitting in the open airwaves. In fact, one of the most pressing concerns for businesses considering wireless computing relates to the security in operations. *PR* refers to the extent to which a functional or psychosocial risk a consumer feels he/she is taking when purchasing and use a product. Kleijnen and Ruyter (2003) further define perceived risks as the extent to which risks are attributed to the mobile services. It greatly affects a user's intention to use a particular product/service (Featherman & Pavlou, 2003; Pavlou & Gefen, 2004). User's perception of unsatisfactory security on the Internet is one of the primary reasons hindering online operation (Zellweger, 1997). From a user's perspective, adapted from Chellappa (2005), we define *PS* as the subjective probability with which users believe their sensitive information (business or private) will not be viewed, stored, and manipulated during work sessions by unauthorized parties in a manner consistent with their confident expectations. And we deem that the relationship between perceived risk and perceived security for user adoption is reversed: the more risks perceived by users, the less likely users are to adopt the MO services; the more security perceived by users, the more likely users are to adopt the MO services.

Based on TAM, IDT, and PCI, as well as such new constructs as perceived risk and perceived security, a conceptual framework for mobile office adoption is proposed (see Figure 1). We argue that PR and PS are negatively related to the intention to use mobile office. Further, other constructs, such as perceived usefulness, complexity, compatibility, communicability, image, and result demonstrability are positively related to the intention to use mobile office.

Figure 1. Proposed framework for mobile office adoption

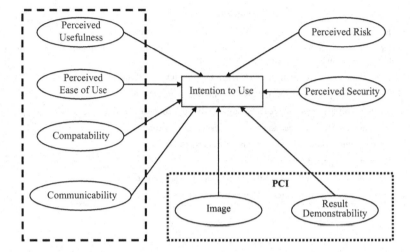

Implications and Research Agenda

The rapid and innovative developments in wireless technologies can be of significant contribution to current and future professional communications. Mobile office technology has the strong potential to extend the office boundary toward an anywhere/anytime model. It is of crucial importance to gauge how MO users would make the decision for technology acceptance and what key factors influence their decision-making. Table 1, containing guidelines for research and practice, is thereby proposed for both researchers and practitioners for further analysis and investigation on MO acceptance and trade-off research. It is necessary for both practitioners and researchers to understand which factor is the most important and which factor is comparatively the least important toward technology adoption.

IS researchers should develop and pursue sound empirical research based on the IS acceptance theories, including TAM, IDT, and PCI, combined with practical field-based research utilizing the case method and surveys of MO users. Such research would introduce a new avenue for innovative technology adoption research and would be of help for practitioners in the field of professional communications to understand the trade-offs that consumers are willing to make for the technology adoption decision.

Mobile office must be a strategic part of a company's IT portfolio, rather than simply a technological tool for tactical productivity gains. Furthermore, the workplace of the future will be an open, collaborative realm, with less reliance on geographic limitations between the physical location of the organization and its employees. We must also pursue practical questions such as (1) which factors are consumers most concerned with when electing to adopt MO for professional communications?, and (2) what is the trade-off that consumers might make for accepting and adopting MO technology?

Table 1. Guidelines for research and practice

What are the objectives?
• Understand how users make the decision for MO technology acceptance.
• Understand which key factors influence MO users' decision making when electing to adopt MO for professional communications. What are the trade-offs?
• Understand the user's requirements, so that appropriate MO technologies can be adopted.
• Understand the impact of the technology on teams and organizations.
• Train individuals and teams so the technology can be applied most effectively.
• Understand the factors that lead to greater success with the technology.
• Train to leverage the technology for the organization's benefit.
• Understand the expected outcomes of various implementation scenarios.
• Provide awareness to employees so that individuals use technologies in best ways.
• Develop "best practices" for MO implementation to guide further usage patterns.

The application of emerging technologies must be accompanied by careful organizational research that allows managers to understand the user's requirements, the impact of the technology on teams and organizations, the factors that lead to greater success with the technology, and the expected outcomes of various implementation scenarios. Without careful *a priori* and *ex poste* analysis, technology can have unintended consequences. The research factors and preliminary agenda detailed in this paper will facilitate greater understanding of this important socio-technical phenomenon, and will contribute to its success. The findings of this stream of research will enable future managers to confidently implement MO with a presumption of positive strategic outcomes for the individual users and also for the entire organization.

References

Chellappa, R. K. (2005). *Consumers' trust in electronic commerce transactions: The role of perceived privacy and perceived security.* Under review.

Cisco. (2002). *Cisco mobile office.* Retrieved August 15, 2005 from http://www.cisco.com/asiapac/mobileoffice/index.shtml

Davis, F. D. (1989). Perceived usefulness, perceived ease of use, and user acceptance of information technology. *MIS Quarterly, 13*(3), 318.

Davis, F. D. (1993). User acceptance of information technology: System characteristics, user perceptions and behavior impacts. *International Journal of Man-Machine Studies, 38*, 475-487.

Featherman, M. S., & Pavlou, P. A. (2003). Predicting e-services adoption: A perceived risk facets perspective. *International Journal of Human-Computer Studies, 59*, 451-474.

Gruman, G. (2005). Taking it to the streets: 3g arrives. *InfoWorld, 27*(10), 30.

Heijden, H. v. d. (2004). User acceptance of hedonic information systems. *MIS Quarterly, 28*(4), 695-704.

IBM. (2004). *Mobile office: The next breakthrough in professional productivity gains.* Retrieved August 15, 2005 from http://www.incentric.com/solutions/solutions/Mobileoffice_The_nextbreakthrough.pdf

Intel. (2004a). *Anytime, anywhere mobile office.* Retrieved August 15, 2005 from http://cache-www.intel.com/cd/00/00/10/28/102829_pp022001_sum.pdf

Intel. (2004b). *Solutions for mobile network operators.* Retrieved August 15, 2005 from http://www.cisco.com/en/US/netsol/ns341/ns396/ns177/networking_solutions_white_paper09186a00801fc7fa.shtml

Karahanna, E., & Straub, D. W. (1999). Information technology adoption across time: A cross-sectional comparison of pre-adoption and post-adoption beliefs. *MIS Quarterly, 23*(2), 31.

Kleijnen, M., & Ruyter, K. d. (2003). Factors influencing the adoption of mobile gaming services. In B. E. Mennecke & T. J. Strader (Eds.), *Mobile commerce technology, theory and applications* (Vol. 11, pp. 202-217). Hershey, PA: Idea Group Publishing.

Liang, T.-P., & Wei, C.-P. (2004). Introduction to the special issue: Mobile commerce applications. *International Journal of Electronic Commerce, 8*(3), 7.

Mahajan, V., & Peterson, R. A. (1985). *Models for innovation diffusion (quantitative applications in the social sciences).* Beverly Hills, CA: SAGE Publications.

Moore, G. C., & Benbasat, I. (1991). Development of an instrument to measure the perceptions of adopting an information technology innovation. *Information Systems Research, 2*(3), 173-191.

Muthaiyah, S., & Ehsan, S. D. (2004). *Readiness towards 3g: Antecedents of 3g adoption and deployment in Malaysia.* Paper presented at the Wireless Information Systems.

North-Smith, L. (2002). *Mobile office Solutions: Real-time access to PIM/e-mail.* Retrieved August 15, 2005 from http://www03.ibm.com/industries/wireless/doc/content/bin/real-time_access.pdf

Pavlou, P. A., & Gefen, D. (2004). Building effective online marketplaces with institution-based trust. *Information Systems Research, 15*(1), 37.

Plouffe, C. R., Hulland, J. S., & Vandenbosch, M. (2001). Richness versus parsimony in modeling technology adoption decisions—understanding merchant adoption of a smart card-based payment system. *Information Systems Research, 12*(2), 208.

Rogers, E. M. (1995). *Diffusion of innovation* (4th ed.). New York: Free Press.

Suoranta, M., & Mattila, M. (2004). Mobile banking and consumer behavior: New insights into the diffusion pattern. *Journal of Financial Service Marketing, 8*(4), 354-366.

Varshney, U., & Vetter, R. (2002). Mobile commerce: Framework, applications and networking support. *Mobile Networks and Applications, 7*, 185-198.

Venkatesh, V., Morris, M. G., Davis, G. B., & Davis, F. D. (2003). User acceptance of information technology: Toward a unified view. *MIS Quarterly, 27*(3), 425.

Wang, X., & Butler, B. S. (2003). *Individual technology acceptance under conditions of change.* Paper presented at the International Conference on Information Systems, Seattle, WA.

Zaltman, G., Duncan, R., & Holbek, J. (1973). *Innovations and organizations.* New York: Wiley and Sons.

Zellweger, P. (1997). Web-based sales: Defining the cognitive buyer. *Electronic Markets, 7*(3), 10-16.

Section III

Global Outsourcing of Business Services

Chapter X

Sourcing and Outsourcing Arithmetic

Tapen Sinha, Instituto Technológico Autónomo de México, Mexico and
University of Nottingham, UK

K. Subhadra, ICICI Bank, India

Abstract

This chapter studies outsourcing from the United States to India. First, we show that outsourcing is not taking most jobs out of the United States. Second, we argue that outsourcing does not contradict trade theory. Third, we analyze how India has come to occupy a preeminent position in outsourcing. Fourth, we show that the Indian dominance is likely to continue well into the next decade. Finally, we discuss some risks associated with outsourcing.

Introduction

The Greek philosopher Seneca said over 2 millennia ago, "There is nothing new under the sun." Outsourcing is nothing new either. It is well known that the Roman Empire had out-sourced tax collection in far-flung places. As a result, a recurrent theme in Edward Gibbon's historical treatise, *The History of The Decline and Fall of the Roman Empire,* is that the decline is attributable, to some extent, to outsourcing.

In the eighteenth and the nineteenth century, England outsourced, to private contractors, the maintenance and operation of streetlights, the management of prisons, and the repair of public highways. However, historically, most outsourcing has been associated with "non-essential" services. PriceWaterhouseCoopers defines outsourcing as "the long-term contracting out of non-core business processes to an outside provider to help achieve increased shareholder value" (http://www.pwcglobal.com). On the other hand, Gartner Group defines it as "the delegation of one or more IT-intensive business processes to an external provider that, in turn, owns, administrates and manages the selected processes based on defined and measurable performance metrics." Unlike PriceWaterhouseCoopers, Gartner avoids any reference to noncore business, it focuses instead on information technology (IT). Outsourcing of strategic business services is relatively new. It started with Eastman Kodak outsourcing information technology (IT) to three external partners in 1989.

During the 2004 presidential election in the United States, it riled the political world so much that the Coalition for Economic Growth and American Jobs suggested that instead of calling the phenomenon "outsourcing," we should use a more neutral term, "worldwide sourcing" (Koffler, 2004).

The loss of white-collar jobs due to outsourcing has prompted many U.S. state governments to ban foreign contractors from bidding altogether. In a telling example, the governor of Indiana canceled a $15 million contract with an Indian company to process state unemploy-ment claims. The next-lowest bidder, an American firm, was eventually given the same job for $23 million (Maranjian, 2004).

In this chapter, *we focus on outsourcing from the United States to India because the United States has become the largest outsourcing country whereas India has become the largest host country.* In that context, we first put outsourcing in proper perspective in terms of job losses. Second, we discuss outsourcing in the context of trade theory. Third, we discuss the reasons and the types of outsourcing. India has become the focus of the entire outsourcing debate because a substantial number of outsourcing contracts in the past 10 years between developed and developing countries have gone to India. Therefore, we discuss how and why India has become such an important source of outsourcing. Finally, we discuss outsourcing risks.

Outsourcing in Perspective

In 2002, John C. McCarthy of Forrester Research estimated that over a period of 15 years, some 3.3 million jobs would go offshore as a result of outsourcing (McCarthy, 2002). Of this 3.3 million, 2.3 million jobs are going to go to India. That is, over 60% of these jobs are going to migrate to India. These figures created a political uproar.

To take one example, in 2003, Delta Air Lines outsourced some of its reservation functions to two Indian companies. It saved about $12 million in costs by the end of 2005. The service providers handled simple reservations, while complex ones were taken care of by agents based in the United States. There were protests, leading some states in the United States to *legislate against* such outsourcing for *government contracts*. What was little noticed was the fact that the job losses would happen over a period of *15 years*.

We need these figures in perspective. The Bureau of Labor Statistics estimates show that seasonally adjusted job losses *every quarter* during 1995-2003 were in the range of 7 and 8 million jobs. Thus, outsourcing is and will stay small potatoes in terms of job losses and creation in the United States. Of course, when trade in services causes job losses domestically, a similar number of jobs are created at the same time. By the same token, it does not make sense to concentrate job losses due to *import* of services alone. We need to examine the corresponding figures for *export* of services. The total value of *export* of private services amounted to $131.01 billion in 2003, whereas the *import* of private services was worth $77.38 billion in 2003. Thus, the U.S. had a $53.64 billion surplus in the trade of services. Farrell (2003) estimates that 1 dollar spent on outsourcing will result in 58 cents of company cost savings, 5 cents of additional U.S. goods and services bought, 4 cents for repatriated earnings (when the outsourcing is to the subsidiary of a U.S. company), and 45 to 47 cents from new jobs created by the outsourcing company. Therefore, at the *global* level, $1 on outsourcing produces $1.12-$1.14 worth of benefits (Phillips, 2004).

Does Outsourcing of Services Contradict Trade Theory?

Many laypeople seem to think that outsourcing of high-tech jobs from the United States to India (*from* a developed *to* a developing country) contradicts trade theory. We argue that trade theory is not contradicted.

Economists have developed models to answer the question of why countries trade. The first classic answer came from David Ricardo in 1821. His explanation was based on comparative advantage. A country with comparative advantage in producing wine would export wine. This does not sound like a profound idea until one considers the essence of comparative advantage. One key insight of Ricardo was that a country may have absolute advantage in producing everything, but it cannot have comparative advantage in producing everything. Thus, it is logically impossible for a country to be importing or exporting everything.

Heckscher (1919) and Ohlin (1928) proposed a different theory. The theory of Heckscher and Ohlin states the following. In the absence of trade barriers and without any cost of transportation, a country would export only those goods that use its more abundant factors of production. A logical extension is "factor price equalization." Under the conditions of Heckscher and Ohlin, if all markets are perfectly competitive, the price of each factor of production will be equalized across countries. Free trade will equalize not only commodity prices but also factor prices, so that all workers earn the same wage rate and all units of capital will earn the same rental return in all countries regardless of the factor supplies or the demand patterns in the countries. Thus, Heckscher-Ohlin theory says that a country will export products that use its abundant factors of production intensively.

In our context, we could translate that theory saying that the United States should export skilled-labor abundant products. This is contradicted by the outsourcing of skilled labor tasks to India (assuming India is not skilled-labor abundant). However, if we go back to Ricardian theory, it says that a country will export goods in which it has a comparative advantage, that is, in which it has the best among its (possibly bad) technologies. Why? Poor productivity in a developing country like India leads to low wages. Therefore, in a product where the productivity is not as bad, the country's low wages allow for exports. This alone can explain *service* exports from India to the United States (Feenstra, 2005). Trade between developed and developing countries arises due to traditional comparative advantage, largely determined by differences in endowment patterns.

Reasons for Outsourcing

Kakabadse and Kakabadse (2000) conducted the first large-scale survey of views about outsourcing by companies. They studied outsourcing practice and its strategic importance among 700 companies in the U.S. and Europe. They discovered that even though most companies were either actively outsourcing or thinking about it, they are doing it for different reasons. Some viewed outsourcing relationships as potential strategic alliances and others saw outsourcing primarily as a way of reducing operating costs, whether in their core business or not. Thus, the first group viewed it as a strategic response of a company whereas the second group saw it as a tactical response to business conditions.

There was also a difference in the response of the American companies and the European companies. The American companies took a wider strategic view of outsourcing: pursuing added value through best practice, improvements in service quality, focus on core competencies, and the use of technology in addition to cost reduction. European companies viewed the practice of outsourcing primarily as a way to cut costs (see also Odindo et al., 2004).

Kinds of Outsourcing

The most natural types of outsourcing take place in the services sector. Of course, not all types of services can be outsourced. An estimated 70% of U.S. service jobs (e.g., retail, restaurant, hotel, and personal-care services) are geographically fixed and not in danger of being outsourced (Farrell, 2003, p. 5). Banking and insurance are the most natural candidates for outsourcing most of their work. In retail banking, many business processes, such as account maintenance, opening accounts, check processing, can be outsourced, as well as administration of funds. For insurance companies, claims processing can easily be outsourced. Similarly, business processes, such as benefits administration, and payroll processing of *any company*, can be outsourced.

There are some other services that do not require face-to-face interaction that also can be outsourced for most businesses. Services that have been successfully outsourced for the past 5 years include telesales, customer service, technical support help desk, e-mail support, fax responses, live but not face-to-face interaction (such as chat room customer service), general telemarketing, and collection of receivables.

The form of outsourcing can be quite different. The multinational company could set up a wholly owned subsidiary (called a *captive*). The first companies to outsource to India such as American Express, GE, or IBM did it by setting up captives. A more symbiotic relation is set up through a joint venture. Many companies that came later into the market offer services in a joint venture setup. Nowadays, outsourcing is being offered through a third party. The third-party operation is much cheaper to run as it is not required to have people working in the operation that are on the payroll of the company. Operating a third-party deal requires a high degree of trust between the company that is contracting out and the company that is doing the operation. Outsourcing can also be done through classic *build-operate-transfer* (BOT) method.

India Calling

How did India become the major outsourcing partner? There were three sequential events in the U.S. that drove it, and another sequence of events in India that made it possible.

First, starting in 1995-1996 and culminating in December 1999, there was the so-called millennium bug problem (also called the Y2K problem). It required fixing the codes of hundreds of thousands of mission critical computer programs before the arrival of the Year 2000. The fear was that critical computer programs being used by banks, power plants, air-line controllers, and other critical systems will reset their internal clocks playing havoc in the international financial markets, not to mention accidents caused by misdirected airline controllers, and nuclear power plants, among others. A vast portion of the work fixing these programs was outsourced to India.

Second, in the late 1990s, the market for software boomed in the U.S. Many companies outsourced their software needs to India. Some were done with captives in India (such as American Express, IBM, or GE). Others were contracted out to external providers.

Third, with the recession of 2000-2001 in the U.S., companies were looking for ways to cut cost. One solution was to farm out back-office paperwork to other countries with cheaper but qualified labor. India became the natural choice.

In all three counts stated, India became the most sought after complement.

Advantage India

Business Climate

One way to measure how attractive India is compared with other countries is to see how India stacks up. Recent studies have put India against Brazil, China, and Russia to highlight the growth areas around the world (Wilson & Purushothaman, 2003). In Figure 1, we compare total number of business articles published in *The New York Times, Wall Street Journal, Washington Post, Los Angeles Times, Chicago Tribune, Forbes, Fortune, BusinessWeek, Time, Newsweek,* and *US News & World Report* during the year 2004. It shows that the number of business news items on India is well below that of its main competitor, China. Even Mexico and Russia had more media coverage in business news. However, when we compare the news items that talked about outsourcing, India dwarfed every other country by a big margin.

Western Media Perceptions

In 2004, Edelman (http://www.edelman.com) published a media audit. In that study, a survey was conducted among the media news leaders with the following question: "When you think of these countries as an emerging market, what comes to mind?" The results are reported in Table 1. India is the *only* country in that group that is associated with the phrase "innovation" and "English Language." Democracy is another feature that prominently appeared whereas China was noted for its lack of democracy. However, economic growth and population size did not seem to feature in the commentary on India, though the phrase "Good Business Environment" did, but the same is the case for all the other countries in the survey. Innovation and the use of English bode well for conducting business in IT, in particular in outsourcing.

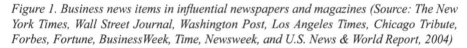

Figure 1. Business news items in influential newspapers and magazines (Source: The New York Times, Wall Street Journal, Washington Post, Los Angeles Times, Chicago Tribune, Forbes, Fortune, BusinessWeek, Time, Newsweek, and U.S. News & World Report, 2004)

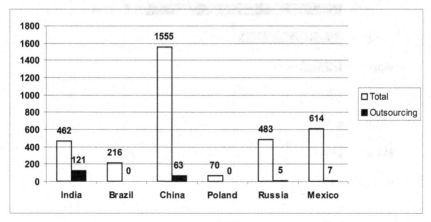

Table 1. When you think of these countries as an emerging market, what comes to mind? (Source: Edelman's India Audit Report, 2004)

India	China	Mexico	Brazil	Russia	Poland
Democracy	*Lack of* Democracy	Good Business Environment	Economy	Trade	Democracy
English Language	Good Business Environment	Economy	Good Business Environment	Economy	Good Business Environment
Innovation	Growth	Democracy			
Good Business Environment	Huge Population				

This perception of the media about the English language advantage of India is no accident; neither is the perception of innovation. For the Y2K problem, India had a ready source of English-speaking computer programmers who could deliver the requisite modification reliably. In the U.S., such programmers were not there at the time in sufficient numbers. This fact has not escaped the attention of the newsmakers.

Human Resource

The available pool of university graduates is an important element in the search for qualified workers to do the job reliably. There too, India has a big advantage over China, its nearest rival in terms of size. Figure 2 shows us that India produces twice as many college graduates as China. Moreover, graduates in India have a better command of the English language than their Chinese counterparts.

Figure 2. Number of university graduates in 2001

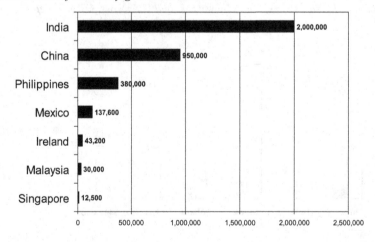

Table 2. Cost comparison between India and the U.S. (Source: McKinsey Quarterly and Asia/Pacific Research Center [quoted in Miller, 2003)

Job Category	India	U.S.
Software Developer	$6/hour	$60/hour
CPA	$15,000/year	$75,000/year
Claims Adjuster	$300/month	$1,500/month
Call Center	$1.50/hour	$10/hour

Pioneering outsourcing companies like American Express, IBM, or GE found that moving the back office to India created value. The human resources are far cheaper than their western counterparts (see Table 2). Depending on the type of service, the cost in the U.S. was 5 to 10 times as high as in India. It should be emphasized that these estimates do not reflect the cost to the companies for getting specific projects done. However, projects that require large input from human resources (for example, debugging programs or reconciling accounts), the difference in cost leads to 50% to 75% cost saving while not sacrificing any quality of the jobs done.

The level of Internet development had already reached a stage so that the delivery of such services became possible in real time. There had also been a dramatic reduction in data transmission cost between 1979 and 2000 by a factor of 10 (http://www.neweconomyindex. org/section1_page13.html).

In addition, the infrastructure in India to handle increased Internet traffic was in place. Upgrading of telephony made it possible to stay connected to the international telephone network 100% of the time. Upgrading of physical infrastructure was accompanied by a general opening up of the Indian economy since 1991. This meant that it became possible for large multinationals to form captive companies in India or pursue long-term contracts with their Indian partners.

Team India

In the past few years, most of the business process outsourcing (BPO) contracts won by Indian players are in IT-enabled services (ITeS). Some of the Indian companies initially started as low-cost services such as call centers. But with time, large companies have started focusing on the high-end services due to high margins in those areas, and are climbing up the value chain. The Indian BPO industry has been mainly dominated by call centers until recently.

The players in the Indian BPO industry can be classified into five categories on the basis of their ownership structure: captive players, third-party service providers, BPO operations by Indian IT companies, U.S. BPO majors, and BPO units by other companies (see Table 3).

Table 3. Types of outsourcing companies

Ownership Structure	Description
Captive Players	The BPO centers are started and managed by the foreign companies. The captive centers usually process only parent company's work. Example: GE operating machine design centers in India.
Third-Party Service Providers	These are the companies started by the group of individuals with funding from venture capitalists. These players generally have to compete with others for every contract. Mostly they compete on the basis of cost. Most companies in India are of this type.
BPO units of Indian IT companies	These are the units started by established Indian IT companies to take advantage of the BPO wave. These companies have advantage of well-established brand name and management of the IT companies. Wipro Spectramind, Nipuna fall into this category.
Subsidiaries of U.S. BPO companies	With many western companies outsourcing their work to India, some of the U.S. BPO companies have started their subsidiaries in India to retain their clients. Examples are EDS, Accenture, Deloitte.
BPO units of Indian companies	Not only IT companies, many companies from other streams also entered BPO industry through their subsidiaries. Examples are HLL, Reliance, ICICI Bank.

The captive players are the companies that are wholly owned subsidiaries of the foreign companies that transferred their processes to India to take advantage of low costs in India. The initial entrants into Indian BPO industry are British Airways, American Express, and GE.

The success of these companies with outsourcing has prompted many western companies to outsource their processes to India. The processes that are outsourced to India include accounting, customer service, data entry, and medical transcription. From the voice-based customer queries, Indian companies have moved up the value chain and started offering services such as payroll management, accounts, and human resource management.

Though many companies were keen to shift their operations to India, they were not keen on establishing their wholly owned subsidiaries in India. For this reason, the Indian BPO industry saw the emergence of third-party vendors, who entered into contracts with the western companies to provide outsourced processes to them at lower costs.

Indian IT companies also entered the business process outsourcing (BPO) business. The Indian IT players, such as Infosys, Wipro, TCS, and Satyam, have entered into BPO industry through their subsidiaries. These companies could easily get outsourcing contracts as they already had established their credentials through their IT work.

To get a foothold in the IT industry in the United States for outsourcing, it was critical for the Indian companies to have worldwide recognition. A readily available yardstick became available in the form of capacity maturity model (CMM) by the Software Engineering Institute (SEI) of the Carnegie Mellon University. There are five different levels of the capacity maturity model; the highest is the Level 5 Certification. It was important for the Indian companies to demonstrate world-class quality. Quality accreditations from international agencies helped them to garner more contracts. Indian companies excelled in getting higher-

Figure 3. Size and growth of Indian software industry

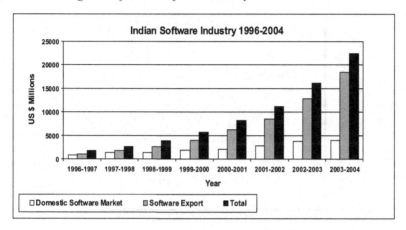

level capacity maturity model certifications. In 2003, SEI published a list of companies with capacity maturity model certifications. Most companies in that list with capacity maturity model levels of 4 or 5 were Indian.

Recognition of India Inc.

The software business in India is booming. Figure 3 shows that between 1996-1997 and 2003-2004, the Indian software industry has grown at an average compound rate of 30%. While the growth of the domestic market has been excellent, the growth of the export market has been spectacular. This trend is set to continue. In 2002, the NASSCOM McKinsey report on Indian software industry predicted that in 2008: (1) The overall IT industry revenues will be worth $140 billion. (2) The IT software and services market capitalization will exceed $225 billion. (3) IT software and services will contribute to over 7.5% of the overall GDP. (4) The software products market will amount to around $18 billion. (5) The software and services sector will create employment for over 2.2 million professionals.

Perceptions of Fortune 500 Companies

What is the source of such phenomenal optimism of the NASSCOM-McKinsey Report? A survey was conducted about the perceptions of the Fortune 500 companies about software business in various countries. The results are reported in the following figures. Figure 4 shows that in vendor sophistication and people sophistication, India stands well above the rest of the countries that are competing with India.

Figure 4. CEO survey of Fortune 500 companies

Outsourcing: Survey of CEOs of Fortune 500
India
Philippines
China
Russia
Mexico
Vendor Sophistication (Number, Quality)
People Sophistication (Number, Cost, Language Skills)

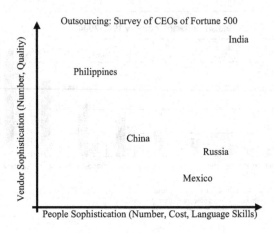

When we add the cost element to this optimistic view about India, it shows that not only does India have high quality of available resources (the only country higher in that count is Israel), but it also has a tremendous cost advantage. It is far cheaper than other countries in its category of quality (see Figure 5).

Figure 5. India has low cost and high quality

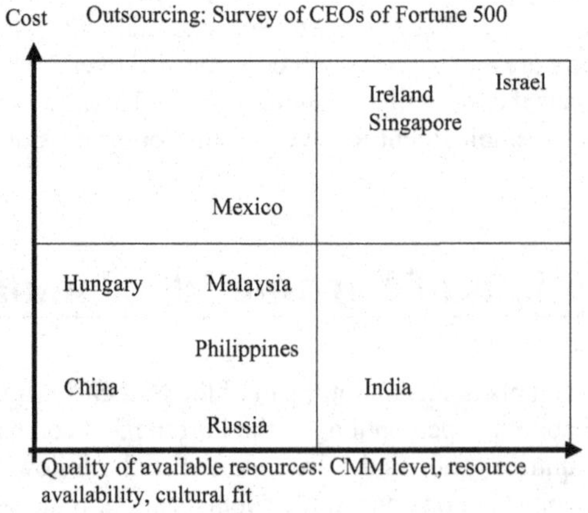

Cost
Outsourcing: Survey of CEOs of Fortune 500
Ireland
Singapore
Israel
Mexico
Hungary
Malaysia
Philippines
China
India
Russia
Quality of available resources: CMM level, resource availability, cultural fit

Outsourcing as a Securitization of Services

Securitization is the process of converting apparently indivisible goods into divisible goods, thereby changing the cost structure of a company. What does outsourcing do to the company? It turns a fixed cost into a variable cost. Just 20 years ago, janitors and the directors used to be fixed costs for a company. Whether there were any sales or not, janitors and directors had to be paid. In the twenty-first century, there has been a change in the business model. The software industry has shown that it is possible to attract managerial talent without a high salary by relocating to countries with cheaper but equally well-qualified employees. Performance based bonuses have become a standard practice not just in IT, but also in all types of business. Similarly, janitorial service is also being contracted out of companies.

Just the way companies have been able to securitize assets and liabilities, they can "securitize" services whether they are part of the core business or not. In the example with janitors and directors, the use of janitors is not a core business. It can be contracted out.

Large insurance companies like AXA and Prudential have contracted out (in a phased manner) the following activities of the company: (1) accounts payable, (2) payroll, (3) benefits administration, (4) employee data management, (5) employee call center, (6) some staffing, (7) training and compensation functions, (8) third-party human resource vendor management, and (9) IT functions that support human resources. Outsourcing such processes was unthinkable just a decade ago. This is exactly what we termed as securitization of services.

Some aspects of the insurance business naturally lend themselves to outsourcing. Consider an insurance company that wants to leave a certain line of business (called a run-off). The company has to earmark certain funds and wait for a number of years before all claims are settled in that line of business. Since human resources have to be tied up for run-off, it has always been a fiscal drag on a company. With outsourcing, an insurance company can leave its run-off business with an outsourced company and immediately redeploy their staff for new core business.

Reinsurance companies require extreme nimbleness to run their business. Since they are less bound by regulation than an insurance company, they can quickly redeploy resources. Not surprisingly, a majority of the top 10 reinsurers have outsourced to India either their entire back-office operation or a substantial part of it.

A recent survey showed that the top concerns of the buyers of outsourcing are the following: (1) on-time delivery, (2) cost effectiveness, (3) end-user satisfaction, (4) timely, quality staffing (of the provider) and (5) service availability of the provider (Diamond Cluster, 2004).

Peering into the Future

Short-Term Backlash

There has been a backlash among the main exporters of BPO: the United States and the United Kingdom. In the U.S., it has taken the form of banning outsourcing of state government jobs. For example, Kansas has adopted a bill seeking to bar outsourcing telephone enquiries about its food-stamp program to India and other countries in May 2004. Arizona, California, Colorado, New Jersey, South Carolina, and Washington are considering banning outsourcing related to medical, financial, or personal information. A survey conducted by the UK-based research agency, Mori, on behalf of the unions of Lloyds TSB Group, has concluded that half of the bank's customers would consider moving their accounts to a different one if they discovered the calls were being managed from India. These are short-term isolated issues.

Long-Term Trends

Business process outsourcing services worldwide reached US$405 billion in 2003. Forecasts based on client survey by the International Data Corporation shows it will grow 11% through 2008, reaching $682 billion.

A. T. Kearney released a study on March 30, 2004, ranking various offshore locations for back-office work. India emerges on top by a wide margin among the 25 countries in Kearney's "Offshore Location Attractiveness Index," which employs 39 criteria to rank the locations. China is ranked second, followed by Malaysia and the Czech Republic. This result is consistent with other surveys by other consulting companies.

For India, BPO employs 0.1% of the labor force, but it contributes 2% of GDP and a substantial 20% of its exports in 2004. There are a number of growth areas: banking (back office work such as accounting work), financial services and insurance (such as claims processing), telecom, healthcare (billing, claims management, accounting), human resources (payroll processing), retail (managing payables and receivables).

How much of it will come to India?

A study released by McKinsey-NASSCOM showed some 140 billion dollars could be coming to India by 2008. The result of their survey is reproduced in Table 3.

Table 3. Estimate of outsourcing market size in India by 2008 (Source: McKinsey NASSCOM Survey, 2002)

Type of service	Value
Customer interaction services	15.0
Finance & Accounting services	15.0
Animation	2.0
Translation, Transcription & Localization	1.2
Engineering & Design	5.0
HR Services	44.0
Data search, Integration and Management	18.0
Remote education	15.0
Total	140.0

Note: Figures in billions of U.S. dollars

Black Clouds in the Long Run

Legislative changes in the United States/United Kingdom pose the biggest threat to this growth of BPO. These changes could take the form of banning transfer of confidential information to a foreign country. This would mean payroll or medical bills cannot be processed outside the country.

Risks of Outsourcing

Outsourcing is not without its risks. When Eastman Kodak decided to outsource many of its core businesses, it did not realize that it lost key skills and capabilities. Short-term advantage was their prime concern at the time. Similarly, IBM outsourced PC-related business too early. It did not recognize that the market was not mature enough. Many innovations were to come.

Modern business is all about "knitting together people, processes and platforms" (Aron, 2003). If the risks of the processes are not properly evaluated and priced, outsourcing will simply not be the right solution. Consider the backlash some companies suffered when they moved their call centers to India. Clearly, these companies did not value the risk properly. The cost due to the loss of unhappy customers can outweigh the benefits of cutting the cost of delivering the service. Similarly, future possible backlash through legislative changes that prohibit "exporting" confidential client information need to be fully evaluated. Therefore, Aron (2003) suggests that instead of outsourcing, business should emphasize on "right sourcing." By outsourcing, companies can lose control of their own processes and the people (both customers and employees). Thus, outsourcing may lead to higher risk and therefore loss of future revenue.

Microlevel risks taken by a company are the following: (1) exposure of sensitive and critical information of a company; (2) exposure of customer information; (3) exposure of a company's intellectual property such as source code, patented processes; (4) relocation of IT equipment from a known, safe environment to an unknown environment; (5) no direct control over business continuity of the outsourced processes (Twing, 2005). Like any other risk management process, the risks are to be identified, measured, and steps for mitigation are to be taken.

Conclusion

Outsourcing of any service requires trust. Indian companies, over the past decade, have worked at earning that trust. It requires a high volume of sophisticated human resources. India has provided such a workforce. The Indian IT industry has been moving from low-end simple tasks to high-end complicated tasks in outsourcing in the form of BPO. Could Indian experience be duplicated in other countries? Many elements in India were present at the right place at the right time. Thus, it would be unlikely that some other country will

Box 1. Terminologies

BPO	Business process outsourcing. An entire line of business such as automobile design or insurance claims management process is farmed out.
IT	Information technology.
ITeS	Information technology enabled services. Services that use information technology intensively.
CMM	Capability maturity model articulated by the Software Engineering Institute (SEI) at the Carnegie Mellon University. The CMM/SEI framework aims to distinguish mature processes from immature processes. Level 5 is the highest grade.

Box 2. List of outsourced services (Adapted from the United Nations Conference on Trade and Development E-Commerce and Development Report, 2003)

Banking Services	Asset Management Services
Account opening services	Account creation
Account information capture	Account maintenance
Customer queries	Transfers and additions
Check clearing	Dividend payments
Check payment reconciliation	Brokerage payment
Statement processing	MIS reporting
ATM reconciliation	Customer service
Investment account management	**Customer Care**
Management reporting	Customer service
Loan administration	Customer analysis
Credit debits card services	Call centers
Check processing	Consumer information services
Collections	Customer relationship management
Customer account management	**Human Resources Services**
Mortgage Services	Payroll and benefits processing
Application verification and processing	Training and development
Disbursals and collections	Retirement investment and benefits management
Payment reconciliation	Hiring and staffing
Account information updates	Recruitment screening
Mortgage loan servicing	Administration and relocation services
Financial Services	Payroll processing
Document management	Compensation administration
Billing	Benefits planning
Shareholder services	Administration and regulating compliance
Claims processing	**Sales and Marketing Services**
Accounts receivable	Telemarketing services
Accounts payable	Direct marketing and sales campaigns

Box 2. continued

General ledger	**Web-Related Services**
Accounting services	Web site designing
Treasury operations management	Web site management
Credit Card Services	Site personalization
Applications screening and card issuance	Site marketing
Customer account management	Search engine, directory optimization and positioning services
Collections and customer follow-up	Catalog/content management
Account queries and limit enhancements	Web analytics
Accounting and payment reconciliation	Database design
Insurance Services	Web security services and integration with CRM
Policy owner services	Back-office systems for inventory management
Claims processing	Web enablement of legacy applications
Transaction & reinsurance accounting	Electronic bill presentment and payment services
Statutory reporting	Graphics/animation
Annuities processing	Web-based e-mail processing
Benefit administration	Web-based help desk
Customer information capture	Web-based chat support
Risk assessment and premium computation	E-learning: Web-based online education services
Policy processing and account monitoring	E-publishing
Claims management	
Payment reconciliation	
Health Care	
Medical transcription services	
Diagnostics	

be able to emulate India's experience. India has already made inroads into core business in some industries especially in financial services. All indicators point to more consolidation in the future.

Acknowledgments

We thank Bradly J. Condon and Rebecca Benedict for their comments. Our thanks to the many participants from the Indian IT Industry, who generously gave their time to discuss various issues. We thank the Asociación Mexican de Cultura AC for supporting this research.

Comments from anonymous referees have allowed us to refocus the chapter. However, we alone are responsible for the opinions expressed. They do not represent the views of the institutions with which we are affiliated.

References

Aron, R. (2003, June 1-14). Sourcing in the right light. *Optimize*. Retrieved January 11, 2005 from http://www.optimizemag.com/issue/020/management.htm?_loopback=1

Condon, B. J., & Sinha, T. (2003). *Drawing lines in sand and snow: Border security and North American economic integration*. M. E. Sharpe.

Diamond Cluster. (2004). *2004 Global IT Outsourcing Study*. Retrieved January 11, 2005 from http://www.diamondcluster.com

Farrell, D. (2003). *Offshoring: Is it a win-win game?* McKinsey Global Institute.

Feenstra, R. (2005, January 16-18). *The future of business outsourcing, Sixth Annual NBER-NCAER Neemrana Conference.*

Heckscher, E. F. (1919). Utrikeshandelns verkan pa inkomstfordelningen (The effect of foreign trade on the distribution of income) *Ekonomisk Tidskrift, 21*, 497-512.

Kakabadse, N., & Kakabadse, A. (2000). Outsourcing: A paradigm shift. *Journal of Management Development, 19*(4), 670-728.

Koffler, K. (2004, March 2). Business coalition rewrites lexicon for jobs outsourcing. *Congress Daily*. Retrieved January 11, 2005 from http://nationaljournal.com

Leavy, B. (2004). Outsourcing strategies: Opportunities and risks. *Strategy and Leadership, 32*, 20-25.

Maranjian, S. (2004, March 11). Thoughts on offshoring and outsourcing. *Motley Fool's News and Commentary*. Retrieved January 11, 2005 from http://www.fool.com/news/commentary/2004/commentary040311SM.htm

McCarthy, J. C. (2002, November 11). 3.3 million US service jobs to go offshore. Whole View Tech Strategy. *Forrester Research*. Retrieved January 11, 2005 from www.forrester.com

Miller, H. (2003, November). *The new competitive reality*. Presentation of the ITAA. Retrieved January 11, 2005 from http://www.itaa.org

Odindo, C. et al. (2004). *Outsourcing in the UK financial services industry: The Asian offshore market*. University of Nottingham School of Business, CRIS Discussion Paper Series—2004.I. Retrieved January 11, 2005 from www.nottingham.ac.uk/business/cris/discussionpapers.html

Ohlin, B. (1928, April). The reparations problem. *Svenska Handelsbanken, 28*, 2-23.

Phillips, M. M. (2004, March 15). More work is outsourced to U.S. than away from it, data show. *Wall Street Journal*. Retrieved January 11, 2005 from http://www.wsj.com

Twing, D. (2005, September). Reviewing the security aspect of outsourcing. *Network World*, 22-31. Retrieved September 30, 2005 from http://www.networkworld.com/newsletters/asp/2005/0905out1.html

Wilson, D., & Purushothaman, R. (2003, October). Dreaming with BRICs: The path to 2050. *Goldman and Sachs, Global Economics Paper No. 99*. Retrieved September 30, 2005 from http://www2.goldmansachs.com/insight/research/reports/report6.html

Chapter XI

Strategies for Business Process Outsourcing:
An Analysis of Alternatives, Opportunities, and Risks

Subrata Chakrabarty, Texas A&M University, USA

Abstract

This chapter provides a comprehensive overview of business process outsourcing (BPO) strategies and analyzes related issues. The discussions in this chapter can serve as an aid to decision makers who face the great dilemma of whether to insource or outsource a process, and additionally how to handle outsourcing to offshore locations. While business processes themselves are activities that need to be performed efficiently, outsourcing them is essentially a strategic decision that can ultimately impact the competitiveness of the client firm. This chapter explores the risks and opportunities associated with the numerous strategies related to outsourcing and offshoring alternatives, business process migration, contracting and alliance building, the role of the vendor, the nature of the relationship, multiclient or multivendor relationships, infusing maturity and ushering transformations in business processes, locating required expertise and quantity of workers, and also utilizing on-demand software services from application service providers.

Introduction

In *business process outsourcing* (BPO), a client's business process is performed by a vendor. Certain business processes of the client are transferred over to the vendor, and the vendor's office then becomes the "back office" for the client's outsourced business processes. The vendors are given the responsibility to manage the client's business processes, such as call centers, emergency hotlines, claims management, helpdesks, data management, document processing and storage, financial services (banks and insurance), payroll, auditing, accounting, travel management systems, various logistics and information systems services (Millar, 1994, as cited in Lacity & Hirschheim, 1995, pp. 4-5; Sparrow, 2003, p. 11). Hence, a BPO vendor needs to have the capability to provide consistent levels of customer service spanning across a range of services and businesses.

Though BPO has inherent risks, it also provides many benefits to the client. Apart from focusing on short-term cost savings and operational efficiencies, it is important that BPO be performed with a strategic mindset, whereby decisions are based on wider business context and help in gaining competitive advantages in the tough external environment (Sparrow, 2003, p. 8). For effective BPO, an organization should segregate its business processes into two broad categories: (1) the ones where its own core competencies are strong and which have strategic significance, and (2) those that can be performed better by a vendor (Adler, 2003, p.53). In most cases, business processes that represent the client's core competencies and have high strategic stakes are best performed in-house. In order to identify its *"core competencies,"* an organization needs to be very clear about where its own strengths lie and identify the processes that truly give the organization its business value. In order to identify processes that are "strategic," the organizations need to be able to identify processes that differentiate it from its competitors in the marketplace, or processes that gives it the competitive advantage (Porter, 1996).

Importantly, the market is dynamic where the demands and competition changes over time and, therefore, the core competencies or the strategic nature of associated business processes may accordingly change. Hence, organizations also need to have a clear vision of their goals and future strategy in the dynamic marketplace and, accordingly, identify its business processes for outsourcing. Failure to do so can make an organization overly dependent on the BPO vendors for its core or strategic business processes, and it would effectively be at the mercy of vendors. The key here is to have complete power and control over one's core and strategic business processes, while gaining maximum advantages out of the various vendors' strengths in noncore business processes. This chapter discusses the various alternative strategies that clients should consider while pursuing BPO.

Strategies: Basics of Outsourcing and Offshoring

Business Process Insourcing and Outsourcing

The two basic strategies in sourcing business processes are *insourcing* and *outsourcing*. While in *business process insourcing* a firm executes business processes on its own, in *business process outsourcing* (BPO) the client firm establishes a contractual relationship and hands over the responsibility of executing the business processes to a vendor. In other words, a company "insources" from within and "outsources" to an external company, that is, *outsourcing* is the sourcing of work across organizational boundaries.

- **Insourcing:** The business processes are performed by the client itself or a client entity (such as a subsidiary or an internal department).
- **Outsourcing:** The business processes are performed by a nonclient entity (such as a vendor/supplier).

When a firm decides to insource its business processes, there are two basic strategies: (1) the "OK as is" strategy where the client feels that it is running its business processes efficiently and satisfactorily, and hence the strategy is to simply continue with the status quo, and (2) the "fix and keep in-house" strategy where the client might be a bit unsatisfied with the efficiency of its in-house business processes, but believes that insourcing is still the best option, and decides to invest in the adoption of better practices to identify and fix the deficiencies (Wibbelsman & Maiero, 1994, as cited in Dibbern, Goles, Hirschheim, & Jayatilaka, 2004, p. 11). Here, firms target the highest efficiency levels (achieved by competitors or vendors), set them as the benchmarks, and are self driven and motivated to achieve those high efficiencies in their business processes.

When a firm decides to outsource its business processes, two basic strategies are (1) the "option to reverse" strategy where business processes are outsourced to a vendor, but it also takes into account the possibility of bringing the outsourced business processes back in-house whenever needed, and (2) the "divest completely" strategy where business processes that are perceived to be best managed by a vendor are outsourced permanently (Wibbelsman & Maiero, 1994, as cited in Dibbern et al., 2004, p. 11). Additionally, it is also important to note that a client's option is not limited to outsourcing to just one vendor, and it can potentially outsource to multiple vendors. Similarly, vendors often provide services to multiple clients. The strategic aspects related to multiple clients and multiple vendors will be discussed later in the chapter.

Making the Insourcing vs. Outsourcing Choice

To evaluate the experiences of organizations with outsourcing, 14 case studies were carried out by Hirschheim and Lacity (2000). The case studies show that when departments executing in-house business processes get the required support from the upper management, they too can improve performance and imitate the various cost-reducing and effi-ciency-enhancing tactics adopted by the vendors, and thus provide a strong alternative to outsourcing. Furthermore, they highlight the risk of lesser control and lower–than-expected service levels that may result from large-scale outsourcing. Moreover, they report that some organizations were considering the discontinuation of outsourcing, which involved getting the outsourced work back in-house by either waiting for the contract period to end or by simply renegotiating/terminating the contract. Outsourcing is not easy, and a great amount of planning along with immaculate execution is needed for it to be completely successful. Based on an extensive review of the academic literature, some of the salient advantages of insourcing and outsourcing are compiled (Ang & Straub, 1998; Aubert, Rivard, & Patry, 1996; Chakrabarty, 2006b; Currie & Willcocks, 1998; Earl, 1996; Jurison, 1995; Loh & Venkatraman, 1992; Loh & Venkatraman, 1995; Nam, Rajagopalan, Rao, & Chaudhury, 1996; Nelson, Richmond, & Seidmann, 1996; Poppo & Zenger, 1998):

Advantages of business process insourcing:

- Insourcing allows greater *control* over the strategic assets and resources that are used in the business processes.

- Possibility of *opportunistic behavior* of a vendor is a major hassle, and insourcing safeguards against this risk.

- Insourcing is best when high *uncertainty* is associated with the business process

- Many business processes require very high amounts of *firm specific knowledge* (busi-ness/technical) for their effective execution. Transferring such knowledge to a vendor not only takes time and effort, but may also compromise the confidentiality of the firm-specific knowledge.

- Negotiating *intellectual property* rights associated with business processes (with a vendor) are always a tricky issue, and insourcing reduces the risk of IP rights viola-tions.

- Not all business processes can be effectively carried out by vendors (no matter what the sales/marketing representatives of the vendors say). Hence, insourcing is sometimes the only option when *competent vendors are absent*.

Advantages of business process outsourcing (BPO):

- BPO can lead to considerable *cost advantages*:
  - The client does not have to invest in the infrastructure or the technology required to execute the business processes and hence saves on capital expenditure.
  - The vendor's economies of scale and economies of scope help in reducing the costs of running the business processes.
  - The very process of bidding for and negotiating the outsourcing contract makes the respective vendors give estimates on the costs involved in executing the busi-ness processes, which in turn makes the costs more predictable for the client.

- BPO allows organizations to focus its *core business,* and outsource the noncore business that take up a considerable amount of management time and resources.

- BPO makes a client's transition to newer business processes easier, wherein the legacy or current business processes are outsourced to a vendor during the transition period.

- BPO gives more flexibility in managing labor:

  ° Any upsurge or downswing in the volume of business process work would entail variations in the required manpower. The client does not need to worry about this because the recruitment and staffing for outsourced business processes would be the vendor's responsibility. A vendor organization can more easily manage variations in manpower needs since it would be executing a huge number of business processes (for various clients) that involve a large number of vendor employees working on similar tasks. The vendor can easily balance out variations in staffing needs across its various BPO projects.

  ° BPO frees up a client's in-house resources (infrastructure, manpower, etc.) from noncore activities, and they can instead be utilized in the development of core competencies and processes that could give the client a competitive edge in the market.

  ° BPO gives the client access to the process and technical expertise of the vendor personnel, which can have a positive impact on the way the client's business processes are executed.

- To stay competitive, most vendors strive to adopt the best *business process maturity* models that can guarantee better quality and service. Hence, clients can benefit from the quality provided by the best-in-class vendors.

Apte and Mason (1995, p. 1258; see also Dibbern et al., 2004, p. 33) proposed that the choice between insourcing and outsourcing can be ascertained by the "strategic importance" and the client's "relative efficiency" in carrying out an activity in-house. Insourcing of business processes is suitable when both the *strategic importance* and the *relative efficiency* of performing the business processes in-house are high. However, if both these factors are low, the BPO is favorable. But what if the *strategic importance* is *high* but the client's *relative efficiency* is *low*? In this case the client has the following options: (1) invest time, money, and effort into increasing the efficiency of these strategic or core competency business processes, (2) ask external consultants or vendors to come to the client site and suggest the necessary changes to infuse efficiency, and (3) consider building a *strategic-alliance* with a vendor who is an expert in executing the relevant business processes. Options (2) and (3) would need the imposition of strict controls that would prevent any compromise on the strategic importance or confidentiality associated with the business processes. And finally, it is suggested that if the business processes are *not of strategic importance* but the organization has *extremely high efficiency* in executing them, then the organization should consider setting up a subsidiary or spin-off that offers its expertise to other organizations in the external market.

It should be noted that firms rarely outsource "everything," and instead adopt a cautious and sensible approach of selectively picking out the business processes that it feels can be best performed by the vendors. This is discussed in the next section.

Strategy for Selective BPO

Is it a good strategy to outsource all business processes? Or is it better if they are all retained in-house? Well, it would be nice if the answers were as simplistic as the questions posed. The outsourcing decision is rarely an all-or-nothing approach. As discussed earlier, an optimum balance is reached between the number of business processes to be outsourced and the ones to be retained in-house. *Selective BPO* is the practice of outsourcing carefully selected business processes to vendors, while retaining the others in-house (Lacity, Willcocks, & Feeny, 1996, pp. 13-14). Clients often *outsource* the business processes that they feel can be better performed by a vendor, but prefer to keep select business processes in-house based on their own strengths and capabilities. This selective approach is based on an analysis of costs and benefits, technology/infrastructure availability, and human resource availability. *Selective BPO* shuns the all-or-nothing approach in favor of a smarter way of outsourcing that involves careful judgment and discernment, and that meets the customer's needs while minimizing risks associated with total outsourcing approaches (Lacity et al., 1996, pp. 13-14). This widely recommended selective approach capitalizes on the strengths of both the client and the vendors.

Strategy for Offshore BPO: Going Global

Offshoring and Outsourcing Classifications

As described earlier, the client's business processes can be executed or managed by entities that are either internal (its own department, subsidiary, or captive center) or external (a vendor). In this world where globalization is having astounding effects on the way business is conducted, where exactly is the location where the client's business processes are being executed? When the client's business processes are being executed in the same country as that of the client, it is known as *onshore sourcing, domestic sourcing,* or simply *onshoring* (Chakrabarty, 2006b). On the other hand, if the business processes are being executed in a country that is different from the client's country it is known as *offshore sourcing* or *global sourcing* (Chakrabarty, 2006b). Hence, offshoring is the transfer of work across geographical boundaries. But then, the question arises whether the business processes are being executed by a client entity (such as a subsidiary or department) or a nonclient entity (a vendor)? Hence, the following possibilities arise (see figure-1):

- **Onshore-insourcing of business processes:** When both the client and the client-entity that executes the business processes (such as its own subsidiary or internal department) are located in the same country it is known as *onshore BPI* (business process insourcing) or *domestic BPI*.

Figure 1. Outsourcing and offshoring

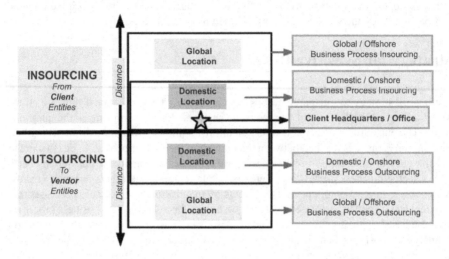

- **Offshore-insourcing of business processes:** When the client entity (such as a subsidiary, department, or captive center) that executes the business processes is located in a country that is different from the client's country it is known as *offshore BPI* or *global BPI*.

- **Onshore-outsourcing of business processes:** When both the client and the vendor that is executing the client's business processes are located in the same country it is known as *onshore BPO* (business process outsourcing) or *domestic BPO*.

- **Offshore-outsourcing of business processes:** When the vendor that is executing the client's business processes is located in a country that is different from the client's country it is known as *offshore BPO* or *global BPO*.

Why offshore Outsourcing is Gaining Prevalence

There are many reasons that are attributed to the growth of offshore BPO, and the major ones can be summarized as follows:

1.   **Business processes can be executed round the clock:** By distributing the work globally across multiple time zones, business processes can be run 24×7. This can lead to a faster execution time in completing any business process cycle (Apte & Mason, 1995, p. 1252; Sinha & Terdiman, 2002) and also allow 24×7 management and supervising that is crucial for business processes. 24×7 services can be a competitive strategy for any client in today's global market.

2. **Cost savings due to high availability of cheap skilled labor:** The predominant cause for the offshoring trend is certainly the cost advantage derived out of the lower pay scales of skilled professionals and the lower cost of living in some developing countries such as India and China. The high supply of skilled labor in such countries boosts the low-cost advantage (Apte & Mason, 1995, p. 1252; Carmel & Agarwal, 2002; Sinha & Terdiman, 2002; Sobol & Apte, 1995).

3. **Modern communication and collaboration technologies:** The Internet has surely promoted the growth of offshoring by providing a platform for the latest communication and collaboration technologies at reasonably low costs (e-mailing, teleconferencing, videoconferencing, instant messengers with text messaging, voice chat and Web cams, etc.). Thanks to these latest technologies, geographical distance is becoming less of a barrier for collaboration and coordination among globally distributed teams, also known as "global virtual teams" (Carmel & Agarwal, 2002, p. 66; Chakrabarty, 2006d).

4. **Business process discipline, maturity and quality improvement:** When a business process is outsourced to a vendor in a different country, the vendor personnel are obliged to understand and adopt the business process completely to make it operationally effective. The vendor personnel would attempt to understand the business process from a "fresh" perspective without any baggage of past or local experiences in the particular business process (Aron & Singh, n.d.). This would throw open the business process to questioning, and possible avenues for improvement. It is important to note that most vendors strive to adopt the best *business process maturity* models that can guarantee better quality and service, and hence attract more clients. Offshore outsourcing of business processes can therefore bring into it the much needed "process discipline" that makes: (1) *the process globally understood*—through removal of any ambiguity and improperly synthesized information, and enforcement of universally understood standards and procedures, and (2) *the tasks in the process optimally sequenced*—through elimination of redundant tasks and modification of defective tasks (Aron & Singh, n.d.). This evaluation of the outsourced business processes from the unadulterated third-party perspective of the offshore personnel, if well utilized (by requesting and acting upon the feedback), can lead to improvements in the business process in terms of discipline, maturity, and quality. Hence, the remoteness of the vendor or offshore personnel can also turn out to be an advantage.

Why Offshore Outsourcing is a Risk

Offshore outsourcing brings in various risks that need to be addressed by the clients and the vendors (Apte & Mason, 1995, pp. 1252-1253; Carmel & Agarwal, 2002, p. 68; Chakrabarty, 2006d; Sinha & Terdiman, 2002; Sobol & Apte, 1995, p. 271), and these risks include:

- **Behavioral risks:** These risks include lack of trust, cultural differences, communication, and coordination issues.
- **Risks due to global laws, norms, and environments:** Getting visas/work-permits for global travel has become difficult and time consuming due to various factors

(such as fears of job loss, and terrorist threats), laws and norms in various nations on cross-border data flow and services are sometimes unclear, and finally there is always a possibility of unstable economic, political, or social environments in any nation (in varying degrees).

- **Information and knowledge related risks:** There is sometimes a risk due to possible violations of intellectual property rights and privacy, since many business processes deal with sensitive data (such as credit card numbers). There is also the difficulty in knowledge transfer from the client to the vendor. The offshore vendor would lack domain knowledge about the client's industry, market, customers, organizational culture, and the nitty-gritty about the way the client operates. How much should the client reveal? How much should be kept confidential? Also, how much time and effort will go into ensuring effective knowledge transfer?

- **Business process management risks:** It might be difficult to control quality and schedule unless proper mechanisms to ensure the same are in place. Also, how quickly, accurately, and efficiently can changes in business processes be affected?

Distributed Consulting and Global Delivery

Offshore BPO is not always "purely offshore." An offshore BPO can have a minor onshore component along with a major offshore component. Often, a need arises to have a small vendor team at onshore in addition to the large number of vendor personnel at offshore executing who are executing the business processes (see Figure 2). While the offshore vendor personnel have the responsibility of carrying out the bulk of the work, the onshore vendor team has the role of coordinating face-to-face with client. This is known as *distributed*

Figure 2. Distributed consulting & global delivery

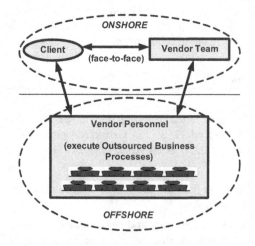

consulting (Kobyashi-Hillary, 2004, p. 153). This method is a widely accepted practice to ensure effective coordination between onshore-based clients and offshore-based vendors.

Companies such as TCS, Infosys (whose BPO arm is called Progeon), and Wipro, all large software service providers (primarily based in India), are now aggressively providing BPO services, and have for long incorporated the concept of distributed consulting into what they call the "*global delivery model*," whereby these large vendors execute the business processes from various global locations for their clients situated at various other global locations (Chakrabarty, 2006b). Table 1 gives some of the BPO services being aggressively offered by these companies. Though India is one of the predominant players in the market, it is mentioned here only as an example, and it is important to realize that numerous organizations from various other countries are also competitively providing BPO services (Kempf, Scholl, & Sinha, 2001).

The vendor's offices, where the client's business processes are executed, are located worldwide (based on various factors such as availability of skilled manpower at low costs), and

Table 1. BPO services

TCS (http://www.tcs.com/bpo/offerings.htm)	Infosys (Progeon) (http://www.infosys.com/bpo/services.asp, http://www.progeon.com/)	Wipro (http://www.wipro.com/bpo/index.htm)
Banking and Financial Services Payment Processing, Loans Processing, Securities Back-office Processing	**Banking** Credit cards, retail lending, mortgage processing, retail banking and account management, cash management, trade services, lease and loan processing, investment banking	**Customer Interaction Services** Customer Services, Telemarketing Services, Technical Support Services, IT Help Desk Services
Telecom Revenue Assurance, Order Management, Digitization of Network Data, Network Service Provisioning	**Securities Industry** Custody and Fund Administration, Brokerage, Asset Management, Investment Research	
Healthcare Clinical Data Management, Statistical Analysis	**Insurance** Life & Pensions, General	**Industry Administration Services** Insurance Processing, Mortgage Processing
Travel and Hospitality Revenue Accounting and Fare Audit, Fare Filing and Distribution, Ticketing & Reservation, Loyalty Program Administration	**Enterprise Services** Accounts payable, accounts receivable, GL and fixed asset accounting, Financial reporting, Sales order management and administration, Procurement Services, HR services	**Business Optimization Services** HR Processing Services, Finance & Accounting Solutions, Procurement Solutions
Insurance New Business Acquisition support, Policy servicing, Claims Management, Distribution Administration	**Telecom** Billing, Service Provisioning **Knowledge Services** Equity Research, Credit Analysis, Fixed Income Research, Bond Analysis, Economic Analysis, Industry analysis and Company analysis	**Knowledge Services**

there is comprehensive networking with the latest telecommunications and collaborative technologies that allow seamless integration of business processes delivered from multiple locations and thereby providing economies of scale and scope. Hence, the "*global delivery model*" is an offshore BPO model that takes advantage of the global talent pool to give the best value to the client in terms of cost and quality.

This section focused exclusively on offshore BPO. However, the strategies discussed throughout the remaining chapter apply to both domestic/onshore BPO and global/offshore BPO.

Strategies for Business Process Migration

Strategy for Migration of Business Processes from Client to Vendor Site

It is interesting to note how some of the vendors are trying to convince the clients to take up the risk of BPO, and it also shows how very confident the vendors are in their ability to execute third-party business processes from a far-off location. For example, the Wipro Web site (http://www.wipro.com/bpo/methodology.htm) tries very hard to market the importance it lays on the smooth transfer of business processes from the client site to the vendor site:

For BPO projects, we follow the Wipro Service Delivery Model, which is a robustly defined framework to manage the complete BPO process migration and transition management and has been developed based on the experience gained from migrating more than 400 remote business processes to India over the past ten years. This proven service transfer platform is designed to ensure process integrity and minimize inherent migration risks. The model includes a tried and tested Transition Toolkit to support transition management by ensuring that there is a documented methodology with formats, tools, guidelines and past learnings in place to aid the transition team in de-risking the transition of a customer's processes and reducing the pain of migration as much as possible. A coordinated project management system captures critical client documentation and incorporates an extensive knowledge base that assists the transition management team in understanding, duplicating, and migrating mission-critical business processes.

The Infosys Web site (http://www.infosys.com/bpo/methodology.asp) gives a good overview of the steps and planning that goes into BPO from the vendor perspective. They provide the following step-by-step approach for BPO execution:

Step1: "*Assessment* – *Build the case and ready the client organization for BPO.*"

Step 2: "*Transition* – *Migrate the processes after mapping processes, creating technology infrastructure and training resources.*"

Step 3: "*Parallel run* – *Phase out the process at the client (site) and put in place measures for ongoing tracking and monitoring.*"

Step 4: "*Steady State* – *Manage the process in the steady state* – *ensure continuity, and continuous quality and process improvement.*"

If a client chooses a vendor that has already been involved in a lot of BPO deals, then the vendor would already be aware of the better ways to migrate the business processes from the client site to the vendor site. However, most business processes are interlinked to other business processes, and (before outsourcing) all these business processes harmonize with each other like parts of a well-oiled machine. BPO is equivalent to dismantling some parts of this well-oiled machine, and then reassembling the removed parts back together in a different fashion. The risk here is that the client cannot afford to trust the vendor completely, and should remain alert on the approaches the vendor takes in transferring the business processes. The outsourced business process may be highly integrated with other business processes at the client site, and efforts must be made by the client to ensure that the *interfacing* between the in-house business processes and the outsourced business processes is satisfactory.

There is something more for the client to ponder about. The vendor takes proactive initiatives to make sure that the client is comfortable with BPO and that the transfer or migration of business processes occurs smoothly. But if someday the client decides to get these business processes back in-house, then would the vendor be as cooperative in ensuring the effective and smooth transfer of the business processes back to the client site?

Strategy for Getting the Business Process Back In-House

What does an organization do when its wants to bring back in-house the business processes that it had previously outsourced? The term *"backsourcing"* was coined for this strategy (Hirschheim & Lacity, 1998). But why would an organization want to bring back business processes that it had previously decided to outsource? There can be a variety of reasons (Hirschheim & Lacity, 1998). On a positive side, it might be something that was actually planned during the initial outsourcing decision itself. For example, it is possible that the organization was going through a major transformation (Sparrow, 2003, p. 10), or needed a major realignment of processes, labor, or work allocation, and had therefore decided that some of its business processes could be temporarily outsourced during that period. On the other hand, the *backsourcing* may be an unplanned compulsion, such as the result of dissatisfaction from BPO experiences (for example, poor customer feedback, high overhead costs, breach of contracts or trust, or simply too many conflicts with the vendor), or as a result of certain business processes turning out to be more strategic and closely associated with the client's core competence than previously thought (irrespective of the performance of the vendor).

The process of bringing back previously outsourced business processes has its own risks and is a challenge for any organization (Hirschheim & Lacity, 1998). During the time the processes were outsourced, the client organization might have lost key resources (such as employees with relevant expertise, infrastructure, and tacit knowledge). Setting up the business processes again and integrating them back into the organization would require significant investments of time, money, and effort.

Strategies for Contracting and Alliance Building

Strategy of Linking Realization of Benefits from BPO to Payments

How can a client ensure that it would, in fact, receive the benefits from BPO being promised by the vendor's marketing team? What if the client does not receive the benefits being promised? One way to get over the dilemma is to contractually link the realization of the promised benefits from BPO to the payments. The contract would attempt to clearly define the specific expectations of the client organization from BPO, and the client would pay the vendor in proportion to the realized benefits. This has been termed as *business benefit contracting* (Millar, 1994, as cited in Lacity & Hirschheim, 1995, pp. 4-5), and it enables the sharing of risks by linking a client's costs to the realization of the expected benefits from BPO. Hence, well-defined client expectations can be embedded in the contract, and detailed evaluations of whether and how much the vendor actually contributed towards the client's performance would have to be carried out (Willcocks & Lacity, 1998, p. 26, pp. 30-31).

However, the major risk lies in not being able to come to mutually agreeable interpretations of the specific benefits or benchmarks that are linked to the payments. For example, the client may put across a pessimistic view of the benefits actually gained from BPO in order to reduce the amount of payments due to the vendor, while the vendor may put across an overly rosy scenario of the benefits gained by the client in order to get the highest possible payments from the client. With the vendor's revenue/profits from its clients being linked to benchmarks, problematic disagreements on the benchmarks may emerge, and hence, due to the difficulties associated with the related measurements and negotiations "business benefit contracting" is difficult to adopt (Lacity & Hirschheim, 1995).

Strategy of Getting the Best BPO Deals with Innovative Contracts

In order to be competitive clients need to get the best out of their outsourcing relationships in terms of costs and value addition. For many of business processes that can be possibly outsourced, there are a plethora of vendors willing to bid for the contracts. It is important for clients to recognize that its bargaining power is probably the highest at the point of drafting and signing the contracts. Hence, the client should always be on the lookout for the best deals to satisfy its needs, and adopting the attitude of a hard bargainer or tough shopper in the contract formulation stage might be the right thing to do. Willcocks and Lacity (1998, pp. 32-33), for example, have discussed "creative contracting," which has ingenious practices, such as short term contracts, flexible pricing, competitive bidding for extra or value-added services, and so forth. By using short-term contracts (even if the intention is to have long-term relationships) the vendor can keep the vendor on its toes, and also renegotiate better terms every time a contract is renewed based on past experiences and future expectations. The risk here is that the vendor may be hesitant in making long-term investments (into manpower or infrastructure) for the outsourced business processes since it would be unsure about the renewal of the short-term contracts.

The client may also ask the prospective vendors the question: "what more can you give us apart from meeting our basic requirements?" In other words what would be the vendor's value addition? What can the vendor do to beat the client's expectations? Hence, the client can induce a competitive spirit among the prospective vendors to gain maximum value from BPO. Moreover, the client may also insist on pricing mechanisms that are flexible and that bring in the possibilities of rewarding the vendor for exceptional performances and penalize the vendor for below expectation performances.

Strategies for Sharing Oownership

Business benefit contracting, which was discussed earlier, is a method of sharing benefits and risks. However, its major deficiency lies in the difficulties involved in defining and measuring the specific benefits or benchmarks in the contract. Sharing of ownership might be a much more effective BPO strategy, and would eventually lead to risk sharing (see Figure 3).

Figure 3. Strategies for sharing ownership

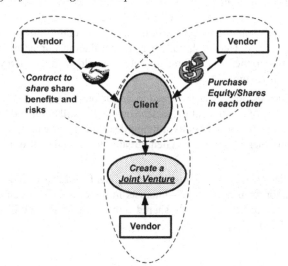

A *strategic alliance or partnership* between a client and a vendor that ensures sharing of risks and rewards may be implemented in the following three forms: (1) contracts that specify clauses on sharing of risks and rewards, (2) creating a joint venture company that would perform the outsourced business processes, and (3) both the client and vendor hold shares or equity in each other (Currie & Willcocks, 1998, p. 124; Sparrow, 2003, p. 12; Willcocks & Lacity, 1998, p. 26, pp. 27-28). As discussed earlier, "business benefit contracting" is an effective risk sharing mechanism based on a contractual agreement linking realization of expected benefits to payments, and "creative contracting" can have pricing mechanisms that reward exceptional performances and penalize poor performances. However, given the difficulties in measuring specific benefits in a mutually agreeable manner, the *sharing of ownership* strategies through *joint ventures* or *share/equity holding* may be better alternatives.

When a client and vendor invest to form a *joint venture*, it truly honors their commitment and dedication towards the success of the BPO endeavor. If the joint venture fails to meet expectations, it is a loss for both the client and the vendor. And similarly, when the joint venture performs well, it is a win-win situation for both the client and vendor. The resources (such as manpower, infrastructure, knowledge, etc.) for the *joint venture* organization can be provided by both the parties. This enables the client to gain access to the vendor's capabilities and skills, to reorganize and induce efficiency into business processes, and to gain new sources of revenue by offering the joint venture's services to the external market (Sparrow, 2003, p. 12). The client does not lose total control of the outsourced business processes since it would have invested in the joint venture, and at the same time it will be assured that the vendor would use its best expertise to bring in operational efficiencies (Currie & Willcocks, 1998). The vendor, on the other hand, would feel more secure and will be willing to invest more time and effort into the venture, since a joint venture is essentially a long-term relationship. However, joint ventures can also fail due to various factors (Reuer, Zollo & Singh, 2002), and the client might have outsourced large amounts of business process work to the failed joint venture. Hence, the risk here is that the outsourced business processes and their contribution to the client's competitiveness would be at the mercy of the success or failure of the joint venture.

If the amount of business processes that need to be outsourced (or some other factor) does not justify the viability of a joint venture, can the ownership still be shared? An *equity holding* deal is the answer. In a share/equity holding deal, the client can purchase substantial equity in the vendor, thereby giving the client greater power and control in its relationship with the vendor.

The vendor may also take an equity position in the client, and that would ensure that both the client and vendor keep each other's interests in mind, thereby leading to a situation where risks and rewards are effectively shared through ownership (Willcocks & Lacity, 1998, p. 26, pp. 27-28).

Strategies on the Role of the Vendor and Nature of the Relationship

Strategy for BPO That Demands Client-Vendor Cooperation

What does an organization do when all the functions related to a particular business process cannot be outsourced? For example, though an organization may outsource its call-center or help-desk activities, it may still need to retain the technical staff that actually fixes the problems reported. There would need to be effective cooperation between the outsourced call centers/help desk and the in-house technical staff to address customer complaints. Hence, to a certain extent, the execution of such business processes would be done jointly by the client and the vendor, and it is known as *cooperative sourcing* (Millar, 1994, as cited in Lacity & Hirschheim, 1995, pp. 4-5). The risk lies in not being able to lay down effective protocols that would ensure high cooperation and easy conflict resolution. For example, in addition to the frequent meetings needed for building cooperation, it is also important to actually document the communications/decisions/schedules/plans made, and enable easy and quick access to such documentation whenever the need arises. Of course, tacit or intangible factors such as trust or personal relationships are very important in ensuring cooperation (Chakrabarty, 2006a). However, such formalization or protocols in the relationship encourages accountability and fixes responsibility, which can lead to better cooperation in executing the business processes.

Strategies for the Number of Clients and Vendors in BPO Relationships

A client may not be able to find a vendor with the capability to perform a wide array of business processes all by itself. In such a scenario, the client may decide to opt for specialized vendors, and the different business processes would be outsourced to the respective specialist vendors (Chakrabarty, 2006c). This is known *multivendor outsourcing* (Gallivan & Oh, 1999, pp. 1-6) or *multisupplier outsourcing* (Currie & Willcocks, 1998) or simply *multisourcing* (Willcocks & Lacity, 1998). Such a one-to-many outsourcing arrangement (one-client-to-many-vendors) would allow a client to engage multiple vendors for various business processes. Let us first discuss the case where *interdependent* business processes need to be outsourced to multiple vendors. For example, though the HR functions and payroll processes may be interdependent, the client may outsource HR-specific processes to one vendor and payroll processes to another vendor. Similarly, there might be other interdependent business processes that are outsourced. Since the processes are interdependent, the division of work and related contracts would be *jointly* negotiated, understood, and agreed upon by the client and *all* the involved vendors (Gallivan & Oh, 1999, pp. 1-6). This form of multivendor outsourcing, where the outsourced business processes are interdependent, would require *all* the vendors and client to cooperate and work together (Chakrabarty, 2006c). The risks would arise out of the difficulties in cooperation, and the need for timely and accurate

Figure 4. Number of clients and vendors in outsourcing

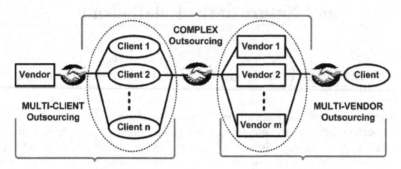

exchange of information amongst the various vendors and the client. The client would have to take the lead in ensuring and verifying that there is proper coordination between the vendors and that the interdependent business processes are being executed harmoniously. On the other hand, the task probably becomes easier when the business processes outsourced to multiple vendors are independent (that is, they are not interdependent). Such an example would be the outsourcing of financial services (banks and insurance) to one vendor, and travel/transportation management to another vendor. Here the client would not have to worry about coordination between the respective vendors.

Importantly, clients can sometimes take advantage of multiple vendors, competing in the marketplace, that provide services for the same business process. For example, there are multiple vendors that offer call center services. In such a scenario, the client can distribute chunks of the same business process to multiple vendors to safeguard against being overly dependent on a single vendor, and thereby negate the possibility of any vendor gaining complete power and control over the client's business process. The client can encourage competition among the vendors to provide the same business process at the best possible value and quality by using "short-term contracts" that are not necessarily liable for renewal with the same vendor. Hence, if a client engages two or more vendors for the same business process, it yields cost advantages due to intervendor competition, and also prevents the risk of a client firm being held hostage by a monopolistic vendor (Klotz & Chatterjee, 1995, p. 1317). Additionally, if the perceived risks associated with any business process are high, then the client can share the risks with the multiple vendors through various ownership sharing mechanisms (such as business benefit contracting, joint ventures, strategic alliances, and equity holding deals, which were discussed earlier).

Just like a single client can engage multiple vendors in a one-to-many relationship, multiple clients can also engage a single vendor in a many-to-one relationship (see Figure 4). In such a *multiclient* outsourcing relationship, multiple clients can pool their requirements and resources to form an alliance, and contract with a single vendor for joint delivery of certain generic business processes. For example, multiple clients can get together and jointly negotiate and bargain for the best possible deal from prospective vendors for all their payroll services. Hence, this leads to buyer economies of scale, increased client bargaining power, and risk sharing. Examples of such relationships have been found in information systems outsourcing, co-marketing, and R&D consortia (Gallivan & Oh, 1999, pp. 1-6).

Lastly, relationships can get even more complex with many-to-many relationships, aptly termed as "complex sourcing" (Gallivan & Oh, 1999, pp. 1-6). This involves multiple clients and vendors in the same outsourcing contract, and can be conceptually interpreted as a combination of the multivendor and multiclient relationships described earlier (see Figure 4).

It is important to note that, most often, a one-to-one or *dyadic* relationship actually exists between a client and a vendor, even though the overall scenario may first point to a multiclient, multivendor, or complex sourcing environment (Gallivan & Oh, 1999, pp. 1-6). For example, a vendor may execute the business processes outsourced by multiple clients, but its clients are independent of each other, with separate contracts between each client and the vendor. Similarly, a client can outsource its business processes to multiple vendors, but its vendors are independent of each other, with separate contracts between each vendor and the client.

Strategy of Utilizing Vendors While Infusing Maturity and Ushering Transformations in Client's Business Processes

Can a client use the expertise of a vendor for infusing maturity or growth into its own business processes? Wibbelsman and Maiero (1994, as cited in Dibbern et al., 2004, p. 11) provided an interesting framework in which the client could use three strategies to retain its business processes in-house over the long term, and use the vendor's expertise to improve them. The three strategies were named as (a) rehabilitation and return, (b) transition assistance, and (c) capability development, and each strategy can be adapted to BPO (see Figure 5). There are subtle differences between the three strategies. "Rehabilitation and return" involves bringing inefficient processes back to life, "transition assistance" involves a changeover to newer processes, and "capability development" involves the strengthening of a client's business processes and core competencies.

In the first strategy of "rehabilitation and return," the vendor (or an external consultant) who has the required expertise in the relevant business processes would assist the client in reforming its business processes at the client site. Here the presumptions are that (1) the client's business processes are in bad shape and need restoration, (2) the client does not want to outsource its business processes, and (3) the client wants to "learn" directly from the experts. This is not strictly "outsourcing" since no business process is really transferred over to the vendor. However, the vendor uses its own expertise to help the client gain operational effectiveness in its business processes by actively suggesting and implementing various changes. Forexample, if the client feels that it is not performing a certain business process (such as data management) efficiently, and at the same time does not want to outsource it (probably because of its strategic nature, security issues, core competence related nature, etc.), then the client can engage a specialist vendor (for data management) that would send over its personnel to the client site on a temporary basis. The vendor personnel would go to the client site, assess the relevant business processes of the client, suggest changes, possibly oversee or actually implement the suggested changes, gauge if the changes are actually leading to desired improvements, and then return. The risk is that the client may not be able to actually replicate the efficiency and effectiveness of vendors in running the business processes. The relevant business process is, in all probability, the core competence of the vendor in which it has developed expertise and tacit knowledge that cannot easily be replicated elsewhere. Additionally, vendors rely on economies of scale and economies of scope to derive cost and quality advantages in the relevant business processes. Many of these factors that help a vendor run certain business processes efficiently cannot be easily replicated on the client site. Of course, the vendor can possibly bring about a greater efficiency in the client's business processes by making suitable recommendations and even implementing them, but it may not match the vendor's own efficiency levels.

In the second strategy of "transition assistance," the client attempts to transition to a newer set of business processes, and uses the assistance of a vendor in various ways during this transition. Here, the client's existing business processes are in good enough shape, but a decision might have been made to changeover to a newer set of business processes. For example, business processes with newer technologies are continually adopted in response to the changing market dynamics. Such a situation demands that while the newer processes are being adopted by the client personnel, the current processes cannot be completely discarded, and need to be kept running during the transition period. Hence, while the client personnel adopt, learn, and transition to the new business processes, the vendor personnel would take the responsibility of keeping the current processes running. Once the client successfully transitions to the newer businesses processes, both the current business processes and the vendor's services would be discontinued. There are two major risks here: (1) the vendor fails to successfully carry out the client's current business processes and hence hurts the client's prospects in the market, and (2) the client fails to transition to the newer system successfully or decides to fall back on the current system. Similar to the "transition assistance" concept, Sparrow (2003, p. 10) speaks about *transformational outsourcing,* where certain activities are

Figure 5. Utilizing vendors while infusing maturity and ushering transformations

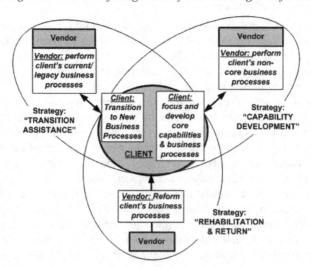

outsourced to the vendor while the client transforms by comprehensive reorganization and optimization of its business processes, and Millar (1994, as cited in Lacity & Hirschheim, 1995, pp. 4-5) speaks about *transitional outsourcing,* where clients usher in a major transition or changeover involving three phases: (a) the outsourcing of legacy processes, (b) the transition to the new processes, and (c) the management of the new processes.

In the third strategy, of "capability development," the focus of the vendor is to build on its core capabilities (and related business processes) that maximize its competitiveness in the marketplace. This implies that the client keeps its focus on its "core" capabilities, and at the same time attempts to add newer capabilities to strengthen this "core" with the aim of making itself more competitive in the marketplace. Additionally, the business processes that are not strictly related to their core capabilities are then candidates for temporary or permanent outsourcing. In other words, the client can focus and build on its strengths (core capabilities) by: (1) handing over some noncore activities to a vendor, and/or (2) making use of a vendor's help to further develop its own core capabilities. After the client has confidently consolidated and built on its core capabilities, the client will have the option of discontinuing or renegotiating the extent of its engagement with the vendor. The risk lies in getting blinded by the urge to focus on the core capabilities and forgetting the importance of monitoring the vendor's activities during that period.

Strategies Based on Required Expertise and Quantity of Workers

When business processes are outsourced to a vendor and/or offshored to another country, important human-resource-related concerns arise. The salaries of personnel vary from organization to organization, and country to country. At the same time, the availability of skilled personnel would vary from location to location. Hence, various factors need to be taken into consideration before business processes are outsourced or offshored (Iyengar, 2005; Karamouzis and Young, 2004). A location with high density of academic institutions would increase the availability and talent pool of skilled professionals in that location, and provide the firms with greater options of hiring fresh talent. Additionally, a location that is a hub for particular businesses or industries would have a greater availability of experienced personnel in those particular businesses. The cost of personnel would vary depending on the supply-demand characteristics, cost of living, and various other economic characteristics of the particular location. India and China, for example, are currently attractive destinations for firms searching for high-quality skills, at low costs, and with high availability (Chakrabarty, 2006d). Aron and Singh (n.d.) provided an interesting classification on the expertise and the number of the workers required for business process outsourcing. They suggest that the various business process tasks can be classified in decreasing order of "worker expertise required" and increasing order of the "number of workers required" as: (a) expert intervention, (b) problem resolution, (c) customer interface services, and (d) data transformation (see Figure 6). Tasks that require high expertise, such as expert intervention or problem resolution, require greater business process understanding from the involved personnel (attained through academic pursuits, training, or work experience), and hence involve greater costs per worker. Alternatively, tasks like data transformation and customer interface services involve greater volumes of work that need to be handled by a larger number of workers.

Figure 6. Business process tasks, expertise, and quantity (Source: Aron & Singh, n.d.)

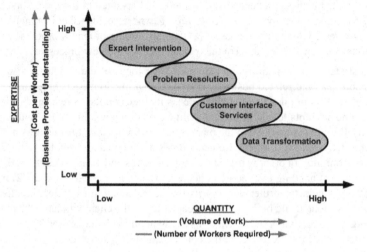

Hence, it is important to consider the following three factors before outsourcing or offshoring business processes: (a) the tasks involved in the business process, (b) the expertise required for the tasks, and (c) the number of workers required. After these three factors have been considered, a decision on the viability of outsourcing to vendors and/or offshoring to another country must be made, based on (1) the availability of workers with the required expertise, (2) the cost of workers with the required expertise, and (3) various other outsourcing and offshoring related considerations discussed in this chapter.

The IT Strategy

IT (information technology) applications or software are often very tightly integrated into business processes, and personnel access and use these IT applications to execute or manage the business processes effectively. For example, the personnel managing the payroll or accounting-related business processes would certainly make use of IT applications, such as spreadsheets and other software, that allow entry, manipulation, and storage of data and also generation of reports of various kinds. The IT applications are commonly off-the-shelf products or are custom developed by software service providers, and need to be purchased. Of course, the software can also be custom developed in-house, which is equivalent to purchasing software from one's own IT department. However, after the purchase, both the off-the-shelf and the custom-developed software need to be hosted on servers and maintained, and for this purpose, the company is forced to hire additional IT staff. This chapter will not go into the aspect of purchasing software products or custom development, since a huge number of books and academic literature is already available on off-the-shelf products and custom development of software, inclusive of insourcing/outsourcing of custom software development (Chakrabarty, 2006a; Nelson et al., 1996; Poppo & Zenger, 1998). However, this chapter will touch the issue of "renting" software, which is a relatively newer and possibly path-breaking concept in the usage of IT in business process management.

Strategy of Renting Remotely Hosted IT Applications for Business Processes

What does an organization do when it does want to take the responsibility of hosting, managing, and maintaining software applications related to its business processes? In other words, what if the organization concerned does not want to have anything to do with the management and technology overhead that goes into "owning" certain software applications that help it run its business processes (which are purchased as a product or custom developed)? IT is, after all, not the core competence of many businesses, and many businesses might find having an in-house IT department as an *overhead* or *cost-center*. An answer to this dilemma is the concept of what is traditionally known as application service providing (ASP), and has been more recently termed in various flavors such as "on Demand" service, "software-as-a-service" (SAAS), "real-time delivery," "application utilities" (Pring & Ambrose, 2004), or "net-sourcing" (Kern, Lacity, & Willcocks, 2002). It has gained greater significance and prominence in recent times due to broadband and other technologies that have made Internet access faster.

This strategy would involve contracting with an application service provider (ASP) whereby the client organization would have access to IT applications hosted by the ASP over a wide area network (WAN), a virtual private network (VPN), or over the Internet (Susarla, Barua, & Whinston, 2003, p. 103). In other words, the client organization would be adopting a strategy of selectively "renting" IS applications rather than "owning" IT software for its business processes (Bennett & Timbrell, 2000, p. 196). Technologically, the difference lies in where the application is hosted (Dewire, 2000, p. 14). Normally, IT applications for any business process would be hosted on the employee's/user's personal computer, or in the organization's own local area network (LAN) or data center (see Figure 7). However, when the application is "rented," it would be hosted in a server or data center managed by the ASP (see Figure 7). IDC (International Data Corp., as cited in Dewire, 2000, p. 14) explains that an organization would rent the IT applications from the ASP "on a subscription basis and can bundle a full range of hosted application services" which can range from "low-end, productivity programs (e.g., word processing) to high-end ERP modules"

A major advantage of this strategy is that the ASP would purchase, customize, and manage IS applications at remote locations and host them for clients over the Internet (or maybe over a WAN, VPN, or extranet), and hence the related overheads and responsibilities would lie entirely with the ASP. Moreover, in the fast-changing software marketplace, the onus of getting the latest software upgrades, keeping the software defect free, securing the software application and data (against hackers and other threats), and ensuring 24×7 operations would be the ASP's responsibility. The client organization just has to make sure that the network connectivity between the organization and ASP is secure and active, and that proper budgeting is done for the software services that are being rented.

Figure 7. ASPs and on-demand software services

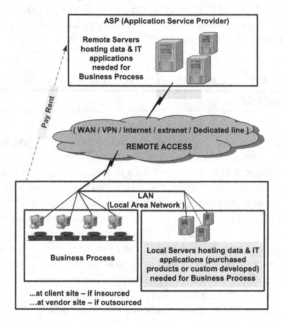

The major risks would be "loss of control" and "reliability" issues. The ASP would be in complete control of the software application, and the client would be dependent on the ASP for reliable access to the software application. ASPs often host software on a centrally managed facility, and provide access to the software application to multiple-client organizations (Dewire, 2000, p. 14). Now, multiple-client organizations might have divergent needs or customization requirements with regard to the software being rented. If it is a simple word processing application, then there would be low chances of divergent needs, but if it is an ERP or some complex application, then the clients might have divergent interests in terms of the software features, upgrades, or customization. In case of conflicting interests among clients, the ASPs may be inclined to give greater importance to larger clients, or arrive at some sort of compromise that does not ensure 100% satisfaction to all clients but is just "good enough." Furthermore, the client organization is completely dependent on the ASP for 24×7 reliable accesses to the software application. Clients should make sure that the contract has clauses that safeguard the client organization from risks resulting from the ASPs unsatisfactory behavior. When IS applications are tightly integrated into business processes, any failure to reliably access an IS application can affect the entire gamut of associated business processes (see Figure 7).

Conclusion

Though BPO has many advantages, it is also fraught with many risks. Effective strategies need to be adopted for successful BPO, along with suitable assessment of risks and maximum utilization of the opportunities. This chapter attempted to provide a comprehensive overview of several BPO strategies, along with an analysis of the associated opportunities and risks, which would be of help both to the practitioners and the academicians.

Note

The author acknowledges the kind guidance and support from the editors of this book. The author may be contacted at schakrabarty@tamu.edu or chakrabartys@yahoo.com.

References

Adler, P. S. (2003). Making the HR outsourcing decision. *MIT Sloan Management Review*, *45*(1), 53-60.

Ang, S., & Straub, D. W. (1998). Production and transaction economies and IS outsourcing: A study of the U.S. banking industry. *MIS Quarterly*, *22*(4), 535-552.

Apte, U. M., & Mason, R. O. (1995). Global disaggregation of information-intensive services. *Management Science, 41*(7), 1250-1262.

Aron, R., & Singh, J. (n.d). *IT enabled strategic outsourcing: knowledge intensive firms, information work and the extended organizational form*. Knowledge@Wharton, Wharton School Publishing. Retrieved Dec 19, 2005, from http://knowledge.wharton. upenn.edu/PDFs/1071.pdf

Aubert, B. A., Rivard, S., & Patry, M. (1996). A transaction cost approach to outsourcing behavior: Some empirical evidence. *Information & Management, 30*(2), 51-64.

Bennett, C., & Timbrell, G. (2000). Application service providers: Will they succeed? *Information Systems Frontiers, 2*(2), 195-211.

Carmel, E. & Agarwal, R. (2002). The maturation of offshore sourcing of information technology work. *MIS Quarterly Executive, 1*(2), 65-78.

Chakrabarty, S. (2006a). A conceptual model for bidirectional service, information and product quality in an IS outsourcing collaboration environment. In *Proceedings of the 39th Hawaii International Conference on Systems Sciences (HICSS-39)*, HI. Retrieved December 5, 2006 from http://ieeexplore.ieee.org/iel5/10548/33361/01579305.pdf

Chakrabarty, S. (2006b). Making sense of the sourcing and shoring maze: The various out-sourcing & offshoring slternatives. In H. S. Kehal & V. P. Singh (Eds.), *Outsourcing & offshoring in the 21ˢᵗ Century: A socio economic perspective* (pp. 18-53). Hershey, PA: Idea Group Publishing.

Chakrabarty, S. (2006c). Real life case studies of offshore outsourced IS projects: Analysis of issues and socio-economic paradigms. In H. S. Kehal & V. P. Singh (Eds.), *Outsourcing & offshoring in the 21ˢᵗ Century: A socio economic perspective* (pp. 248-281). Hershey, PA: Idea Group Publishing.

Chakrabarty, S. (2006d). The journey to new lands: Utilizing the global IT workforce through offshore-insourcing. In P. Yoong & S. Huff (Eds.), *Managing IT professionals in the Internet age* (pp. 277-318). Hershey, PA: Idea Group Publishing.

Currie, W. L., & Willcocks, L. P. (1998). Analyzing four types of IT sourcing decisions in the context of scale, client/supplier interdependency and risk mitigation. *Information Systems Journal, 8*(2), 119-143.

Dewire, D. T. (2000). Application service providers. *Information Systems Management, 17*(4), 14-19.

Dibbern, J., Goles, T., Hirschheim, R., & Jayatilaka, B. (2004). Information systems outsourc-ing: A survey and analysis of the literature. *ACM SIGMIS Database, 35*(4), 6-102.

Earl, M. J. (1996). The risks of outsourcing IT. *Sloan Management Review, 37*(3), 26-32.

Gallivan, M. J., & Oh, W. (1999). Analyzing IT outsourcing relationships as alliances among multiple clients and vendors. In *Proceedings of the 32ⁿᵈ Annual International Confer-ence on System Sciences*, HI.

Hirschheim, R. A., & Lacity, M. C. (1998). Reducing information systems costs through insourcing: Experiences from the field. In *Proceedings of the 31ˢᵗ Annual Hawaii International Conference on System Sciences*, HI (pp. 644-653).

Hirschheim, R. A., & Lacity, M. C. (2000). The myths and realities of information technol-ogy insourcing. *Communications of the ACM, 43*(2), 99-107.

Iyengar, P. (2005, March 11). *How to assess cities in India for your IT outsourcing needs* (ID No. G00126067). Gartner Research.

Jurison, J. (1995). The role of risk and return in information technology outsourcing deci-sions. *Journal of Information Technology, 10*, 239-247.

Karamouzis, F., & Young, A. (2004, June 30). *India maintains its offshore leadership posi-tion* (ID No. G00121630). Gartner Research.

Kempf, T., Scholl, R. S., & Sinha, D. (2001, October 5). *Cross-border collaboration: A service aggregator model for offshore IT services (Executive Summary)* (ID No. ITSV-WW-EX-0037). Gartner Research.

Kern, T., Lacity, M. C., & Willcocks, L. P. (2002). *Netsourcing: Renting business applica-tions and services over a network*. New York: Prentice Hall.

Klotz, D. E., & Chatterjee, K. (1995). Dual sourcing in repeated procurement competitions. *Management Science, 41*(8), 1317-1327.

Kobyashi-Hillary, M., (2004). *Outsourcing to India:Tthe offshore advantage*. Berlin, Germany: Springer-Verlag.

Lacity, M. C., & Hirschheim, R. A. (1995). *Beyond the information systems outsourcing bandwagon: The insourcing response*. Chichester: Wiley.

Lacity, M. C., Willcocks, L. P., & Feeny, D. F. (1996). The value of selective IT sourcing. *Sloan Management Review, 37*(3), 13-25.

Loh, L., & Venkatraman, N. (1992). Determinants of information technology outsourcing: A cross-sectional analysis. *Journal of Management Information Systems, 9*(1), 7-24.

Loh, L., & Venkatraman, N. (1995). An empirical study of information technology outsourcing: benefits, risks, and performance implications. In *Proceedings of the 16th International Conference on Information Systems*, Amsterdam, The Netherlands (pp. 277-288).

Nam, K., Rajagopalan, S., Rao, H. R., & Chaudhury, A. (1996). A two-level investigation of information systems outsourcing. *Communications of the ACM, 39*(7), 36-44.

Nelson, P., Richmond, W., & Seidmann, A. (1996). Two dimensions of software acquisition. *Communications of the ACM, 39*(7), 29-35.

Poppo, L., & Zenger, T. (1998). Testing alternative theories of the firm: Transaction cost, knowledge-based, and measurement explanations for make-or-buy decisions in information services. *Strategic Management Journal, 19*, 853-877.

Porter, M. E. (1996, November-December). What is strategy? *Harvard Business Review*, 61-78.

Pring, B., & Ambrose, C. (2004, November 3). *Vendors vie for competitive position in ASP market* (ID No. G00124388). Gartner Research.

Reuer, J. J., Zollo, M., & Singh, H. (2002). Post-formation dynamics in strategic alliances. *Strategic Management Journal, 23*, 135-151.

Sinha, D. & Terdiman, R. (2002, September 5). *Potential risks in offshore sourcing* (ID No. ITSV-WW-DP-0360). Gartner Research.

Sobol, M. G., & Apte, U. M. (1995). Domestic and global outsourcing practices of America's most effective IS users. *Journal of Information Technology, 10*, 269-280.

Sparrow, E., (2003). *Successful IT outsourcing*. London: Springer-Verlag.

Susarla, A., Barua, A., & Whinston, A. B. (2003). Understanding the service component of application service provision: An empirical analysis of satisfaction with ASP services. *MIS Quarterly, 27*(1), 91-123.

Willcocks, L., & Lacity, M. (1998). *Strategic sourcing of information systems*. Chichester: Wiley.

Section IV

Web Delivery of
College Level Courses

Chapter XII

Developing and Delivering Online Courses

Jayavel Sounderpandian, University of Wisconsin-Parkside, USA

Manohar Madan, University of Wisconsin-Whitewater, USA

Abstract

Distance education, which started out with closed circuit TV technology, has evolved into completely online courses. Not surprisingly, online education has emerged as a major form of e-business. This chapter offers helpful suggestions for those who are planning to develop and deliver online courses, either as part of an existing degree program or as a new totally online degree program. Wherever needed, an online MBA program is used as an example. The chapter considers such things as mission, curriculum planning, curriculum control, marketing, scheduling, course development, expectations from students and faculty, and strengths and weaknesses of online education.

Introduction

Traditional classroom (or face-to-face, or F2F) instruction requires the students and instructor to be at the same place at the same time. In other words, the instructor and the students are place bound and time bound. Early forms of distance education[1] removed the need for them to be place bound. The earliest form of distance education started with the closed-circuit TV technology, where the audio and video signals of an instructor's lecture were transmitted to a distant location so that students at that location could also "attend the class." A clear advantage of this technology was that it eliminated or greatly reduced commuting needs for students and instructors. Later, the signals were compressed and carried via closed circuit or broadcasted using a satellite so that the signals could be delivered to several remote locations efficiently. Consequently, compressed video became a popular technology for distance education.

The advent of Internet changed the technology radically so that asynchronous communication could be utilized. Reading materials and activities of a course could be stored at a Web site for secure access from anywhere at any time. Students and instructors could "come to the class" individually at a time convenient to them and carry out all classroom activities. This turned out to be a great convenience to them, because not only are they not place bound but now they are also not time bound. As a result, demand for online education grew rapidly. Today, a Google search of the phrase "online education" produces more than a billion hits. Worldwidelearn.com, DirectoryofSchools.com, USNews.com and GetEducated.com are good Web sites to get a list of available online degree programs. For a survey of literature on distance education, including online education, see Bryant et al. (Bryant, Kahle, & Schafer, 2005).

MBA has been a popular degree program since the 1960s, and it still enjoys a high demand. It is no wonder that online MBA programs are increasing in popularity, because the advantages of being not place bound and not time bound are especially attractive to business employees. Private and public schools have raced to claim their share of the online market. Crawford (2005) reports an estimate of 125,000 online MBA students in the year 2005. A list of well-recognized MBA programs can be found at the Web site, BusinessWeek.com, and online MBA programs at GetEducated.com. Since many online programs are constantly being added and deleted, most lists are not up-to-date.

Online training of employees has also been increasing rapidly. Corporations have found it more cost effective to train their employees using online programs. Such programs eliminate the need for employees to travel, saving a sizeable amount of money for the company. For details on the advantages of online training of employees, see Blake et al. (Blake, Gibson, & Blackwell, 2005).

Consonance with the Mission

A university interested in starting an online degree program should first examine if such an action is in line with its mission. The university may have an obligation to its on-site students as laid out in its mission. Starting an online program should not in any way jeopardize that obligation. A reason for concern is that the new program will need substantial investments during the beginning years, and some recurring needs for resources in later years. In return, of course, the online program promises to generate sufficient revenues in future years. However, Folkers (2005) has cited several examples of failures of online education. Such examples and their reasons for failure will have to be analyzed to ensure that the contemplated online program will succeed and existing on-site programs will not be adversely affected. Folkers (2005) also provides a detailed discussion of incorporating online education as part of higher learning.

An additional consideration with respect to the mission is whether the online program is benefiting the clientele intended in the mission. For instance, suppose the mission implies service to only a regional population. The economics of an online program may require admitting a large proportion of students from outside the region. Whether this affects the mission of serving the region should be carefully examined. It could be that by offering an online program that educates nonregional students, a university generates substantial additional income that can be used to educate regional students F2F. In this case, the online program will be justified. The institution may also consider amending the mission in light of online opportunities.

For certain programs, the mission may call for maintaining a minimum quality level, usually in the form of maintaining an accreditation. For MBA programs, the accreditation by AACSB International (Association for Advancement of Collegiate Schools of Business, International) is valued highly. The accreditation standards call for certain minimum requirements in starting new programs and maintaining the quality of an existing program that is newly delivered online. The standards are refined continually, and the current information can be found at the AACSB Web site (http://www.aacsb.edu). At the time this article was written, the standards for every new program required the following.

Demand Analysis

A justification for starting a new program requires a proof of healthy demand for the program. This may be done in several ways. One way is to conduct a survey of the intended market. Another way is to analyze the demand for existing similar programs at other comparable schools and apply it to the intended program at the intended location.

Resource Analysis

As already explained, the new program will need financial, instructional, and administrative resources. These requirements should be estimated, and resources must be identified.

Learning Goals

For any new program, a set of learning goals should be finalized. Learning goals should be established not only for each course, but also for the whole program. AACSB is keen on program-level learning goals, and expects detailed processes for assurance of learning. These processes are discussed next.

Assurance of Learning

For each program level learning goal, processes should be in place to ensure that at least some minimum percentage of students are achieving those goals before they graduate. The assurance that a particular student has achieved a particular goal can come about through embedded exercises and exam questions in selected courses. The assessment of a student's achievement of a goal should be verified by a group of faculty members rather than by a single person, preferably including some outsiders. When the number of students in the program is large, sampling a representative set of students and assessing only the sampled students is admissible. A detailed discussion of assurance of learning is presented in a subsequent section.

Organizational Structure

Developing and delivering online courses involve many personnel whose efforts need to be coordinated. It also involves a considerable amount of monetary investment. Needless to say, the whole process needs to be systematically organized. The commonly observed organization structure is shown in Figure 1. At the top we have the Project Management Team, which typically consists of representatives from university administration, faculty, and technical services. This team is responsible for managing the whole project, with special attention to budgets and deadlines. Below it are the Curriculum Planning and Control Committee, the Technical Services Committee, and the Marketing and Public Relations Committee. The functions of Curriculum and Technical Services Committees are described in some detail. The Marketing and Public Relations Committee is responsible for building the image of the program and recruiting students.

The developers of individual online courses report to the Curriculum Planning and Control Committee, and the Web technicians report to the Technical Services Committee. The Project Management Team should be aware of possible turnover of personnel, especially among the Web technicians, and must be prepared to manage it.

The organization chart in Figure 1 applies only to the course development phase. After the courses are developed and the program is started, other entities such as course instructors, business services, and student information system come into play.

Figure 1. Organization chart for online course development

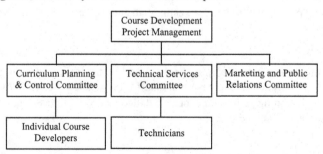

Revenue Allocation

The financial side of online course development and delivery can be different from that of onsite development and delivery due to the differences that exist between the two modes. Essentially, there are the following cost centers that would need to share the revenue:

- Program administration
- Instruction
- Technical services
- Student information system
- Student services
- Business services
- Marketing

Program administration is the owner of the enterprise and holds the equity. The administration needs to arrive at a formula for sharing the revenue among the cost centers. The formula may include fixed payments plus a percentage of the revenues. For example, at the course development stage, the instructors who develop the course are paid a fixed amount, usually according to a negotiated contract. When a course is offered, the instructor is usually paid a fixed amount to teach that course. Some universities may pay an additional bonus on a per-student basis, recognizing the fact that the teaching effort increases with the number of students in the class. Occasionally, an instructor may be paid a bonus for teaching excellence that is reflected in, say, the students' feedback on instructor performance.

Similarly, at the beginning of a course, a fixed amount of effort from technical services department is needed to set up the Web site. Additionally, as the course proceeds, the technical effort needed for the course increases with the number of students in the course. The technical service department is therefore paid a fixed sum plus a per-student fee.

Student information system keeps track of student enrollments and grades. Student services include advising, financial aid, and counseling. These services will incur both fixed and per-student costs. Finally, the marketing department may be paid a fixed fee for running the advertisements and recruiting students. The department may be paid a fixed amount per year for advertising efforts and a per-student amount for students recruited by that department.

Curriculum Planning

If an existing F2F program is being planned for online delivery, then no new curriculum needs to be designed. But if the planned online program is completely new, then the whole curriculum of the program needs to be carefully designed. The first step is to finalize the learning goals for the curriculum as a whole, which will serve as a guide for developing individual courses. Because the overall curriculum plan drives all the individual courses, this plan is very important. It should be designed by a Curriculum Planning and Control Committee of faculty members, with representation from each functional area of the program.

The curriculum plan for an MBA program will typically include foundation courses, core courses, and elective courses. The foundation courses are needed for those who enter the program without a business background, such as science or engineering graduates. Those who have a recent undergraduate degree in business are usually waived from foundation courses.

The core courses are required of all students. They are expected to cover all the functional areas of business, and additionally, essential components such as ethics, leadership, communication, global economy, and information technology. Finally, there should be opportunity for the students to integrate their knowledge gained from various functional areas and apply them to tackle real or hypothetical business problems. Real-world case studies are routinely employed for this purpose. An important requirement of the core courses is that together they should cover all the concepts that are necessary to achieve the learning goals set for the program.

Electives are meant to give a student the opportunity to specialize in an area that he/she wishes. AACSB requires at least a total of 30 credits for core and elective courses put together. If a

Figure 2. The concepts vs. courses matrix

	Required Courses									
	ACCT 701	ACCT 702	FIN 731	FIN 732	HRM 741	HRM 742	MIS 721	MKT 751	MKT 752	...
Accounting										
Double Entry Method	x									
Financial Statements	x		x							
Costing Methods		x								
Activity Based Costing		x								
Transfer Pricing		x								
GAAP	x	x		x						
...										
Finance										
Time Value of Money	x		x							
Financial Ratios		x	x	x						
Cost of Capital			x	x						
Working Capital Mgmt				x						
Financial Markets				x						
Financial Institutions				x						
Investment				x						
...										
Human Res. Mgmt.				An x mark in the matrix entry implies the topic on the row is covered in the course on the column.						
Info. Systems										
Marketing										
Business Strategy										

school has a total of 30 credits in its MBA program, it is common to see anywhere between 9 to 15 credits of electives.

A simple technique that may be used to summarize the essential part of the curriculum plan is the concepts vs. courses matrix. Though simple, the matrix proves to be an effective tool. The rows in the matrix represent the concepts (or topics) that are planned to be covered in the program. The columns are the required courses in the program. (See Figure 2.) The entries in the matrix are either a check mark to show that a concept is covered in the corresponding course, or a number that represents the hours that an average student spends on that topic by completing the program. Such a matrix gives a nice summary of the curriculum with respect to the concepts planned in the curriculum. It helps not only the implementation of the plan, but also the maintenance of the whole curriculum. For instance, if a course is revised for any reason, the matrix can be used to ensure all the concepts that are necessary to keep in the revised version. In the next section, we shall see how to implement this plan.

Curriculum Implementation and Maintenance

Curriculum control is necessary for any program, whether it is online or F2F, for proper implementation. Fortunately, curriculum control is a lot easier in online programs, because the content can be easily verified by just looking into the course Web site.

Figure 3. Course overview form

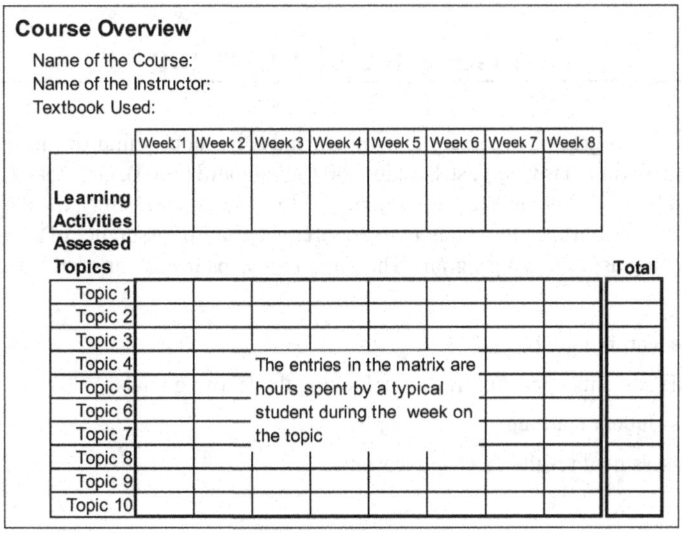

Course Overview

Name of the Course:
Name of the Instructor:
Textbook Used:

	Week 1	Week 2	Week 3	Week 4	Week 5	Week 6	Week 7	Week 8	
Learning Activities									
Assessed Topics									**Total**
Topic 1									
Topic 2									
Topic 3									
Topic 4		The entries in the matrix are							
Topic 5		hours spent by a typical							
Topic 6		student during the week on							
Topic 7		the topic							
Topic 8									
Topic 9									
Topic 10									

The process of collecting data for concepts vs. courses matrix is as follows. For every required course, the instructor of the course submits a course overview form to the school. (See Figure 3.) At the top of the form there are details such as course name and number, semester, instructor name, and textbook used. Below this information is a matrix where the rows are the concepts and the columns are the weeks of the course. If there are 8 weeks of classes, then there will be eight columns in the matrix. The instructor of the course enters, at the top of each column, the list of activities that the students perform that week, and the description of the concept along the rows. (Later in this chapter it will be seen that every course is to be assigned a "faculty-in-charge" of its content. If the instructor is not the faculty-in-charge, then the instructor will consult the faculty-in-charge in designing the course content and filling in the course overview form.) The entries in the matrix are the number of hours an average student spends on each topic. By collecting this information for all required courses, the coverage of the concepts can be summarized. A spreadsheet format is very convenient for this purpose.

All course overview forms are organized as worksheets within a single workbook, and a summary sheet in the front adds the number of hours spent on each concept. The summary sheet thus provides a listing of concepts and the emphasis placed on each concept in the program. This information is very valuable for curriculum control. Each sheet workbook can serve as a record of course content that can be communicated to any other instructor who is asked to teach the same course. The individual course sheets and the summary sheet should be continually updated.

It should be noted that the course overview forms and the summary are only "inputs" to the students. More actions and documentation are needed to achieve assurance of learning. In the case of MBA programs, the accrediting body, AACSB, is less interested in the inputs, and a lot more interested in assurance of learning. This brings us to the next section on assurance of learning.

Assurance of Learning

Assessment of a program is necessary to maintain and continuously improve its quality. The literature on assessment is very vast. Suskie (2004), Walvoord (2004), Gronlund (2005), and Palomba and Banta (1999) are standard references for assessment. Lately, the emphasis has shifted to learning from teaching. Thus, one should concentrate on assurance of learning rather than the teaching aspects in a program. The important steps in assurance of learning are:

1.   Define learning goals.
2.   Provide students opportunities for achieving the learning goals.
3.   Assess student learning.
4.   Use assessment results to assure learning.

Learning goals are defined using Bloom's taxonomy (Bloom, 1984). For MBA programs, AACSB recommends four to eight such goals at the program level. At the individual course level, there will be separate sets of goals. The difference in program-level learning goals

(PLLGs) compared to course-level learning goals (CLLGs) is that PLLGs are to be tracked more closely than CLLGs. One way to track PLLGs is to create a (fake) online course using the software Desire2Learn (D2L) for assurance of learning, and enroll all active students in it. D2L allows an online grade book that can be set up to track the progress of each student against each PLLG. This makes for an efficient way to assure that every student achieves every PLLG.

The second step is to provide opportunities to students to achieve the learning goals. For example, if attaining public speaking skills is a goal, then it is not enough to just ask the students to speak at a public forum. The curriculum should include a required course where students are taught public speaking principles. The concept vs. course matrix in Figure 2 can help to ensure that learning opportunities exist in the curriculum for every goal.

The next step is assessment of each learning goal. One way to assess CLLGs of core courses is to employ the standardized tests offered by the Educational Testing Service (ETS). ETS offers tests for many majors including business administration at the undergraduate and graduate levels. Such tests are called Major Field Tests, and are available at reasonable cost. The advantage of the Major Field Tests is that they have external validation, and can be used to compare one institution with another or the national average. Interested readers should consult the ETS Web site (http://ets.org) for the availability and details of standardized tests in a desired major.

The final step closes the loop. Results from the assessment of student achievement should be formally compiled and used for continuous improvement of the curriculum. A committee comprising faculty and other stakeholders should look at the compiled results, locate deficiencies in student performance, and formulate action plans to remove those deficiencies.

Almost all the literature on assurance of learning or assessment assumes onsite courses rather than online courses. Online courses may need some special treatment. Marks et al. (Marks, Sibley, & Arbaugh, 2005) discuss numerous aspects of online courses and how they may affect student learning. Such studies can help a school formulate special plans for assurance of learning. They can also help to formulate action plans for improving the curriculum after receiving a formal assurance of learning report.

Technical Support

Offering online courses need extensive technical support from a technical department. Technical support is crucial to the success of the program. Typically, the technical support provider is responsible for the following tasks.

Maintain the Web Servers

The service provider has to use reliable hardware as Web servers. The servers should have sufficient capacity to handle the peak projected demand for Internet communication, assuming all the students are online at the same time.

Provide Course Development Support

Faculty members will have to work closely with technicians in developing the Web pages of a course. If the page requires advanced features such as video and audio files, the needed support will be correspondingly more. Additionally, there will be ongoing revisions to the course content. Processes must be in place to take care of revisions.

Place the Courses Online

When a course is developed, it will have to be made available at the desired URL. The technicians should place the courses at the URL in a timely manner so the instructors can check it well ahead of the first day of classes.

Provide Technical Support to Students

One important benefit of online education is the temporal flexibility, that is, providing choice of time of learning to the students (Demirdjian, 2002). As online learning requires significant use of technology, students will invariably face technical problems. Hence, students will require assistance from qualified technicians to answer their questions on a 24/7 basis.

Maintain Uniformity of Web Pages Across Different Courses

Students would expect/prefer standardization of format of lectures, assignments, discussions, and exams in all courses. The technicians are expected to convey to the faculty their schemes for formatting the different items in course Web pages, and maintaining uniformity of pages across all courses.

Conduct Student Surveys for Feedback

Online courses require more frequent monitoring than on-site courses. It is customary to conduct a course evaluation at least twice, midway through the course and at the end, in order to facilitate continuous improvement. Since this needs a survey to be conducted online, the technicians are once again involved.

As can be seen from the list of duties for technical staff, it is very important to have qualified and reliable technical support. A school may or may not have such capability within the campus. While on-campus technical support is common, many schools do use commercial outfits for the purpose. If a school is planning to employ a commercial outfit, needless to say, the outfit should be selected carefully.

Marketing Plans

The need for marketing an online degree program cannot be overemphasized. A typical online program may have the ability to attract a number of potential students outside the region. A good marketing plan should include advertising at popular Web sites. In the case of MBA, this could be Businessweek.com. There are also specialized Web sites such as GetEducated.

com and Onlinedegrees.net. Of course, the university must have its own attractive Web site. Many students will check a program's Web site to estimate the quality of the program.

To attract regional students, it is necessary to resort to traditional methods of marketing and promotion. Printing well-designed brochures and mailing them to local businesses and potential students is a must. Additionally, the university should conduct open houses and other forms of informational sessions. Offering scholarships is another way to attract students who may otherwise go elsewhere.

Since many potential students may be outside the region, the university must use recruiting agents who travel to other campuses and educational fairs, domestic and foreign, to advertise the program or conduct informational sessions.

A recent phenomenon is the emergence of commercial agencies that offer recruiting services. In populous countries such as India and China, such agencies provide local expertise in recruiting efforts. Such agencies bring significant efficiencies in recruiting and tend to be quite successful in identifying and attracting a sizeable number of prospective students who satisfy the specified admission requirements.

Scheduling

Another important part of the plan for a new program is the scheduling of courses. The required courses and electives have to be offered so that a typical student can graduate within a reasonable time. Indeed, it is best to list the courses that a typical student would take in each semester. Aggregating this over all students, who may enter into the program at different times, one can arrive at the courses that need to be offered each semester. Depending upon the number of students in the program, this requirement sets a minimum frequency and minimum number of sections of each course. This plan, in turn, determines the teaching capacity needed. Thus, the number of courses required to graduate, the number of students in the program, the time taken by an average student to graduate, and the planned schedule for offering the courses determine the capacity needed. The university should ensure that the capacity can be made available without disrupting other programs.

The time to graduate is an important parameter. To understand its implication, consider a program with a total of 32 credits (which is common in MBA programs). Suppose the curriculum consists of 16 two-credit courses, which we shall designate as A1, A2, A3, A4, B1, B2, ..., D4. Courses usually have a prerequisite structure. We will assume a simple prerequisite structure: A1 is a prerequisite for A2; A2 is a prerequisite for A3, A3 is a prerequisite for A4, B1 is a prerequisite for B2, ..., D3 is a prerequisite for D4. Each course runs for 8 weeks, and a semester is 16 weeks long. Suppose a student can handle only one course at a time, and thus takes two courses per semester, which are offered one after the other in the same semester. Consider the case of 25 new students entering the program every year. When a steady state is achieved, the scenario that evolves in terms of courses offered and enrollment in each course over a period of 1 year may be depicted as in Figure 4. The table is read as: 25 first year students enroll in Course A1 in the first half of fall semester and in course A2 during the second half, and so on. After completing Courses A1 through A4, a student becomes a second-year student and moves on to B courses.

Figure 4. The scenario where an average student takes 4 years to graduate

Total 100 students	Fall Semester		Spring Semester	
25 I year Students	A1	A2	A3	A4
25 II year Students	B1	B2	B3	B4
25 III year Students	C1	C2	C3	C4
25 IV year Students	D1	D2	D3	D4

Figure 5. The scenario where an average student takes 2 years to graduate

Total 50 students	Fall Semester		Spring Semester	
25 I year Students	A1 B1	A2 B2	A3 B3	A4 B4
25 II year Students	C1 D1	C2 D2	C3 D3	C4 D4

Notice that the university will have, at any time, a total of 100 active students, and will need to track that many students. With the same capacity, the same curriculum, the same number of students admitted per year, and the same schedule of course offerings, now suppose a student can take two courses at a time. Then the students will need only 2 years to graduate, and the scenario will be as shown in Figure 5. This table is read as: 25 first year students enroll in courses A1 and B1 in the first half of the fall semester, courses A2 and B2 in the second half and so on. Notice that now there are only 50 active students to keep track of. Encouraging students to take more courses at the same time can reduce some cost for the university for the same throughput. (This is indeed a strategy advocated in operations management to reduce work-in-process inventory.)

The relationship between various parameters can be summarized using some equations and formulas.

Let

C = total credits required for graduation

c = credits that a typical student takes in a year

T = the average time to graduate.

Then $T = C/c$ years.

Let

e = the rate of enrollment in students/year

S = the average number of active students in the program

Then $S = e(C/c) = eT$.

Some of these parameters will be useful in computing certain costs. For example, if a student information system costs x dollars per student per year, then the annual cost of the system for a given program will be $xS = xeT = xe(C/c)$. This goes to show that as c increases the cost decreases. Since many other administrative costs also follow the same pattern, it is safe to say that there will be cost savings as c increases. It is generally believed that because online courses avoid commuting, students are willing to take more credits in a year, implying c will be larger and, therefore, many types of administrative costs will be less for online courses,

Let

k = average class size for a course.

Then the minimum number of sections of the course to be offered in a year = e/k.

Let

y = cost per credit of teaching a section of a course (assumed to be the same for every course).

Then total annual teaching cost = $y (e/k) C$,

Because the cost is inversely proportional to k, there is a tendency to increase k. It has therefore become a common practice to use k as one of the measures of quality of education at an institution. The maller the value of k, the higher is the perceived quality.

Let

z = tuition fee per credit.

Then the total annual revenue = $zSc = zeC$. Since S and c are related, it is better to use the expression zeC to analyze interrelationships. Note that z and C are easily controlled by the university. Because a university may increase one or both of them in its enthusiasm to increase revenue, the value of zC, which is the total tuition for the whole program, is used in rating a program. Higher the value of zC, more cautious the students will be in enrolling in the program.

Revenues from tuition fees and government grants are to be compared against the costs. The costs include the cost of instructors, technical staff, academic and administrative overhead, technical overhead, and curriculum development costs. It is difficult to give any guidelines about these costs because they vary widely depending on the type of university. A cost that is unique to online courses is the cost of course development. Even this cost can vary widely. Boettcher (2002) provides an estimate that it can vary anywhere from $92,000 to $368,000!

The school should carefully estimate its costs. Needless to say, a comparison of total revenues and total costs is necessary for financial control and success of the program.

Course Development

The process of developing courses is extensive and it has great influence on the quality of the curriculum. It therefore has to be controlled well, and will require a lot of effort.

The first step in developing a course is to train the developers. (It is assumed that the university has already designed the content of the whole curriculum and the individual courses, as described under the sections on curriculum planning and curriculum control. It is also assumed that the technical support has been hired, as described in the section on technical support.) Training will require assistance from technicians as well as content specialists. Technical training requires the developers to learn the essentials about the software that is going to be used for creating course Web sites. Types of technology necessary to deliver online courses are listed by Folkers (2005). Currently, commonly used software is Desire2Learn or D2L. Additionally, the developers also learn some pedagogical and technical aspects of developing online courses. For instance, the developers need to know the strengths and weaknesses of online courses (most of which are discussed later in this chapter). They need to know what type of technical feature, such as quiz or discussion, is suitable for different topics. Some technical features are discussed later in the chapter.

While scheduling the development of a course, it may be noted that at least one semester's time is necessary to develop one course by a trained developer combined with an experienced technician. A conservative approach is to combine one summer and the following semester as the scheduled to time to develop a course.

The course development schedule and the first-time course-offering schedule should be coordinated properly. Specifically, they should be coordinated in such a way that the first cohort of students is able to take the courses as planned and graduate as planned. This constraint can put some strain both on the university and the students when it comes to electives. The university may be forced to develop many elective courses in a short time, and many students may be forced to take an elective course just because it is the only one being offered.

When a course is developed, the usual practice is the university pays the developer a contracted amount of remuneration and the course becomes the property of the university. The university can then use either the developer or any other instructor to teach the course. This raises some important issues. A developer may not be willing to share the course material with another instructor interested in teaching the course. On the other hand, the potential instructor, who is not the developer, may not like to teach the course designed by another person. Another issue is the maintenance of course content. After a course is developed, any changes in the content must be consistent with preserving integrity of the content. One way to deal with this issue is to have a "faculty-in-charge" for each course, who may be the developer. This person has the authority over changes to the content. Sometimes, content change becomes mandatory, as in the case when the textbook goes to a new edition. In any case, a course should be updated at least once in 5 years. In reality, most courses are updated once in 3 years. The university has to be aware of these issues and make them clear to the faculty.

To ensure good quality of a course, a good practice is to have at least two faculty members involved in developing a core course. The reason is to have some kind of peer review. The team of developers can inspect each other's work and offer constructive criticism. As in any academic product, peer review is the key to quality. Also, having more than one faculty member involved in the development of a course offers the flexibility in scheduling.

For an elective course, whenever possible, more than one faculty member should be used to develop the course. Often this may not be possible, because only one faculty member may have the expertise in the specialized area. In such cases, the university may have an additional constraint to deal with while scheduling courses.

What is Expected of the Faculty

The faculty developing online courses need to develop lectures using multimedia technology, systems facilitating online discussions and assignments, exams and projects appropriate for online mode of delivery. As online courses are inherently asynchronous in nature, it is important for a faculty delivering an online course to post alert messages regularly. It is a useful practice to urge students to access the course regularly and frequently. It is important to communicate with the students that although they have the flexibility to learn the material at any convenient time, the students have to do it within the specified deadline in order to keep up with the pace of class.

Even though the online mode of delivery provides a faculty, the flexibility to interact with students at any convenient time, a common practice is to set a reasonable time limit within which they can expect responses to their questions. Similar practice should be adopted by the faculty regarding grading and returning of grades, and providing timely feedback to the students. It is useful to communicate such policies to the students very early in the course so that students have realistic expectations on receiving feedback.

Group exercises could include assignments such as discussions on topic areas and research projects. Group exercises have a different dynamics in online courses. As the students do not have opportunity to interact with other students as readily as in an on-site mode of delivery, the faculty may have to form initial groups of students based on profile information of the students. Student inputs/preferences can be taken into consideration in forming groups. Students may have clear preferences of group members, as they may have had the opportunity to develop working relationships with some of the students while participating in other online courses in the program.

Participation in group-discussion assignments should be within a clearly specified time window. Real-time discussions tend to be problematic if the students are dispersed in different geographic locations. A faculty should monitor discussions periodically and provide feedback and guidance to make discussions meaningful.

A faculty needs to develop assignments and exams for the course and make them available at specified times through a standardized mode of technology. The technology should facilitate administering of the exam at a specified time. In addition, the technology should allow students to be able to complete their assignments and exams and submit them effectively. Finally, given the time and distance constraints on online delivery, the faculty has to take special care to maintain integrity of exams and assignments.

What is Expected of the Students

In addition to the commonly required computer technology in education, students in an online course need to have easy access to Internet technologies. Students need to access the course Web site regularly and complete all course activities as required. Students have to pay special attention to observing deadlines, as deadlines have a different nature in online courses when compared to traditional onsite courses. For example, deadlines in an online course may not necessarily fall on a periodic basis similar to onsite courses, where deadlines commonly fall on a particular day(s) of the week throughout the semester.

The time and location flexibility in the learning process in an online course adds a level of complexity in managing group projects. Students have to make special efforts to work successfully in groups. Conflicts may be a lot harder to manage in an online environment compared to onsite classes. Finally, students have to make a special effort to preserve the integrity of assignments and exams. This is especially important if the online courses do not require students to take their exams in a supervised environment.

A weakness of online education is that cheating can be easier online than F2F. (This point is elaborated later in the next section.) Many universities require the students to sign an honor code.

Strengths and Weaknesses of Online Courses

There are many strengths and weaknesses of online courses. Demirdjian (2002) provides a detailed description of benefits and disadvantages of online education. In this section, we provide a brief description of strengths and weaknesses from the standpoint of faculty and students.

Strengths

Let us first look at the strengths from the standpoint of the instructors of online courses. The asynchronous nature of the delivery provides significant flexibility, preparation, and delivery of the courses. The instructor has the ability to modify the course content, and carry out course activities, such as grading or monitoring discussions, at any time from anywhere.

Curriculum control is easier with online than onsite courses, because the course content is very visible, and there is a complete record of what happened during the previous offering of a course. The instructor can study this record and plan modifications to the content or the conduct of the course very efficiently. Onsite courses do not have a record, and a mistake can recur easily. Continuous improvement is thus much easier with online courses than onsite courses.

It is easy to enforce deadlines in online courses. Exams can be made available only during a particular time window. The online folders into which students submit their assignments and tests can be made to appear or disappear at predetermined times. A time stamp is automatically made on every submission.

It is easy to track student participation in online courses. The instructor can select and view all the online activities of a particular student. The system can provide statistics such as how often a student logged on to the course Web site and how long he/she stayed online. Overall statistics, such as which day of the week the students are most active, can also be obtained, Such data can not only help with grading, but also can provide a basis for course modifications.

The quality of discussion can be enhanced significantly in online courses. In an online discussion, a student has more time to organize his/her thoughts, compose his/her messages, and post them at his/her convenience. It is also seen that this improves the writing skills of the students. In onsite classes, a student has only a limited amount of time to voice his/her opinion. At times, especially in the case of business managers, it is indeed desirable that a person is able to respond to a question on the spot. If such a skill is deemed necessary in an online class discussion, the format of the discussion can be changed from the usual bulletin board to online chat.

It is easy to have a guest lecture or a guest instructor in an online course. The guest can be anywhere physically and can communicate asynchronously. In other words, the guest is neither time bound nor place bound. A prominent guest can be invited to a class at significantly reduced cost. If the guest agrees, the guest lecture can be repeated in the next offering of the course at no additional cost.

Next, let us look at the strengths of online courses from the standpoint of the students. The asynchronous nature of the course provides flexibility and convenience to the students. Onsite classes tend to be rigid in the sense that students cannot continue with the program if they are required to change locations of their workplace. Online programs allow the students to move to different locations and still continue with the program. Many MBA students tend to travel on their job more often than other students. Thus, online courses are particularly suitable for MBA students.

Although a course may have set tasks for every week, within a week the students have a lot of freedom. They can read or listen to a lecture any number of times, because the lecture file is available online. In the F2F mode, students get only one chance to listen to a lecture in the classroom. An online audio file can be stopped and started, or even "rewound" and replayed any number of times.

Students will find classroom discussions more effecting online than F2F. In the F2F mode, students do not get enough time to think about the question and organize their thoughts. At the end of the class they might think of things that they should have said during the discussion. In an online discussion, students get sufficient time to assemble their thoughts and post them. They also get good practice in writing effectively.

Administrators also gain several advantages. They can review, at any time during the course or at the end of the course, how well it is progressing, or progressed, by reviewing all that has happened—discussions, quizzes, exercises, homework, and exams—during the course. Reviews of F2F courses in this much detail are difficult at best. Administrators can maintain uniformity of course content, irrespective of who is teaching the course, by maintaining the course content the same in all offerings of the course.

Weaknesses

Online courses have several inherent weaknesses. The most serious is the issue of preventing academic dishonesty of the students. It is difficult to check against cheating in exams and assignments. To mitigate this problem, some schools require the students to take, at least, the final exam at a test site so that the test can be proctored. However, this defeats the purpose of not having to be place and time bound. Some students may find it difficult to go to the test site at an appointed time. In the case of assignments, because there will be too many of them in a course, it is not possible to ask the students to go to a site at an appointed time to complete an assignment. As mentioned in the previous section, some schools ask the students to sign an honor code to take care of this issue.

A special kind of cheating is the availability of paper mills that sell term papers on any subject, for a fee. Instructors should actively guard against such cheating practices. Austin and Brown (2002) present a set of resources available to locate paper mills. Also, turnitin. com is a popular Web site for instructors in this regard.

Online courses also result in reduced personal contact with other students and faculty in the course. A common complaint is that online education is dehumanizing. The asynchronous nature of the course delivery is the source of many strengths, and strangely, it is also a source of one particular weakness. It makes it difficult to enforce timely participation of students through timely intervention. It is easier to persuade and counsel a student in F2F courses than in online courses. As a result, the attrition rate in online programs is generally greater than those in F2F programs.

Concluding Remarks

Online education has emerged as the most successful form of distance education. It frees students from being place and time bound. It is estimated that, currently, there are more than 125,000 students enrolled in online MBA programs alone. Online education is thus a major form of e-business. This chapter provides some guidelines on starting an online degree program. Though not exhaustive, these guidelines cover most of the important aspects of online programs.

The chapter covered several aspects of online program development, starting with how consonance with the mission is important. Under curriculum planning and curriculum control, several useful guidelines have been provided. Next, the importance of assurance of learning was pointed out. In the case of MBA program, some aspects of AACSB accreditation requirements were pointed out. These guidelines are transferable to other programs as well.

The tasks of technical support were explained, both during course development and course offering. The need for marketing plans, and the costs involved, were noted. In the case of scheduling of course offerings, several parameters that affect the program administration were highlighted. Useful guidelines for course development were suggested.

The attention then turned to faculty and student expectations, and strengths and weaknesses of online courses. Numerous strengths and some weaknesses of online mode of delivery were described. It is hoped that this coverage is helpful to those who are planning the development of an online program. It should also be noted that online education is advancing in scope and technology rapidly, and one should be in constant touch with the latest developments to keep oneself current.

References

Austin, M., & Brown, L. (2002). Internet plagiarism: Developing strategies to curb student academic dishonesty. In L. Foster, B. Bower, & L. Watson (Eds.), *Distance education: Teaching and learning in higher education* (pp. 258-267). Boston: Pearson Custom Publishing.

Blake, C., Gibson, J. W., & Blackwell, C. W. (2005). What you need to know about the web. *SuperVision, 66*(9), 3-7.

Bloom, B. S. (1984). *Taxonomy of educational objectives.* Boston: Allyn and Bacon.

Boettcher, J. (2002). How much does it cost to put a course online? It all depends. In L. Foster, B. Bower, & L. Watson, (Eds.), *Distance education: Teaching and learning in higher education* (pp. 258-267). Boston: Pearson Custom Publishing.

Bryant, S. M., Kahle, J. B., & Schafer, B. A. (2005). Distance education: A review of the contemporary literature. *Issues in Accounting Education, 20,* (3), 255-272.

Crawford, K. (2005). A degree of respect for online MBAs Web-based programs lack Ivy prestige, but they can boost aspiring executives' fortunes. *Business 2.0, 6*(11), 102-103.

Demirdjian, Z. S. (2002). The virtual university: Is it a panacea or a Pandora's box? *Journal of American Academy of Business, 1*(2), 172-178.

Folkers D. A. (2005). Competing in the marketspace: Incorporating online education into higher education - An organizational perspective. *Information Resources Management Journal , 18*(1), 61-77.

Gronlund, N. E. (2005). *Assessment of student achievement.* Boston: Allyn and Bacon, Inc.

Holsapple, C. W., & Lee-Post, A. (2006). Defining and promoting e-learning success: An information systems perspective. *Decision Sciences Journal of Innovative Education,* I, (1), 67-85.

Marks, R. B., Sibley, S. D., & Arbaugh, J. B. (2005). A structural equation model of predictors for effective online learning. *Journal of Management Education, 29,* (4), 531-563.

Palomba, C. A., & Banta, T. (1999). *Assessment essentials: Planning, implementing, and improving sssessment in higher rducation.* New York: John Wiley & Sons, Inc.

Suskie, L. (2004). *Assessing student learning: A common sense guide.* Boston: Anker Publishing Company, Inc.

Walvoord, B. E. (2004). *Assessment clear and simple: A practical guide for institutions, departments, and general education.* New York: John Wiley & Sons, Inc.

Chapter XIII

The Business of Online Education

Dirk Baldwin, University of Wisconsin-Parkside, USA

Bradley Piazza, University of Wisconsin-Parkside, USA

Abstract

Many observers have predicted a revolution due to online education. Opportunities exist to save money due to the lack of brick and mortar, and travel necessary to take classes in a traditional setting. Besides costs savings, several studies show that online education has significant benefits including support for self-paced learning and better discussion between learners and teachers. The opportunities for online learning have spurred growth in the business of online education. Entrepreneurs see opportunities for increased market share, while others perceive a threat. The design of an online program is not easy, however. This chapter summarizes pedagogical and business dimensions that must be addressed in order to develop an effective online educational program. The chapter also discusses tactics that will help organizations compete in the online education industry.

The Business of Online Education

In a relatively early book regarding electronic commerce (e-commerce), Choi, Stahl, and Whinston (1997) described e-commerce in terms of three dimensions: product, process, and agent. Each of these dimensions can take on a digital or physical form. Pure e-commerce, according to Choi et al., takes place when all three dimensions are digital. For example, purchasing downloadable music through the Internet is pure e-commerce because the search, purchase, delivery, and product are all digital. Because educational materials, such as lecture notes and exercises, can be found, stored, and delivered in digital form, it is not surprising that several people predicted a revolution in education. In 1997, the management expert, Peter Drucker, stated (Gubernick & Ebeling, 1997, p. 84): "Universities won't survive. The future is outside the traditional campus, outside the traditional classroom. Distance learning is coming on fast." In 2001, Arthur Levine, president of Columbia University's Teachers College, echoed this prediction. While discussing online education, Levine asked (Washburn & Press, 2001, p. 1): "If we can do all that…why do we need the physical plant called the college?"

While this predicted revolution has not completely materialized, there is ample evidence that online education is growing significantly. In a 2002 study of 274 institutions, 71% responded that they offer some fully online courses and 80% offered hybrid courses that combine in-class with virtual instruction (Arabasz, Pirani, & Fawcett, 2003). In addition, the success of online universities, such as the University of Phoenix and Capella University, attest to the interest in online learning.

Undergraduate business programs and MBA degrees, in particular, have seen a dramatic rise in online classes. According to a 2003 study, 51% of public universities offer an online business degree program (Golden, 2006). The rapid movement to online business degree programs can be attributed to many factors including corporate demand, opportunities for a greater market share, and the potential threat posed by private online business degree programs (Folkers, 2005).

Institutions of higher education are not the only source of online education. Vocational schools, K-12 schools, certification programs (e.g., real estate licensing, project management certificates), special purpose courses (e.g., drivers permit courses) and corporate training have developed significant online presence. In an IDC India study, corporate e-learning is predicted to grow to $21 billion by 2008 (*Financial Times*, 2005).

The rise of online education poses opportunities and challenges for education providers. In this chapter, we review these opportunities and challenges, discuss various considerations for developing online programs, and describe strategies for competing in the online educational marketplace.

Benefits and Challenges of Online Education

Numerous articles and entire journals are devoted to online education. Trade journals and academic research commonly discuss the effectiveness, strategies for success, benefits, and weaknesses of online education. Inexperience with digital technology, the novelty of teaching outside the traditional classroom, the reluctance of teachers to support online education, the rise of educational competition, and the shift to teaching working students motivate many of these studies and articles.

At least some of the benefits associated with online education are similar to the benefits of distance education. Distance education began as early as 1840 when Sir Isaac Pitman developed correspondence courses (Blake, Whitney, & Blackwell, 2005). These courses delivered learning materials through the mail to those who did not have the means or time to travel to traditional schools. As technology changed, the methods for delivering correspondence courses evolved. Instructional films were first used in 1910; a few organizations experimented with radio-based delivery in the 1930s; and some form of television-based education has existed since the 1940s. As satellite, cable, and other forms of networks began to appear in the 1970s through 1990s, educational institutions experimented with technology such as video conferencing and instructional CDs (Williams, Nicholas, & Gunter, 2005). It is only natural that the Internet became a source for distance education in the 1990s.

Similar to Pitman's original motivation, businesses and government, today, are interested in efficiently delivering education to learners in locations other than a centralized location. High levels of skill and knowledge are required to perform knowledge work and, by some estimates, 50% of knowledge and skills become outdated in 3 to 5 years (Blake, et al., 2005). Yet, the cost of travel and infrastructure to deliver this education is a disincentive. Cadence Design System, the world's largest supplier of electronic design automation technologies and engineering services, reports savings of $260,000 per training session (excluding airfare) through the use of Web-based training of its sales staff (Stroud, 2005). Ford provides a similar justification for its Web-based training program (Pollitt, 2005). A 2005 Bersin and Associates survey of US organizations found that 28% of training hours were delivered online (*Business Wire*, 2006).

Articles related to online learning cite many benefits, including (see Bernard, 2005; Blake et al., 2005; Bryant, Kahle, & Schafer, 2005; Demirdjian, 2002; Pollitt, 2005; Stroud, 2005):

- An effective way to deliver education that improves a learner's knowledge and skills
- A cost-effective way to reach learners that are geographically dispersed
- Supports asynchronous learning where learners participate at times that are convenient for them
- Supports self-paced learning
- Supports adaptable learning materials that can be updated immediately in response to new knowledge and events
- Supports modularity so that learners can design a learning experience that is customized to their individual needs
- Allows learners to participate in the comfort of their home or office
- The available tools and the possibility of anonymity support interactions among learners and between learners and the instructor.
- Supports immediate feedback through automated grading of a learner's answers

- Supports the development of e-portfolios (electronic documents of the students work); students can use the portfolios as part of a job application package. Instructors can use the e-portfolio as part of assessment

The same articles identify several difficulties associated with online learning, including:

- High participant attrition rates; students must be self-motivated
- The need to access appropriately configured computer systems
- The challenge of technology phobia by some learners and teachers
- The need for faculty training
- High development costs; the development of e-learning courses is labor intensive
- The increased opportunity for dishonesty by learners because of the inability to verify who is doing the work

Perhaps the most important question related to online learning is, "Is online learning effective?" Although there have been positive (Grandzol, 2004) and negative results (Orr & Bantow, 2005), the research to date mostly shows that online education is no more or less effective than traditional classroom education (Bryant et al., 2005). Ultimately, the success of an online program will depend upon how well it is designed in relation to the needs of the learner, and how well it is positioned in relation to online and traditional educational competitors.

The Dimensions of an Online Learning Curriculum

The design of an online educational program is a complex endeavor. In order to organize research relevant to distance education, Bryant et al., (2005) highlight four main components: The educational organization, teacher, learner, and communication medium. While these dimensions are important for pedagogical decisions, other dimensions are relevant in light of the online learning marketplace. In the following paragraphs, we describe issues and decisions related to the relationship between the educational organizations, teachers, learners, communication methods, curriculum, feedback, media designers, administrative support system, and marketing. Table 1 summarizes some of the key decisions by highlighting the relationship among the various dimensions.

The educational organization is the unit that brings together the teachers, learners, and the curriculum. From a business standpoint, this is the unit that strives to achieve success in the educational marketplace. Educational organizations include universities, 2-year schools, K-12 schools, as well as specialized trainers. This organization probably, but not necessarily, owns the curriculum that will be delivered. The educational organization makes the decisions that influence the success of the dimensions in Table 1.

Table 1. The dimensions and issues to consider by an e-learning provider

	Educational Organization	Teacher	Learner	Media Designer	Curriculum	Communication Method	Feedback	Administration	Marketing
Educational Organization	Collaboration/ partnerships Articulation agreements								
Teacher	Full-time employees vs. adjunct teachers Qualifications Training teachers	Joint teaching of courses Promoting collaboration Teaching mentors							
Learner	Learner independent of the educational organization or a student within the organization. Admission requirements. Support for other educational functions (e.g., advising)	Type of interaction (face to face, online real time, online nonreal time, No direct interaction) Self-paced vs. teacher paced.	Support for teamwork and student discussion groups.						

Table 1. continued

	Educational Organization	Teacher	Learner	Media Designer	Curriculum	Communication Method	Feedback	Administration	Marketing
Media Designer	In-house vs. outsourced. Roles of media designer: Create media, serve as help desk.	Teacher creates or modifies media (e.g., Web site) vs. specialized media designers.	Types of access and interaction supported for students	Single source for media design vs. collaboration amongst different media designers.					
Curriculum	Degree of ownership of curriculum. Who controls curriculum?	Ability to change course content.	Ability to design courses based on individual needs.	Single media designer for all classes vs. different designers for different classes. Consistency of user interface across curriculum.	Relationship between class work (e.g., prerequisites, degree programs, isolated classes)				
Communication Method	Types of communication methods supported by organization. Should organization support traditional classes and online classes?	How does teacher communicate with students (e.g., e-mail, discussion groups, slide presentations, taped lectures)?	How do learners communicate with teachers (e.g., e-mail, phone, discussion groups, and messages)?	Media designers role in creating communication methods (e.g., taping lectures, creating bulletin boards)	Determining best way to communicate for a particular course or curriculum. Same for all courses or, differs by course.	Interaction between communication methods. Web-based notes to discussion to video.			

Table 1. continued

	Educational Organization	Teacher	Learner	Media Designer	Curriculum	Communication Method	Feedback	Administration	Marketing
Feedback	How to provide feedback to educational organization.	How to provide feedback to teacher from all parties involved.	Feedback to learner (automatic, instant, teacher controlled)	Provide feedback to media designer on what works or does not work.	Who provides feedback, who receives feedback, and how is feedback provided about the curriculum?	Feedback about communication method. Type of communication method to use for feedback.	Multiple formats of feedback allowed?		
Administrative support system.	Outsourced or in-house? Determine budget, tuition, fees	Maintain payment and personnel records.	Registration and payment of tuition/fees. Admissions. Financial aid.	Evaluation of media providers. Payment to media providers.	Responsible for displaying and supporting registration.	Media for handling administrative functions such as admissions, registration, and payment.	Feedback provided about administration. How accomplished, who provides feedback?	Levels of administration. Interaction between different administrative functions (Strategic, management, operational)	
Marketing	How do you market the educational organization?	How do you attract teachers?	How do you attract students?	Do you outsource marketing to media designers?	How do you market specific courses or programs?	What communication methods do you use for marketing (traditional, online)?	How do you evaluate the success of a marketing effort?	Establish budget and administrative structure to support marketing.	Can you collaborate on marketing across organizations?

In most traditional educational settings, the learners and the teachers "belong to" the educational organization. Teachers work full-time or part-time for the organization, and students are admitted to the school. However, this situation is not required. An educational organization may contract with another organization to deliver classes to that organization. For example, ESI International delivers online project management training for many corporations. In a university or K-12 environment, articulation agreements can be reached that will allow students from one school to take online courses from another organization. In the traditional environment, articulation agreements are commonly reached with nearby institutions because students must be physically present to take the course, but in the online world, relationships can be established between organizations that share other common characteristics; physical proximity is less of an issue.

Similarly, physical proximity is not necessarily a requirement for teachers. Online education allows educational organizations to employ qualified teachers from any location that has Internet access. At the extreme, some online courses do not need "real time" instructors at all. Students can access instructional materials, take exams, and receive feedback through intelligent educational software.

The relationship between the teacher, learner, curriculum, communication method, and media designers must be carefully considered. Within the boundaries defined by the course objectives, professors at traditional universities design the course contents, determine how the contents will be communicated, and determine how the learners will be assessed. Professors are not only teachers, but scholars who develop and update course material based upon their own expertise. Materials, such as textbooks, are one communication method used in the course. Simulating this situation in online teaching requires that the professor have control over the online curriculum and communication methods.

Unfortunately, several factors in online education work against the traditional model. First, many professors do not possess the technical ability to develop quality online material. Expertise is required to create Web sites, develop dynamic instructional media (e.g., an animated PowerPoint or Flash application), and create online assessment material. Second, a consistent and professional user interface is frequently used as a surrogate for the connection students feel to the physical university campus. That is, online educational organizations like a consistent look to all their educational offerings. For these reasons, specialized media designers are employed to create online material. These media designers may be in-house or outsourced. Rather than developing separate educational media for each professor, economies of scale suggest that the same media be used for all sections of a course. The professor therefore can lose some control over the content, delivery, and assessment of the course. The standardization of course content and delivery is less likely an issue in K-12 education, corporate training, and vocational education. Ideally, standardization in these cases leads to consistent quality independent of the instructor.

Besides issues related to curriculum and delivery, online educational organizations must maintain the business functions of any educational organization. These functions include administrative functions such as admissions, registration, and marketing. Educational organizations must determine their target audience (e.g., students who will take some courses online vs. students who will take all courses online) and their niche (e.g., image of the educational organization vs. image of a particular program). Decisions regarding the various dimensions of online education must not only be made to create a quality educational program, they must be made in light of increased competition for the educational dollar.

Competition in the Online Educational Marketplace

Historically, competition in training programs and education was limited to those institutions that were in close regional proximity. Today, regional proximity is still important, but the emergence of online training and education has removed the geographic boundaries that once offered some protection against a large number of competitors. For example, US students studying to be lactation consultants have the option of taking online courses in medical terminology and nutrition from an Australian medical school. Educational organizations with a strong brand identity or niche have an opportunity to expand their customer base. Smaller, regional organizations may feel threatened by this increased competition.

Michael Porter's (1979) classic model, "A Model for Industry Analysis," identifies five forces that can be used to analyze strategic threats and opportunities in the educational marketplace: supplier power, buyer power, threat of substitutes, barriers to entry and degree of rivalry.

Supplier Power

Online instructors are a primary supplier for online education. Online instructors are frequently responsible for developing the content of the course, in addition to moderating the class discussions and providing an assessment of student work and progress. The media designers, both for the course Web site and for the platform (e.g., Desire 2 Learn, Blackboard) that the content is delivered through, are also suppliers to the industry. In addition, there could be 24-hour support staff available for answering technical questions that arise from the learners.

To some extent, educational organizations can use suppliers to add a level of product differentiation. A course offered by a renowned expert could distinguish one organization from another. Currently, there appears to be less opportunity to distinguish an online educational organization through Web site design or platforms. The suppliers of delivery platforms are somewhat limited. For example, many universities use Blackboard, WebCT, or Desire 2 Learn (D2L). The look and feel of the Web sites associated with online education is fairly similar. An organization could distinguish itself through in-house or exclusive contract development of unique computer-aided instruction software. Regional educational organizations, however, may not have the resources to develop a unique identity through these content delivery methods.

The suppliers significantly impact the costs associated with online education. In the short run, traditional educational organizations must pay for brick and mortar associated with the school. They must also compensate the designers and technical staff for online education. This compensation adds to the costs of delivery, and ultimately results in a higher price for the buyer. Nontraditional organizations, without the brick and mortar infrastructure, should see a cost advantage.

Switching costs must be taken into account if one is considering making a change with a supplier. As with most industries, the relationships that are formed from conducting business can make it very difficult to change.

Buyer Power

The buyers in this industry are the students who are looking for courses or entire online degree programs. From the marketing perspective, the buyer or consumer is oftentimes believed to have a degree of leverage. In the education industry, this belief is certainly true. The consumers have many options for education. There are multiple colleges and universities as well as organizations that deliver online training or education. In addition to the many online options, there is always the possibility of attending onsite programs. This assumes, of course, that there is an institution within the regional proximity of the consumer.

Brand identity can help the buyer make a decision. If the delivering institution has far-reaching and positive brand identity, it is likely that the buyer will consider pursuing the class or degree at that institution. The opposite is also true. If the delivering institution has only regional identity and/or a negative perception in the mind of the buyer, it is unlikely that it will be chosen. Brand identity may partially explain the recent growth in the number of students enrolling in online courses offered by large, doctoral-granting, public universities. The University of Maryland reported 51,405 students enrolled in online courses in 2005 compared to 9,696 in 1998 (Golden, 2006). The University of Massachusetts emphasizes the quality of its brand through a recent advertising slogan: "Because Quality Matters."

The switching costs for the buyer may be high, particularly for students who are pursuing a complete online degree. The costs of transferring from an online program to an onsite program include the transferability of credits and residency requirements of the institutions. Residency refers to the number of credits that must be completed at an institution in order to be awarded the degree.

Threat of Substitutes

Substitute products are those products that can be used to satisfy the same needs as that of the original product. Several substitute products exist with regards to online education or training. As examples, a buyer can choose a traditional classroom delivery method, companies or organizations can choose to deliver in-house training, and a consumer could decide not to pursue any education or training.

The traditional classroom environment can be an acceptable substitute if there is a college or university within geographical proximity. There may also be a degree of price elasticity in place, particularly if the classroom option is at a public institution. It may be the case that the public institution can deliver the course or courses at a much lower tuition rate than the online option. If there is no regionally located institution, or there is no price elasticity, the threat is lessened.

The ability of companies to deliver in-house training is only a threat if the company can find a cost-effective way of delivering the training. If there is in-house expertise, the costs may be much less than if an outside consultant needs to be brought in for the training.

All consumers have the option of not making a decision. In this case, the consumer may choose not to pursue any education, online or classroom. For work training this may not be an acceptable option if the training is mandated by the organization. If the training is optional, it becomes a valid threat.

Barriers to Entry

The barriers to entry into the industry of online delivery of courses, degrees, or training programs are significant. The first barriers are financial and human resource. In particular, this is true for small, public educational institutions. If the institution is trying to deliver on-campus degree programs and also deliver online courses or degrees, they begin to find themselves stretched very thin in both financial resources and personnel. This is particularly true if the programs delivered online are substantially different from those being delivered onsite. There are significant start-up costs involved when developing new courses and programs. For example, if the instructor is granted release time to develop a course for online delivery, an adequate replacement needs to be found for the course that he or she is not teaching. This results in the need for additional human resource assistance, which leads to an increase in financial pressure. If the programs are identical except for the method of delivery, there may not be significant costs involved in course development, but there will still be a financial burden brought about from the limits on teaching loads.

Another barrier is whether or not the online delivery consists of a few courses only or the entire set of courses needed for a degree. The barrier here is getting other departments to offer their courses online. For example, if a business school decides to pursue online delivery of courses with the intention of being able to attract buyers who want the entire set of courses online, then all the departments that contribute to the degree must be willing and able to deliver their courses online. Success requires significant financial and human resource capacity in these other departments.

The learning curve experienced by institutions that are beginning to offer online opportunities is significant. It takes time for faculty to learn how to effectively develop and deliver courses through this medium, particularly if they have not done it in the past. Proper marketing of the courses, from the pricing to the promotion, is different than that of the traditional classroom experience. Finding a way for the students in the online courses to feel "connected" to the campus is difficult, especially if the delivering campus is not within the student's region.

If there is very little or no brand identity for the delivering institution, it becomes even more difficult to expand on a national or even international level. If the identity is already present, this barrier may be less.

Final barriers are any institutional policies that may impede the delivery of education via a different method. There may also be policies in-place from outside accrediting bodies. Any policies that are in existence will need to be overcome prior to entering the industry. New educational organizations, niche training organizations, and nonaccredited organizations may see less of a barrier in these cases. However, these types of organizations will face significant barriers regarding staffing the courses, developing the courses, and establishing an identity.

Degree of Rivalry

The final dimension of Porter's model is the degree of existing rivalry. Currently, many universities offer some form of online courses. The EDUCAUSE Center for Applied Research reports that 87% of doctoral institutions and 95% of 2-year colleges offer classes online. Interestingly, only 27% of baccalaureate universities offer online classes. Similarly, a quick perusal of the Internet reveals hundreds of companies offering online training. The sheer number of universities and business in the marketplace might suggest a shakeout. However, many industry experts believe that the demand for online courses will outstrip supply (Golden, 2006). Students (industry or university students) well versed in Internet access will increasingly expect that at least some courses be placed online. The failure of a university or other provider of education to enter the online teaching arena could result in a loss of overall market presence. The natural question is how can an educational organization compete given so much competition?

Strategies for Online Education

Competing successfully in the online education marketplace is a daunting task, especially if the organization is a small regional supplier of education or training. Financial, technical, and human resources must be marshaled and organized. The curriculum must be developed, and the media to deliver the curriculum created. Administration and marketing of the program must also be planned and implemented. The specific strategies and steps for competing effectively in the online market depend upon the size, brand identity, niche, and resources of the educational organization. Nevertheless, we propose three general strategic steps for competing successfully.

1. *Develop a strategic plan that includes online education as a factor.* Online education is not likely a fad that will disappear. Some faculty members at traditional educational organizations are highly opposed to this form of education. Even if the organization decides not to enter the online arena, the long-range plan should be aware that their competition is increasing because of online education. In addition, many learners are acquiring online skills and, over time, an increasing percentage is likely to favor at least some courses to be delivered online.

The Wisconsin Virtual Academy is a K-8 online public education curriculum run by the Northern Ozaukee School District. The program is a public e-school that does not charge tuition and loans a computer to school families. The program is marketed to all Wisconsin parents. Even if other school districts do not offer a complete online curriculum, the other districts and private schools must be aware of its presence, and market a program that is seen to have other advantages. Similarly, universities, vocational schools, and training programs must identify their niche within the online environment. The niche may or may not include online components, but it needs to be marketable and seen by many as an advantage over other online competitors.

The process of creating a strategic plan related to online education is similar to the process used to develop most other strategic plans (see Luecke, 2005). First, the organization develops or updates a vision and mission. Second, the environment is assessed, and a strengths, weakness, opportunities, and threats (SWOT) analysis is performed. The SWOT analysis should include the opportunities associated with the online education market as well as the threats. The technology environment should also be evaluated to look for new ways to use technology to support education. Third, a strategic direction should be articulated. This direction should indicate the niche you plan to target. Fourth, goals and measurable objectives should be specified. The objectives could include measures referring to the revenue, profit, number of courses, number of students, number of degree programs, and number of faculty associated with online education. Fourth, a strategy or action plan should be developed to achieve the objectives. The action plan must include a budget, identify technology associated with online learning, and identify how the organization plans to motivate and train teachers to teach in an online environment. Finally, an implementation plan should be specified that indicates how the action plan will be implemented and tracked.

2.   *Identify your student segment in your strategic plan.* While online education provides the opportunity for a national or global presence, national or global boundaries do not need to define the segment. The school's mission statement should identify the students and region it primarily serves. Some educational organizations with significant brand identity may indeed focus on a general student body from across the globe, but regional universities can still define a regional market (Wood, Tapsall, & Soutar, 2004). A regional educational organization will have better knowledge of the educational needs of the region. The opportunity for onsite as well as online education may be seen as a significant benefit for many students. Regional educational organizations may also enjoy a price advantage because of in-state tuition rates.

Educational specializations may also be used to define a student segment. Online education may make a narrow segment profitable that was not profitable when the organization was confined to a building within a certain geographic region. 360water is a Columbus, Ohio company that offers classes in areas such as math, drinking water disinfection, water analysis, and safety, to operators in the water and wastewater industry. Similarly, universities with specialized expertise may be able to offer online courses that would not be easily duplicated by other universities.

3.   *Form partnerships.* Partnerships can be used to help overcome the resource requirements and risks prevalent in the online education industry. For example, the University of Wisconsin-Parkside is partnering with Learning Innovations to help deliver MBA and undergraduate business courses. Learning Innovations provides expertise and human resources related to online support and online curriculum development. UW-Parkside has also partnered with three other University of Wisconsin schools to create an MBA consortium. Members of the consortium jointly develop and offer MBA classes. The partnership helps overcome human resource limitations in each school. The consortium markets its program across the state and is beginning to market worldwide. Some students will complete their entire degree program online, while others take some courses online and take other courses in the traditional classroom. The consortium expands the time courses are offered and the available electives for MBA students. In addition to degree program partnerships, educational organizations can form individual class partnerships with universities across the world. These part-

nerships would allow students to take classes from recognized experts even though the expert is not physically located at the university offering the degree.

Besides partnering with other educational organizations and suppliers, partnerships with learners can also be formed. An educational organization may contract with a corporation or other group to offer education to its employees and members. For example, Health-e-learning is listed on the International Board of Lactation Consultant Examiners Web site as offering online continuing education. This type of partnership can help create a strong customer base.

Universities may form similar types of partnerships. MBA programs, for example, that have existing partnerships with corporations to deliver customized or onsite courses, may be able to capitalize on their knowledge of the corporation. Online courses could be developed that contain special instruction that fits the required expertise and background of students from the corporation or industry. This strategy could provide a competitive advantage over other universities that may have greater brand recognition.

Conclusion

Like many areas of business, the business of education is becoming increasingly competitive and undergoing continual change. Different observers of education see online education as an opportunity to improve education, harmful to quality education, an opportunity to increase market share, and a threat to take market share. However, most observers believe that online education will continue to grow, and will increasingly become an important part of the educational landscape. Success in online education requires the design of a quality educational program. This design must take into account characteristics of the teacher, learner, curriculum, media designer, educational organization, communication method, feedback, administration, and marketing. The design of a quality program is not enough to achieve success, however. Organizations must develop long-range plans that take into account competitors, suppliers, customers, and substitutes related to online education. Educational organizations must carefully define their student segment, and can look to form partnerships that help them compete in the online education arena.

References

Arabasz, P., Pirani, J., & Fawcett, D. (2003). *Supporting e-learning in higher education: research study from the EDUCAUSE center for applied research*. Retrieved October 21, 2005 from http://www.educause.edu/ecar.

Bernard, G. (2005). Why e-learning affects us all. *The British Journal of Administrative Management, 24.*

Blake, C., Whitney Gibson, J., & Blackwell, C. (2005). What you need to know about the Web. *SuperVision, 66*(9), 3-7.

Bryant, S., Kahle, J., & Schafer, B. (2005). Distance education: A review of the contemporary literature. *Issues in Accounting Education, 20*(30), 255-272.

Business Wire. (2006, January 12). Bersin & Associates announces comprehensive research study of learning management systems market; Overall market growth of 28% in 2005; Despite mergers still no clear market leader. *Business Wire.*

Choi, S., Stahl, D. O., & Whinston, A. B. (1997). *The economics of electronic commerce.* Indianapolis: Macmillan Technical Publications.

Demirdjian, Z. S. (2002). The virtual university: Is it a panacea or a Pandora's box? *Journal of American Academy of Business, I*(2), 172-178.

Financial Times. (2005, April 30). Learn and let e-learn (Corporate e-learning will grow to $21 billion globally by 2008). *India Business Insight, Global News Wire-Asia Africa Intelligence Wire.*

Folkers, D. A. (2005). Competing in the marketspace: Incorporating online education into higher education—an organizational perspective. *Information Resources Management Journal, 18*(1), 61-77.

Gajilan, A. (2000, November). An education revolution: Investors like Michael Milken and Larry Ellison are betting that Chicago's Unext can change the face of college online. *Fortune Small Business, 29.*

Galloway, D. (2005). Evaluating distance delivery and e-learning. *Performance Improvement, 44*(4), 21-27.

Golden, D. (2006, May 9). Degrees@StateU.edu: Online university enrollment soars as quality improves; Tuition funds other projects. *Wall Street Journal,* B1.

Grandzol, J. R. (2004). .Teaching MBA statistics online: A pedagogically sound process approach. *Journal of Education for Business, 79*(4), 237-244.

Gubernick, L., & Ebeling, A. (1997, June). I got my degree through e-mail. *Forbes,* 84-92.

Luecke, R. H. (2005). *Harvard business essentials: Strategy—create and implement the best strategy for your business.* David J. Collis (Subject Advisor). Boston: Harvard Business School Press.

Orr, S., & Bantow, R. (2005). E-commerce and graduate education: Is educational quality taking a nose dive? *The International Journal of Educational Management, 19*(7), 579-586.

Pollitt, D. (2005). E-learning delivers management skills to Ford's North American dealers. *Human Resource Management International Digest, 13*(4), 13-15.

Porter, L. (2004). *Developing an online curriculum: Technologies and techniques.* Hershey, PA: Information Science Publishing.

Porter, M. E. (1979). How competitive forces shape strategy. *Harvard Business Review, 57*(2), 137-145.

Stroud, T. (2005, August). Web conferencing: The future of training? *Training Journal*, 26-29.

Wang, Y. (2003). Assessment of learner satisfaction with asynchronous electronic learning systems, *Information and Management, 41*, 75-86.

Washburn, J., & Press, E. (2001, January 1). Digital diplomas. *Mother Jones*. Retrieved October 25, 2006 from http://www.newamerica.net/index.cfm?pg=article&DocID=132

Williams, P., Nicholas, D., & Gunter, B. (2005). E-learning: What the literature tells us about distance education. *Aslib Proceedings, 57*(2), 109-122.

Wood, B. J. G., Tapsall, S. M., & Soutar, G. N. (2005). Borderless education: Some implications for management. *The International Journal of Educational Management, 19*(5), 428-436.

Section V

Risk Management

Chapter XIV

E-Business
Risk Management
in Firms

Ganesh Vaidyanathan, Indiana University South Bend, USA

Abstract

In order to understand the different types of e-business risks, this chapter uses a framework focusing on five dimensions of e-businesses. This chapter examines e-business risk management in a broader context by integrating various functions within firms. Primary consideration is given to characteristics of the integrated supply chain functionalities of a firm and their associations with information technology (IT), business models of firms, business processes that have become important to e-business, services that have been interlocked into e-business, the relative importance of partnerships, trust, and the necessity of adaptation in managing the supply chain in order to attain competitive advantage. The purpose of this chapter is to understand how to identify and manage various online risks.

Introduction

E-business has paved a path for new growth potential for many businesses around the globe. E-business is emerging as the medium of choice in trade, and is replacing traditional commerce. Some of the brick-and-mortar companies have made e-business the solution of the future. Corporations can now trade goods and services, ranging from steel to medical equipment, with potential unknown buyers and sellers using online technology. These trading hubs might be further enhanced in the future to deliver substantial value to their members, including greater liquidity, better pricing, better quality, better delivery time, efficient transactions, and better quality assurance. Why is it that the many e-businesses have not performed as expected? Despite very optimistic projections for business-to-business e-commerce, businesses have been very cautious to embrace the technology as well as using e-business to their maximum advantage. Is this due to perceived risks inherent or associated with e-business? The perceived risks are multi-faceted and includes security and privacy (Mercuri, 2005), privacy assurance (Moores, 2005), credibility and information asymmetry (Ba & Pavlou, 2002), reliability, damage and loss of systems (Dillon & Pate-Cornell, 2005; Straub & Welke, 1998), supply chain (Spekman & Davis, 2004), decision-making processes (Pathak, 2004), poor business models (Grover & Saeed, 2004), and online services (Lange, Davis, Jaye, Erwin, Mullarney, Clarke, & Loesch, 2000; Orr, 2005). These risks have played a role in impeding the growth and acceptance of e-business.

Risk may be defined as a factor, thing, element, or course involving uncertain danger in a firm, while challenge is a test of a firm's abilities or resources in a demanding but stimulating undertaking. In this study, we focus on risks. Risk has been defined by various scholars in many ways. Cox and Rich (1964) refer to perceived risk as the overall amount of uncertainty perceived by a consumer in a particular purchase situation. Cunningham (1967) recognized the risk resulting from poor performance, danger, health hazards, and costs. Jacoby and Kaplan (1972) classified consumers' perceived risk into the following five types of risk: physical, psychological, social, financial, and performance. Murphy and Enis (1986) define perceived risk as customer's subjective assessment of the consequence of making a purchasing mistake. Ahn, Park, and Lee (2001) define perceived risk as the overall amount of uncertainty or anxiety perceived by a consumer in a particular product/service when the consumer purchases online. Using these definitions, risk is identified in the five dimensions that include technology, process, business models, services, and fulfillment in this study.

One of the critical factors playing a major role is the risk associated with online commerce in general. The purpose of this chapter is to provide an analysis of e-business risk management in a broader context that examines the integration of the functions within firms in the context of suppliers and customers at a firm level. A conceptual insight to e-business risk management will be developed with an understanding of the strategic aspects of business philosophy. Primary consideration is given to characteristics of the integrated supply chain functionalities of a firm and their associations with information technology (IT), business models of firms, the business processes that have become important to e-business, services that have been interlocked into e-business, and the relative importance of partnerships, trust, and the necessity of adaptation in managing the supply chain in order to attain competitive advantage. A review of the literature and an analysis of the characteristics and implications of the e-business risks in the context of changing global markets emphasize the importance of strategically managing the e-business initiatives of the firm. The remaining sections in this study are arranged as follows. The next section discusses how traditional businesses have transformed themselves to online businesses. The third section conceptualizes a framework of risks in e-businesses. The following sections expand each one of these risks. The final section discusses the management of risks and presents a summary of the five risk dimensions.

Background

This section briefly describes both the traditional and online business models. The differences between these two models convey how e-business risk is really different from traditional risks. The traditional buy and sell business can be established as a process, as illustrated in Figure 1 (adapted from Vaidyanathan & Devaraj, 2003). The buyer approves a vendor using certain criteria, seller approves a customer using credit feed from credit bureaus and other selection criteria, buyer orders goods and services through purchase order, seller accepts the purchase order, both parties guarantee payment and receipt of goods using a letter of credit, seller sends an invoice and the buyer accepts the invoice, seller initiates the order by shipping the goods using a logistics provider, buyer accepts the goods/services, buyer verifies goods and services for quality, buyer approves payment, gets financed if needed, makes payments using financial institutions, and seller accepts payments. In some cases, disputes are resolved after dunning, and payments are collected using external legal and collection agency services.

This process works well regardless of whether the supply chain and backend computer services are connected or not. The performance and efficiency of the process depends on the presence or absence of connectivity. If the supply chain and back-end services function efficiently, the traditional process will perform very well (Vaidyanathan & Devaraj, 2003). In

Figure 1. Traditional buy/sell process

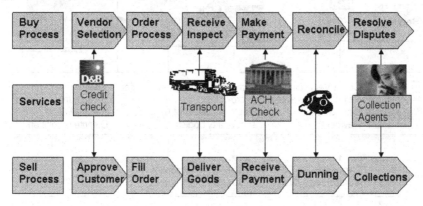

the traditional process, there are four different players: buyers, sellers, suppliers, and service providers. As we can see in Figure 1, the financial institutions and other service providers, such as logistic providers, collection agents, and legal firms, constitute the service providers. Financial institutions offer services such as financing the buyer and financing the seller, as well as being the intermediary for payment processing that traditional checks, wire transfer, credit cards, smart cards, and electronic fund transfer. On the consumer side of the buy/sell process, the financial institutions are also involved in credit and debit payment networks. Service providers offer logistics, warehousing, global transportation, inventory management, and all other fulfillment needs. The suppliers are material suppliers, contract manufacturers, and computer hardware, infrastructure, and software providers who support the traditional sellers. The balanced traditional model has certain risks like credit-card fraud and identification thefts. The service providers such as financial institutions, logistics providers, credit bureaus, insurance companies, banks providing letter of credits, have mitigated most of these risks. In the traditional model, the service providers charge the buyers, sellers, and suppliers to mitigate their business risks (Vaidyanathan & Devaraj, 2003). The evaluation of the risks of technology and enhancing the technologies to new, emerging technologies may mitigate certain technology risks.

Online business or e-business has transformed this traditional buy/sell process as seen in Figure 2 (adapted from Vaidyanathan & Devaraj, 2003). The fundamental buy/sell process does not change significantly online; however, new risks have been introduced (Vaidyanathan & Devaraj, 2003). There is perception that online businesses are faster, and this has changed the relationship between suppliers and sellers. Buyers expect faster fulfillment and suppliers have to work in maximum synchronization with the buyers. As with the traditional model, this online transformation of buy/sell process works very well when the supply chain and backend services are integrated and work together seamlessly. The performance and efficiency

Figure 2. Online buy/sell process

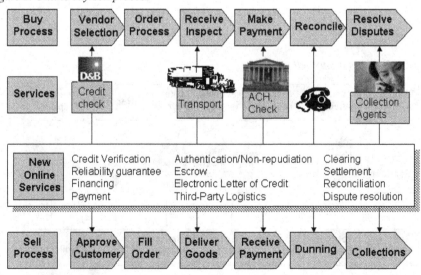

of the online process depends on the presence of this connectivity. If the supply chain and back-end services function well, the online process will be efficient and will perform as expected for the online community of buyers and sellers. In this new online buy/sell process, there is now an extra player who plays a critical role, as shown in Figure 2. This is the required online service provider. These service providers are essential in bringing together the online buyers and sellers. These new online service providers offer credit verification services, digital authorization and authentication services, online financing, online payments, online business intermediations, Internet hosting, and Internet collaborative tools to buyers, sellers, and suppliers. There are also other new service providers such as online financial transaction companies, online insurance companies, and online logistics providers who have newer business models and new business processes. The traditional service providers of insurance, finance, and logistics have also set up these new online services. Therefore, the online scene has the traditional buyers, sellers, traditional service providers, suppliers, and the new online service providers (Vaidyanathan & Devaraj, 2003). In addition, some of these new online service providers have collaborated with traditional service providers to form intermediaries. E-marketplaces that provide online buy/sell transactions are examples of these new online service providers.

Some of the new online service providers have established their new processes, new technology, new fulfillment needs, and new business models. The traditional buyers, sellers, suppliers, and the service providers have also changed their business models to suit the new online method of doing business. Moreover, they have modified their processes, introduced new processes, and introduced new technology to do online business. By introducing these new processes, new business models, new fulfillment requirements, new online services, and new technologies, the buyers, sellers, suppliers, customers, and traditional and online service providers have been introduced to new risks.

Figure 3. Concerns of a global trader

Seller	Buyer
Does the buyer have buying power?	Will the seller keep his promise?
Does the buyer have authority?	Does the seller have authority?
Will I get paid?	Will I receive the goods in good condition?
Is the product up to expectations?	Is the product up to expectations?
How can I maximize price?	How can I minimize cost?
Will the sale go through?	Will the sale go through?
Will I retain loyalty?	Will the quality be maintained?
What are the regulations and rules?	What are the regulations and rules?
Are there "rogue" buyers?	Are there "rogue" sellers?
Alternative buyers?	Alternative sellers?
What is buyer's reputation?	What is seller's reputation?
How good is the security?	How good is the security?
Is the contract good in that country?	Is the contract good in that country?
How good is the Letter of Credit?	How good is the Inspection report?
How can we avoid litigation?	How can we avoid litigation?
Will the payment be on time?	Will the delivery be on time?
What are my total exposures?	What are my total exposures?

Throughout the supply chain network, there are substantial risks. There is risk that goods will be stolen or damaged. There is risk that they arrive in time but with inferior quality. There is risk that the warehouse burns down or is destroyed by natural disasters. In 1995, an earthquake hit the port town of Kobe in Japan. This earthquake destroyed hundreds of buildings and shut down Japan's largest port for more than 2 years. This disaster forced thousands of firms to change their production and distribution strategies just to survive. Automotive plants had to halt production, as parts were unavailable for a period of time. Furthermore, labor strikes, machine breakdowns, political instability, and customer changes also contribute to supply-chain failure (Kilgore, 2004). Supply-chain problems have more impact on stock price (Singhal, 2000). Some of the concerns of buyers and sellers in a sup-ply-chain network are illustrated in Figure 3. The concerns reside in technology, process, business models, services, and fulfillment needs. The next section introduces a framework of these new risks.

Conceptual Framework

Electronic business has paved a path for new growth potential to many businesses around the globe. Electronic business is emerging as the medium of choice in trade, and is replacing traditional commerce. The rise and then the fall of B2B vertical and horizontal exchanges within the electronic marketplace have been well documented. Current B2B models have three fundamental flaws (Wise & Morrison, 2000): (1) Economics, not quality, is being pursued by the current models; (2) sellers are being pressurized by price wars, profitability, and customers; and (3) customer priorities have not been considered. However, these are not the only fundamental flaws of e-business.

Although we have encountered the positive effects of B2B business, some studies have drawn attention to certain aspects of risk. Some of the risks associated with e- business are due to weak procedures in software development process, deficiencies in electronic busi-ness protocols and other technology-related problems (Muiznieks, 1995). There are hosts of other electronic business risks that must be addressed, such as accidental or erroneous processing of business transactions (Ratnasingham, 1998).

A study illustrated that there are administrative threats in the form of risks, such as password sniffing, data modification, spoofing, and repudiation (Bhimani, 1996). Risks associated with fraud are due to the rapid growth of electronic business companies in general, as well as the rapid growth of electronic business lacking internal controls and good business sense (Baker, 1999). Many studies point electronic business risks toward information technology (IT) and/or security (Kolluru & Meredith, 2001; Salisbury, Pearson, Pearson, & Miller, 2001).

A model of traditional and electronic business to build trust in electronic business envi-ronments has been established (Papadopoulou, Andreou, Kanellis, & Martakos, 2001). A model, using global electronic business processes, has been presented by Caelli (1997). This latter model includes integrated schemes by financial institutions and consumers, open standardization, international standards for security and technology, and international agree-ments on legal, social, and economic systems. However, these models have not explicitly considered the elements of risk. A framework for trust requirements in electronic business was developed (Jones, Wilikens, Morris, & Masera, 2000). Although the framework does not view trust with respect to risk, it does identify complexities in the world of electronic business. The complexities that are identified relate to technology, process, and services. These complexities may be extended to business models and fulfillment needs as well. The literature regarding measurement of risk attitude of management concluded that decision makers can be simultaneously risk seeking and risk averse in different domains, that is, context-specific (Shapira, 1995).

Since there is an established perception that online businesses are faster, the relationship between suppliers and sellers has changed. Buyers expect faster fulfillment and suppliers have to work in maximum synchronization with the sellers. As with the traditional model, this online transformation of buy/sell process works very well when the supply chain and back-end services are connected and work together. The performance and efficiency of the online process depends on the presence of this connectivity. If the supply chain and back-end services function well, the online process will be efficient and will perform as expected by the online community of buyers and sellers.

Some of the brick and mortar companies have made electronic business the solution of the future. Corporations can now trade goods and services, ranging from plastics to medical equipment, with potential unknown buyers and sellers using online technology. These trading hubs might be further enhanced in the future to deliver substantial value to their members, including greater liquidity, better pricing, good quality and better delivery time, faster transactions, and better quality assurance. By creating these trading hubs, electronic marketplaces are initially focusing on gaining a critical mass of buyers and sellers in order to establish themselves as the leader in their particular core competencies. The electronic marketplaces are currently preoccupied with experimenting with different types of business models such as sell-side auctions, buy-side auctions, and pure exchange formats. In the B2B exchange market segment, the ability to be the first in the business, that is, gain the first mover advantage, is the paramount goal.

The new online risks have been either partially mitigated or not mitigated at all. Firms that face these risks need to address both their internal and external environments. For instance, one such external environment factors are the standards. Much of the impetus for standard setting comes from the threat to B2B network posed by hackers and foreign governments (Vijayan, 2001). The global expansion of Internet use, combined with the global threats of increasing presence of hacker tools and the decreasing difficulty of use, argues for a permanence of constant risk. Organizations need to take responsibility for their protection of data and intellectual property. They need to achieve cooperation with other parties involved. They need to understand the weaknesses of the e-business systems that they are dependent on (McCrohan, 2003). The involvement of senior managers in risk awareness and risk assessment initiatives is required to mitigate the risks (McCrohan, 2003).

Many primary services crucial to the success of e-business have entered the scene. These services include guaranteed transaction services, financing services, quality assurance, integrated shipping, foreign exchange, and international fund transfers. Traditional service providers and new entrants have taken the reins to offer these primary services online. Internet consulting firms believe in potential growth despite recent setbacks. New business models are evolving. New buy and sell processes will make an impact on electronic business and some of them may fail. New technologies are paving a road for growth and some of them will be questionable. New fulfillment needs will arise and some of them will go unanswered.

Figure 4. Conceptual framework

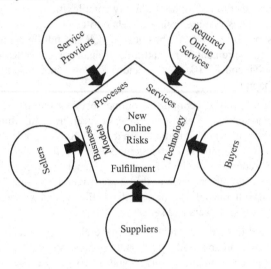

With the advent of these online services, new technologies, new processes, new business models and new fulfillment needs, new online risks, have surfaced, and these risks have accounted for some of the uncertainty associated with electronic business.

A framework for evaluating online risks is needed to analyze the impact of electronic business in the business-to-business (B2B) world. The traditional processes of buying and selling can be viewed as a model with conventional risk mitigation instruments including escrow, insurance, and contracts. As global B2B trade progresses using the electronic business as its medium of choice, an array of new business models, new processes, new fulfillment needs, new services, and new technology have emerged, resulting in a new set of online risks. These new online risks have created an imbalance in the traditional buying and selling process. A framework for examining the various risks in the online B2B buy and sell process was presented (Vaidyanathan & Devaraj, 2002). This chapter will expand that basic framework with the new insights, and include the entire major research that several scholars have provided in recent years. This study will include the risk environment with an analysis of how these firms can understand the risks and mitigate them. The next section expands on these five dimensions of risks.

Five Dimensions of New Online Risks

The new online risks may be attributed to the following five dimensions that have emerged for online B2B business: new services, new business models, new processes, new technologies, and new fulfillment needs. These five dimensions play an important role in this framework and, in fact, may be used to define the role of online B2B business. Figure 4 (adapted from Vaidyanathan & Devaraj, 2003) illustrates the five dimensions of this framework. These dimensions, consisting of services, business models, processes, technologies, and fulfillment needs, are offshoots of their traditional roles. They have been transformed to accommodate the online business scene. In each one of the dimensions, there are a number of types of risks. These types of risks are illustrated as a summary in Table 1. The next sections define each one of the types of risk in detail.

New Services

The rise of the e-business has changed the way that many organizations function and exist. E-services need to be included in the e-business models to make the business models robust. E-services, as compared to offline services, have grown rapidly, and the Internet has provided tremendous opportunities for service companies to offer quality services (Surjadjaja, Ghosh, & Antony, 2003). These services that have been offered by the service providers are often disparate and companies have to invest in integration of the services and systems. An example of an e-service is the experience of buying a ticket on the Internet. As seen in

Table 1. Risk types in dimensions

Risk Dimension	Risk Type
Services	Service failure risks
	Service-specific security risks
	New jurisdiction risks
	Intangible property risks
	Obsolete assumption risks
	Online fraud
	Poaching
	Third-party liability risk
Business Models	Performance risks
	Financial risks
	Financial transaction risks
	Lack of trust
Technology	Security
	System failure risk (availability, reliability)
	Data integrity risks
Processes	Risks due to misfit between new processes and existing organizational processes and organizational structure
	Product quality risks
	Process Integration risks
Fulfillment	Order fulfillment risks
	Other supply chain management risks

Figure 2, these new online services are conceptually the traditional services like banking, shipping, insurance, logistics, credit services, and so forth. During an e-service encounter, the customers are restricted to hearing and viewing whereas, in traditional service, customers can experience the service using all senses. However, traditional service is restricted by distance and opening hours, whereas e-service has substantially removed these barriers (Surjadjaja et al., 2003).

Empirical studies demonstrate that buyers perceive services to be riskier than products (Mitchell & Greatorex, 1993). Disparate services increase risk exposure. Furthermore, these services are threatened by internal factors including lack of standards, lack of regulations and rules, and lack of support systems. This contrasts with traditional service industries that have deep-rooted support systems, rules, regulations, and standards. The external factors that threaten the new online services are volatile online political sanctions, natural hazards, legal issues, environmental issues, and other political instabilities.

Several risks arise from these online services that include service failure risks, service-specific security risks, new jurisdiction risks, intangible property risks, and obsolete assumption risks. Jurisdiction on Internet sales is still ambiguous and sellers may find themselves in expensive litigation in distant forums (Lange et al., 2000). The intangible property rights create new risks both in the nature of uncertainty regarding existing transactions and in attempting to control risk of future transactions (Lange et al., 2000). Courts will have to determine whether the risks created by the use of new technology should be borne by the party who puts the technology into use, or whether the interest in innovation has for the potential benefit to third parties supports denial of liability (Lange et al., 2000). In the event of failure in the e-service, service recovery redresses loss to customers. Customers who experience a service failure can become more demanding and lose confidence with the firm that is offering the services or the firm who uses a third-party service. However, if service recovery is carried out satisfactorily, it can turn dissatisfied customers into satisfied customers (Ahmad, 2002), with a consequent decrease in negative word of mouth (Sparks & Bradley, 1997). In contrast, unsuccessful service recovery leads to a decline in customers' confidence, lost customers, negative word of mouth, negative publicity, and the direct cost of having to reperform the service (Berry & Parasuraman, 1992).

In banking, online fraud is a real problem (Streeter, 2005). The U.S. is a hotbed of online fraud, according to a report just published by the FBI and the National White Collar Crime Center (NWCCC). The same report claims a staggering 94.1% of all online fraud complaints reported to the Internet Fraud Complaint Center. These frauds include bogus invoices, cramming, slamming, loan scams, phishing, and so forth. According to a new survey, high fraud rates continue to plague electronic commerce Web sites, with criminals expected to steal $2.6 billion from online merchants. Suspicious merchants are now rejecting a far higher percentage of orders, meaning a steep increase in lost sales due to accidental rejection of legitimate orders (Sullivan, 2004).

Poaching is a contractual relationship risk where information that is transferred between parties for purposes specified in the contract is deliberately used by the receiving party for purposes outside the contract, to its own economic benefit, and to the detriment of the party that provided the information (Clemens & Hitt, 2004). This is a form of transactional risk and is one component of opportunistic behavior and abuse of power, when a client cannot monitor performance and when a client has become dependent upon a vendor's services. The rise of outsourcing and of interfirm activities that entail the transfer of intellectual property increases the risk of poaching (Clemens & Hitt, 2004).

Third-party liability exposure seems to be theoretical but can become a reality (Sclafane, 2000). The services risks are particular to Internet service provider (ISP) or application service provider (ASP). If interrupted, these services pose a problem to other businesses as well. For example, if AOL goes down, there is a significant business interruption to Amazon or eBay. Web-based storage services allow business users to store their documents and other digital files on third-party servers. Since most of these service users are small and medium enterprises (SME), data protection is absolutely critical in these instances for their survival (Aber, 2004). Web-based storage services ensure businesses to focus on their core business, and operate even if crises, outages, or disasters occur in their main offices. They also offer real-time collaboration and file sharing between SME and their partners in supply chain (Aber, 2004).

As firms expose applications to internal and external users, it is critical that these exposed interfaces are well defined, easy to use, and meaningful to the service consumer. This means that they must more closely reflect business concepts and requirements (documents, processes) rather than low-level technical concepts (APIs, data types, and platforms). Interfaces exposed in this way are referred to as business services. These e-services consist of three layers. The first layer consists of software standards and protocols that include Extensible Markup Language (XML) and simple object access protocol (SOAP) that allow information to be exchanged easily among Web applications. The second layer builds upon the protocols and standards, and forms a service grid managed by third parties that facilitate transport of messages and identify available services and assuring reliability and consistency as well. The third level comprises of a diverse area of application services, from credit card processing to production scheduling, that automate individual business functions (Hagel, 2002). Web services-specific security is still in rudimentary stage. Standards bodies like the W3C and OASIS are working diligently toward a solution, but Web services on the Internet today are completely defenseless against cyberterrorists and hackers. This level of exposure is far too risky for most IT executives. We will discuss the risks of business models in the next section.

New Business Models

New business models have emerged on the online scene. Portal models, such as dynamic pricing, free products and services, demand-sensitive pricing, and so on, may add further risks. Products and services have made their way to the e-business to be sold by original manufacturers, certified resellers, and sometimes noncertified resellers as well. The original manufacturer or service provider may find it attractive to channel their marketing and sales efforts using e-marketplaces or exchanges, only to find that the owners of the e-marketplaces or exchanges have different business models than their conventional marketing and sales practices. When the business models of the original manufacturer are not aligned with the certified resellers or noncertified resellers, the original manufacturers will be exposed to various new risks. The business models are threatened by internal factors, like loss of revenue, due to the cost of poor image, and so forth. In this case, these business models are threatened by socio-psychological external factors including trust, privacy, confidence, and other such factors. Businesses going global online have new exposures that are different from traditional ones. There are new regulatory exposures that they never thought about before.

The complexity of the business and the complex nature of risk itself is one of the concerns of the risk industry (Kaiser, 2002). The high consolidation levels within industries has translated into big channel conflicts and led to cannibalization of their own business (Kaiser, 2002). In many parts of the world, as in Latin America, sellers are in a much better position than buyers, and unless there is a steep rise in competition among sellers, the buyers will be at a disadvantage (Sinha, 1999). The most significant aspect of e-business is the transfer of power from the supplier to the buyer (Kaiser, 2002). There are risks associated with the seller credibility due to the availability of an overwhelming number of retailers, which is partially due to the perceived low entry and set-up costs business models (Biswas & Biswas, 2004; Peterson, Balasubramanian, & Bronnenberg, 1997). It becomes difficult for the customer to distinguish between "fly-by-night operators" and regular "honest" suppliers in e-business (Biswas & Biswas, 2004). This higher level of uncertainty would, in turn, increase the overall perceived risks (Biswas & Biswas, 2004). Some companies, like Fingerhut, abandoned strategic positioning for some of their new customers due to new business models and failed. The management also failed to adequately analyze their ability to sustain competitive advantages of the many online businesses in which they invested (Phan, Chen, & Ahmad, 2005).

Performance risk and financial risks have received strong attention (Grewal, Gotlieb, & Marmorstein, 1994) in growing markets. Performance risk is the uncertainty and consequence of a product not functioning at some expected level (Shimp & Bearden, 1982). Performance risks are likely to be higher in e-business since customers are unable to physically inspect the product before purchase (Biswas & Biswas, 2004; Lal & Sarvary, 1999). Financial risks are the uncertainty and monetary loss one perceives to be incurring if a product does not function at a certain expected level (Grewal et al., 1994). There exists transaction risks, which is the uncertainty associated with giving information such as credit card number to the seller during the course of a transaction. Consumers have higher levels of perceived performance, financial, and transaction risks in e-business (Biswas & Biswas, 2004). Retailer reputation, perceived advertising expense, and warranty have been shown as consumer risk perception signals in e-business conditions for products (Biswas & Biswas, 2004).

The strong ties associated between the high levels of trust and the banking industry have not yet been translated to its full potential (Yousafzai, Pallister, & Foxall, 2005). Trust has been identified as the key enabler to e-business (Keen, Balance, Chan, & Schrump, 2000). Lack of trust and privacy are risks and uncertainties that exist in e-business (So & Sculli, 2002). Customers are reluctant to adopt e-business, especially in online banking applications, because of trust (Lee & Turban, 2001). Trust has been looked upon as the major obstacle in e-business models (Gefan et al., 2003). Another risk is perceived reputation of a firm. Until executives actively manage the perceptions of their company with as much rigor as they apply to managing financial, operational, or technology risk, a company's most important intangible asset—its reputation—will be at risk (Resnick, 2004). The blemish in reputation may be due to any number of reasons, one of them being loss of confidence and trust due to online business models of the firm.

Privacy is infringement by online retailers by sharing or selling or renting personal information to other companies, contacting without consent, and tracking habits and purchases.

System security includes concerns about potentially malicious individuals who breach firms' systems to acquire personal, financial, or transactional information. Frauds are concerns regarding any fraudulent behavior by either customer or supplier, including nondelivery or misrepresentation of ordered goods (Miyazaki & Fernandez, 2001). Trust is crucial to e-business, but e-businesses are failing to support ways of assuring it (Moores, 2005). Privacy seals, like TRUSTe, CPA Webtrust, and BBBOnline, are Web assurance seals to persuade buyers that the particular Web site can be trusted. The result in a recent study points out that many do not fully comprehend the form and function of the privacy seals and deciding to trust the site with the privacy seal (Moores, 2005). The results suggest that the seals have failed to play their intended role, and the buyers have to be educated with the process and assurance of these seals.

Technology can be the stimulus for the growth of e-business. Technology alone cannot be the stimulus. The transformation to online business is a complex social, technological, political understanding (Davison, Vogel, & Harris, 2005). However, technology has its own risks, as presented in the next section.

New Technology

E-business uses emerging technologies. Most of these technology applications may not have been tested for scalability, security, and availability. The integration with other software products has also been a challenge. Integration of various systems and software has exposed the integrated system's vulnerabilities. These vulnerabilities may highlight unique risks caused specifically by integration. Furthermore, security risks have been well documented in the literature (Kolluru & Meredith, 2001; Salisbury et al., 2001). The internal factors that threaten new technologies are complexity of systems and integration of systems, while the external factor that threatens the technologies is security.

Security refers to the technical safety of the network against fraud or hackers (Surjadjaja et al., 2003). Recent information thefts have left a mark on the risks of third-party data. About 145,000 consumers nationwide were placed at risk by a recent data theft at the database giant ChoicePoint. Personal information on 310,000 people nationwide has been stolen from LexisNexis, which compiles and sells personal and financial data on U.S. consumers. This is not a technology problem and is a legal problem (Schneier, 2005). These frauds and thefts would not have been public if it were not for the California law mandating public disclosure of such events (Schenier, 2005). Hacker attacks and rapidly spreading viruses, worms, and Trojans impact an organization causing anything from loss of productivity to loss of reputation (Nyanchama, 2005).

In addition, increased networking, mobility, and telecommuting have introduced serious technical issues and potential security problems (Dillon & Pate-Cornell, 2005). Fundamentally, the Internet and its infrastructure, system access, security, open standards, information access, reliance, integrity of data and information, complexity, interdependence, and interconnectivity, all lead to exposures.

New technologies have created new products, for example, capturing procurement habits of customer database. These technologies have led to intangible property rights and contracts. Unclear or overreaching agreements are risk exposures to these new products (Lange et al.,

2000). IT has enhanced product marketing and distribution. If the experiences of Web site marketing simulations do not match the real experiences of the buyer, this new media way of marketing can create risks (Lange et al., 2000). Technology failure risks include lack of system functionality, system unavailability, loss of data integrity, loss of data confidentiality, and security of systems in general. IT systems crash when large waves of orders overload processing capacity. Business interruptions lead to financial risk as well as market share risk (Phan et al., 2005). Furthermore, standardization in exchange of data is lacking in industry (Kaiser, 2002), raising risks in integrity of data.

Other risks include antiquated network backbone, development of "spaghetti" code, poor configuration control, expensive conversion of data, noncompliance with embraced methodologies, no or lack of standards, poorly articulated requirements, and incompatible development tools. Most companies are focusing on how to use new technology by improving processes in order to increase productivity, reduce cost, and seek reliable partnerships in order to compete in e-business (Zhang, 2005). The new processes have been exposed to risks as well, and are illustrated in the next section.

New Processes

Businesses generally engage in three main processes (Klamm & Weidenmier, 2004): (a) acquiring and paying for resources, (b) converting resources into goods/services, and (c) acquiring customers, delivering goods and services, and collecting revenues. New e-business processes to enhance these three main processes have surfaced to fill a real business need. Companies that have emerged onto the online scene have changed the old processes to build new business models. Integration of external partner process with internal process has created new reengineered processes. These new processes may expose new risks. The creation of real-time process for e-business may also expose new risks. New outsourcing processes may also create risks for the business. In response to perceived risks, many existing businesses redesigned their processes for e-business conditions. Some emerged successfully, while many others failed (Phan et al., 2005). Some of these new processes are threatened by internal factors such as stringent product specifications for specific market needs. The processes are also threatened by external factors such as perceived quality of products and services.

The new processes in e-business include routine activities automated by computers for higher speed and reliability; business processes and services to extend across different organizations; the agility in business processes to be able to quickly adapt to customers needs and market conditions; and business functions desired to be readily shareable at a small granularity level (Zhang, 2005).

A new trend in e-business is to enable a business to dynamically connect arbitrarily complex e-services provided by different vendors in order to create a new service (Zhang, 2005). It is difficult to implement this process because it requires complicated coordination among various vendors based on exchange of data and process information (Zhang, 2005). In order to enable interoperability, it is important that vendors agree on basic common standards, and there is a lack of these standards. These process integrations give rise to new e-business risks. The return process is an essential criterion in any e-business operation (Curtis, 2000; Strauss & Hill, 2001). This is especially true if buyers need to see, touch, smell, and test a product before deciding whether to retain or return it (Surjadjaja et al., 2003). New audit and internal control procedures have given rise to new exposures (Yu, Yu, & Chou, 2000).

New technology leads to implementing new, better, improved, and standardized internal business processes (Barnes et al., 2003). These new levels of technically complex processes lead to contextual risk in e-business environment (Pathak, 2004). Streamlining approvals through electronic processes may remove existing internal controls and potentially increase the risk (Pathak, 2004). As issues of fulfillment and the need for new technology to be integrated increased in e-businesses, risks in integrating e-business capabilities into existing business processes increased (Krell & Gale, 2005). This is because of the misfit between new processes and existing organizational processes and organizational structure (Krell & Gale, 2005). Integrating complex systems in firms have caused firms to abandon projects either in the middle of the project or after a futile attempt (Cliffe, 1999). The objective of complex ERP implementation is to integrate information systems across all functional areas and to pursue a long-term sustainable competitive advantage. Failing to integrate the processes into ERP systems can lead to failure of ERP implementation and thus connectivity to e-business.

These new business models, new processes, new online services, and new technologies have created exposure to businesses. In the next section, fulfillment risks are explored.

New Fulfillment

The perception of online fulfillment has changed. Products and services are needed almost in real time in this online world. E-business may bring in sales from many new channels of marketing. The integration of these real-time sales orders with the existing supply-chain management and order fulfillment may increase risks. Inefficient fulfillment integration with external distribution providers may also expose risks. The internal factor that threatens the new fulfillment needs is supply-chain management. The external factor that threatens the fulfillment is the real-time demand for products and services.

Fulfillment refers to the delivery of products and services on time and, as specified, within a service level agreement (Surjadjaja et al., 2003). Order fulfillment risks, such as lost orders, shipment delays, and shipments of incomplete orders, can be detrimental to business health (Phan et al., 2005). Orders may take long to assemble, and Web partners have to pay for express shipments (Phan et al., 2005). Experience in order fulfillment and ample warehouse capacity do not automatically translate into success in e-business (Phan et al., 2005). Because e-business requires linkages between front-office and back-office operations with the supply chain, lack of integrated fulfillment systems create risks (Phan et al., 2005).

Factors of fulfillment can be viewed in the logistics framework proposed by Vaidyanathan (2005). The framework includes global servicing, global transportation, global warehousing, global inventory management, logistics, and information sharing. Fulfillment also includes inventory management, warehousing, and "e-fulfillment centers" (Reynolds, 2000), and coping with seasonal variations in demand (Ridley, 2002). The challenges are in delivering digital products and services where issues such as copyrights and data protection need to be addressed and resolved before delivering digital products and services. Of course, the delivery of physical products has its own challenges. Due to all these challenges, online businesses without strong financial resources and networks can experience difficulties in managing the fulfillment needs (Surjadjaja et al., 2003).

Risk in a supply chain is the potential occurrence of an incidence associated with inbound supply in which the result is the inability of the purchasing firm to meet customer demand (Zsidisin, 2000). Spekman and Davis (2004) illustrated a six-factor risk framework for supply chain. The first factor is the obsolete or unwanted inventory that can rise due to lack of communication with the supply-chain partners. An example would be of Cisco's inventory dilemma when the firm wrote off $2.5 billion in inventory. The second factor is associated with the flow of information. The third factor is with the supply chain's flow of money, and relates risks associated with stable pricing, hedging, letters of credit, timely payment of bills, and so forth. These three factors affect both inbound and outbound flows of the supply chain including risks on quality, product design, production, supplier development, supplier stability, logistics, and any other physical activity that affects supply chain's ability to meet its objectives. The fourth factor is the security of the firm's internal IT and the risks relating to who has access to the information and sharing of information. The fifth factor is associated with the relationships forged among supply chain partners, and the tendency of the partners to act in their self-interest. The sixth factor of risk relates to the supply-chain members' reputation and corporate social responsibility.

Moreover, supplier capacity constraints, process changes in production and design, inability to reduce costs, unanticipated delays, and supply disruptions (Zsidisin, Panelli, & Upton, 2000) can become a part of the risks in the six-factor risk framework. Many e-marketplaces have failed to deliver on promises that were made (Murtaza et al., 2004). There is a general concern of security ad standards in the supply-chain management. There are no common supplier qualification criteria, no consistent item coding schemes, and no technology integration guidelines (Murtaza et al., 2004). Furthermore, integration of systems to provide efficient supply chain is of concern as well (Murtaza, 2004). Antitrust laws are another major challenge, since highly successful e-marketplaces can run the risk of limiting competition unfairly, even though the laws improve efficiencies (Murtaza, 2004).

Risk Management

The risks of e-business are generally very similar to the risks of doing traditional business. The primary difference is that risks from e-business arises from and relates to novel contractual exchanges. Mitigating and management of e-business risks essentially start with identifying all the associated risks. Once all the risks are identified, then the risks need to be quantified using frequency and severity of risks. Once the e-business risks are quantified, the next task is to mitigate the risks by effective means. Then the risk management needs to be made into a process within the company. This is accomplished by adopting and using contract management policies. As with any process, the contract management needs to be monitored continuously. We will explore this four-step process in this section.

Identifying Risks

Risk analysis begins with the identification of assets and all possible threats to the identified assets (Jung, Han, & Suh, 1999). The firm needs to understand the requirements of the business processes, as well as to include concerns over financial loss, damage to reputation, loss of intellectual property, devaluation of goods, and regulatory requirements, among other business-specific risks.

The process of searching for risks may be iterative. A list of risks associated with each objective, key parameter, major deliverable, or principal activity may be prepared. It is essential that every aspect of the five dimensions is analyzed. This list preparation should be from first principles without the use of checklists or prompts, to avoid constraining the process of discovery. After this, the exercise should be repeated with the help of the risk matrix and other prompt aids. A brainstorming session to review the risks previously identified and to flush out further risks needs to be undertaken. Having identified all the risks, the identified risks need to be classified and grouped for further evaluation.

Quantifying Risks

Firms must understand their internal and external failure modes, including knowledge of how specific system compromises or failures can affect a business process and its relative risk. Usage of tools such as failure mode and effects analysis (FMEA) can be used to identify and quantify risks (Bongiorno, 2001; Carbone & Tippett, 2004; Chrysler Corp., Ford Motor Co., & General Motors Corp., 1995). Many firms have used FMEA in process development and product development. Usually, input is solicited from many experts across the organization. The input can be sought from customers and suppliers to understand the risks of supply chain. The FMEA is then used for troubleshooting and corrective action. The standard FMEA evaluates failure modes for occurrence, severity, and detection (Chrysler Corp., Ford Motor Co., & General Motors Corp., 1995). The experts, in their opinion, give input to the occurrences, severity, and detection of risks. The risk priority number (RPN) is then calculated as product of occurrences, severity, and detection.

Mitigating Risks

The quantified risks need to be aligned with the goals of the company. The quantified risks need to be mitigated using correcting measures if plausible, by developing compensating controls, by insuring the risk, and, in most cases, by developing a detection method for these failure modes.

E-services will be successful if more factual product service information is provided; shopping convenience, product value, and customer relations are emphasized; and customer needs, such as better purchasing experience, are understood (Verma, Iqbal, & Plaschka, 2004). In one instance, the government of Singapore initiated their e-business using e-services that allow the different government agencies to share components such as payment gateways, electronic data exchange, authentication, and other security features in the development of e-services. This reduced both the incremental cost for implementation of new e-services as well as the time needed for design and development. It also retains the flexibility to change business requirements in services easily, and offers services via multiple concurrent channels. Singapore citizens and businesses can obtain faster, more convenient access to government services as compared to waiting in line. This fast, efficient, and cost-effective implementation of e-services Singapore recognized as "Innovative Leaders," along with Canada and United States in recent report on global e-government. They used Sun Microsystems's Public Services Infrastructure (PHI), which allows the different government agencies to share components such as payment gateways, electronic data exchange, authentication, and other security features in the development of e-services (Sun Microsystems, 2001).

Structural assurance and situational normality mechanisms both have an impact on customers' trustworthiness perceptions, suggesting that firms need to use a portfolio of strategies to build customers' trust (Yousafzai et al., 2005). To improve the customers' confidence and to mitigate psychological risks associated with security, more Web sites are advertising a secure transaction sign (for example, VeriSign). VeriSign is effectively selling confidence, facilitated by the strong market reputation of Microsoft. In addition to VeriSign, many Web sites use the symbols of various accreditation bodies (such as ATOL, IATA and ABTA, BBBOnline). Firms can always secure Web services to a partner through existing network security technologies such as Virtual Private Networks (VPNs), Public Key Infrastructure (PKI), and digital certificates. Among various remedies to promote trust and reduce online fraud, online escrow services have been implemented as a trusted third party to protect online transactions and Internet fraud (Hu, Lin, Whinston, & Zhang, 2004). Courts need to recognize that in the information age, virtual privacy and physical privacy have no same boundaries (Schneier, 2005).

Data-mining capabilities are crucial for e-business. For example, Toys-R-Us has established affiliations with Amazon.com, leveraged from data collected from online customers with a company with a trusted brand (Phan et al., 2005). Being a component of information security management, vulnerability management is effective when defined with a risk management approach. To be effective, vulnerability management must incorporate key elements of effective processes such as policies, accountabilities, communication, and continuous improvement (Nyanchama, 2005).

Buyers can buffer against supply risks by developing multiple sources of supply and carrying safety stock (Giunipero & Eltantawy, 2004). In order to manage risk effectively, purchasers are moving to adopt closer relationships with key suppliers and expect the suppliers to provide solutions and compliment or enhance the buying firm's core competencies (Giunipero & Eltantawy, 2004). Joint buyer-supplier efforts may reduce risks in the supply process, and this type of collaborative supply management effort increases product reliability and reduces risks in product introduction (Giunipero & Eltantawy, 2004). For example, Chrysler minimized supply-chain risks by implementing long-term trading agreements and sharing the benefits of mutual involvement in design and development of products that Chrysler purchases (Viehland, 2002).

Firms need to develop policies regarding use of forms and conditions in which standard clauses may be negotiated. They have to monitor sales and distribution channels to determine that appropriate forms are being used and that contract policies are followed. In addition, the firms have to develop and administer policies on early dispute mitigation and alternate dispute resolution (Lange et al., 2000).

Managing Risks

A recent survey by nCircle, a provider of enterprise-class vulnerability and risk-management solutions, polled 1,700 CIOs, CSOs, and security directors for the Vulnerability and Risk Management Trend survey (Government Technology, 2005). The survey results indicate that many businesses still lack the information they need to determine the effectiveness of their security ecosystem:

- Sixty percent of respondents were unable to determine whether their network security risk was decreasing or increasing over time.

- Fifty-eight percent of respondents stated they are unable to generate reports about applications or vulnerabilities on their network by region business unit or business owner.

- Fifty-two percent of respondents stated they have no way to verify and manage compliance with their own internal security policies.

The prime objective of risk management is to minimize the impact and probability of occurrence of risks in firms. Firms must put in place detective controls and operational monitoring so that, when a failure mode occurs, it is detected without delay and the appropriate response is enacted. Effective institutionalization of e-risk management requires five additional factors (Lange et al., 2000):

- Implement an initial review and risk assessment of a firm's e-business risk exposures to include legal, network security, human resources, management personnel, and others, and make sure that the company's policies and procedures are followed.

- Establishing clear lines of authority for contract administration, a firm can best control the assumption of unintended business risks, and by implementing periodic reviews by outside control, bring multiple perspectives and best practices.

- Fine-tune contracts and substantially revise to reflect the technology and services relevant to e-business.

- Cover insurances with all the possible exposures due to e-business.

- Keep current with legal, technological, and market developments.

To have successful e-commerce ventures, firms need to show strength in four areas. These four areas revolve around their business models—their external environments and their corporate strategies, structures, systems, and resources. Based on the evaluation of these inputs, they must develop proper e-business leadership, strategies, structures, and systems (Epstein, 2005). A framework that helps a decision maker consider security issues early in the project has been developed by Dillon and Pate-Cornell (2005). This framework has a proactive approach, as it allows planning for contingency and setting priorities in resource allocation considering the system life cycle. Another methodology using case-based reasoning (CBR) was introduced to analyze IT risks (Jung et al., 1999). The learning component enables the software to update the case base dynamically in a fast-changing e-business environment.

Conclusion and Future Research

Even the insurance firms are in their rudimentary stage in enterprise risk management (ERM) (Oliva, 2005). A few firms have hired or appointed chief risk officers (CROs) and are embracing strategies and technologies to manage risk companywide, but most insurers are behind the curve. ERM needs to be embraced as a competitive strategy and linked to allocation of capital and growth goals. Critical success factors going forward will include (Oliva, 2005):

• Identifying, measuring, monitoring, mitigating, and financing all aspects of risk

• Instituting procedures for handling risk

• Computing and allocating capital based on risk tolerances

The framework presented in this article can help us understand the various risks involved in B2B commerce. The conceptual framework presented examines risk from five critical dimensions—services, business models, technology, fulfillment, and processes. Online businesses can benefit from a careful consideration and analyses of these five factors that are primary sources of risk. Such a planned risk analysis exercise can provide insights to practitioners of e-business, procurement managers, marketing managers, IT managers, as well as academicians. It remains to be seen if understanding and mitigating risk will indeed be the turning point for B2B commerce. E-business may be the most important value-creating activity for many businesses. The key is in its implementation (Epstein, 2005) and how these companies mitigate risks as well.

References

Aber, R. (2004, July 12). Managing risks with online storage. *Entrepreneur.*

Ahmad, S. (2002). Service failures and customer defection: A closer look at online shopping experiences. *Managing Service Quality, 12*(1), 19-29.

Ahn, J., Park, J., & Lee, D. (2001). *Risk focused e-commerce adoption model—a cross-country study.* Working paper, last revised June 2001.

Ba, S., & Paulou, P. A. (2002). Evidence of the effect of trust in electronic markets: Price premiums and buyer behavior. *MIS Quarterly, 26*(3), 243-266.

Baker, C. R. (1999). An analysis of fraud on the electronic business. *Electronic Business Research: Electronic Networking Applications and Policy, 9*(5), 349-359.

Barnes, D., Hinton, M., & Mecgkowska, S. (2003). Focusing failures in competitive environments: Explaining decision errors in the Monty Hall game, the acquiring of a company problem, and multiparty ultimatums. *Journal of Behavioral Decision Making, 16*(5), 353.

Berry, L. L., & Parasuraman, A. (1992). Prescriptions for a service quality revolution in America. *Organizational Dynamics, 20*(4), 5-15.

Bhimani, A. (1996). Securing the commercial electronic business. *Communications of the ACM, 39*(6), 29-35.

Biswas, D., & Biswas, A. (2004). The diagnostic role of signals in the context of perceived risks in online shopping: Do signals matter more on the web? *Journal of Interactive Marketing, 18*(3), 30-45.

Bongiorno, J. (2001). Use FMEAs to improve your product development process. *Project Management Network, 15*(5), 47-51.

Caelli, W. J. (1997). Information security in electronic business. In *PACIS'97—The Pacific Asia Conference on Information Systems*, Brisbane, Australia (pp. 1-5).

Carbone, T. A., & Tippett, D. D. (2004). Project risk management using the project risk FMEA. *Engineering Management Journal, 16*(4), 28-35.

Chrysler Corp., Ford Motor Co., and General Motors Corp. (1995). *Potential failure mode and effects analysis (FMEA) reference manual* (2nd ed.), equivalent to SAE J-1739.

Clemons, E. K., & Hitt, L. M. (2004). Poaching and the misappropriation of information: Transaction risks of information exchange. *Journal of Management Information Systems, 21*(2), 87-107.

Cliffe, S. (1999) ERP implementation. *Harvard Business Review, 77*, 16-17.

Cox, D. F., & Rich, S. U. (1964). Perceived risk and consumer decision making—the case of telephone shopping. *Journal of Marketing Research, 1*(4), 32-39.

Cunningham, S. M. (1967). The major dimensions of perceived risk. In D. F. Cox (Ed.), *Risk taking and information handling in consumer behavior* (pp. 82-108). Boston: Graduate School of Business Administration, Harvard University.

Curtis, J. (2000, February). Next generation customer service. *E-business*, 62-67.

Davison, R. M., Vogel, D. R., & Harris, R. W. (2005). The e-transformation of western China. *Communications of the ACM, 48*(4), 62-66.

Dillon, R. L., & Pate-Cornell, M. E. (2005). Including technical and security risks in the management of information systems: A programmatic risk management model. *Systems Engineering, 8*(1), 15-28.

Epstein, M. J. (2005, March). Implementing successful e-commerce initiatives. *Strategic Finance*, 23-29.

Gefan, D., Karahanna, E., & Straub, D. (2003). Trust and TAM in online shopping: An integrated model. *MIS Quarterly, 27*(1), 51-90.

Government Technology News. (2005). Retrieved from http://www.govtech.net/magazine/channel_story.php/94696

Grewal, D., Gotlieb, J., & Marmorstein, H. (1994). The moderating effects of message framing and source credibility on the price-perceived risk relationship. *Journal of Consumer Research, 21*(7), 145-153.

Grover, V., & Saeed, K. A. (2004). Strategic orientation and performance of Internet-based businesses. *Information Systems Journal, 14*(1), 23-42.

Guinipero, L. C., & Eltantawy, R. A. (2004). Securing the upstream supply chain: A risk management approach. *International Journal of Physical Distribution & Logisitics Management, 34*(9), 698-713.

Hagel, J. (2002, November). Web services: Technology as a catalyst for strategic thinking. *Harvard Management Update*, 3-4.

Hu, X., Lin, Z., Whinston, A. B., & Zhang, H. (2004). Hope or hype: On the viability of escrow services as trusted theirs parties in online auction environments. *Information Systems Research, 15*(3), 236-249.

Jacoby, J., & Kaplan, L. B. (1972). The components of perceived risk. In *Proceedings of the 3rd Annual Conference of the Association for Consumer Research* (pp. 382-393). Association for Consumer Research.

Jones, S., Wilikens, M., Morris, P., & Masera, M. (2000). Trust requirements in e-business. *Communications of the ACM, 43*(12), 81-87.

Jung, C., Han, I., & Suh, B. (1999). Risk analysis for electronic commerce using case-based reasoning. *International Journal of Intelligent Systems in Accounting, Finance & Management, 8*, 61-73.

Kaiser, T. (2002). The customer shall lead: E-business solutions for the new insurance industry. *The Geneva Papers on Risk and Insurance, 27*(1), 134-145.

Keen, P., Balance, C., Chan, S., & Schrump, S. (2000). *Electronic commerce relationships: Trust by design.* Upper Saddle River, NJ: Prentice Hall.

Kilgore, J. M. (2004, April). *Mitigating supply chain risks.* Presented at the 89th Annual International Supply Chain Conference.

Klamm, B. K., & Weidenmier, M. L. (2004). Linking business processes and transaction cycles. *Journal of Information Systems, 18*(2), 113-125.

Kolluru, R., & Meredith, P. (2001). Security and trust management in supply chains. *Information Management and Computer Security, 9*(5), 233-236.

Krell, T., & Gale, J. (2005). E-business migration: A process model. *Journal of Organizational Change Management, 18*(2), 117-131.

Lal, R., & Sarvary, M. (1999). When and how is the Internet likely to decrease price competition? *Marketing Science, 18*(4), 485-503.

Lange, S. K., Davis, J. K., Jaye, D., Erwin, D., Mullarney, J. X., Clarke, L. L., & Loesch, M. C. (2000). *E-Risk: Liabilities in a wired world.* Cincinnati: The National Underwriter Co.

Lee, M., & Turban, E. (2001). A trust model for consumer Internet shopping. *International Journal of Electronic Commerce, 6,* 75-91.

McCrohan, K. F. (2003). Facing the threats of electronic commerce. *The Journal of Business and Industrial Marketing, 18*(2), 133-145.

Mercuri, R. T. (2005). Trusting in transparency. *Communication of the ACM, 48*(5), 15-19.

Mitchell, V. W., & Greatorex, M. (1993). Risk perception and reduction in the purchase of consumer services. *The Services Industries Journal, 13,* 179-200.

Miyazaki, A. D., & Fernandez, A. (2001). Consumer perceptions of privacy and security risks for online shopping. *The Journal of Consumer Affairs, 35*(1), 27-44.

Moores, T. (2005). Do consumers understand the role of privacy seals in e-commerce? *Communications of the ACM, 48*(3), 86-91.

Muiznieks, V. (1995, November). The electronic business and EDI. *Telecommunications,* 45-48.

Murphy, P. E., & Enis. B. M. (1986). Classifying products strategically. *Journal of Marketing, 50*(3), 24-42.

Murtaza, M. B., Gupta, V., & Carroll, R. C. (2004). E-Marketplaces and the future of supply chain management: Opportunities and challenges. *Business Process Management Journal, 10*(3), 325-335.

Nyanchama, M. (2005, July/August). Enterprise vulnerability management and its role in information security management. *Information Security Management,* 29-56.

Oliva, V. (2005, March). Predictions 2005: Insurance industry force-fed transformation. *Gartner Report,* 1-10.

Orr, B. (2005). Identify fraud, round two. *ABA Banking Journal, 97*(6), 64-65.

Papadopoulou P., Andreou A., Kanellis P., & Martakos, A. (2001). Trust and relationship building in electronic business. *Electronic Business Research: Electronic Networking Applications and Policy, 11*(4), 322-332.

Pathak, J. (2004). A conceptual risk framework for internal auditing in e-commerce. *Management Auditing Journal, 19*(4), 556-564.

Peterson, R. A., Balasubramanian, S., & Bronnenberg, B. J. (1997). Exploring the implications of the Internet for consumer marketing. *Journal of Academy of Marketing Science, 25*(4), 329-346.

Phan, D. D., Chen, J. Q., & Ahmad, S. (2005, Summer). Lessons leaned from an initial e-commerce failure by a catalog retailer. *Information Systems Management,* 7-13.

Ratnasingham, P. (1998). The importance of trust in electronic business. *Electronic Business Research: Electronic Networking Applications and Policy, 8*(4), 313-321.

Resnick, J. (2004). Corporate reputation: Managing corporate reputation - Applying rigorous measures to a key asset. *Journal of Business Strategy, 25*(6), 30-38.

Reynolds, J. (2000). eCommerce: A critical review. *International Journal of Retail and Distribution Management, 28*(10), 417-44.

Ridley, H. (2002, January). The ghost of e-christmas past. *e-Business*, 12-13.

Salisbury, W. D., Pearson, R. A., Pearson, A. W., & Miller, D. W. (2001). Perceived security and World Wide Web purchase intention. *Industrial Management and Data Systems, 101*(4), 165-176.

Schneier, B. (2005). Risks of third-party data. *Communications of the ACM, 48*(5), 136.

Sclafane, S. (2000, March). Emerging third-party risks lurk online. *Property & Casualty Risk & Benefits Management*, 15.

Shapira, Z., (1995). *Risk taking: A managerial perspective.* New York: Russell Sage.

Shimp, T. A., & Bearden, W. O. (1982). Warranty and other extrinsic cue effects on consumers' risk perceptions. *Journal of Consumer Research, 9*(7), 38-46.

Singhal, V. (2000, December). Putting price on supply chain problems: Study links supply chain glitches with falling stock prices. *Georgia Tech Research News.*

Sinha, T. (1999, December). The Internet, insurance, and Latin America. *Texas Business Review*, 4-5.

So, M. W. C., & Sculli, D. (2002). The role of trust, quality, value and risk in conducting e-business. *Industrial Management & Data Systems, 102*(3), 503-512.

Sparks, B. A., & Bradley, G. L. (1997). Antecedents and consequences of perceived service providers effort in the hospitality industry. *Hospitality Research Journal, 20*(3), 17-34.

Spekman, R. E., & Davis, E. W. (2004). Risky business: Expanding the discussion on risk and the extended enterprise. *International Journal of Physical Distribution & Logistics Management, 34*(5), 414-433.

Straub, D., & Welke, R. J. (1998). Coping with systems risk: Security planning models for management decision making. *MIS Quarterly, 22*(4), 441-469.

Strauss, J., & Hill, D. J. (2001). Consumer complaints by e-mail: An exploratory investigation of corporate responses and customer reactions. *Journal of Interactive Marketing 15*(1), 63-73.

Streeter, W. W. (2005, April). Call me paranoid. *ABA Banking Journal*, 4.

Sullivan, B. (2004, November 11). Online fraud costs $2.6 billion this year. *MSNBC*, 2004.

Sun Microsystems. (2001). *Singapore government public eServices infrastructure delivers one-stop services on demand, based on Sun ONE.* Sun Success Story. Retrieved from http://www.sun.com/br/government/PSi_final.pdf

Surjadjaja, H., Ghosh, S., & Antony, J. (2003). Determining and assessing the determinants of e-service operations. *Managing Service Quality, 13*(1), 39-53.

Vaidyanathan, G. (2005). A framework for evaluating third-party logistics. *Communications of the ACM, 48*(1), 89-94.

Vaidyanathan, G., & Devaraj, S. (2003). A five factor framework for analyzing online risks in E-business. *Communications of the ACM, 46*(12), 354-361.

Verma, R., Iqbal, Z., & Plaschka, G. (2004). Understanding customer choices in e-financial services. *California Review Management, 46*(4), 42-67.

Viehland, D. W. (2002, May). Risk e-business: Assessing risk in electronic commerce. *Decision Line,* 9-11.

Vijayan, J. (2001, September 25). Group pushes for B2B standards. *Computer World.* Retrieved from http://www.computerworld.com/governmenttopics/ government/legalissues/ story/0,10801,51191,00.html

Wise, R., & Morrison. D. (2000). Beyond the exchange: The future of B2B. *Harvard Business Review,* 86-96.

Yousafzai, S. Y., Pallister, J. G., & Foxall, G. R. (2005). Strategies for building and communicating trust in electronic banking: A field experiment. *Psychology & Marketing, 22*(2), 181-201.

Yu, C., Yu, H., Chou, C. (2000). The impacts of electronic commerce on auditing practices: An auditing process model for evidence collection and validation. *International Journal of Intelligent Systems in Accounting, Finance & Management, 9,* 195-216.

Zhang, D. (2005). Web services composition for process management in e-business. *Journal of Computer Information Systems, 45*(2), 83-91.

Zsidisin, G. A., Panelli, A., & Upton, R. (2000). Purchasing organization involvement in risk assessments, contingency plans, and risk management: an exploratory study. *Supply Chain Management: An International Journal, 5*(4), 187-197.

Chapter XV

Electronic Risk Management

Tapen Sinha, Instituto Tecnológico Autónomo de México, Mexico and
University of Nottingham, UK

Bradly Condon, Instituto Tecnológico Autónomo de México, Mexico and
Bond University, Australia

Abstract

Doing business on the Internet has many opportunities along with many risks. This chapter focuses on a series of risks of legal liability arising from e-mail and Internet activities that are a common part of many e-businesses. Some of the laws governing these electronic activities are new and especially designed for the electronic age, while others are more traditional laws whose application to electronic activities is the novelty. E-business not only exposes companies to new types of liability risk, but also increases the potential number of claims and the complexity of dealing with those claims. The international nature of the Internet, together with a lack of uniformity of laws governing the same activities in different countries, means that companies need to proceed with caution.

Introduction

Within 48 hours after Katrina came ashore, a number of Web sites cropped up claiming that they are for hurricane relief. At the click of a computer Web site, you could donate money for the victims. Some of them even allowed you to donate money through a Red Cross Web site. Unfortunately, many of them turned out to be fraudulent. When you thought you were going to the Red Cross Web site, you would be taken to a different one and your credit card information would be stolen and sold to the highest bidder. In the electronic parlance, this process is called "phishing" (see Appendix for terminologies).

Electronic information transfer has become the backbone of our information society. Therefore, it is not surprising that it has also increased the risks coming from electronic sources. The main risk comes from the Internet. For many businesses, and for many individuals, the benefits of being connected to the Internet have increased so much that not being connected to the Internet is no longer an option.

Companies who conduct transactions over electronic channels face a number of risks. Some of these risks, such as viruses, flow from the nature of modern technology. Others, such as theft, are age-old risks that have taken on new twists in the electronic age. For example, banks transfer huge amounts of money by wire, making them easy and lucrative targets for fraud, extortion, and theft. Other financial institutions, such as credit card companies, are prone to the same hazards. Software companies sell their products in electronic format. Copying files and programs is easy and cheap, making software companies particularly vulnerable to theft of their products. Electronic retailers that do all of their business online, such as Amazon.com, are subject to a wide array electronic risks associated with electronic money transfers and Web sites. However, even bricks and mortar companies face numerous risks emanating from (electronic) viruses, hackers, and the online activities of employees. These legal and technological risks associated with e-business—which may be referred to collectively as electronic or cyber risks—are the subject of this chapter.

The aim of this chapter is to survey a broad array of electronic risks that can cause their victims to lose money. It is beyond the scope of this chapter to provide advice on how to manage each and every one of these risks. Rather, this chapter seeks to raise awareness of a variety of risks so that readers will become conscious of the need to develop electronic risk management strategies. The best advice in this regard is to invest in expert advice. For example, where litigation risk exists, consult a lawyer early on regarding strategies to adopt that will avoid litigation or minimize the cost and risk of litigation should it become unavoidable. Where loose lips increase risks, develop strategies for managing the content of correspondence, whether traditional or electronic, such as educating and monitoring employees. Where the problem is primarily a technical one, invest in the necessary technology and expertise. Finally, where insurance is available to manage the financial risks associated with doing business electronically, buy it.

A Global Problem of Viruses

Computer viruses have become synonymous with electronic risk on a global scale. The method of electronic infection has changed dramatically. In 1996, e-mail attachments were responsible for 9% of infections whereas 57% of infections came from floppy disks. In 2000, 87% infections came from e-mail attachments and only 6% came from floppy disks. By 2004, the rate of infections from e-mail attachments had topped 99% of total infections (Source: ICSA Labs Virus Prevalence Survey, various years). As a result, in 1997, only 30% of all institutions used virus protection for e-mails whereas by 2004, the use of virus protection had almost reached universality (ICSA Labs Virus Prevalence Survey 2004, Figure 15). However, the rise of the use of virus protection has not reduced the rate of infection. Figure 1 shows how the rate of infection has changed over a period of 9 years. Despite the near universal use of antivirus software, the rate of infection has increased more than eleven-fold. The biggest jump in infection came between 1998 and 1999. It has not decreased since (see Table 1).

The number of problems and the associated cost of computer viruses have gone up steadily over the past decade. DARPA created the Computer Emergency Response Team Coordination Center (CERT/CC) in November 1988 after the computer worm Morris worm struck. It is a major coordination center dealing with Internet security problems run by the Software Engineering Institute (SEI) at Carnegie Mellon University. CERT/CC has compiled a comprehensive list of security "incidents" that have occurred since 1995 (see Table 2). The trend is showing an exponential rise of such incidents over time.

Table 1. Computer infection rates 1996-2004 (Source: ICSALabs.com)

Infection Rates	Per 1000 Computers
1996	10
1997	21
1998	32
1999	80
2000	90
2001	103
2002	105
2003	108
2004	116

Table 2. Number of incidents reported by CERT 1995-2003 (Source: http://www.cert. org)

Year	No. of Incidents
1995	2,412
1996	2,573
1997	2,134
1998	3,374
1999	9,859
2000	21,756
2001	52,658
2002	82,094
2003	137,529

Note: A CERT "incident" may involve one, hundreds, or thousands of sites. Some incidents may involve ongoing activity for long periods of time.

Table 3. Annual financial impact of major virus attacks 1995-2003 (Source: http://www. computereconomics.com)

Year	Worldwide Economic Impact (US$)
2003	$13.5 Billion
2002	11.1 Billion
2001	13.2 Billion
2000	17.1 Billion
1999	12.1 Billion
1998	6.1 Billion
1997	3.3 Billion
1996	1.8 Billion
1995	500 Million

How much do such viruses cost the world? Estimates are available for 1995-2003. It shows that the cost went up quite rapidly between 1995 and 2000, but then there was no clear increase over time. One reason for such a recent slowdown is the widespread use of antivirus programs implemented by businesses as well as individuals.

The damage caused by computer viruses is not uniform across all viruses. A few viruses (and their variants) cause most of the damage. The undisputed world champion was a virus codenamed ILOVEU (see Table 4). It was created by a person in the Philippines. Yet, the most damage it caused was in the developed world. It propagated during the weekend of

February 2000 around St. Valentine's Day. The biggest recent attack, in August 2005, was caused by a worm code named Zotob. It took out the computer system of CNN live. It spread through the entire Internet over the weekend. Within 2 weeks, the police in Morocco arrested an 18-year old as the main coder of the worm at the request of the Federal Bureau of Investigation. However, given that there is no extradition treaty in these matter between the United States and Morocco, it is highly unlikely that the person would be extradited to the United States.

The Spam-Virus Nexus

Being connected to the rest of the world through the Internet in general, and through e-mails in particular, has a cost. The cost comes in the form of spam. Spam is unsolicited e-mail. The problem of spam has become extremely large. In July 2004, spam accounted for more than 95% of all e-mails (see Figure 1). MessageLabs published a report in 2004 in which it noted that "more than 80% of global spam originates from fewer than 200 known spammers in the USA. Many are based in the small town of Boca Raton in Florida, one of three states in the U.S. which have no spam legislation in place" (Source: http://www.MessageLabs. com). In addition to being a nuisance, spam also represents a big source of electronic risk. Among the devastating viruses, SoBig.F (see Table 4) spread mainly through spam. Thus, spam can not only be a nuisance by itself, but can also carry a payload of viruses.

Table 4. Financial impact of major virus attacks since 1999 (Source: http://www.computereconomics.com)

Year	Code Name	Worldwide Financial Impact ($US)
2004	MyDoom	$4.0 Billion
2003	SoBig.F	2.5 Billion
2003	Slammer	1.5 Billion
2003	Blaster	750 Million
2003	Nachi	500 Million
2002	Klez	750 Million
2002	BugBear	500 Million
2002	Badtrans	400 Million
2001	CodeRed	2.75 Billion
2001	Nimda	1.5 Billion
2001	SirCam	1.25 Billion
2000	ILOVEU	8.75 Billion
1999	Melissa	1.5 Billion
1999	Explorer	1.1 Billion

Figure 1. Spam has become a huge segment of e-mails

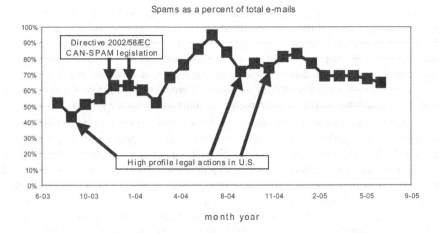

Spams as a percent of total e-mails

Figure 1 suggests that some electronic risks can be diminished with adequate legal protection. However, there are limits to what can be achieved through the enactment of new criminal and civil laws to deal with illicit electronic activities, just as there are limits to what the law can achieve more generally. Civil litigation is an expensive and uncertain process. Judgments can be difficult to enforce against defendants that are determined to avoid payment. Criminal laws have not eliminated crime. The global nature of the Internet means that laws have to be coordinated and enforced across international borders, introducing further complications. As a result, managing electronic risk requires a blend of risk reduction and legal strategies.

A Catalog of Risks and Legal Problems

The most common electronic risks are the following: (1) business interruptions caused by hackers, cybertheives, viruses, and internal saboteurs; (2) employer liability stemming from the inappropriate employee use of e-mail and Internet; (3) claims that products and services advertised on the Web fail to deliver; (4) Web-related copyright and trademark lawsuits; (5) patent infringement costs; (6) fraud-extortion hybrid.

General Legal Issues

Given the international scope cyberspace, several general legal issues arise. The first is how to address conflicts between the laws of different jurisdictions. Whose law governs when the parties involved live in different countries and the transaction occurs in cyberspace? Many Web sites now use online contracts that specifically provide whose law will govern the transaction. These online contracts generally require the user to click their agreement with the terms of the contract before they are allowed to proceed with the transaction.

A related issue is choice of forum. Where do you sue for breach of contract? Many online contracts also provide the answer to this question. However, where there is no contract involved, such as in cases of fraud or negligence, the issues of conflict of laws and choice of forum may not have clear answers. Moreover, the choice of forum that is of the most benefit to the party who is suing for damages will be the jurisdiction in which the assets are located that will serve to satisfy any award for damages. Alternatively, the plaintiff may prefer to sue in its own jurisdiction due to convenience or familiarity with the system.

If a plaintiff chooses to sue in a particular jurisdiction, that does not resolve the matter. In each jurisdiction, courts apply their own rules to determine whether to exercise jurisdiction over the defendant in a given case. For example, many U.S. courts base the decision to accept jurisdiction in Internet transactions on the nature and quality of the commercial activity. If a foreign defendant enters into contracts with residents in the jurisdiction that involve knowing and repeated transmission of computer files over the Internet, the court will accept jurisdiction. On the other hand, if the defendant merely operates a passive Web site that posts information that is accessible to users in other jurisdictions, the court will not exercise jurisdiction (Gasparini, 2001).

One crucial question is, who do you sue? In cases involving employees, it is generally wise to sue both the individual and the employer. In determining who to sue, several questions must be considered. Who has liability? Who has assets that can be seized to satisfy a judgment awarding damages? Where are the assets? What is the procedure to seize the assets in the jurisdiction in which they are located? Are the assets accessible? For example, are they held in the name of the responsible person and in a jurisdiction where the judgment can be enforced? In some jurisdictions, enforcing judgments may be problematic. For example, in Mexico, bank secrecy laws may prevent a determination of what assets are available to satisfy a judgment. In addition, enforcing the judgments of courts from one country in a second country can be problematic where the second country has no procedure for recognizing the awards of foreign courts.

Another important consideration is litigation risk. Litigation is costly and the outcome is uncertain. Even if the plaintiff secures judgment in his favor, enforcement may not be possible. If the party claiming damages is not able to collect from the guilty party, the cost of litigation is wasted. This leads to another important question. Is the guilty party insured? Does the insurance contract provide coverage for actions that generated legal liability? Should it?

Business Interruptions

Any kind of business interruption is costly. It can increase cost of doing business or reduce revenue or both. It does not matter if it stems from strikes, fire, power failure, hackers or saboteurs. Electronic risk is increasingly becoming a bigger threat to business.

For example, a hacker overwhelmed several large Web sites through multiple distributed denial-of-service (DDOS) attacks. The culprit hijacked various computers throughout the world to bombard target servers with seemingly legitimate requests for data. It is estimated that the DDOS attacks, which interrupted the sites' ability to efficiently conduct their business, caused over $1.2 billion in lost business income. (http://www.insurenewmedia.com/html/claimsexample.htm)

This raises several legal issues. The denial of service that occurs when the server fails could expose the business to claims for damages for breach of contract from clients. In the contract, the server agrees to provide the service. If the interruption of service causes financial loss, for example, due to lost business, the administrator of the server may be liable for the loss. Liability will depend on the terms of each contract. For example, if a *force majeure* clause excuses the server from performing the contract in the event of power outages or hacker attacks, there will be no liability.

The denial of service could also give rise to a claim for damages based on the negligence of the server administrator. Where the server can be protected against hacker attacks by readily available technology, the failure of administrator to employ the technology to protect client access to the service would be negligent.

Another issue is whether the server may sue the hacker for damages. However, this may be a moot point if the hacker cannot be located, lives in a jurisdiction where the law does not allow for such a legal claim to be filed, or has no assets with which to satisfy the claim for damages (for example, teenage hackers with poor parents).

Inappropriate Use of E-Mail and Internet

Inappropriate use of e-mail and Internet can expose employers to claims for damages in three principal areas of law—human rights law, privacy legislation, and civil liability for damages caused by employees to fellow employees or third parties under negligence and libel laws.

In addition to the foregoing liability risks, e-mail communications are a rich source of evidence in any kind of legal dispute, which means that employees need to be careful about what they communicate electronically. Poorly managed written communications in e-mails and letters can come back to haunt any business that later finds itself enmeshed in litigation, accused of corporate fraud, or audited for SEC compliance. It is technically possible to recover e-mail messages that have been "deleted" in e-mail programs, making it difficult to destroy this type of evidence. As a result, these messages may be uncovered during a civil litigation procedure known as pretrial discovery in common-law jurisdictions such as Canada and the United States. This data needs to be managed well, both in terms of limiting its creation in the first place and in terms of reducing the cost of its retrieval should it need to be produced in pretrial discovery. (Just imagine the cost of teams of lawyers sorting through millions of e-mails.)

Many jurisdictions give employees the right to sue for sexual harassment under human rights legislation. A common inappropriate use of e-mail consists of sexual harassment of one employee by another. For example, a manager and his employer could be sued for communicating sexual messages via e-mail to a subordinate. The same act can create a cause of action for a civil suit against both the manager and the employer who allowed the act to take place. In litigation, reliable evidence that the harassment really took place becomes a central issue. When the means of communication is e-mail, that evidence is more readily available, increasing the risk of an award of damages against the employer.

Electronic communication raises the risks of violating general privacy legislation and professional rules regarding privileged information. One of largest health insurers in the United States inadvertently sent e-mail messages to 19 members containing confidential medical and personal information of 858 other members. Although the company immediately took steps to correct the problem, the company was exposed to lawsuits alleging invasion of privacy. Similarly, lawyers must take care not to violate solicitor-client privilege, which can expose them to both disciplinary proceedings in the profession and claims for damages from the client (Rest, 1998).

Internet telecommuting raises the risk that an employer's internal network will be exposed to "backdoor attacks" that exploit the telecommuter's connection and threaten confidential information belonging to a client or third party. In such cases, employer liability will probably depend on whether the employer provided adequate protection from such an attack (Maier, 2001).

Employee use of company e-mail to promote personal business is another source of legal problems. Where the actions of the employee can be considered part of the normal course of their employment duties, the employer may be held liable for the actions of the employee. For example, the employer may be liable for allowing its system to be used for the communication of the slanderous message. In the United States, however, the Communications Decency Act of 1996 has made Internet providers immune from liability for publishing a defamatory statement made by another party and for refusing to remove the statement from its service (King, 2003).

The employer may be held liable for failing to properly supervise employee use of e-mail and Internet. For example, an employee who uses e-mail to sexually harass a fellow employee can expose a company to lawsuits. Using the company's e-mail and Internet system to further criminal acts can also expose the company to liability. In such cases, traditional law regarding employer liability extends to e-risk cases.

Under the common law doctrine of *respondeat superior*, the employer is responsible for employee acts that are within the scope of employment or further the employer's interests. However, the employer cannot be held liable if the personal motives of the employee are unrelated to the employer's business. (Nowak, 1999) For example, in Haybeck vs. Prodigy Services Co., Prodigy Services was not held liable for the actions of a computer technical advisor when he used the company computer to enter Internet chat rooms and to lure his victim with offers of free time on Prodigy. The employee was HIV-positive and intentionally had unprotected sex without disclosing his infection. Where an employee's improper use of e-mail or Internet falls outside the scope of employment, the employer cannot be held liable under this doctrine.

However, the employer may still be found liable for negligently retaining or supervising an employee. Under the doctrine of negligent retention, an employer may be liable for hiring an unfit person in circumstances that involve an unreasonable risk of harm to others.

The employer will be held liable for the acts of an employee where the employer knew or should have known about the employee's conduct or propensity to engage in such conduct. Moreover, the employer has a duty to set rules in the workplace and to properly supervise employees. (Nowak, 1999) Thus, there is a risk of liability if the employer has knowledge of facts that should lead the employer to investigate an employee or to implement preventive rules for all employees.

The key issue is whether the employer could have reasonably foreseen the actions of the employee. For example, in the Prodigy case, the court held that the employer was not liable for negligent retention because the plaintiff could not show that Prodigy had any knowledge of his activities. Nor was there an allegation that technical advisors commonly have sex with customers without revealing that they carry communicable diseases. However, in Moses vs. Diocese of Colorado, a church parishioner in Colorado successfully sued the Episcopal diocese and bishop for injuries she suffered having sex with a priest from whom she sought counseling. Sexual relationships between priests and parishioners had arisen seven times before and the diocese had been notified that greater supervision of the priests might be necessary. The court found the diocese negligent for not providing more supervision when it knew that such relationships were becoming more common.

Similarly, employers may be held liable for negligent supervision of employee use of e-mail and Internet if they know that their employees visit pornographic Internet sites and use e-mail for personal communications. In such circumstances, they have a duty to provide rules of conduct for employees and to monitor compliance. If they administer their own networks, they should monitor employee use of the system where incriminating communications may be stored. It would be difficult to argue that they are unaware of employee activities when contradictory evidence is stored on the company system. Employers should use software that blocks access to pornographic Internet sites and that screens e-mails for key words. However, they should also advise employees that their computer use is being monitored, to avoid liability for invasion of employee privacy.

A company's monitoring practices may be justified by the potential liabilities created by employees' misuse of e-mail and the Internet. However, the company's potential liability for invasion of employee privacy must also be considered. While employees in the United States have little privacy protection in this area, European employers must take reasonable precautions to protect their employees' privacy when they monitor their e-mail or Internet usage. (Rustad & Paulsson, 2005). Even in the United States, however, employers should take care not to violate labor laws by unduly restricting their employees' communications regarding labor rights (O'Brien, 2002).

Companies can reduce or eliminate the risk of liability for employees' use of electronic communication by implementing an effective Internet policy. Such a policy should (1) warn employees that their communications may be monitored; (2) require employees to sign consent forms for monitoring; (3) limit employee Internet access to work-related activities; (4) establish clear rules against conducting personal business on the company system; (5) define and prohibit communications that may be considered harassment of fellow employees and third parties or violate human rights laws; (6) forbid employees using another employee's system; (7) implement a policy on the length of time documents are retained on a backup system; and (8) ensure all employees understand and will follow the policy. (Nowak, 1999) To limit exposure to e-risk, insurers should insist that clients implement an effective Internet policy as a condition of coverage.

Sloan (2004) offers a series of practical suggestions for avoiding litigation problems. His advice includes the following recommendations: (1) Instead of using e-mails, it is preferable to use telephones when possible. (2) E-mails should not be sent immediately. Once sent, e-mails cannot be called back. If a cooling period is implemented, they can be recalled. (3) The distribution of e-mails should be limited. The default e-mail option should not include the possibility of sending it to a large group within a company all at once. (4) Within a company, sarcasm and criticism can do a lot of damage to the company's health. They should be avoided. (5) Swearing is a bad idea in an e-mail. This should be avoided at all cost.

Failure of Product

Failure of a product to deliver can come from many different sources. For example, an antivirus software may fail to protect the customer from a particular virus leading to loss of mission-critical data for the company. Recently, a number of Web site development companies have been sued for being negligent with their design, which allowed hackers to enter and use computer portals for unauthorized use.

False claims regarding the characteristics of products and services can give rise to three types of legal actions. If it is a case of fraud, criminal laws would govern. Criminal legal procedures differ from civil law suits in two important respects. The cost of filing a criminal complaint is negligible because the investigating police and the prosecutor are paid by the state. This provides a low financial threshold for the unhappy customer. However, defending a criminal charge is just as costly as defending a civil action for the business person who commits the fraud. However, a criminal case generally results in no damages award. Instead, the guilty party may be subject to fines and/or imprisonment. The customer thus has a low financial threshold for filing charges, but is likely to receive no financial reward at the conclusion of the proceedings, except in cases where courts order the defendant to pay restitution.

In many jurisdictions, consumer protection legislation gives customers the right to return a product for a refund where the product is not suitable for the purpose for which it is intended. As long as the business provides the refund, the cost to the business is relatively low because its liability ends with the refund. Should the business refuse to refund the purchase price, the customer may sue and be entitled to legal costs as well. However, where the value of the transaction is low, the cost of suing will exceed the amount owing, making it impractical to pursue.

In common law jurisdictions (such as Australia, Canada, England, and the United States), false claims regarding a product or service may give rise to a civil action for negligent misrepresentation. In a case of negligent misrepresentation, the customer could claim compensation for damages caused by the customer's reliance on the company's representation of what the product or service would do.

Traditional principles of agency may expose reputable companies to liability where they sponsor the Web sites of smaller firms. If the company creates the appearance of an agency relationship, and a consumer reasonably believes the companies are related, the consumer can sue the sponsor for the harm caused by the lack of care or skill of the apparent agent. This is so even where no formal agency relationship exists (Furnari, 1999).

Fraud, Extortion, and Other Cybercrimes

The Internet facilitates a wide range of international crimes, including forgery and counterfeiting, bank robbery, transmission of threats, fraud, extortion, copyright infringement, theft of trade secrets, transmission of child pornography, interception of communications, transmission of harassing communications and, more recently, cyberterrorism. However, the division of the world into separate legal jurisdictions complicates the investigation and prosecution of transnational cybercrimes (Goldstone & Shave, 1999).

There are numerous examples. In one case, eight banking Web sites in the United States, Canada, Great Britain, and Thailand were attacked, resulting in 23,000 stolen credit card numbers. The hackers proceeded to publish 6,500 of the cards online, causing third-party damages in excess of $3,000,000 (http://www.aignetadvantage.com/bp/servlet/unprotected/claims.examples). In another case, a computer hacker theft ring in Russia broke into a Citibank electronic money transfer system and tried to steal more than $10 million by making wire transfers to accounts in Finland, Russia, Germany, The Netherlands, and the United States. Citibank recovered all but $400,000 of these transfers. The leader of the theft ring was arrested in London, extradited to the United States 2 years later, sentenced to 3 years in jail, and ordered to pay $240,000 in restitution to Citibank. In yet another case, an Argentine hacker broke into several military, university, and private computer systems in the United States containing highly sensitive information. U.S. authorities tracked him to Argentina and Argentina investigated his intrusions into the Argentine telecommunications system. However, Argentine law did not cover his attacks on computers in the United States, so only the United States could prosecute him for those crimes. However, there was no extradition treaty between Argentina and the United States. The U.S. persuaded him to come to the United States and to plead guilty, for which he received a fine of $5,000 and 3-years probation (Goldstone & Shave, 1999).

In these types of scenarios, the hackers could be subject to criminal prosecution in the victim's country but not in the perpetrator's home country. Even if subject to criminal prosecution in both countries, extradition may not be possible. Moreover, criminal proceedings would probably not fully compensate the banks for their losses or that of their customers. Indeed, the customers might be able to file claims against the banks for negligence if they failed to use the latest technology to protect their clients' information from the hackers.

A further complication arises when there are conflicts between the laws of different countries. For example, hate speech (promoting hatred against visible minorities) is illegal in countries such as Canada, but protected by the constitution in the United States. A court may order the production of banking records in one country that are protected by bank secrecy laws in another. For example, in United States vs. Bank of Nova Scotia, the Canadian Bank of Nova Scotia was held in contempt for failing to comply with an order that required the bank to violate a Bahamian bank secrecy rule.

The jurisdictional limits of the authorities in each country also complicate investigations. For example, a search warrant may be issued in one country or state to search computer data at a corporation inside the jurisdiction, but the information may actually be stored on a file server in a foreign country, raising issues regarding the legality of the search. International investigations are further complicated by the availability of experts in foreign countries, their willingness to cooperate, language barriers, and time differences (Goldstone & Shave, 1999).

Another cybercrime that is currently theoretical is cyberterrorism. While there have been no cases to date, there are likely to be in the future. A bill passed by the New York Senate defines the crime of cyberterrorism as any computer crime or denial of service attack with an intent to ... influence the policy of a unit of government by intimidation or coercion, or affect the conduct of a unit of government (Iqbal, 2004).

Web-Related Intellectual Property Rights Infringement

Intellectual property infringements are a significant liability risk for Internet business and may lead to expensive litigation. For example, computer bulletin board companies have been sued for copyright infringement (in Religious Technology Center vS. Netcom Online Communication Services, Inc.) and for copyright infringement, trademark infringement, and unfair competition with respect to video games (in Sega Enterprises Ltd. vs. Maphia). (Richmond, 2002) In another case, an online insurance brokerage created a hyperlink that seemingly transferred its clients to additional pages on the site itself. It was later discovered that the brokerage "deep-linked" its users to the Web pages of various insurance companies, creating a seamless navigational experience. The insurance companies sued the online brokerage for copyright and trademark infringement (http://www.insurenewmedia.com/html/claimsexample.htm). With litigation of intellectual property claims against e-commerce ventures on the rise, the risk is increasing for insurance companies as well (General & Cologne Re, 1999).

Patent infringement claims are quite common. In the past, Microsoft had faced a whole slew of them (including the well-publicized ones from Xerox about the use of mouse as a computer interface). Computer software always builds on past programs. Therefore, the line between what is legal and what is not is not very clear (see, for example, http://www.borland.com/about/press/2001/webgainsuit.html for a recent lawsuit by Borland against WebGain).

Cybersquatters have led to the further development of trademark law. In the early days to the Web, cybersquatters registered Web sites using the names of well-known companies and celebrities. Many made substantial amounts of money later selling the name back to the company or individual. However, their joy ride ended with cases such as Madonna's, who successfully sued to claim the Web site name without paying the cybersquatter.

Intellectual property law protects legal rights such as those related to copyrights, patents, and trademarks. Intellectual property law has been globalized by several international agreements. Countries that are members of the North American Free Trade Agreement (NAFTA) (Canada, the U.S., and Mexico) and the World Trade Organization (WTO) (148 countries) are required to have laws providing both civil and criminal procedures for the enforcement of copyright and trademarks. In this regard, the requirements of NAFTA Chapter 17 and the WTO Agreement on Trade-Related Intellectual Property Rights (TRIPS) are virtually the same.

Table 5. Pirated software in use and the losses due to piracy in 2003 and 2004 (Source: Second Annual BSA and IDC Global Software Piracy Study, 2005)

	% software pirated	% software pirated	Loss due to piracy in millions of $US	Loss due to piracy in millions of $US
Country	2004	2003	2004	2003
Australia	32%	31%	409	341
China	90%	92%	3,565	3,823
Hong Kong	52%	52%	116	102
India	74%	73%	519	367
Indonesia	87%	88%	183	158
Japan	28%	29%	1,787	1,633
Malaysia	61%	63%	134	129
New Zealand	23%	23%	25	21
Pakistan	82%	83%	26	16
Philippines	71%	72%	69	55
Singapore	42%	43%	96	90
South Korea	46%	48%	506	462
Taiwan	43%	43%	161	139
Thailand	79%	80%	183	141
Vietnam	92%	92%	55	41
Austria	25%	27%	128	109
Belgium	29%	29%	309	240
Cyprus	53%	55%	9	8
Czech Republic	41%	40%	132	106
Denmark	27%	26%	226	165
Estonia	55%	54%	17	14
Finland	29%	31%	177	148
France	45%	45%	2,928	2,311
Germany	29%	30%	2,286	1,899
Greece	62%	63%	106	87
Hungary	44%	42%	126	96
Ireland	38%	41%	89	71
Italy	50%	49%	1,500	1,127
Latvia	58%	57%	19	16
Lithuania	58%	58%	21	17
Malta	47%	46%	3	2
Netherlands	30%	33%	628	577
Poland	59%	58%	379	301

Table 5. continued

Portugal	40%	41%	82	66
Slovakia	48%	50%	48	40
Slovenia	51%	52%	37	32
Spain	43%	44%	634	512
Sweden	26%	27%	304	241
United Kingdom	27%	29%	1,963	1,601
Bulgaria	71%	71%	33	26
Croatia	58%	59%	50	45
Norway	31%	32%	184	155
Romania	74%	73%	62	49
Russia	87%	87%	1,362	1,104
Switzerland	28%	31%	309	293
Ukraine	91%	91%	107	92
Argentina	75%	71%	108	69
Bolivia	80%	78%	9	11
Brazil	64%	61%	659	519
Chile	64%	63%	87	68
Colombia	55%	53%	81	61
Costa Rica	67%	68%	16	17
Dominican Republic	77%	76%	4	5
Ecuador	70%	68%	13	11
El Salvador	80%	79%	5	4
Guatemala	78%	77%	10	9
Honduras	75%	73%	3	3
Mexico	65%	63%	407	369
Nicaragua	80%	79%	1	1
Panama	70%	69%	4	4
Paraguay	83%	83%	11	9
Peru	73%	68%	39	31
Uruguay	71%	67%	12	10
Venezuela	79%	72%	71	55
Algeria	83%	84%	67	59
Bahrain	62%	64%	19	18
Egypt	65%	69%	50	56
Israel	33%	35%	66	69
Jordan	64%	65%	16	15

Table 5. continued

Kenya	83%	80%	16	12
Kuwait	68%	68%	48	41
Lebanon	75%	74%	26	22
Mauritus	60%	61%	4	4
Morocco	72%	73%	65	57
Nigeria	84%	84%	54	47
Oman	64%	65%	13	11
Qatar	62%	63%	16	13
Reunion	40%	39%	1	1
Saudi Arabia	52%	54%	125	120
South Africa	37%	36%	196	147
Tunisia	84%	82%	38	29
Turkey	66%	66%	182	127
UAE	34%	34%	34	29
Zimbabwe	90%	87%	9	6
Canada	36%	35%	889	736
Puerto Rico	46%	46%	15	11
United States	21%	22%	6,645	6,496

TRIPS requires members to make civil judicial procedures available to right holders, including minimum standards for legal procedures, evidence, injunctions, damages, and trial costs (TRIPS Articles 42-49). Rights holders may thus seek court injunctions to stop the illegal activity and have the perpetrator ordered to pay the costs of the legal action. The owners of intellectual property may sue producers and vendors of pirated goods for damages. While this is important, in many cases it is not a practical option for companies to pursue. Civil litigation is a costly and lengthy process, and seeking payment of any damages that might be awarded can be problematic. Nevertheless, the global expansion of intellectual property law remedies, together with the global nature of the Internet, is sure to increase intellectual property litigation around the globe.

TRIPS also requires members to provide criminal procedures and penalties in cases of intentional trademark counterfeiting or copyright piracy on a commercial scale. Penalties must include imprisonment or fines sufficient to provide a deterrent, consistent with the level of penalties applied for crimes of a corresponding gravity. Where appropriate, remedies must also include the seizure, forfeiture, and destruction of the infringing goods (TRIPS Article 61).

As tough as this may sound, such criminal laws do not have a great impact on the enforcement of intellectual property laws in many developing countries. While authorities may occasionally conduct well-publicized raids on highly visible commercial operations, corruption and the lack of adequate human and financial resources means the vast majority of infractions still go unpunished. These practical and legal limitations inherent in intellectual property protection mean that producers of easily copied intellectual property, such as software, are likely to continue to experience worldwide problems with piracy, as the following table shows (Table 5). The amount of money at stake, together with the globalization of intellectual property laws, means that owners of intellectual property are likely to devote more of their own resources to the enforcement of their property rights in the coming years.

Insurance

In August 2000, St Paul insurance company commissioned a survey of 1,500 risk managers in the United States and Europe, along with 150 insurance agents and brokers. Only 25% of all U.S. companies and 30% of European companies had set up formal structures (such as a risk management committee) to identify and monitor technology risks.

Online attack insurance costs between $10,000 and $20,000 per million-dollar coverage. Main coverage takes the following forms: protection against third-party liability claims from the disclosure of confidential information when a hacker strikes or denial of service when a computer virus attacks. Another common coverage is electronic publishing liability, which can offer protection from third-party lawsuits for defamation, libel, slander, and other claims stemming from information posted on the company Web site.

While many of the legal sources of liability for online activity are not new (such as intellectual property infringements, defamation, and invasion of privacy), the accessibility of the Internet has increased the rapidity and scale of these actions and, thus, the potential liability. As a result, some believe that e-commerce will emerge as the single biggest insurance risk of the 21st century, for three reasons. First, the number of suits involving Internet-related claims will be exponentially greater than in pre-Internet days. Second, the complexity of international, multi-jurisdictional and technical disputes will increase the legal costs associated with these claims. Third, the activities giving rise to Internet-based claims will present new arguments for both insureds and insurers about whether they the liability is covered by the policy (Jerry & Mekel, 2002). For example, traditional first party insurance for physical events that damage tangible property may not help an Internet business whose most valuable property exists in cyberspace with no physical form (Beh, 2002). Even if a company has an insurance policy that covers its activities on the World Wide Web, there is a significant risk that it won't be covered outside the United States or Canada (Crane, 2001).

Conclusion

Like the more traditional marketplace, doing business on the Internet carries with it many opportunities along with many risks. This chapter has focused on a series of risks of legal liability arising from e-mail and Internet activities that are a common part of many e-businesses. Some of the laws governing these electronic activities are new and especially designed for the electronic age, while others are more traditional laws whose application to electronic activities is the novelty.

E-business not only exposes companies to new types of liability risk, but also increases the potential number of claims and the complexity of dealing with those claims. The international nature of the Internet, together with a lack of uniformity of laws governing the same activities in different countries, means that companies need to proceed with caution. That means managing risks in an intelligent fashion and seeking adequate insurance coverage. The first step is to familiarize themselves with electronic risks and then to set up management systems to minimize potential problems and liabilities.

Acknowledgments

We thank the Instituto Tecnológico Autónomo de México and the Asociación Mexicana de Cultura AC for their generous support of our research.

References

Beh, H. G. (2002). Physical losses in cyberspace. *Connecticut Insurance Law Journal, 9*(2), 1-88.

Crane, M. (2001). International liability in cyberspace. *Duke Law and Technological Review, 23*(1), 455-465.

Furnari, N. R. (1999). Are traditional agency principles effective for Internet transactions, given the lack of personal interaction? *Albany Law Review, 63*(3), 544-567.

Gasparini, L. U. (2001). The Internet and personal jurisdiction: Traditional jurisprudence for the twenty-first century under the New York CPLR. *Albany Law Journal of Science & Technology, 12*(1), 191-244.

General, & Cologne Re. (1999). *Global casualty facultative loss & litigation report: A selection of Internet losses and litigation, 3*, 12-17.

Goldstone, D. & Shave, B. (1999). International dimensions of crimes in cyberspace. *Fordham International Law Journal, 22*(6), 1924-1945.

Iqbal, M. (2004). Defining cyberterrorism. *Marshall Journal of Computer & Information Law, 22*(1) 397-432.

Jerry, R. H. II, & Mekel, M. L. (2002). Cybercoverage for cyber-risks: An Overview of insurers' responses to the perils of e-commerce. *Connecticut Insurance Law Journal, 9*(3), 11-44.

King, R. W. (2003). Online defamation: Bringing the Communications Decency Act of 1996 in line with sound public policy. *Duke Law and Technology Review, 24*(3), 34-67.

Maier, M. J. (2001). Backdoor liability from Internet telecommuters. *Computer Law Review & Technology Journal, 6*(1), 27-41.

Marron, M. (2002). Discoverability of deleted e-mail: Time for a closer examination. *Seattle University Law Review, 25*(4), 895-922.

Nowak, J. S. (1999). Employer liability for employee online criminal acts. *Federal Communications Law Journal, 51*(3) 467-488.

O'Brien, C. N. (2002). The impact of employer e-mail policies on employee rights to engage in concerted. *Dickinson Law Review, 103*(5), 201-277.

Pederson, M., & Meyers, J. H. (2005). Something about technology: Electronic discovery considerations and methodology. *Maine Bar Journal, 12*(2), 23-56.

Rest, C. L. (1998). Electronic mail and confidential client/attorney communications: Risk management. *Case Western Reserve Law Journal, 48*(2), 309-378.

Richmond, D. R. (2002). A practical look at e-commerce and liability insurance. *Connecticut Insurance Law Journal, 8*(1), 87-104.

Rustad, M. L., & Paulsson, S. R. (2005). Monitoring employee e-mail and Internet usage: Avoiding the omniscient electronic sweatshop: Insights from Europe. *University of Pennsylvania Journal of Labor and Employment, 7*(4), 829-922.

Sloan, B. (2004, July). Avoiding litigation pitfalls: Practical tips for internal e-mail. *Risk Management Magazine,* 38-42.

Appendix: Terminologies

Firewall: A firewall is a barrier that enforces a boundary between two or more computer networks. It is similar to the function of firewalls in building construction. A firewall controls traffic between different zones of trust. Two extreme zones of trust include the Internet (a zone with no trust) and an internal network (a zone with high trust). Setting up firewalls requires understanding of network protocols and of computer security. Small mistakes can render a firewall worthless as a security tool.

Hackers: In computer security, a hacker is a person able to exploit a system or gain unauthorized access through skill and tactics. This usually refers to a black-hat hacker. Two types of distinguished hackers exist. A Guru is one with a very broad degree of expertise, a Wizard is an expert in a very narrow field.

Malware: Malware is a software program that runs automatically against the interests of the person running it. Malware is normally classified based on how it is executed, how it spreads, and what it does.

Phishing: Phishing (also known as carding and spoofing) is an attempt to fraudulently acquire sensitive information, such as passwords and credit card details, by masquerading as a trustworthy person or business in an apparently official electronic communication, such as an e-mail. The term phishing alludes to to "fishing" for users' financial information and passwords.

Spam: Spam refers to unsolicited messages in bulk. It can refer to any commercially oriented, unsolicited bulk mailing perceived as being excessive and undesired. Most come in e-mail as a form of commercial advertising.

Spoofing: See *phishing*.

Spyware: Spyware is a malicious software intended to intercept or take control of a computer's operation without the user's knowledge or consent. It typically subverts the computer's operation for the benefit of a third party.

Virus: A virus is a self-replicating program that spreads by inserting copies of itself into other executable code or documents. A computer virus behaves in a way similar to a biological virus. The insertion of the virus into a program is called an infection, and the infected file (or executable code that is not part of a file) is called a host. A virus is a malware.

Worm: A computer worm is a self-replicating computer program. A virus needs to attach itself to, and becomes part of, another executable program. A worm is self-contained. It does not need to be part of another program to propagate itself.

About the Authors

Jayavel Sounderpandian is a professor of quantitative methods at University of Wisconsin-Parkside, USA. He received his master's and doctoral degrees in business administration from Kent State University, Kent, OH, USA, and his bachelor's degree in mechanical engineering from Indian Institute of Technology, Madras, India. He teaches operations management, business statistics, and decision analysis at undergraduate and graduate levels. Before joining the academia, he worked as an engineer for 7 years at Hindustan Aeronautics Ltd., Bangalore, India. His research interests include decision analysis and supply chain management. He has published numerous research articles and textbooks.

Tapen Sinha is the ING Comercial America Chair Professor at the Instituto Tecnológico Autónomo de México (ITAM) in Mexico City. He is also a Special Professor at the School of Business, University of Nottingham, UK. He has a PhD in economics from the University of Minnesota. He is the founder-director of the International Center for Pension Research, ITAM and an associate of the Centre for Risk and Insurance Studies at the University of Nottingham. Professor Sinha has published over 100 papers and 5 books. He has been a consultant for a number of multinational companies and governments of different continents.

* * *

Dirk Baldwin is an associate professor of management information systems and the department chair of Business at the University of Wisconsin-Parkside, USA. Professor Baldwin conducts research related to multiple view systems, decision support systems, and strategic issues related to IT. He has published in journals such as *Journal of MIS*, *IEEE Transactions on System, Man, and Cybernetics*, and *Journal of Cases on Information Technology*. He has coauthored books on MS Access. Professor Baldwin is chair of the Information Technology Practice Center and was named Wisconsin Idea fellow by the University of Wisconsin System Board of Regents.

Srinivas Bhogle heads the Information Management Division at National Aerospace Laboratories (NAL), Bangalore, India. He obtained his PhD in 1983 from the University of Paris V under the supervision of Claude Berge. He graduated from the Indian Statistical Institute, Kolkata, in 1978 specializing in operations research. Bhogle leads NAL teams developing interactive information portals, digital repositories and aviation information products, and writes extensively about R&D developments outside NAL. Bhogle has taught courses on information systems at Bangalore University and elsewhere for a decade, guided over 200 student projects, and authored about 75 articles, reviews, and reports.

Rajendra V. Boppana is a professor of computer science at the University of Texas at San Antonio, USA. He received the B Tech degree in electronics and communications engineering from Mysore University, India, in 1983, the M Tech degree in computer technology from the Indian Institute of Technology, Delhi, in 1985, and the PhD degree in computer engineering from University of Southern California, in 1991. Dr. Boppana's research interests are in parallel and distributed computing, performance evaluation, computer networks, and mobile computing and communications. Dr. Boppana published extensively and served on the program committees of several conferences in these areas. His current and previous research has been supported by several grants from NSF, DOD, and other federal funding agencies.

Subrata Chakrabarty is pursuing his PhD at Mays Business School, Texas A&M University, USA, since Fall 2004. His research and consulting interests include global sourcing of information systems (IS), quality assurance and control, global project management, business processes in the IS industry, and strategic and organizational issues related to offshoring and outsourcing. Before pursuing his PhD, he worked for more than 2 years at Infosys Technologies (India) on projects for clients in the U.S. and UK. He completed his undergraduate degree in India, and received the 1st rank in his college. He is a "certified software quality analyst" (CSQA). His hobbies include swimming, painting, and cartooning.

Suresh Chalasani is an associate professor of the Department of Business at the University of Wisconsin-Parkside, USA. Professor Chalasani specializes in supply chain management systems, e-commerce systems, technologies for e-commerce systems, parallel computing, and bioinformatics applications. Professor Chalasani is a senior member of IEEE. He published nearly 70 research papers in journals such as *IEEE Transactions on Computers*, *IEEE Transactions on Parallel and Distributed Systems*, *IEEE Transactions on Communica-*

tions, Parallel Computing, and in several conference proceedings. His work on distributing traffic for parallel computing systems was patented by the IBM Corporation. He served on program committees for numerous conferences. Dr. Chalasani was a recipient of multiple research and instructional grants from the National Science Foundation and the University of Wisconsin System.

Bradly Condon (BA, University of British Columbia, 1985), (LLB, McGill University, 1988), (LLM, University of Calgary, 1993), (PhD, Bond University, 2004) is professor of International Trade Law at the Instituto Tecnológico Autónomo de México (ITAM) and is senior fellow, Tim Fischer Centre for Global Trade and Finance, School of Law, Bond University, Australia. Dr. Condon is author or coauthor of four books and numerous academic articles on international trade law and economic integration.

Stephen Hawk is an associate professor of MIS in the School of Business at Technology at the University of Wisconsin-Parkside, USA. His recent publications include articles on offshore software development, the software industry in Russia, e-commerce in developing countries, and MIS curriculum issues. He has published in *MIS Quarterly Executive, Decision Sciences, Electronic Commerce Research, Information Technology for Development, Journal of Information Technology Education, IEEE Transactions on Engineering Management, Information and Management*, and *International Journal of Man-Machine Studies*. His PhD is from the University of Wisconsin-Madison.

Rajeeva Laxman Karandikar is a professor at the Indian Statistical Institute, New Delhi, India. His areas of research and interest include stochastic calculus, semimartingales, stochastic differential equations, Markov processes, diffusion processes, martingale problems, filtering theory, linear and nonlinear, finitely additive probability theory, limit theorems, white noise calculus: finitely additive approach, financial applications of stochastic processes, Boltzman equation and associated stochastic process, evolutionary game theory, psephology in the context of Indian elections, cryptography, block ciphers, Monte Carlo simulation and MCMC. He has published extensively in these areas and has published two books.

Giorgos Laskaridis holds a degree in informatics from the Department of Informatics, University of Athens, Greece, and is now a PhD candidate in the same department. As a research fellow for the Department of Informatics, University of Athens, he has participated in several European and national RTD projects. His research interests are in the fields of electronic services, e-government, software engineering, and system analysis and design. He has published journal and conference publications in the field of e-services and e-government. He is currently advisor to the Secretary General, General Secretariat for Information Systems of the Hellenic Ministry of Economy and Finance.

Xin Luo is a PhD candidate of MIS at Mississippi State University, USA. He obtained his BA from Sichuan Normal University (China), MBA from The University of Louisiana, and MSIS from Mississippi State University. His research interests center around information security and assurance, innovative technology management, and cross-cultural issues. He has published journal papers in *Communications of the ACM*, *Information Systems Security*, and *Journal of Internet Banking and Commerce*, in addition to several book chapters and national and international conference proceedings including AMCIS, DSI, IRMA, and ISOneWorld, and so forth.

Manohar S. Madan is a professor of operations and supply chain management at the University of Wisconsin-Whitewater, Whitewater, WI, USA. Manohar received his PhD in business administration from the University of Tennessee, Knoxville, Tennessee, USA. He teaches courses in the area of operations management and supply chain management. Manohar has extensive international teaching experience. Specifically, he has taught business courses in Hong Kong and the West Indies. He has published articles in journals such as *International Journal of Operations and Production Management*, *IIE Transactions*, *Journal of the Operational Research Society*, and *International Journal of Production Research*.

Nikos Manouselis is a researcher at the Informatics Laboratory of the Agricultural University of Athens, Greece. He has a Diploma of Electronics & Computer Engineering, a Master of Operational Research, as well as a Master of Electronics & Computer Engineering, from the Technical University of Crete (Greece). Mr. Manouselis has been previously affiliated with the Informatics & Telematics Institute of the Centre for Research & Technology (Greece), as well as the Decision Support Systems Laboratory and the Multimedia Systems & Applications Laboratory of the Technical University of Crete (Greece). His research interests involve the design, development, and evaluation of electronic services, and their applications for the agricultural sector.

Penelope Markellou is a computer engineer and researcher in the Department of Computer Engineering and Informatics at the University of Patras, Greece, as well as in the Research Academic Computer Technology Institute (RACTI). She obtained her PhD in "Techniques and Systems for Knowledge Management in the Web" (2005), and her MSc in "Usability Models for E-Commerce Systems and Applications" (2000) from the University of Patras. Her current research interests focus on algorithms, techniques, and approaches for the design and development of usable e-applications including e-commerce, e-learning, e-government, and business intelligence. She has worked on many R&D projects both national and European, has published several research papers in national and international journal and conferences, and is coauthor of seven book chapters and four books.

Kathleen Mykytyn is a lecturer and researcher in the Department of Management at Southern Illinois University, Carbondale, USA. She received her Master of Science in Information Systems from the University of Texas at Arlington, and she has taught information systems-related courses at several universities. For more than 10 years, she has conducted research in the area of information systems and the law, with current emphasis involving e-commerce systems, intellectual property, and jurisdictional issues. Her research has been published in *MIS Quarterly*, *Information & Management*, *Journal of Management Information Systems*, *Management Decision*, and *Knowledge, Technology, and Policy*.

Peter Mykytyn is a professor of management information systems in the Department of Management at Southern Illinois University, Carbondale, USA. He received his PhD degree from Arizona State University in Computer Information Systems. He has published his research in over 25 journal articles, including *Information Systems Research, MIS Quarterly, Journal of Management Information Systems, Information & Management,* and *Journal of Strategic Information Systems.* Dr. Mykytyn's research interests include the relationship between information technology and a firm's competitive advantage, use of group-support technologies in organizations, and the relationship between intellectual property, information technology, and organizational effectiveness and performance.

Angeliki Panayiotaki obtained her Diploma of Computer Engineering and Informatics from University of Patras, Greece (1996) and her MSc of "Advanced Information Systems" from University of Athens (2000). She is currently working as a researcher (PhD student) at the Computer Engineering and Informatics Department of the University of Patras and also at the General Secretariat for Information Systems of the Hellenic Ministry of Economy and Finance. Her research interests focus on personalization, Web mining, and interoperability techniques applied in the e-commerce, e-government and e-health domains. She has published several research papers in international and national conferences and is coauthor of four book chapters.

Bradley Piazza is the assistant dean in the School of Business and Technology at the University of Wisconsin-Parkside, USA and teaches in the marketing area. He completed his Master of Science in Management with a concentration in International Business at the University of Wisconsin-Milwaukee, USA. Through UW-Parkside, Piazza has been very active in the development of an online MBA program with three other University of Wisconsin System schools. He also advises student teams that are working on "live" projects for companies and organizations within southeastern Wisconsin. Some examples of projects are marketing plans, new product launch plans, and competitor analysis.

Sundar G. Sankaran is a senior signal processing engineer at Atheros Communications, Inc. He has many years of experience in designing physical layer of wireless communication systems, including Wi-Fi, WiMAX, and a proprietary fourth-generation system. He has published 14 papers in refereed conferences and technical journals. He earned a PhD degree in Electrical Engineering from Virginia Tech. He also serves as an adjunct lecturer in the department of electrical engineering at Santa Clara University.

K. Subhadra is currently an officer at the ICICI Bank in Hyderabad, India. She has received her bachelor's degree from Osmania University. She also has an MBA. She has worked for a number of years at the ICFAI as a Research Associate. She was a research fellow at the Indian Institute of Risk Management in Hyderabad. She has 10 years of research experience in software industry and in financial industry.

Athanasios Tsakalidis obtained his Diploma of Mathematics from the University of Thessaloniki, Greece (1973), his Diploma of Computer Science (1981), and his PhD (1983) from the University of Saarland, Saarbrucken, Germany. He is currently a full professor in the Department of Computer Engineering and Informatics, University of Patras and the R&D-Coordinator of the Research Academic Computer Technology Institute (RACTI). His research interests include data structures, graph algorithms, computational geometry, expert systems, medical informatics, databases, multimedia, information retrieval, and bioinformatics. He has published several research papers in national and international journals and conferences, and is coauthor of the *Handbook of Theoretical Computer Science* and other book chapters.

Ganesh Vaidyanathan is an assistant professor of Decision Sciences at IUSB, and has conducted research in the areas of e-commerce, supply chain management, project management, knowledge management, technological innovation, and IT value. He has authored over 20 publications in journals such as *Communications of the ACM* and four patents in various computer science areas. Dr. Vaidyanathan has held executive positions at eReliable Commerce, Inc., Honeywell, General Dynamics, Lockheed Martin Inc., and Click Commerce Inc. Dr. Vaidyanathan launched products that include security, payment processing, procurement, logistics, ERP, SCM, and data warehousing. He has consulted with Fortune 100 companies including United Airlines, Mitsubishi, Motorola, and Honeywell in technology, business, and process reengineering. Dr. Vaidyanathan holds a PhD with a focus on artificial intelligence, robotics and computer engineering from Tulane University and an MBA from the University of Chicago.

Merrill Warkentin is professor of MIS at Mississippi State University, USA. He has published over 125 research manuscripts, primarily in computer security management, e-commerce, and virtual collaborative teams, which have appeared in books, proceedings, and journals such as *MIS Quarterly, Decision Sciences, Decision Support Systems, Communications of the ACM, Communications of the AIS, Information Systems Journal, Journal of End User Computing, Journal of Global Information Management, Journal of Computer Information Systems*, and others. Professor Warkentin is the coauthor or editor of four books, and is currently an associate editor of *Information Resources Management Journal* and *Journal of Information Systems Security*. Dr. Warkentin has served as a consultant to numerous organizations and has served as national distinguished lecturer for the Association for Computing Machinery (ACM). Previously, Dr. Warkentin held the Reisman Research Professorship at Northeastern University in Boston, where he was also the director of MIS and E-Commerce programs. Professor Warkentin holds BA, MA, and PhD degrees from the University of Nebraska-Lincoln.

Weijun Zheng is an assistant professor of MIS in the School of Business at Technology at the University of Wisconsin-Parkside, USA. His recent research includes electronic marketplace, information system value, and organizational signaling, power and IT in organization. He received his PhD from the University of Oklahoma.

Index